Advanced Information and Knowledge Processing

Series Editors
Professor Lakhmi Jain
Lakhmi.jain@unisa.edu.au
Professor Xindong Wu
xwu@cs.uvm.edu

T0140351

For other titles published in this series, go to
www.springer.com/series/4738

Gian Piero Zarri

Representation and Management of Narrative Information

Theoretical Principles and Implementation

Springer

Gian Piero Zarri
Present Affiliation
Virthualis Project
Politecnico di Milano
Milano, Italy
zarri@noos.fr

AI&KP ISSN: 1610-3947
ISBN: 978-1-84996-723-5   e-ISBN: 978-1-84800-078-0
DOI 10.1007/978-1-84800-078-0

British Library Cataloguing in Publication Data
A catalogue record for this book is available from the British Library

Printed on acid-free paper

Springer Science+Business Media
springer.com

Preface

This book corresponds to a (provisional – see the "Conclusion," Chapter 5) assessment of more of 30 years of work about the possibility of dealing in an "intelligent" and "automated" way with *narratives* – in short, with the description of the modalities according to which *some "characters" (not necessarily human) "behave."* The results obtained up to now in this context, i.e. the Narrative Knowledge Representation Language (NKRL), will be described here in the best possible complete way. Note, however, that, for clarity's sake, (i) we will avoid as much as possible introducing in the text any cumbersome axiomatic details and, on the other hand, (ii) we have not conceived this book as a practical "manual" of NKRL. We will, nevertheless, supply regularly, in the following chapters, precise indications on where to find the missing "formal" and "operational" information.

All the Web addresses mentioned in the book, both in the text and in the References, were checked for accuracy in November 2007.

The origin of the work described here can be retraced back to 1974, when, after 10 years of professional activity distributed among industry (automation of industrial processes) and academic research at the Centre of Cybernetics and Linguistics Activities of the University of Milan directed by Silvio Ceccato, I was hired as a researcher by the French National Centre for Scientific Research (CNRS) and assigned to a small team of historians and linguists, specialized in the French Middle-Age period and fond of computer science techniques. Given my interests and skills in both computer science and artificial intelligence techniques, two colleagues, Carla Bozzolo and Monique Ornato, suggested I profit from the extensive "biographical" (in the largest meaning of this word) material they had amassed about the main characters of that period to try to build up a computerized system for (i) representing this material in computer memory in the most complete and faithful way; (ii) making use of the stored representations to find all the possible "intelligent" connections among these characters. Thanks to the financial support of the French DGRST (*Direction Générale de la Recherche Scientifique et Technique*, General Direction of the Scientific and Technical Research) the project RESEDA was born (RESEDA: *REseau SEmantique DocumentAire*, Semantic Network for Information Retrieval).

RESEDA's "metalanguage" was far from having the complexity (and the comprehensiveness) of the present NKRL, but many of its fundamental features were already present. We can mention, first, the use of a complex form of knowledge representation going well beyond the usual, simple "object–property–value" models and centered on the use of semantic predicates and roles – the latter surely reminiscent of Ceccato's "correlators." Another important aspect in common with NKRL was the (at least partly) *use of primitives*, both for reducing the risks of combinatorial explosion and for avoiding the ambiguities linked with the intensive use of natural language (NL)-like expressions. RESEDA was, from the beginning, favorably received by the artificial intelligence community [Ornato and Zarri, 1976]; see also the three communications accepted at IJCAI (the International Joint Conference on Artificial Intelligence) in 1977, 1979 and 1981 [King *et al.*, 1977; Zarri, 1979, 1981]. Thanks to additional grants from INRIA (*Institut National de Recherche en Informatique et Automatique*, National Research Institute for Computer Science and Automation) and other French public and private bodies, a complete, running prototype of the RESEDA system was built up, including non-toy knowledge bases of rules and biographical data, a complete backward-chaining inference engine adapted to the particular characteristics of the complex RESEDA's knowledge representation, tools for mass memory storage and update, etc. Given the unavailability at CNRS during the 1970s of advanced symbolic computer tools able to deal with important amounts of data, the system was implemented in VSAPL. On March 2nd, 1984, an official presentation of the complete prototype to the CNRS Scientific Direction put an official end to the project. For a retrospective description of the main technical characteristics of the RESEDA project, see, for example, Zarri [1995] – see also the tribute paid to the originality of this project by J.-P. Genet in his Preface to an "erudite" book about French Middle Age history published recently by Monique Ornato [Ornato, 2001].

The years between 1984 and the early 1990s have mainly been years of theoretical reflection that have seen the progressive transformation of RESEDA's metalanguage into NKRL; a trace of this progressive shift can be found in Zarri [1992a]. We can mention here, for example, the passage from five to seven primitive semantic predicates, with the corresponding increase of the number of exploitable "narrative" structures (what are now known as NKRL's "templates," i.e. the formal description of general classes of events), the final formalization of the specific "sub-language" (AECS) for building up complex arguments of the predicates, the generalization of the "binding structures," etc. Even more important, this restructuration has also implied the addition to the language of a *full, standard ontology* (a hierarchical structure coded according to the classical "binary" approach) in order to represent adequately the concepts and their instances – RESEDA's metalanguage was only endowed with a partially structured "lexicon." With the reorganization of the "catalogue" of templates into a *second ontology* – the "ontology of events," where the nodes (the templates) are represented by *n*-ary structures – NKRL then assumed its

*definitive, characteristic configuration based on the contemporaneous presence of
two hierarchical structures*, i.e. binary for concepts and *n*-ary for templates.

Implementing concretely all the features of the new language in order to
produce a complete and running NKRL environment has been a long-term
effort, carried out for the most part in the framework of five R&D projects
partially financed by the European Commission between 1990 and 2005. Of
course, in these 15 years, the "theoretical" developments of the language have
been continued in parallel with the implementation work, dealing in particular
with the setting up of the particularly sophisticated inference procedures
described in Chapter 4.

The first two projects (1991–1995) – NOMOS, Esprit Project 5330, in the legal
domain, and COBALT, LRE (Linguistic Research and Engineering) Project
61011, in the corporate domain – have been mainly developed within a generic
Common Lisp framework, making use, in case, of specialized environments like
CRL (Carnegie Representation Language). A turning point from the viewpoint of
the NKRL implementation has been represented by a new Esprit project, CON-
CERTO (Esprit 29159), which dealt with the advanced management of news
stories (1998–2000). The CONCERTO consortium was, in fact, convinced of
the necessity to have NKRL implemented in Java to profit fully from its advanced
characteristics. A re-implementation in Java (and Java2 successively) of the
NKRL modules was then started: at the end of the project (December 2000), a
basic Java environment for NKRL was in place, including tools for the setting up
of the knowledge bases and a first version of the NKRL *InferenceEngine* modules;
see Chapter 4. This work was continued in the subsequent EUFORBIA project
(2001–2003), in the "filtering of inappropriate Internet information" domain –
EUFORBIA was the 26505 IAP (Internet Action Plan) Project – and finished, at
least partially (see the "Conclusion" in Chapter 5 and Appendix A), thanks to the
PARMENIDES project (2003–2005) in a "temporal data mining and terrorism
news stories" context, Esprit project 39023. Work accomplished within this last
project is particularly important for at least two reasons:

- The set up of a complete and efficient implementation of the possibility
  of executing the NKRL inference procedures in an *integrated way*; see
  Chapter 4.
- The complete restructuring of the NKRL environment into *two pre-commer-
  cial versions*, i.e. a file-oriented and an ORACLE-supported one.

Some "commercial" applications of the NKRL technology have also been
implemented during recent years, e.g. in the "beauty care" and "tutoring"
domains.

The next, most important moves, see again the "Conclusion" in Chapter 5 for
more details, will now concern mainly:

- the setting up of a *complete solution* for accelerating the semi-automatic
  construction of NKRL knowledge bases trough the syntactic/semantic analysis of NL texts – partial results have already been obtained in this context;

- the transformation of the actual prototype(s) into full commercial products –
  the *first steps* in this direction have already been taken.

Even if I am the main driving force behind both the RESEDA and NKRL
projects and the *only one responsible for all the conceptual, technical and implementation choices* accomplished in this context, it is evident that several people
have contributed, both from a theoretical and a practical point of view, to the
fulfillment of their aims. Besides Carla Bozzolo and Monique Ornato already
mentioned – Monique has been especially instrumental in the setting up of the
first versions of RESEDA's metalanguage – I would like to mention here
the following people: Pedro Abreu, Christophe Assemat, Saliha Azzam, Luc
Bernard, Pieter De Vries, Marthe Faribault, Luca Gilardoni, Marie Hayet,
Sébastien Hourcaillou, James Henry Ingrouille, Sarah Jacqmin, Margaret
King, Dehbia Laradi, Georges Lee, Ruddy Lelouche, Béatrice Marin, Jeremy
Martin, John McNaught, Vincent Meissonnier, Bernard Nallet, Fátima Pires,
Patricia Sandjong, Lionel Stouder, Peizheng Wu, Lucia Zarri-Baldi, Anne
Zwiebel. May the people I have forgotten to quote here forgive me for this
omission.

Gian Piero Zarri

Contents

Chapter 1
Basic Principles

This book is about the Narrative Knowledge Representation Language (NKRL); NKRL comprises:

- *a knowledge representation system* for describing in adequate detail and in computer-understandable format the *essential content (the "meaning") of complex narrative information*;
- a system of *reasoning (inferencing) procedures* that, thanks to the richness of the representation system, is able automatically to establish *"interesting" relationships among the represented narrative items*;
- an *implemented software environment* that allows the user (i) to *encode* the original information in the terms of the representation language to create "NKRL knowledge bases" in specific application domains and (ii) to *exploit* these bases *intelligently* by questioning and inferencing.

Before explaining the details of the knowledge representation and inference systems in the next three chapters, we will introduce here the "theoretical" framework of this work and some general principles that have inspired its practical implementation.

Section 1.1 will explain what we mean exactly, in the context of this work, when we speak about multimedia (text, image, sound, videos, etc.) "nonfictional narrative" documents or, in short, "nonfictional narratives." We will also emphasize, on the one hand, the "ubiquity" of this particular type of narrative information and its economic importance and, on the other hand, the exigency of producing not only "theoretical" systems, but also "running" systems in order that this economic importance can be concretely exploited. In Section 1.2, we will examine some past and current Knowledge Representation solutions that could be used to represent in a satisfactory way the "meaning" of the nonfictional narratives. In particular, we will see that: (i) it can be very hard to describe in full this type of information making use of the usual "binary," Semantic Web (SW) languages in the W3C style (RDF, OWL); (ii) real "*n*-ary" languages are required for this aim. Section 1.3 will summarize the main points expounded in this chapter.

G.P. Zarri, *Representation and Management of Narrative Information*,
DOI 10.1007/978-1-84800-078-0_1, © Springer-Verlag London Limited 2009

1.1 Narrative Information in an NKRL Context

First, we will mention some theoretical results obtained in the framework of "narratology" research, and we will then try to define informally the meaning of terms like "event" and "elementary event" in an NKRL context.

1.1.1 Narratology and NKRL

Studying all sorts of multimedia "narratives" constitutes the object of a full theoretical discipline, the "narratology."

Traditionally, the term "narratology" is considered to have been coined in French (*narratologie*) by Tzvetan Todorov in the first pages of his *Grammaire du Décaméron* [Todorov, 1969]. According to Todorov, narratology's aim is mainly to produce *an in-depth description of the "structure" of the narratives*, i.e. the narratologist is in charge of dissecting narratives into their component parts in order to establish their functions, their purposes and the relationships among them. Narratology's golden age (its "classical" period) was in the 1970 s and 1980 s. It has recently experienced a surge of popularity visualized through the flourishing of all sorts of "specialized narratologies," from the psychoanalytic narratology to a feminist narratology, a cognitive narratology, etc. A good introduction to the full domain is Jahn [2005].

Several humanistic disciplines, from stylistic to literary techniques, are in a strict relationship with narratology. But we can note immediately that at least two disciplines that can be associated with this domain, namely "storytelling" and "eChronicles," are also of import from Artificial Intelligence (AI) and Computer Science (CS) points of view. They have acquired a particular importance in recent years.

"Storytelling" [e.g. Soulier, 2006] concerns, in general, the study of the different ways of conveying "stories" and events in words, images and sounds in order to entertain, teach, explain, etc. "Digital storytelling" concerns in particular the ways of introducing characters and emotions in the *interactive entertainment domain*: it is of interest, then, for videogames, (massively) multiplayer online games, interactive TV, virtual reality, etc.; see Handler Miller [2004]. Digital storytelling is related to another computer-based variant of narratology called "narrative intelligence," a specific sub-domain of AI that explores *topics at the intersection of AI, media studies, and human computer interaction design* (narrative interfaces, history databases management systems, artificial agents with narratively structured behavior, systems for the generation and/or understanding of histories/narratives, etc.); see Mateas and Sengers [2003].

An "eChronicle" system can be defined in short as a way of recording, organizing and then accessing *streams of multimedia events* captured by individuals, groups, or organizations making use of video, audio and any other possible type of sensor. The "chronicles" gathered in this way may concern any sorts of "narrative," like meeting minutes, conference records, wedding videos, surveillance videos, football games, visitor logs, sales activities, "lifelogs" obtained from wearable sensors, etc. The technical challenges concern the ways of *aggregating the events into coherent "episodes" and of providing access to this sort of material at the required level of granularity*. A unifying indexing system employing an event-based domain model is used, in general, to introduce a *conceptual layer* onto the *metadata layer* proper to each repository. Note that (i) the users of the eChronicle repositories are not concerned with the original data sources and that (ii) *exploration, not "normal" querying*, is the predominant way of interaction with these repositories. Details can be found, for example, in Güven et al. [2005] and Westermann and Jain [2006].

1.1.1.1 "Fictional" and "Nonfictional" Narratives

Having verified that narratology is not totally extraneous to AI and CS research, we can now examine whether narratology's results can be used to better define the characteristics, aims and limits of a computerized language/environment, NKRL, that has "narrative" as the first term of its name.

An intuitively evident dichotomy proper to narratology concerns the differentiation between "fictional" and "nonfictional" narratives; see Jahn [2005]:

- A *fictional narrative* has mainly an *entertainment value*, and represents "... an imaginary narrator's account of a story that happened in an imaginary world"; a novel is a typical example of fictional narrative.
- A *nonfictional or factual narrative* presents, on the contrary, "... a real-life person's account of a real-life story." Factual narratives (like news stories) are then concerned, for example, with an author's *credibility problems*, given that a nonfictional narrative should represent, at least in principle, "... an evidence of what happened in the real world."

As a first delimitation of the domain of interest, we can then say that NKRL deals mainly with *multimedia nonfictional/factual narratives*, and more precisely with the very large category of *"economically relevant" multimedia information* embodied in "documents" like "corporate knowledge" documents (memos, policy statements, reports, minutes, etc.), news stories, normative and legal texts, medical records, many intelligence messages, surveillance videos, actuality photographs for newspapers and magazines, material (text, image, video, sound, etc.) for eLearning, etc., as well as a great majority of the nonfictional documents stored on the Web. "Economically relevant" means that the information considered has an (at least implicit) *commercial value*, and that people *could then be willing to pay for a system able to process in an "intelligent" way this information and/or for the results of the processing*. With respect to the "multimedia" term, we can note immediately that, even if a large amount of nonfictional narratives are represented by natural language (NL) texts, *this is not necessarily true.* A photograph representing a situation that, verbalized, could be expressed as "The US President is addressing the Congress" is not of course an NL document, yet it surely represents a narrative. The economical interesting, nonfictional narratives taken into account by NKRL are then embodied, in general, within *multimedia documents represented under the form of texts, images, videos, sounds, etc.*

The topics addressed by NKRL, then, coincide at least partly with those proper to the eChronicles domain evoked above, though with some important differences:

- NKRL is particularly interested in the *economic relevance* of the nonfictional narratives dealt with, while eChronicles are more oriented towards recording everything a person can do *at the personal level*, including *entertainment and social activities in a Web 2.0 style*;
- eChronicles stress the possibility of *a massive, automatic recording in digital form* of these personal activities making use of all the possible sorts of sensors, while NKRL emphasizes the *quality and exactness* of the coding and the *related possibilities of in-depth reasoning*;
- the *depth of internal representation is completely different*, with NKRL mainly making use of a *high-level model in a knowledge representation style*, while the internal model of eChronicles is fundamentally represented, notwithstanding the added indexing (conceptual) operations, by the *rough output directly produced by the multimedia sensors*.

For more details about the relationships between NKRL and eChronicles, see Zarri [2006].

To conclude this section, we will note that the decision to confine NKRL to the domain of nonfictional narratives *has nothing to do with the possible, technical internal limitations of NKRL*. In fact, this decision is mainly linked with (i) the wish to emphasize the "practical" aspects of the NKRL work and (ii) that of limiting, from a very pragmatic point of view, the amount and the subject matter of information to deal with. As we will see in Chapters 2 and 4, NKRL (considered under the form of a *general CS/AI environment*) is *largely indifferent* with respect of the specific types of narrative, fictional or nonfictional, to be represented and processed. The nonfictional specialization of NKRL is then more evident at the *ontological and semantic level*, i.e. when examining the specific narrative contents inserted in the two NKRL ontologies; see Chapter 3. However, note that, in this latter chapter, when we examine some of the specific narrative structures NKRL can manage, we will meet there, for example, favorable/negative behaviors of "personages," motivations, experience of positive or negative situations, transfers of knowledge, changes of activities, trips, availability of material or intellectual resources, production of concrete or abstract resources, etc., i.e. *narrative structures that might be definitely used also in the context of some "… story that happened in an imaginary world."*

1.1.1.2 Informal Definition of an NKRL "Narrative"

Other theoretical results of narratology can now help us to make precise the meaning of the term "narrative" in an NKRL context. A dichotomy frequently encountered in these sorts of study says that, within a narrative, it is necessary to make a distinction between a generic "story level" and the "discourse level":

- The first concerns *what* is really "narrated," and is formed then by a specific *stream of elementary events*. These involve characters (agents, patients, beneficiaries, etc.), describe real or imaginary happenings, and are connected together by specific *coherence links* that assure the uniqueness of the overall narrative.
- The "discourse" concerns *how* a particular story is narrated, i.e. the stylistic choices of the author that determine the particular form of the final narrative, e.g. including the choices dictated by the exigency of taking into account a particular social, political or cultural framework.

From an NKRL point of view, we can say immediately that we are *quite exclusively interested in the proper "story level" of narratives*. All the possible differentiations about the style of communication between an author or narrator and their audience – "overt narrator" versus "covert narrator," "homodiegetic" narrative (when the story is told by a narrator who is present as a character in the story itself) versus "heterodiegetic narrative," etc.; see Jahn [2005] – are not (or very little – see below) taken into consideration by NKRL. We can then state that dealing with "narratives" in an NKRL context means, as a *first approximation*, finding a way of *representing correctly, in the presence of "narrative" phenomena, the underlying "stream of elementary events" and their specific "coherence"* aspects. We can note that the "discourse" level, apart from being fundamental for literary analysis and production, is also essential for any form of *"automatic generation" of narratives*. This last aspect is outside the present NKRL's scope, even if some downgraded forms of "automatic generation" could be useful to produce some "friendly" forms of NL reply from the answers in internal format supplied by the query/inferencing tools (see Chapter 4).

We can now see briefly if one of the classic theories in the narratology domain, *Mieke Bal's analysis of the narrative phenomena* [Bal, 1997] can be useful to introduce further precisions about the characteristics of the above "story level."

Bal sees narratives as structured into *three layers* called "fabula," "story proper," and "narrative"; note that only the first of these three terms, "fabula" (a Latin word: fable, story, tale, play) is now considered as standard in the narrative domain. Thus, the lowest layer, i.e. fabula, concerns a series of *logically and chronologically related events* (corresponding to the above "stream of elementary events") that describe the activities or the experiences of given characters. The second level is what Bal calls the "story," which consists of a particular subset of the fabula contents rearranged in a new sequence according to given purposes, e.g. to inform a user about the background of a series of events. It is then possible *to derive a number of different "stories" (following Bal's terminology) starting from a given fabula.* The third layer, the level of the final "narrative," is how the "story" is eventually expressed according to a given language or media form, e.g. as a verbal exchange, a picture, a novel, or a film. A variant of this classification – which we prefer because it allows us to avoid any ambiguity associated with the term "story" that we have defined above by its opposition with "discourse" – has been proposed by Swartjes and Theune [2006]. According to them, the lower layer is still the *fabula level* as defined by Bal, Bal's story level is called (with the same meaning) the *plot level* and, in accordance with CS's practices, the narrative proper layer is called simply the *presentation layer*.

From an NKRL point of view, we can now say that dealing with the *"story level" of a narrative* (in opposition again to its "discourse level") in reality means taking (at least partly) into account *all three layers described above*. In Chapter 2 we will describe a *general model* for representing in a machine-understandable way the main characteristics of that "stream of elementary events," with their *logical and chronological connections*, which corresponds to the *proper fabula level*. Chapter 3 will show how this general model is employed to implement the conceptual structures used to encode *specific classes of elementary events*, e.g. the events related with some sort of physical or mental displacements, the production of artifacts or the manifestation of specific attitudes towards living beings/things/situations. Chapter 4 will then deal, essentially, with the *plot layer*, i.e. with the *extraction of specific subsets of the NKRL representations at the fabula level* to answer specific user queries or to validate, for example, specific hypotheses about the causal chaining of events/streams of events – in short, for *inferring new useful information from that represented at the basic (fabula) level*. Subsets pertaining to different fabulae can be mixed to better answer the user's requirements. Given that NKRL is mainly interested in an "intelligent information retrieval" form of exploitation of the fabula material than, as already stated, in the exploitation of this same material for "generation" purposes, *the presentation layer concerns only the usual forms of displaying to the user the results of the plot activities.*

It is then evident that *representing correctly the fabula aspects is of paramount importance for the success of the NKRL's effort.* For simplicity's sake, we will now assimilate an NKRL "narrative" with its "fabula level"; we will then state that, eventually, *an NKRL narrative is a logically connected stream of nonfictional elementary events; in particular, this stream represents some form of "economically relevant" information.* Subsets pertaining to different narratives can be extracted (and, in case, combined) at the "plot" and "presentation" levels to satisfy specific requirements of the users. A narrative, as defined above, is characterized by the following general characteristics (independently, by the way, of any "economically relevant" or not consideration):

- One of the features defining the "connected" character of the elementary events of the stream concerns the fact that these events are *chronologically related*, i.e. narratives *extend over time*. This *diachronic* aspect of narratives (a narrative normally has a beginning, an end and some form of development) represents, indeed, one of their most important characteristics.

- *Space* is also very important in the narrative domain, given that the elementary events of the stream occur generally in well-defined "locations," real or imaginary ones. The connected events that make up a narrative are then both *temporally and spatially bounded*. Bakhtin [1982] speaks about "chronotopes" when drawing attention on the fact that *time and space in narratives are strictly interrelated*.

- A simple chronological succession of elementary events that take place in given locations cannot, however, be defined as a narrative without some sort of *semantic coherence* and *uniqueness of the theme* that characterize the different events of the stream. *If this logical coherence is lacking, then the events pertain to different narratives*: a narrative can also be represented by a single "elementary event."

- When the constitutive "elementary events" of a narrative are verbalized in NL terms, their *coherence* is normally expressed through *syntactic constructions like causality, goal, indirect speech, coordination and subordination*, etc. In this book, we will systematically make use of the term *connectivity phenomena* to denote these sorts of clue, i.e. to denote what, in a stream of events: (i) leads to a *"global meaning" that goes beyond the simple addition of the "meanings" conveyed by a single elementary event*; (ii) defines *the influence of the context* in which a particular event is used on the meaning of this individual event, or part of it. For the NKRL solutions used to deal with these sorts of phenomena, see Section 2.3. In a computational linguistic-oriented context, see also the LINK constructions introduced by TimeML [Pustejovsky et al., 2005], in particular TLINK (representing the temporal relationships holding between events) and SLINK (subordination links).

- Eventually, narratives concern *the behavior or the condition of some "actors"* (persons, characters, personages, figures, etc.). They try to attain a specific result, experience particular situations, manipulate some (concrete or abstract) materials, send or receive messages, buy, sell, deliver, etc. In short, *they have a specific "role" in the event* (in the stream of events representing the global narrative) – see, in a very peculiar "narratology" context, the famous seven roles (the hero, the villain, the princess, etc.) described by Vladimir Propp [1968] in *Morphology of the Folktale*. Note that these actors or personages are not necessarily human beings; we can have narratives concerning, for example, the vicissitudes in the journey of a nuclear submarine (the "actor," "personage," etc.) or the various avatars in the life of a commercial product.

1.1.2 The Notion of "Event" in an NKRL Context

Having defined the NKRL narratives as, in short, *spatio-temporally bounded streams of elementary events*, it would now be necessary to define what it is meant as "elementary event" in an NKRL context. Unfortunately, narratology (where the notion of "event" is, essentially, considered as an "intuitive" one) is not of much help in this context.

Limiting ourselves, for the moment, to a strict formal (and operational) point of view, *the formalized equivalent of an NKRL "elementary event" corresponds simply to a spatio-temporal instantiation – called a "predicative occurrence" – of one of the (pre-established) n-ary structures called "templates" (already evoked in the Preface) that identify general categories of basic events like "moving a physical object" or "living in a given place" (or "being injured")*. NKRL's templates (actually, about 150 – see Chapter 3 for a detailed description of many of them) are structured into a hierarchy (HTemp, the "hierarchy of templates," that corresponds then to the NKRL "ontology of events"). To represent in NKRL's format one of the recurrent examples in the theoretical discussions about events, "Brutus stabs Caesar" (e.g. see Davidson [1967a]), we will simply *retrieve from the general "catalogue" of NKRL templates represented by HTemp* the specific template Produce:HumanBeingInjuring – see a detailed discussion about the characteristics of this template and of the related ones in Sections 3.2.2.3 and 3.2.2.6. This particular template is structured around the *deep predicate* PRODUCE that defines then the "general conceptual category" of the elementary event to be represented. We will then instantiate the template by substituting to the variables that, introduced by roles, constitute the arguments of the deep predicate (and by complying with the constraints on the possible values that can be bound to these variables) the "individual" BRUTUS_ as "filler" of the SUBJ(ect) role, the "concept" human_being_injuring as filler of the OBJ(ect) role, CAESAR_ as filler of the BEN(e)F(iciary) role, the concept stabbing_ as filler of the MODAL(ity) role, plus ROME_ as location of the subject and of the source, the ides of March of 44 BC, etc. The details concerning the construction of the "predicative occurrences" will be supplied in Chapter 2.

To enlighten now *some general and "theoretical" aspects* of this purely formal and functional approach, we can try to situate it with respect to two modern theories about the notion of "event" – with the caveat, of course, that *any theoretical, in-depth analysis of this highly controversial notion would be totally out of scope here*. For some preliminary information on the "event" problem, see the useful "Introduction" of Casati and Varzi's [1996] anthology about "events."

1.1.2.1 A Kimian-like Analysis

We can say, first, that (at least to a first approximation) the formal interpretation of *elementary event* as expounded above seems to be *rather compatible* with Jaegwon Kim's [1993, 1996] notion of *monadic event*. According to Kim, a "monadic" event is identified by a triple $[x, P, t]$, where x is an object that exemplifies the n-ary property or relation P at time t (where t can also be an interval of time); monadic means that the n-ary property P is exemplified by a single object *x* at a time. We can note immediately that a controversial aspect of this theory concerns the fact that, since Kimian events are just an exemplification of the properties of an object over some duration of time, *there are, at least in principle, as many events going on in this time interval as there are properties exemplified* – even if these properties seem to be nothing than *additional specifications of what appears to be in reality a single event*. Kimian events are then *very fine-grained.*

In the NKRL interpretation of Kim's triples, *the single "object" x corresponds, systematically, to the filler of the SUBJ(ect) role of the corresponding formal event* (predicative occurrence): *x* matches then the "individual" BRUTUS_ in the above example. We can derive some first, interesting conclusions from this (at least partial and provisional) identification of the "NKRL's elementary events" with Kim's monadic event:

- An NKRL predicative occurrence (a formal NKRL representation of an elementary event), to be well-formed, *requires that the SUBJ(ect) role always exists and that it could be correctly filled*; see section 2.2.2.2 in this context.
- A "property" *cannot be the filler* of the above *SUBJ*(ect) role, given that this will be contradictory with both the Kimian definition of a monadic (elementary) event and with the intuitive meaning of the notion of event. This conclusion is very important, from a practical point of view, for *constraining the formal expression of the different templates of NKRL.*
- As stated before, given that in a predicative occurrence (an instantiated template) the roles are there *to introduce the arguments (variables) of the deep predicate*, the necessary existence of a SUBJ(ect) role implies *the necessary existence of this deep predicate in a well-formed occurrence* – even if the notion of "predicate" does not appear in the Kimian formalism, see the next section.
- Moreover, a well-formed, NKRL predicative occurrence must be *always characterized by the presence of a specific time t or of an interval of time* (Section 2.2.2.4).

With respect now to the "constitutive," *n*-ary property *P* (in the above example, the Brutus' property exemplified by his stabbing of Caesar at time *t*), this is formally represented in NKRL by the *set of additional roles and fillers* (and, in case, locations, modulators, temporal codes, etc. – see again subsequent chapters) that, in a well-formed predicative occurrence, are *normally added* to the predicate and the pair represented by the SUBJ(ect) role and its filler(s). We can add two remarks here.

- The first concerns one of the *most common criticisms* addressed to Kim's theory (and related with the criticism concerning the *too fine-grained nature* of the Kimian events), i.e. *the lack of precise criteria for determining which specific properties can be considered as constitutive of an event*, e.g. see Brand [1997:335]. This criticism is *irrelevant* in an NKRL context. Given that

NKRL's elementary events are *instances of precisely predefined "templates,"* the "legal" property *P* associated with a specific elementary event is, as stated above, *exactly defined by the set of predefined NKRL features (roles, fillers, etc.)* that, in the "father" template, go along with *the basic core* represented by the association between a predicate and a SUBJ(ect) role.

- On the other hand, since the NKRL elementary events can only be concretely represented as instances of one of the (presently about) 150 general templates, there exists a concrete risk that several of these events cannot be represented at all (even if they correspond precisely to Kimian monadic events) because of the lack of a corresponding template to be instantiated. We can note in this respect:
  - The "upper level" templates included in HTemp are represented by *very general conceptual structures* in the style of "behave," "exist," "move" or "produce" and *according to the more general meaning of these notions*; see Chapter 3. It seems, then, *relatively rare* that a concrete event cannot be able to find an *at least partial representation* under the form of instantiation of one of these very general templates. The concrete risk consists instead of the possibility that, to make reference to the Kimian formalism, *x* could be correctly represented, but not its constitutive *n*-ary property *P*, given the lack (at this level of extreme generality) of the *specific set of roles, fillers, locations, etc. needed to represent completely all the "properties" of the elementary event under consideration.*
  - However, as we will see in subsequent chapters, HTemp is *not a static structure*, and new complete templates *can always be added to the existing ones* when required by specific NKRL applications. This is easily done *by specializing (customizing) the present templates or by creating totally new templates* following strictly the formal model of the existing ones. Accordingly, the number of elementary events that can be formally described in NKRL *systematically increases as new applications are taken into account.*

1.1.2.2 A Davidsonian-like Analysis

Apart from the problems linked with the possibility of too fine-grained events, the Kimian formalism does not emphasize sufficiently what, in our opinion, is *one of the fundamental constituents of an "elementary event"* – and, by the way, of an NKRL template – i.e. *the existence of this sort of "conceptual predicate" that, as stated above, determines the "general conceptual category" of the specific event.* The need (and function) of a predicate like this becomes more evident when taking into account another theory particularly popular in the linguistic domain that has led to a definition of events under the form of "Davidsonian events" [Davidson, 1967b]. These have a "true existence" like the physical objects and, like these latter, have spatio-temporal locations and properties.

What is of a particular interest for us in this theory is the specific *Davidsonian formalism.* According to this (originally introduced in the context of the specific "action verbs"), each verb is *associated with an existentially quantified event-token variable*. In this way, the Davidsonian representation of "Brutus stabs Caesar" becomes $\exists e.\text{stab}(e, b, c)$, where e is the *event variable* and the global meaning of the formalism is: "there is an event e such that e was a stabbing of Caesar (c) by Brutus (b)." Besides the explicit representation of a "stabbing" predicate, another important "linguistic" consequence of the introduction of the quantified event-token variable concerns the possibility of *explaining how a large number of adverbial modifications and modifying phrases can be attached to verbs and described in terms of predication of events*. If the sentence to be represented was: "Brutus stabbed Caesar in Rome on the Ides of March of 44 BC," then the Davidsonian representation would in fact be $\exists e[\text{stabbed}(e, b, c)$ & $\text{In}(e, l)$ & $\text{On}(e, t)]$.

We can add that, according to the so-called *"neo-Davidsonian approach"* [e.g. Higginbotham, 1985, 2000; Parson, 1990], Davidson's suggestion of introducing, for the verbs of action, a "hidden" argument place for events *has been extended not only to verbs in general, but also to adjectives, nouns and preposition when they have a "predicative" function*. Moreover, and this is particularly interesting from an NKRL point of view, while Davidson introduced event arguments as *an additional argument of given verbs*, the neo-Davidsonians assume that the event argument is *the only argument of the (verbal) predicate*. This implies, then, *the introduction of "thematic roles"* for expressing the relation between events and their participants. The formalization of "Brutus stabs Caesar" now becomes $\exists e[\text{stab}(e)$ & $\text{agent}(e) = b$ & $\text{object}(e) = c]$, which has some *interesting similarities* (the use of "roles," for example) with the NKRL formalization of the same elementary event outlined at the beginning of this section.

We can derive from the above "Davidsonian" analysis at least the following two conclusions:

- The need of keeping in the formalization of an elementary event the *explicit representation* of some sort of "generalized predicate" (verbs for Davidson, but also adjectives, nouns, etc. for the neo-Davidsonian when they have a *predicative function*).
- According to the neo-Davidsonian again, the opportunity to make use in this formalization of *"thematic" (conceptual) roles*.

The above discussion, then, has emphasized the strict relationship between predicates and events. However, we must note that, in NKRL terms, predicates are "deep predicates," totally independent from "surface" syntactic considerations of, for example, the active or passive type; see some "classical" AI papers on the subject [e.g. Bruce, 1975; Goldstein and Papert, 1977; Rosner and Somers, 1980]. In the NKRL analysis of the "Brutus stabs Caesar" event, the "deep" representation obtained — there is a "PRODUCE OBJ(ect) human_being_injuring" event having BRUTUS_ as SUBJ(ect) and CAESAR_ as BEN(e)F(iciary) — is not only congruent with the common sense analysis of the above elementary event, but this analysis would not change at all in the presence, at the "surface" level, of terms like "knifes" or "pierces" instead of "stabs," or of a passive form like " Caesar is stabbed by Brutus." We can also note that the symbolic labels of the different "conceptual roles," like SUBJ(ect), SOURCE or MODAL(ity), are purely conventional and correspond more, at least partly, to the pragmatic habits of NKRL's creators/users than to precise NL equivalences. For example, SUBJ(ect) has very few characteristics in common with the syntactic "subject" of a sentence, and could also have been called ACTOR, FOCUS, MAIN _PROTAGONIST or similar.

According to what is stated above, the presence of a "deep predicate" accompanied by roles and arguments is necessary to identify an NKRL elementary event. Connversely, *to any "deep predicate" that is possible to isolate (pragmatically using, for example, neo-Davidsonian criteria) within a narrative there corresponds necessarily an NKRL elementary event.* This implies that the NKRL representation of narratives is a (relatively) analytical one; note, however, the difference with Kim's position, where the recognition of events is linked with *the identification of their (possibly nonessential) properties.* We can also note, incidentally, that the "Problem of Adverbial Modification" [e.g. Kim, 1993] is not really a problem in NKRL, and that "stroll" and "leisurely stroll" give rise to the same elementary event, where the filler of the MODAL(ity) role is more precisely SPECIF(ied) in the second case– see Chapter 2.

Returning, then, to the "Brutus stabs Caesar" example, if the *complete narratives to be represented* were in the style of "Caesar died because of the Brutus' stabbing" or "Brutus stabbed Caesar in order to kill him" or similar, then an NKRL analysis would always lead to the *preliminary identification of two separate, formal elementary events* (two separate predicative occurrences derived from two different templates of the HTemp catalogue). These latter *would then be associated* to represent exactly the whole narrative making use of the NKRL tools ("binding occurrences" in this case; see Section 2.3.2) expressly created to represent the *connectivity phenomena.* According, then, to a *first, rough analysis*, in the first example we will make use of an NKRL elementary event obtained as an instance of the template Exist:Death (see Section 3.2.2.2) and having CAESAR_ as filler of the SUBJ(ect) role. This would be linked, through a CAUSE binding operator, to the instance of Produce:HumanBeing-Injuring already discussed. In the second example, the "injuring" elementary event would be associated again (through a GOAL binding operator in this case) with a second elementary event, an instance now of the template Produce: HumanBeingKilling (Section 3.2.2.6). For a discussion of the modalities used for dealing with "wishes, intentions, planning activities, etc.," see Section 3.2.2.1.

1.1.2.3 Final Notes on the Linguistic Theories about "Events"

We can conclude this short discussion about "events" by noticing that theoretical studies in this context are now particularly copious in the linguistic domain, where, according to Tenny and Pustejovsky [2000: 4], events tend to be studied "... as grammatically or linguistically represented objects, *not as events in the world*" (emphasis added). In this paper, Tenny and Pustejovsky supply an interesting account of the history of "events" following a strict linguistics perspective. Even if we are mainly interested, on the contrary, in finding some sort of computationally useful representation of the *deep meaning* of the *real-world events*, we are also, of course, *particularly attentive to any "linguistic" results that can enlighten or confirm our pragmatic intuitions* – e.g. see the above Davidsonian analysis.

We are not very favorable, however, to the use of *"surface" linguistic considerations to solve problems that concern, in reality, "deep" conceptual knowledge representation issues*. Very often, these "surface" tools are also extremely analytical; to give only an example, see the use (introduced in Vendler [1967]) of the opposition between "imperfect gerundial nominals" and their "perfect" counterparts to suggest distinctions among "facts" (imperfect) and "events" (perfect), *where this grammatical distinction supposedly reflects a semantic one*; see also Bennett [1988: 8]. We do not feel very comfortable, then, with views like that expressed in Jackendoff [1990], where he introduces *a strict a priori parallelism between his own specific "conceptual representation" of events and the syntactic representations of some related sentences at the NL level*. More precisely, he states that any *"meaning"* problem cannot be dealt with properly without also examining in depth the *"correspondence" problem*, where the latter concerns the construction of a *solid theory of the relations between conceptual structures and syntax*. We consider, on the contrary, that the setup of a formal notation for expressing conceptual contents can be developed *quite independently* from the search for an optimal form of correspondence (e.g. see Jackendoff's interpretation of the "θ-criterion") with the *surface form these contents can assume in a particular NL*. Clearly, in our approach, the correspondence problem still exists, but this is tackled *a posteriori and in a totally pragmatic way*, e.g. by finding practical tools to accelerate the extraction of NKRL-coded information from the NL sources; see also Chapter 5.

1.2 Knowledge Representation and NKRL

In previous sections we have defined, at least informally, what we mean for "nonfictional narratives of an economic interest"; the discussion about the (NKRL) notion of events has also allowed us to supply some preliminary information on the knowledge representation principles (like deep predicates, roles, etc.) that NKRL uses to encode these narratives. We must now (i) define these principles in a complete and accurate way (their concrete application will be described in detail in Chapters 2 and 3) and (ii) justify their adoption by examining the possible alternatives offered by standard knowledge representation and CS research.

We can immediately note here that "traditional" narratology is not very helpful with respect to the possibility of supplying *detailed representation models* for our nonfictional narratives. The existing CS applications in this domain (with the exception of very specific treatments in the eChronicle style – see Section 1.1.1) seem, in fact, more interested in the setting up of some ad hoc tests intended to prove or verify particular theoretical assumptions than in proposing a complete, operational model of the domain. Moreover, many of these applications are essentially of a *literary* nature and deal, then, with *"fictional"* narratives. We can also relate to this "literary/fictional" context some specific AI applications that deal with the old dream of generating fictions by computer; see Mehan [1977] and, more recently, Callaway and Lester [2002]. Note, for completeness' sake, that recent initiatives aimed at providing a meaningful set of classes and relations to facilitate the annotation of heterogeneous multimedia items using SW techniques are also sometimes associated, in the literature, with the "narrative" domain, e.g. see the OntoMedia project [Tuffield et al., 2006; http://eprints.ecs.soton.ac.uk/12695].

1.2.1 *"Standard" Ontologies and the "n-ary" Problem*

The standard *ontologies of concepts*, both in their "traditional" (see Noy et al. [2000]) and "SW (W3C, World Wide Web Committee)" versions (see McGuinness and van Harmelen [2004]), *are not very suitable for dealing with narratives.*

1.2.1.1 Introducing the *n*-ary Problem

Basically, ontologies organize the "concepts" (which, for simplicity's sake, we can identify here with the *important notions* to be represented in a given application domain – see Section 2.1) into a hierarchical structure, able to supply an elementary form of definition of these concepts through their mutual generic/specific relationships ("IsA" links). A more precise definition of concepts is obtained by associating with them a set of *properties* or *attributes* expressed as *binary relationships* of the "property/value" type – independently from the syntactic details, this way of defining concepts by specifying their attributes is practically the same in a "traditional" frame context and when using a set of "property" statements to define a "class" (a concept) in a W3C language; see Section 3.1.1.2. The combination of these two basic representational principles, i.e. structuring a set of related concepts by way of generic/specific relationships and specializing these concepts by adding to them properties under the form of binary relationships, is largely sufficient to provide a *static, a priori* definition of a given ontology.

Note that the *impossibility of making use of relations other then binary (i.e. taking only two arguments) to define properties is a constitutive characteristic of SW languages like RDF and OWL*, which is why these sorts of language are often denoted as *binary*. To mention a well-known RDF example [e.g. Manola and Miller, 2004], let us suppose we want to represent in RDF a situation where someone named John Smith has created a particular Web page. We will then make use of the following RDF triple: <http://www.example.org/index.html (*argument1*), creator (*property*), john_smith (*argument2/value*)>. Adding additional information about the situation, e.g. by stating that the Web page was created May 15, 2004, and that the page is written in English, amounts to add two additional statements: <http://www.example.org/index.html (*argument1*), creation_date (*property*), May 15, 2004 (*argument2/value*)> and <http://www.example.org/index.html (*argument1*), language (*property*), English (*argument2/value*)>. From our "event representation" point of view, the basic remark to make about this sort of representation concerns the fact that *the triples obtained are conceptually independent*, i.e. it is possible to speak *separately* about the creator of the Web page, the fact that the page was in English, and that this page was created May 15 *without affecting at all the complete understanding of any single piece of information.*

The technique of describing properties under the form of binary relationships is well known, as well as its formal characteristics. It is not surprising, therefore, that researchers *have tried to make it a universal principle, useful in any possible conditions, including the description of events.*

Unfortunately, *this is not true in general.* Let us consider, in fact, the straightforward and well-known example concerning a very simple narrative like "John has given a book to Mary." In this example, "give" is now an n-*ary (ternary) relationship* that, to be represented in a *complete and unambiguous way*, asks for some form of complex syntax that goes beyond the "binary" approach. In this syntax, the *arguments of the predicate*, i.e. "John," "book" and "Mary," must be *differentiated* by means of some sorts of "*conceptual or thematic roles*," e.g. such as "agent of give," "object of give" and "beneficiary of give" respectively – see also the previous discussion about the "Davidsonian events" in Section 1.1.2.2. For representing the "meaning" of nontrivial narrative documents, the notion of "role" should then be necessarily added to the traditional "generic/specific" and "property/value" representational principles in order to specify the *exact function* of the different components of an event within the *formal description* of this event – more details on the (NKRL) notion of "role" are given in Section 2.2.2.2. Moreover, as we have seen in previous sections, *a narrative cannot be reduced to the simple "elementary event" level*: we must go up at least to the "fabula" level, i.e. we must take into consideration that *a narrative is a connected stream of nonfictional elementary events.* In practice, this means that we must take care of those *connectivity phenomena* (like causality, goal, indirect speech, coordination and subordination, etc.) that, as already stated, link together the basic "elementary events" in the connected stream. It is very likely, in fact, that, dealing with the sale of a company, the global narrative to represent is something like: "Company *X* has sold its subsidiary *Y* to *Z because* the profits of *Y* have fallen dangerously in recent years *due to* a lack of investments," or, returning to our previous example, that "John gave a book to Mary yesterday *as a* present for her birthday," or that, dealing with the relationships between companies in the biotechnology domain, "*X* made a milestone payment to *Y because* they decided to pursue an in vivo evaluation of the candidate compound identified by *X*," etc.

Giving that narratives make use of high-level notions like those of "role" and "connectivity phenomena," *the traditional, "binary" approach is insufficient to describe them correctly as soon as they reach a minimum level of complexity.*

We can note, in this respect, that a *common mistake* made by the supporters of a generalized binary approach consists in saying that the definition of specific *n*-ary languages for managing complex structures in the "narrative" style *is not at all necessary* given that any *n*-ary relationship, with $n > 2$, can always be reduced, in a very simple way, to a *set of binary relationships*. See, on this point, some long-lasting discussions on the Conceptual Graphs Email list, http://news.gmane.org/gmane.comp.ai.conceptual-graphs, and the archives of the W3C "Semantic Web Best Practices and Deployment Working Group" at http://lists.w3.org/Archives/Public/public-swbp-wg/. We will now discuss this topic in some detail in order, among other things, to explain more precisely what we mean by "*n*-ary relationships" and why these sorts of relationship are needed to describe events.

Formally (and leaving aside, for simplicity's sake, the problems introduced by temporal information), we can say that any *n*-ary "narrative" relation $R(t_1, \ldots, t_n)$ can be represented, with the aid of the existential quantifier, as:

$$(\text{exists } e)(R(e) \ \& \ Rb_1(e, t_1) \ \& \ Rb_2(e, t_2) \ \& \ldots \ \& \ Rb_n(e, t_n)) \qquad (1.1)$$

In Eq. (1.1), *e* must be understood as an event or situation of type R; in a triadic situation involving a predicate like "give," we have GIVE(*e*); see again the Davidsonian and neo-Davidsonian approaches. Rb_1, Rb_2, ... Rb_n is some fixed set of binary relations, corresponding to "agent of give," etc. in the previous example. To use an RDF-like formalism, they could then be represented, in this example, as something in the style of <give (*argument1*), agent_of_give (*property*), john_ (*argument2/value*)>, <give (*argument1*), object_of_give (*property*), book_ (*argument2/value*)> and <give (*argument1*), beneficiary_of_give (*property*), mary_ (*argument2/value*)>. This sort of decomposition is not only *formally interesting*, but could also be *important for many practical problems*, e.g. for storing efficiently *n*-ary relationships into standard databases, or for interoperability's sake.

However, the decomposition represented in Eq. (1.1) *does not eliminate* the need for argument *e*, which is *still necessary to assure the coherence of the overall representation*. This means that, in spite of the formal decomposition of the n-*ary (ternary) relationship* "give" in RDF-like statements, the obtained result is – at the difference of what we have seen above in the "Web page" example – *totally meaningless when the three RDF-like, binary statements are not taken contemporaneously into account*. As already stated above, statements like

<http://www.example.org/index.html, creator, john_smith>, <http://www. example.org/index.html, language, English>, etc. *are, on the contrary, perfectly "meaningful" in themselves.*

To pass from a knowledge representation context to a more familiar (*n*-ary) relational databases context, the *conceptual irreducibility of an* n-*ary (ternary) relationship* can be easily understood by supposing of decomposing a relationship in the GIVE style into three two-column tables named "agent," "object" and "beneficiary," where the first column is reserved to the predicate. Now, to recover the *global information* (the full "meaning" of the "John has given a book to Mary" elementary event) we are forced to *join* again the three two-column table on the column that represents the predicate (GIVE). All the above should explain why, if we want to execute some "reasoning" about a GIVE-like event, recognizing the existence of binary relationships between a given book or a human being and this event *is not really useful* without (i) having a way of "reconstructing" the original ternary meaning of GIVE and (ii) taking then into account that the binary relationships among GIVE and its three "arguments," "John," "book" and "Mary," are labeled in different ways, e.g. as "agent," "object" and "beneficiary."

To sum up – with reference also to a recent trend concerning the conversion of pre-existing high-level (*n*-ary) knowledge representation languages into the (apparently more fashionable) W3C (binary) languages – an important point to emphasize here is that, notwithstanding the formal transformation from *n*-ary to binary, *the* n-*ary languages are still* n-*ary after the "translation" has been realized*, just as the GIVE relationship above is still ternary even if formally reduced to a set of binary relationships. This means that, to exploit in full the representational power of *n*-ary languages like NKRL, Conceptual Graphs (CGs) [Sowa, 1999] or CycL [Witbrock et al., 2004] (e.g. for executing complex inference operations), *the original* n-*ary inferencing tools of those languages must necessarily be used.* As a consequence, these languages – after their possible conversion into (W3C) binary format for the practical reasons mentioned above – *must in fact be "translated back" into the original format* n-*ary to get the best of their characteristics and then to avoid the usual "binary" limitations.*

1.2.1.2 The W3C Suggestions

The discussion above should have demonstrated the need to dispose of *"true"* n-*ary languages to deal adequately with high-level conceptual structures like those proper to the great majority of narrative multimedia documents.* Unfortunately, we note that suggestions in this context are *quite scarce* in a SW (W3C) context – the W3C languages represent today one of the most popular paradigms in the knowledge representation domain. The most well-known W3C *n*-ary proposal is described in a "working paper" produced by the W3C Semantic Web Best Practices and Deployment Working Group (SWBPD WG, now closed effective 29 September 2006) about "Defining *N*-ary relations on the Semantic Web"; for the last version, see Noy and Rector [2006]. Note that the authors explicitly mention the fact that this paper concerns only "work in progress."

This paper proposes some extensions to the binary paradigm to allow the correct representation of these four "narratives":

(a) "Christine has breast tumor with high probability";
(b) "Steve has temperature, which is high, but failing";
(c) "John buys a 'Lenny the Lion' book from books.Example.com for $15 as a birthday gift";
(d) "United Airlines flight 3177 visits the following airports: LAX, DFW, and JFK."

Example (d) has been added to the previous three in the more recent versions of the document.

Even leaving aside the fact that only four, very particular "narratives" are examined, without any convincing justification for that choice, the technical solutions expounded in this paper are not very convincing and have aroused several criticisms. First of all, the title is clearly misleading, given that only example (c), "John buys a 'Lenny the Lion' book ..." concerns really a case of an *n*-ary relationship *involving contemporaneously several individuals that play several roles within the global situation* – this example is not very different indeed from the "John has given a book to Mary" example above. On the contrary, the first two examples, (a) "Christine has breast tumor ..." and (b) "Steve has temperature ...," concern cases *where a "standard" binary relationship must be better specified through the addition of properties*. The relationship (has_diagnosis to adopt the label used by the authors) between "Christine" and "breast tumor" is characterized by the "high probability" property, and the relation has_ temperature in Steve's example is contemporaneously "high" and "failing." Example (d) has, once again, nothing to do with *n*-relationships: it is a case of *binary relationship* where one of the arguments consists of an ordered list of individuals rather than a single individual.

In all these examples, the general principle used by the authors to solve the different representation problems is to make use of some sort of *reification* of the binary/*n*-ary relationships. Surprisingly enough, they assert that the reification is implemented *through the use of two different "representation patterns,"* where the first – used, according to them, to solve examples (a), (b) and (c) – should be based on *representing the relation as a class instead of a property*, and the second – used to solve example (d) – should consist in *using lists for arguments in a relation*. In reality, they realize the reification operations making use (i) *of fictitious (and inevitably ad hoc) "individuals"* under the form of RDF "blank nodes" (made-up resources not identified by a URI) to solve the (a), (b) and (d) examples and (ii) a sort of *NKRL-like solution* that makes use (implicitly) of the notion of "role" to solve the *n*-ary example (c).

To enter now into some details, Fig. 1.1 reproduces the solution proposed in the working paper for the first example, (a): "Christine has breast tumor with high probability."

Fig. 1.1 W3C solution for
adding properties to binary
relationships

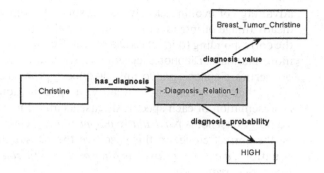

The extra individual inserted (_:Diagnosis_Relation_1) is an instance of a
new class Diagnosis_Relation having as properties diagnosis_value and
diagnosis_probability, restricted respectively in OWL to someValueFrom the
class Disease and allValuesFrom the class Probability_values. An identical
solution has been adopted to represent the second example, (b): the extra
individual inserted is now _:Temperature_Observation_1, instance of a new
class Temperature_Observation having as properties temperature_value and
temperature_ trend. The solution used for (d) is not really different, and it is
based again on the introduction of extra individuals, e.g. UA_1377_1, to identify
the first flight segment to LAX airport. These individuals are instances of the
class FlightSegment having next_segment and destination as properties.

We can note immediately that:

- As observed by some critics, the solution adopted for this first class of
  examples is *not very practical* in the case of real-world applications. It
  implies, in fact, the *continuous, cumbersome addition of new RDF/OWL
  classes and individuals* to solve a relatively simple problem – the addition
  of properties to some binary relationships – that can be dealt with in an
  easiest and more economical way. For example, see the NKRL solutions
  (that refer to an earlier version of the W3C *n*-ary working paper) for cases
  (a), (b), and (c) at http://lists.w3.org/Archives/Public/public-swbp-wg/
  2004Oct/0132.html. In all these solutions, the "property's addition" problem
  is solved (making a straightforward use of the SPECIF(ication) operator –
  see Section 2.2.2.3) *without the involvement of any reification or insertion of
  extra individuals*. With respect now to example (d), see Section 2.2.2.4
  (locations) and Section 3.2.2.4 (Move: templates) for the *NKRL representation (without addition of arbitrary items) of a trip involving an ordered
  sequence of steps.*
- Even accepting the particular reification methodology proposed in the Noy
  and Rector's note, *its "concrete" implementation is particularly unfortunate*
  and shows well all the practical limitations associated with the attempt
  of forcing the innate binary "nature" of the W3C languages. The label
  chosen for the extra individual, i.e. _:Diagnosis_Relation_1, maybe has the

advantage of evoking clearly the reasons of its introduction, but also the disadvantage of introducing in the general ontology of a given application the corresponding (odd) class Diagnosis_Relation at the risk of duplicating a more standard Diagnosis class. The strict logical separation of the two properties diagnosis_value and diagnosis_probability is *very questionable*, given that the second is, in reality, a specification of the first one. The representation of each specific disease as an ad hoc individual, see Breast_ Tumor_Christine, is *particularly inopportune*: a class, Breast_Tumor, should be the correct choice in this case; see the possibility of having, in similar situations, *a concept (class) as filler of a specific role in the NKRL representation of narratives*, etc.

Figure 1.2 reproduces the solution proposed in the W3C note for the (real) *n*-ary example (c), "John buys a 'Lenny the Lion' book from books. Example.com for $15 as a birthday gift." In this case, Purchase_1 is considered as an individual instance of the general class Purchase characterized by the properties has_buyer, has_seller, has_object, has_purpose, has_amount. Likening these properties to "roles" that, associated with the predicate Purchase, introduce the arguments of this particular predicate (John, books.example. com, Lenny_The_Lion, etc.) according to the specific narrative to represent, *we have here a representation for* n-*relationships that could evoke some sort of downgraded NKRL approach*; see again http://lists.w3.org/Archives/Public/public-swbp-wg/2004Oct/0132.html for the complete NKRL representation. We could note, moreover, that example (c) could also be advantageously represented under the form of *two* elementary events linked by a (second-order) GOAL "binding relationship" (see Section 2.3.2), the first used to represent the "purchase" and the second to represent the "gift."

As we will see, however, in the next section, the *main conceptual difference* between a representation like that of Fig. 1.2 and an NKRL representation of a narrative lies in the fact that (to guarantee the logical coherence of the overall representation, its "compactness" and "uniqueness") the last one is *globally reified and identified by a specific symbolic label*. On the contrary, this function is assured in representations like that of Fig. 1.2 by the *arbitrary* reification of the

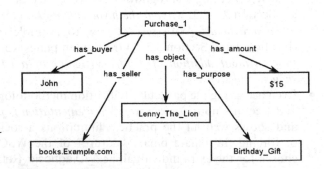

Fig. 1.2 The W3C representation of a "true" *n*-ary relationship

single predicate (**Purchase_1**) *with an evident lack of generality and a reduced practical efficiency.*

We can also note, eventually, that the W3C note says nothing about the way of dealing, in concrete situations, with those *connectivity phenomena* already evoked in previous sections.

1.2.2 A Plain "n-ary" Solution and Some Related Problems

A simple solution to the *n*-ary problem is, in reality, long known: it is based (also see previous sections) on the notions of "conceptual predicate" and "conceptual role" – or "thematic role" in a more linguistic-oriented wording. Returning, then, to the "John gave a book..." example above, a complete representation that captures all the "essential meaning" of this elementary narrative (elementary event) amounts to:

- Define JOHN_, MARY_ and BOOK_1 as *individuals*, instances of general *concepts* like human_being and information_support or of more specific concepts. Concepts and instances (individuals) are, as usual, *collected into a standard "binary" ontology* (built up using a tool like, for example, Protégé; see Chapter 2).
- Define an *n*-ary structure built around a *deep (conceptual) predicate*, e.g. like MOVE or PHYSICAL_TRANSFER, and associate the above individuals (the arguments) to the predicate through the use of "*conceptual roles*" that specify their *function* within the global narrative. JOHN_ will then be introduced by an AGENT (or SUBJECT) role, BOOK_1 by an OBJECT (or PATIENT) role, and MARY_ by a BENEFICIARY role. Additional information, like "yesterday," could be introduced, for example, by a TEMPORAL_ANCHOR role, etc.
- *Reify* the *n*-ary structure obtained by associating with it *a unique identifier under the form of a "semantic label,"* to assure both (i) the logical-semantic coherence of the structure and (ii) a rational and efficient way of storing and retrieving it.

Formally, an *n*-ary structure defined according the above guidelines can be described simply as

$$(L_i(P_j(R_1a_1)(R_2a_2)\dots(R_na_n)))$$ (1.2)

where L_i is the symbolic label identifying the particular *n*-ary structure (e.g. the structure corresponding to the formal representation of "John has given a book..." elementary event), P_j is the conceptual predicate, R_k is the generic role and a_k the corresponding argument (the individuals JOHN_, MARY_, etc.). Note that, in the decomposition represented by Eq. (1.1), the binary relationships Rb_i correspond to the (R_ia_i) cells of Eq. (1.2) taken *individually*.

As already stated, the main point here is that *the whole conceptual structure represented by Eq. (1.2) must be considered globally*.

1.2.2.1 Previous *n*-ary Conceptual Realizations

Many solutions that can be reduced formally to Eq. (1.2) or that are equivalent to this sort of representation have been suggested in the last 60 years in the AI and knowledge representation domains. We will examine some of them here, privileging those that have a clear interest from an NKRL point of view.

First of all, we would like to mention here that one of the first concrete "materializations" of the notion of (thematic, conceptual, etc.) "role" is represented by Silvio Ceccato's *correlators* that he used, in the context of his experiments of mechanical translation (MT), to represent both fictional and nonfictional narratives as *recursive networks of triadic structures*; see Ceccato [1961, 1967]. Ceccato, a philosopher, epistemologist and linguist, was the Director of the Centre for Cybernetics and Linguistic Activities of the University of Milan in Italy from 1957 to 1974.

In Ceccato's approach to MT (Correlational Analysis), "correlators" (about 120) included conjunctions and prepositions, punctuation marks, and relationships like subject–predicate, substance–accident (i.e. noun–adjective), apposition, development–modality (i.e. verb–adverb), etc. A very interesting point is that correlators were conceived as *mental categories* (the activity of "correlating" corresponded in fact to *thought itself*), making of Ceccato one of the precursors of any "conceptual" and "deep" approach to knowledge representation. The two arguments of the correlator, the "correlata," could be other mental categories, already completed correlational structures, substances, individuals, physical things, etc. Another interesting point to mention is that, to deal with the MT polysemy problem, Ceccato proposed the use of a *sfera nozionale* (sphere, network of notions) where terms proper to ordinary life were related by basic conceptual relations – 56 in the 1962 version [Ceccato, 1966] – like "member: part," "species: genus," "part: whole" and more unconventional relationships such as "thing supported: support," "thing produced: place of production" or "thing contained: container." In this way, "sleep" could be linked both to "bed" (activity: usual place) and to "night" (activity: usual time), with "bed" linked in turn to "bedroom" (object: usual place), and to "furniture" (species: genus), etc. Some observers, like John Sowa, see in this sort of tool one of the first concrete examples of "semantic network," which should then predate the classical Quillian's [1966] thesis on semantic memory.

We can now mention right away two *n*-ary AI and knowledge representation systems that have been often associated with NKRL, the Conceptual Dependency Theory of Roger Schank [Schank, 1973; Schank and Abelson, 1977] and Sowa's CGs [Sowa, 1984, 1999]. Their "core" representation principle, making use of predicates and roles, can be in fact assimilated to Eq. (1.2). We can remark that these two conceptual systems claim, at least implicitly, to have a

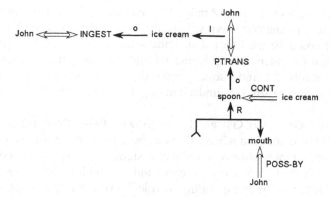

Fig. 1.3 A Conceptual Dependency example

universal coverage, while NKRL, more humbly, intends to *deal only with nonfictional narratives from a strict "engineering" point of view*.

Conceptual Dependency – see the example of Fig. 1.3, Schank's [1973: 201] representation of the narrative "John ate the ice cream with a spoon"– tries to capture the "deep meaning" of linguistic utterances under the form of "conceptualizations" corresponding formally to events. Conceptualizations consist in combinations of "predicates" (chosen from a set of 12 "primitive acts") associated with states, changes of state and primitive "causation"; they make use of a set of seven roles or conceptual cases: Object (in a state), Object (of a change of state), Object (of an action), Actor, Recipient/Donor, From/To and Instrument. The (well-known) primitive acts [Schank and Abelson, 1977: 12–14] are ATRANS (transfer of abstract relationships like possession, ownership or control), PTRANS (transfer of the physical location of an object), PROPEL (application of a physical force to an object), MOVE (movement of a body part of an animal by this animal), GRASP (the grasping of an object), INGEST (the taking in of an animal to the inside of that animal), EXPEL (the expulsion of an object from the body of an animal), MTRANS (the transfer of mental information), MBUILD (construction of new information from old information), SPEAK (the actions of producing sounds), ATTEND (the action of attending or focusing a sense organ like ear or eye towards a stimulus).

We note that, in contrast to NKRL representations of elementary events, which try to limit themselves to the encoding of the *essential components of their "deep meaning,"* Schank's representations are strongly *introspective*, in accordance with the "psychological" trend characteristics of the first years of AI. For example, in Fig. 1.3, the (redundant) transfer towards "the mouth of John" is added. In this figure, POSS-BY and CONT represent "propositional dependencies"; the letters "o" (object), "I" (instrument), and "R" (recipient/donor) denote the "roles" or "conceptual cases." An in-depth comparison between the notion of "primitive" in conceptual dependency and NKRL is given in Chapter 2.

Some attempts to translate Schank's ideas into running computers programs have been realized by Schank's students and collaborators. We can mention here programs like SAM, Script Applier Mechanisms [Cullingford, 1981], written to investigate, in Schankian terms, how the knowledge of context (the script mechanism) could be used to aid in understanding stories, PAM [Wilensky, 1978], devoted to understanding stories by understanding the intentions of the characters involved, and some programs devoted to use Schank's conceptual approach for NL understanding [Riesbeck, 1975; Birnbaum and Selfridge, 1981].

Conceptual Graphs (CGs) are based [Sowa, 1984, 1999] on a powerful graph-based representation scheme that can be used to represent *n*-ary relationships between complex objects in a global system. A CG is a finite, connected, bipartite graph that makes use of two kinds of nodes, i.e. "*concepts*" and "*conceptual relations*" (corresponding to roles); *every arc of a graph must link a conceptual relation to a concept.* "Bipartite" means that every arc of a CG associates necessarily one concept with one conceptual relation: *it is not possible to have arcs that link concepts with concepts or relations with relations.* A formal definition of CGs can be found, for example, in Chein and Mugnier [1992].

A well-known example of a CG, corresponding to the narrative "John is going to Boston by bus," is shown in Fig. 1.4.

In this figure, each box corresponds to a "concept node" and each oval to a "relation node." An arc with an arrowhead pointing toward an oval marks the *first argument* of the relation and an arc pointing away from an oval marks the *last argument*. If a relation has only one argument, then the arrowhead is omitted; if there are more than two arguments, then the arrowheads are replaced by integers 1, ..., *n*. The graph of Fig. 1.4 includes four concepts, each characterized by a "type label" making reference to their "type of entity" (i.e. their position within the ontology proper to the particular application): Person, Go, City and Bus. Two of the concepts are associated with "constants" that identify individuals: John and Boston. Each of the conceptual relations (conceptual roles) has a *type label* that represents the type of relation: Agnt for the agent of going, Inst for the instrument, and Dest for the destination. The CG as a whole indicates that the person John is the agent of an instance of going with Boston as the destination and a bus as the instrument.

For practical purposes, CGs are often expressed in a sort of "linear" notation; the last version in this context is called CG Interchange Format (CGIF); see Table 1.1. CGIF is a *fully conformant dialect of Common Logic*, and has been standardized in the Final Committee Draft of the proposed ISO standard for Common Logic; see [*Common Logic*, 2007]. Common Logic is a *framework for a*

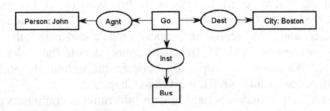

Fig. 1.4 A simple example of a CG

Table 1.1 CGIF form of the example of Fig. 1.4

[Go: *x] [Person: John] [City: Boston] [Bus: *y]
(Agnt ?x John) (Dest ?x Boston) (Inst ?x ?y)

family of logic languages, based on first-order logic, intended to facilitate the exchange and transmission of knowledge in computer-based systems. Other examples of Common Logic dialects are CLIF and XCL; all these allow the use of *n*-ary relations when appropriate. As is apparent from Table 1.1, concepts are represented in CGIF by *square brackets* and conceptual relations by *parentheses.* A character string prefixed with an asterisk, such as *x, is a "defining label." This may be referenced by a "bound label" ?x, prefixed with a question mark, according to the *coreference labels* principle. See also the "variables" system of NKRL in the following chapters and, once again, the Davidsonian and neo-Davidsonian representations mentioned in Section 1.1.2.2.

An important aspect of CGs concerns the *"second-order" (nested graphs) extensions* that allow them to deal with "contexts" and that represent *CGs' solution to the "connectivity phenomena" problem.* Figure 1.5 reproduces the solution proposed by Sowa [1991: 166–167; 1999: 485–486] for the representation of another well-known CG example, corresponding to the sentence "Tom believes that Mary wants to marry a sailor." In this figure, Tom is an "experiencer" (Expr role) that Believe(s) a proposition: on the contrary, another experiencer, Mary, wants a Situation that is described by nested graphs. The latter says that Mary (represented by the concept [T]) marries a sailor. As Sowa states, negation, modalities, and the "patients" or "themes" of verbs like "think" and "know" are linked in general with contexts of the type Proposition; times, locations, and the patients and themes of verbs like "want" and "fear" are linked with contexts of type Situation. The *coreference link* represented by the dotted line says that the concept [T] in the Situation box refers to the same individual as the concept [Person: Mary] in the Proposition box. *The way contexts are nested determines the scope of the quantifiers.* In Fig. 1.5, Sailor is *existentially quantified* inside the situation that Mary wants, which is in turn *existentially quantified* inside Tom's belief. The CGIF representation that corresponds to Figure 1.5 is given in Table 1.2.

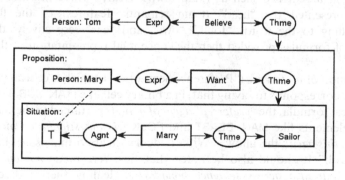

Fig. 1.5 Graphical representation of contexts (nested graphs)

Table 1.2 CGIF form of the example of Fig. 1.5

[Person: *x1 "Tom"] [Believe *x2] (Expr ?x2 ?x1)
(Thme ?x2 [Proposition:
     [Person: *x3 "Mary"] [Want *x4] (Expr ?x4 ?x3)
     (Thme ?x4 [Situation :
          [Marry *x5] [Agnt ?x5 ?x3) (Thme ?x5 [Sailor])])])

CGs and their formal characteristics will be discussed again in Chapter 3 (ontologies) and in Appendix B (representation of "plural" situations).

Having mentioned Schank's Conceptual Dependency Theory in the previous paragraphs, we cannot avoid mentioning another popular theory of the 1960 s and 1970 s, i.e. Wilks' Preference Semantics [Wilks, 1975 a, 1975 b], which finds its origin in the work of Margaret Masterman and the Cambridge Language Research Unit (CLRU). We have mentioned before Silvio Ceccato as (among other things) one of the pioneers of MT. Margaret Masterman, the founder (1955) of the CLRU, was another of these pioneers. Her work is particularly interesting even in the present context, given *she strongly believed that investigating the "meaning," not grammar or syntax, was the key to understanding sentences*, passing, for example, through the construction of an *interlingua based on a finite set of primitive semantic components*. An anthology of her papers has recently been published by Wilks; see Masterman [2005].

Returning to Wilks' Preference Semantics, to produce a conceptual representation of a given text according to this approach, the text was first partitioned at punctuation markers and "function words" (prepositions and conjunctions) into fragments, and each fragment was then tested against a fixed list of *bare templates*. Bare templates were in the form of *triples of semantic features* expressed as "actor/action/object" relationships, where "actor," "action" and "object" constitute the "head" of *lexical formulas* corresponding to senses of the English words (one formula for each sense). Lexical formulas were structured in turn as *binary trees of semantic primitives* (about 70) used to express semantic entities, states, qualities, actions and including cases like TO (direction) SOUR (source) GOAL (goal or end) LOCA (location) SUBJ (actor or agent), OBJE (patient of action), IN (containment) POSS (possessed by), etc. For example, the bare template MAN HAVE THING could match a sentence such as "John owns a car," where MAN, HAVE and THING represented the "head" (main semantic features) of the formulas corresponding to the words "John," "own" and "car" respectively; the final sequence of formulas provided then the conceptual representation of the input sentence.

The notion of *preference* ("Preference Semantics"), which is central in Wilks' approach, corresponds to saying that, in a binary cell like (*ANI SUBJ) used in a given lexical formula, the *"preferred" agent of actions* pertained to the class (*) of animate elements like MAN, BEAST and FOLK *without stipulating mandatory features of this agent*; this allowed Wilks to deal with abnormal usages like "cars drink petrol." It should also be noted that ties were made *not only within sentences, but also across sentence boundaries*, dealing then with cases of "connectivity phenomena" (e.g. causal links) through the use of "common sense inference" rules. An interesting, recent revisiting of Wilks' Preference Semantics theory can be found in Spärck Jones [2007].

Several *n*-ary theories have also been proposed within a general "Semantic Network" context; see Lehmann [1992]. We will limit ourselves to a mention of Lenhart K. Schubert's suggestion that goes back to the beginning of the 1970 s; see Schubert [1976]. Figure 1.6 reproduces the full and simplified *atomic proposition* introduced by Schubert to represent the elementary event "Joe gave a cup to Mary." In the full notation, the PRED link relates the central *proposition node* (represented by a circle) to a *predicative node* (GAVE), where a suitable number of links to *concept nodes* like Joe and Mary denote *the arguments of the predicate*. The latter are marked by letters like A, B and C that correspond clearly to *roles*; it is interesting to note that the "simplified" representation of Fig. 1.6 matches exactly the (very recent) W3C representation proposed for *n*-ary relations; see Fig. 1.2.

Among the current *n*-ary solutions of AI origin we can mention Topic Maps (TMs). Their key notions [Rath, 2003] *concern "topics," "occurrences" and "associations."* A topic is used to represent *any possible specific notion that could be interesting to speak about*, like the play Hamlet, the playwright William Shakespeare, or the "authorship" relationship: a topic, then, *reifies* a subject, making it "real" for a computer system. There is, then, no restriction on what can be represented as a topic. Topics can have *names*, and each individual topic is *an instance of one or more classes of topics ("topic types")* that may or may not be indicated explicitly. They can also have *occurrences*, i.e. information resources – specified as a text string that is part of the TM itself, or as a link to an external resource – that *are considered to be relevant in some way to the subjects the topic reify*. Links from topics to occurrences can, for example, be "discussed-in," "mentioned-in" or "depicted-in." Finally, topics can participate in *relationships with other topics, called "associations"*: an association consists of a number of *association roles* each of which has a topic attached as a "role player." The association role defines how its role player topic takes part in the association.

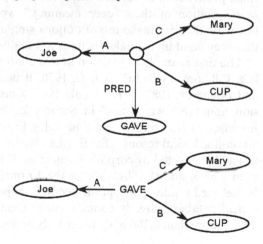

Fig. 1.6 Schubert's representation of *n*-ary relationships

Topics, then, have three sorts of *characteristics*: "names," "occurrences," and "roles" played as members of associations. The allocation of the characteristics is considered to be valid within a certain "scope," or "context." TMs can also be *merged*, at the discretion of the user or of the application (at runtime), or as indicated by the TM's author at the time of its creation.

TMs have often been considered as a *downgraded version* of other conceptual proposals, like Semantic Networks, CGs, or even NKRL; however, with respect to NKRL, for example, they have the advantage of using an XML syntax [Garshol and Moore, 2006] and of being already involved in a process of ISO standardization. An important study carried on by a specific task force consists in providing guidelines for users who want to combine usage of the W3C's RDF/OWL family of specifications with that of the ISO's family of TM standards, and in particular to produce *guidelines for transforming TMs into RDF/OWL representations and vice versa*, e.g. see the survey by Garshol et al. [2005] about the existing proposals for integrating RDF and TMs data.

In the context of the "current" *n*-ary AI-like proposals we can also mention CYC, which will be discussed in some depth in Section 3.1.1.2. Its proper knowledge representation language CycL – used to describe information in the enormous CYC knowledge base that consists of more than a million hand-entered "logical assertions" (facts, axioms and rules) about all the aspects of the world – *makes use in fact of multiple-arity relations* [e.g. Ramachandran et al., 2005]. No CycL predicate or function currently takes more than five arguments.

Eventually, in a description logics context, a specific language called DLR for dealing with *n*-ary relations has also been mentioned [Berardi et al., 2001], along with details about its use for reasoning on UML (unified modeling language) class diagrams. The basic conceptual elements of DLR are "concepts" and "*n*-ary relations."

Even if (as already stated in the previous sections) the linguistic approaches are often more interested in the description of the syntactic–semantic relationships proper to the "surface" aspects of the narrative documents than in the representation of their "deep meaning," we must acknowledge that many linguistic theories make use of notions similar to to the notion of "role" and that they build up formal structures not really dissimilar from Eq. (1.2).

The first example to mention in this context is, obviously, Case Grammars [e.g. Fillmore, 1968, 1977; Chafe, 1970; Bruce, 1975; Cook, 1979; Spärk Jones and Boguraev, 1987; Barker et al., 1997; Anderson, 2006]; also see the discussion about NKRL "roles" in Section 2.2.2.2. Fillmore's approach is *now revamped* in the context of the Berkeley FrameNet project, aimed at creating an on-line lexical resource for English, based on case grammar (frame) semantics and supported by corpus evidence; see Fillmore et al. [2001], Ruppenhofer et al. [2006] and the Web site of the FrameNet project (http://framenet.icsi. berkeley.edu/index.php?option = com_wrapper&Itemid = 126). The FrameNet lexical database already contains more than 10,000 lexical units (November 2007): more than 6,100 of them are fully annotated, making use of 825 semantic frames. Jackendoff's [1990] thematic roles have already been mentioned above in the context of the discussion about Kimian and Davidsonian events.

Kamp's Discourse Representation Theory (DRT) [Kamp and Reyle, 1993] is a theory about the *dynamic interpretation* of NL through a two-stage process: (i) the construction of semantic representations under the form of discourse representation structures (DRSs) and (ii) a model-theoretic interpretation of those DRSs. Kamp's work is of interest from our point of view mainly for the solutions he suggests (e.g. through "embedding functions" similar to the context solutions proposed by Sowa; see above) for *all sorts of context-related problems* – even if these problems and solutions concern mainly a "surface" linguistic context, e.g. see Kamp's proposals for solving the inter- and intra-sentential anaphoric relations between indefinite noun phrases and personal pronouns.

Again in a linguistic context, we have already mentioned the recent trend that concerns dealing with "events" like *grammatical objects* [Tenny and Pustejovsky, 2000] in the sense that the semantics of events should depend from the syntactic structures of verbs. We can also mention that the "story trees" of Mani and Pustejovsky [e.g. Mani and Pustejovsky, 2004], introduced from a computational linguistics and text summarization perspective, have some similarities with the "binding structures" of NKRL used to deal with connectivity phenomena.

A recent *practical* system of "linguistic" origin is the "Text Meaning Representation" (TMR) that is part of an implemented theory of NL processing, OntoSem (Ontological Semantics) [Nirenburg and Raskin, 2004; Nirenburg et al., 2004; Java et al., 2005]. TMR presents some *interesting similarities* with NKRL, which will be examined in some depth in Section 3.2.1.

1.2.2.2 Possible Problems Affecting Existing *n*-ary Solutions

Given the (apparent) profusion of *n*-ary results that could, at least in principle, be used to represent the elementary events that compose the "event stream" of our narratives, we can wonder why should we propose a specific NKRL formalism for these events. A first remark concerns the fact that, in spite of the evident conceptual similarities of all the above solutions, *a real consensus about their underpinning principles is very far from emerging*. We can note, for example, that:

- No *reasonable agreement* exists on the *list of roles*; see also Section 2.2.2.2.
- *Predicates are primitives* in Schank's Conceptual Dependency and NKRL, then lowering the number of possible combinations among the components of Eq. (1.2), but they are *totally free* in, for example, Schubert, Sowa or in all the linguistic theories.

We can also mention quantities of more specific problems, for example, the different ways of encoding the arguments a_k in Eq. (1.2). These can require, in fact, to be represented making use of *complex structures implying the need for specific conceptual operators*. If, for example, the example at the beginning of

Section 1.2.2 becomes "John has given a book *and some flowers* to Mary," then a correct representation of the argument introduced by the OBJECT/PATIENT role must in fact (i) include an operator in the COORDINATION style and (ii) find a way of SPECIFYING "flowers" (a plural...) as "some." NKRL deals with these problems by making use (see Chapter 2) of *binding operators* and *expansions*. Different solutions have been adopted in other systems, like CGs or TMs; see also the solutions in a Schankian style reproduced in Fig. 1.3. The same remarks can be made about the representation of the connectivity phenomena.

Passing now from the general principles to the examination of the *single, current and implemented possible solutions* examined in this chapter – ignoring, then, the "historical" proposals and those that are largely theoretical, like many of the "linguistic" or "narratology oriented" proposals – it is difficult to find a system that complies completely with our *very concrete and specific aims*.

In this context, we have already excluded the eChronicle-like systems because *they lack a real knowledge representation aspect*: this is essential, on the contrary, for our conception of narrative information, where the possibility of *automatically inferring interesting relationships among the involved entities* is particularly crucial; see Chapter 4. The W3C solutions have an *insufficient representational power* to satisfy our aims. As already stated, TMs are often considered as a hybrid, downgraded knowledge representation system where, among other things, the *reasoning capabilities seem to be relatively elementary ones*.

The universal ambitions of CYC [Lenat and Feigenbaum, 1991] (even if now considerably reduced) and the gigantic dimensions of its knowledge base with all the related *consistency problems* contrast deeply with the very specific, practical and well-delimited aims of NKRL. For consistency in CYC, see Johnson and Shapiro [2001] for example; for a description (and criticism) of CYC's ontology, see Section 3.1.1.2. A detailed analysis of the origins, developments and motivations of CYC can be found in Bertino et al. [2001: 275–316].

From a very specific, "narrative" point of view, we can add that the knowledge representation language of CYC, CycL (an *n*-ary language, as already stated) *seems not very suitable for representing all the different facets of narratives*. This is linked with *its uniform use of the same representation principle (substantially, a frame system rewritten in logical form) to represent entities that, in the narrative case, are conceptually very different* (general concepts, individuals, elementary events and general classes of events, dynamic instantiation of concepts and events, connectivity phenomena, rules, etc.). All these narrative categories, in fact, are represented in NKRL by making use of very different tools (binary and *n*-ary structures, labeled lists of reified arguments, etc.). Note that the CycL's "uniqueness syndrome" seems to be a widespread sort of disease, very common in the knowledge representation milieus.

Moreover, the real effectiveness of the commercial implementations of CYC (distributed by the Cycorp Company and used mainly in the context of US Government-supported projects) has often been questioned. See, in this

context, the comments of the evaluators about the results of the recent
HALO project (http://www.projecthalo.com/halotempl.asp?cid = 2133), where
it appears that Cycorp has "beaten" well-known R&D organizations or commercial enterprises like SRI or Ontoprise, but also that its real "understanding" of
the problems dealt with appear to be extremely low. HALO concerns "... the
development of a 'Digital Aristotle' – a staged, long-term research and development initiative that aims to develop an application capable of answering
novel questions and solving advanced problems in a broad range of scientific
disciplines."

CGs *undoubtedly have many points in common with NKRL, and the author of
this book is particularly sympathetic with John Sowa's work.* However, even CGs
seem unable to fit completely with respect to the "nonfictional narrative"
objectives of NKRL as declared in the first sections of this chapter.

As with every existing knowledge representation system, CGs have endured
all sorts of "academic" criticisms – including that of placing an excessive deal of
faith in the theories of the 19th century logician Charles Sanders Pierce. For
example, Guarino [2001] charges heavily CGS with respect to their (supposed)
lack of rigor from a logical and epistemological point of view. More down-to-
earth criticisms have been put forward. For example, the well-known saying
that goes "a picture is worth a thousand words" must sometimes be taken with a
pinch of salt: try to imagine a narrative text (e.g. a news story) of a medium
complexity and length (about a page of written text) represented integrally in
terms of conceptual graphs like those represented in Figs. 1.4 and 1.5. The
evident impracticability of such an approach led Sowa to introduce, from the
beginning, a *linear form of representation for CGs –* we have already seen that
CGIF is the last version produced in this context. There are, however, some
problems in translating a graphic representation into a linear one, given that
there is *no unique way to break a two-dimensional notation into a corresponding
linear notation.* As a result, there exist *multiple linear forms that correspond to a
unique CG.* We can also mention that some doubts have been expressed within
the CGs community itself about the generality and the efficiency of the second-
order structures needed to ensure connectivity, e.g. PROPOSITION and SITUA-
TION (see Fig. 1.5); for example, see Nazarenko's [1993] criticism, mentioned in
Section 3.2.2.4. Eventually, it was necessary to wait until the publication of the
1999 book to have a *precise list of the conceptual relations*; however, note that, in
the CG community, worries still seem to exist about the exact "meaning" of
many of them and their modalities of use; in this context, also see Lukosc et al.
[1995]. There are, for example, some ambiguities concerning the choice between
ATTR (Attribute) and CHRC (Characteristic), or AGNT (Agent) and EXPR
(Experiencer) (see again Figs. 1.4 and 1.5), etc.

We have two specific remarks about the *concrete possibility* of making use of
CG tools for dealing with our nonfictional narratives.

The first concerns the fact that several (very heterogeneous) tools and
environments for developing CG applications exist; however, they are in general *quite experimental, and implement only reduced subsets of the CG theory.*

Some of these tools, like CharGer [Delugach, 2005], CGWorld [Dobrev et al., 2001] and DNAT [Uhlir et al., 2004], are essentially *user interfaces and editing platforms* able to "produce" CGs and CG-based annotations – note that, at least in principle, DNAT annotations and graphs can afterwards be processed using standard tools like RDF and OWL. Others, like CoGITaNT, a library of C++ classes, *allow the execution of some standard canonical operations for creating and modifying CGs*; see Genest and Salvat [1998] and http://cogitant.sourceforge. net/library/index.html. CoGITaNT includes, among other things, the possibility of *implementing "if–then" rules where antecedent and consequent are in the form CGs*, and to make use of *CG-implemented constraints*. Notio [Southey and Linders, 1999] is a *Java API* for constructing CG tools and systems. Rather than attempting to provide a comprehensive CG toolset, Notio provides an *API specification from which different underlying implementations may be built up*. The most recent versions of the Amine Platform [Kabbaj et al., 2001, 2006] allow, among other things, the execution of *some advanced information retrieval operations on a knowledge base in the form of CGs*. With respect now to Corese (a COnceptual REsource Search Engine) [Corby et al., 2004], this tool corresponds to an RDF engine implemented in CG terms that enables the processing of RDF and RDFS statements within the CG formalism. In this case, *the original* n-*ary properties of CGs are downgraded to the usual binary, W3C-like ones*, and this lessens considerably the interest for this sort of system. A list of Corese's applications can, however, be found at: http://www-sop.inria.fr/ teams/edelweiss/wiki/wakka.php?wiki = CoreseApplications.

Sonetto [Sarraf and Ellis, 2006], a rule-based, business product information management system, is an *interesting, recent commercial system making use of a CGIF-like form of representation* that has nothing to share with the previous environments and tools. It is based, in fact, *on a proprietary mode*: (i) on Gerard Ellis's work on the unification of conceptual graphs [Ellis, 1995]; (ii) on the Ripple Down Rules (RDR) framework for dynamic rule acquisition [Compton et al., 2006]. Commercialized by the UK IVIS Group, Sonetto is currently used for retail management by Tesco plc, the third-largest retailer in the world. From an NKRL point of view, this work is interesting because of the *similarities between the problems, and the solutions adopted, for dealing with the unification of (NKRL or CG) conceptual structures* – see also, in this context, the recent work of Corbett [2003] that adds to the standard CG unification procedures the possibility of dealing with constraints, leading then to the implementation of *unification algorithms very similar to those used in the Filtering Unification Module of NKRL, Fum*; see Section 4.1.

Apart from the feeling that work in a CG context *seems to concern largely a pure "academic" domain* – from this point of view, Sonetto appears really as an exception even if, apparently, other "undisclosed" commercial applications of CGs exist – a second important remark concerns the fact that there is *a fundamental difference between the NKRL- and CG-based approaches to the set up and managing of* n-*ary structures*. Even if CGs have, in fact, the possibility of *defining general "standard" conceptual structures for describing complex* n-*ary, narrative-like phenomena* – similar, then, to the NKRL "templates" mentioned in Section 1.1.2 and described in detail Chapter 3 – and despite the title of one of Sowa's papers, "Using a lexicon of canonical graphs in a semantic interpreter" [Sowa, 1988], *an exhaustive and authoritative list of these structures under the form of "canonical graphs" does not exist, and its construction seems never to have been planned.* The practical consequence of this state of affairs, then, is the need, whenever a concrete application of CGs theory must be implemented, *to define anew a specific list of "canonical graphs" for this particular application.*

On the contrary, a fundamental (and apparently unique) characteristic of NKRL is given by the fact that its catalogue of "templates" (including, as already stated, about 150 *n*-ary basic conceptual structures, which are very easy to extend and customize) is in practice *part and parcel* of the definition of the language. Given the risks of *combinatorial explosion* proper to the *n*-ary domain – they derive from the high number of possible associations among predicates, roles and arguments that come up when passing from binary expressions in the $Rb_i(e, Arg_i)$ style (see Eq. (1.1)) to *n*-ary expressions like Eq. (1.2) – this approach is extremely important for practical applications. In particular, it implies that: (i) a system-builder *does not have to create himself* the structural and inferential knowledge needed to describe and exploit the events proper to a large class of narratives (see Chapter 3); (ii) *it becomes easier to secure the reproduction or the sharing of previous results.* In the CG literature, *practical indications* on how to *concretely choose and combine* the P_j, R_k and a_k terms in Eq. (1.2) are difficult to find.

Thus, some good reasons seem to exist for trying to produce an *original, operational, standardized and realistic solution* for the representation and the "intelligent" management of nonfictional narratives of an economic interest.

1.3 In the Guise of Winding Up

In this chapter we have tried (i) to explain the meaning of the term *nonfictional narratives*, (ii) to emphasize the importance of having at our disposal *efficient CS tools* for dealing with these sorts of multimedia document, (iii) to supply some *basic principles* underpinning the solution, NKRL, illustrated in this book for the management of these narratives, and (iv) to *give reasons* for making use of this specific solution. More precisely:

• When trying to define the term "nonfictional narratives," we have seen that a specific discipline, "narratology," deals with the "structure" of the narratives, i.e. attempts to dissect narratives into their component parts in order to establish their functions, their purposes and the mutual relationships. Narratology differentiates between "fictional narratives" (which, like a novel, have mainly an entertainment value and represent an imaginary narrator's account of a story that happened in an imaginary world) and "nonfictional" or "factual narratives" (e.g. news stories, which present on the contrary a real-life person's account of real-life events). Even if NKRL's tools could be used in general to deal with any sort of narrative, we concentrate explicitly on the domain of "nonfictional narratives."

- This last domain is of a *high economic importance*. Examples of nonfictional narratives concern, in fact, the "corporate knowledge" documents, the news stories, the normative and legal texts, the medical records, many intelligence messages, surveillance videos, actuality photographs for newspapers and magazines, material (text, image, video, sound, etc.) for eLearning, etc. Even if large amounts of nonfictional narratives are embedded in NL texts, this is not *necessarily true*; see the example of a photograph representing a situation that, verbalized, could be expressed as "The US President is addressing the Congress." In general, then, the economically interesting, nonfictional narratives taken into account by NKRL are *multimedia documents that can be practically embodied into texts, images, videos, sounds, etc.*

- Even if CS applications that can be reduced to a general narratology context exist, they are not *very effective* as a possible framework for representing and "intelligently" managing nonfictional narratives. They are, in fact, either mainly of interest to fictional and literary applications (e.g. automatic generation of fictions) or they lack those knowledge representation components (e.g. see the eChronicle applications) that are *indispensable for executing "intelligent" querying/inferencing operations.* Theoretical research in the narratology domain can, however, help us to define and circumscribe our domain of interest better.

- From this last point of view we can say, first of all, that we are concerned more with the *story level* (i.e. what is really "narrated") than with the *discourse level* (how a particular story is narrated, i.e. the stylistic choices of the author that determine the particular form of the final narrative) of the nonfictional narratives. If we reduce this "story level" to its lower, essential layer – the "fabula" layer, according to Mieke Bal's theories – *our (nonfictional) narratives represent concretely a logically connected stream of nonfictional elementary events that describe the activities or the experiences of given "characters,"* in the most general meaning of this term. When the *temporally and spatially bounded elementary events* that make up this stream are verbalized in NL terms, their *logical coherence* is normally expressed through syntactic/semantic *connectivity phenomena*, like causality, goal, indirect speech, coordination and subordination, etc.

- Trying now to characterize the notion of elementary event, we can say that, from a strict formal (and operational) point of view, the *formal NKRL equivalent of an "elementary event" corresponds simply to a spatio-temporal instantiation – called a "predicative occurrence" – of one of the (pre-established) n-ary structures called "templates" that identify general categories of events like "moving a physical object," "living in a given place," "sending a message," "producing a document," etc. (or "being injured").* NKRL's templates (actually, about 150) are structured into a hierarchy (HTemp, the "hierarchy of templates") that corresponds then to an "ontology of events."

- To represent in NKRL's format the elementary event "Brutus stabs Caesar," we will then *retrieve from the general "catalogue" of NKRL templates represented by HTemp* the specific template Produce:HumanBeingInjuring. This is structured around the *deep predicate* PRODUCE that defines the *general conceptual category* of the elementary event to be represented. We will then *instantiate* this template by substituting to the *variables* that, introduced by *roles*, constitute the *arguments* of the deep predicate the *individual* BRUTUS_ as "filler" of the SUBJ(ect) role, the *concept* injuring_ as filler of the OBJ(ect) role, CAESAR_ as filler of the BEN(e)F(iciary) role, the *concept* stabbing_ as filler of the MODAL(ity) role, etc.

- This formal definition is *not contradictory* with some popular theories about the *notion of events*: it can be interpreted in their context and we can draw useful lessons from this identification. For example, we have seen that the formal representation of the NKRL "elementary events" complies with the general structure of Jaegwon Kim's "monadic events," and that the Davidsonian and neo-Davidsonian theories and formalisms correspond well to the importance attributed to "predicate" and "roles" in the NKRL formalism.

- An important point to emphasize concerns, however, the fact that NKRL's predicates are always *deep predicates* (see the PRODUCE predicate above): *to each deep predicate that it is possible to recognize within the general stream representing the "narrative" there corresponds an "elementary event."* "Deep" means that the predicate *is more related to a sort of "common sense" general predicative function than to a specific morpho-syntactic, "surface" item.* The notion of "stabbing" used to characterize "Brutus" stabs Caesar" as an elementary event could also be rendered, then, at the linguistic level as "knifing" or "piercing," and is *totally independent from "surface" syntactic considerations in the style of, for example, active or passive voice.* In contrast with many "linguistic" theories, we consider that the set up of a formal notation for expressing the conceptual content of events can be developed *quite independently from the search for an optimal form of correspondence with the surface form these events can assume in a particular NL.*

- Having described the nonfictional narratives as "streams of events," and having supplied some formal and "theoretical" characteristics of the "elementary events" that make up the stream, we must now examine whether, among the existing (or past) knowledge representation systems proposed (mainly) in an AI context, *we can find useful suggestions about how to represent and link together the elementary events of the stream.* We can note immediately that the sort of knowledge representation to be retained cannot be the usual, "binary" one, based on a "property-value" type of approach, like the examination of the trivial narrative "John has given a book to Mary" clearly demonstrates ("give" corresponds to a ternary relationship). To represent elementary events *in general*, an n-*ary sort of representation* like that reproduced in Eq. (1.2) – *where, among other things, the notion of "role" is used* – must then be adopted.

- This immediately excludes the possibility of having NKRL based on *some sort of W3C language like RDF and OWL, given that the latter are intrinsically binary ones*. Some recent attempts to extend the W3C languages in an *n*-ary direction are not particularly convincing.
- Many *n*-ary solutions equivalent to that represented by Eq. (1.2) have been proposed in the past (see Ceccato, Schank, Schubert, Wilks, etc.). *n*-ary solutions are actually used by some knowledge representation systems, e.g. see TMs, CYC, CGs. We can note immediately that, in spite of some evident conceptual similarities among these solutions, *no standard approach has emerged so far about the way to implement the essential components of Eq. (1.2) in practice*. For example: (i) no universal agreement exists on the list of roles; (ii) predicates are primitives in Schank's conceptual dependency and NKRL, but are totally free in, for example, Schubert, Sowa or in the *n*-ary linguistic approaches. The same can be stated about the way of encoding the arguments of the predicate in Eq. (1.2) when these arguments imply the presence of complex structure, or the way of representing the "connectivity phenomena."
- More specifically, none of the existing *n*-ary solutions seems to be able to fit the "nonfictional narratives" bill completely. TMs have often been considered as a hybrid, downgraded knowledge representation system where, among other things, the *reasoning capabilities* seem to be relatively elementary ones. The universal purposes of CYC and the extremely large dimensions of its knowledge base with all the *related consistency problems* contrast deeply with the reduced ambitions of NKRL. From a very specific, "narrative" point of view, even if the representational power of the knowledge representation language of CYC, i.e. CycL (substantially, a frame system rewritten in logical form), is surely equivalent to that of Eq. (1.2), this language seems to be *too rigid and uniform to adapt itself to the representation of the different facets (general concepts, elementary events and general classes of events, dynamic instantiation of concepts and events, connectivity phenomena, etc.) of the narrative phenomena*. Moreover, the real effectiveness of the commercial implementations of CYC has often been questioned.
- In spite of some possible, "minor" representational defaults of CGs – like a particularly convolute solution to the problem of the connectivity phenomena (interrelation of graphs) or some ambiguities about the exact "roles" of some conceptual relations – *it is easy to see that CGs and NKRL share many representational problems and many of the corresponding solutions*.
- However, the "general philosophy" of the two approaches is very different. Even without bearing in mind the fact that CGs present themselves like a sort of "universal" system, while NKRL is focused on the solution of the specific "narrative" problems, *it seems evident that work in a CG context concerns mainly the "academic" domain and that NKRL work, on the contrary, has more of an "engineering" and "practical" flavor*.
- This becomes particularly evident when we consider the fact that (even if CGs obviously have the possibility to define "standard" conceptual

structures similar to the NKRL "templates") *an exhaustive and authoritative list of these structures under the form of "canonical graphs" does not exist, and its construction seems never to have been planned.* On the contrary, a fundamental (and apparently unique) characteristic of NKRL concerns the fact that its catalogue of "templates" is, in practice, *part and parcel* of the definition of the language. Given the risks of *combinatorial explosion* proper to the *n*-ary domain, this approach is extremely important for practical applications given that: (i) a system builder does not have to create themselves the structural and inferential knowledge needed to describe and exploit the events proper to a (sufficiently) large class of narratives; (ii) it becomes easier to secure the reproduction or the sharing of previous results.

Chapter 2
The Knowledge Representation Strategy

This chapter explains in a detailed way the main encoding principles underpinning the NKRL style of knowledge representation. It describes NKRL as a sort of *general environment* to be used to represent formally all sorts of narratives; *specific solutions* used to represent *particular kinds of narrative knowledge* (particular narrative "contents") will be detailed in Chapter 3. After reading Chapter 2, interested people should be able (i) to understand the characteristic NKRL (external) code that has been used in the framework of all the existing NKRL applications; (ii) to encode themselves in NKRL's terms at least in some simple example of nonfictional narrative.

Following Section 2.1, which is devoted to the description of the general, *"architectural" organization of the "basic" NKRL language* and to the introduction of its four *"components,"* Section 2.2, will give a detailed explanation of the *data structures* used for these components. Section 2.3 will deal with the *"second-order"* structures used in NKRL to take into account those *connectivity phenomena* that, as we have seen in Chapter 1, are so important for the correct representation of narrative information. A short conclusion, Section 2.4, will end the chapter.

2.1 Architecture of NKRL: the Four "Components"

From an "architectural" point of view, we can see the *"basic"* NKRL language (i.e. without considering the second-order tools at the moment) as structured into *four connected "components,"* even if the differences among these components are somewhat blurred in the implementation software. Each of them *takes into account a particular category of narrative phenomena*, making use of specific knowledge representation tools that can be considered as the *best fitted* for modeling these phenomena. The four components are *definitional, enumerative, descriptive* and *factual*; we provide a general description of their main characteristics below.

- The *definitional component* concerns the formal (binary) representation of both the *general* (like "human being," "amount" or "artifact") and the

G.P. Zarri, *Representation and Management of Narrative Information*,
DOI 10.1007/978-1-84800-078-0_2, © Springer-Verlag London Limited 2009

specific notions (like "business person," "taxi," "city" or "demand for ransom") that must be considered for taking correctly into account the narrative information proper to the different application domains. The NKRL formal representations of these notions are called *"concepts"* – denoted in general as C_i. NKRL concepts are inserted into a *generalization/specialization directed graph structure* (often, but not necessarily, reduced to a tree) that, for historical reasons, is called HClass(es), "hierarchy of classes." The data structures of the NKRL concepts correspond relatively well to the analogous structures that can be built up using the usual environments for the creation of ontologies like Protégé [Noy et al., 2000], WebODE [Arpírez et al., 2003] or OntoEdit [Sure et al., 2002]. In the *concrete NKRL structures expressed in "external" NKRL format*, the concepts are "named" making use of *(lower case) symbolic labels* like human_being, business_person, taxi_, city_, ransom_demand, etc. To discriminate between concepts and other categories of the language also represented in practice by lower case "names," e.g. the "modulators" (see Section 2.2.2.4), the symbolic labels denoting the concepts always include at least an "underscore" symbol.

- The *"enumerative component"* concerns the formal representation of the *instances I_i (specific examples) of the notions (concepts) pertaining to the definitional component* – as we will see in Chapter 3, not all the NKRL concepts can be endowed with instances. The formal representations in NKRL's terms of such instances take the name of *"individuals"*; individuals are then created *by instantiating the properties of the concepts of the definitional component*. Individuals are characterized by the fact of *being countable (enumerable)* and of always being associated, often in an implicit way, with a *spatio-temporal dimension*. Within the actual NKRL structures, each individual owns a *unique conceptual label* (JOHN_SMITH, PARIS_, RANSOM_DEMAND_4): two individuals associated with the same NKRL description but having different labels will be considered as different individuals. In the "external" format of NKRL, individuals are represented in upper case. To discriminate between individuals and other categories of the language also denoted in upper case, like predicates and roles (Section 2.2.2.2), their symbolic labels always include at least an "underscore" symbol.

- The *"descriptive component"* concerns the formal representation of *general classes of elementary events* like "moving a generic object," "formulate a need," "be present somewhere," "starting a company," "committing acts of violence against someone," etc. As we have already stated in Chapter 1, the *formal (n-ary) representations of these general classes in NKRL terms are called "templates", t_i.* Note that the term "elementary event" is used in NKRL to denote also, in general, all the fuzzy, associated notions like state, situation, period, episode, history, process, action, etc.; see also Zarri [1998]. The general classes of elementary events (templates) of the descriptive component are *obtained by abstraction/generalization from sets of specific, elementary narrative "events" (in the general meaning evidenced before) that we can observe (or imagine) in the real world.* Within the concrete NKRL structures, templates are denoted in "external" format by symbolic labels such as the Produce:HumanBeingInjuring already met in Section 1.1.2; see Chapter 3 for details. Templates are inserted into an inheritance hierarchy (in this case, a simple tree) that is called HTemp (hierarchy of templates).

- The "factual component" provides the formal representation (as instances of the templates of the descriptive component) of the different, possible elementary events that can be isolated within a narrative. As already stated, these formal representations are called "predicative occurrences", c_i. A predicative occurrence is then the NKRL representation of an elementary narrative information like "Tomorrow, I will move the wardrobe," "Lucy was looking for a taxi," "Peter lives in Paris," "Company X, located in Geneva, has taken the control of Company Y," etc. The elementary events (the predicative occurrences) eventually concern the description of a particular set of interactions among individuals (and, in case, concepts) – see the interaction between Lucy and a particular wardrobe in the example before, or between Brutus and Caesar in the "stabbing" event of Chapter 1– where: (i) the "semantic category" of the set of interactions is defined by the particular "deep predicate" ("stabbing") associate with the event; (ii) in conformity with the Kimian analysis of Chapter 1, the set of interactions is delimited from a spatio/temporal point of view. This implies, among other things, that a specific "duration" (a specific temporal interval that can be "empty" in the case, for example, of a "future" or "hypothetical" event) will always be associated with a predicative occurrence. Within the concrete NKRL representations in external format, occurrences are denoted (usually) by a sort of "pointed" notation, introduced in Section 2.2.2.2.

With respect, for example, to a description logics' perspective [Baader et al., 2002], we note that *the definitional component in NKRL corresponds roughly to Tbox and the enumerative component to Abox.* Tbox contains, in fact, *intensional knowledge that describes the general properties of concepts*; ABox contains the *corresponding extensional knowledge.* No description logics structures *correspond, on the contrary, to the descriptive or factual structure of NKRL* that constitute then, from a data structure point of view, the main innovation introduced by this last language.

We can conclude this section by emphasizing that, in NKRL, the concepts (definitional component) and their instances (individuals, enumerative component) are *kept conceptually distinct* – even if *they are represented using, in practice, the same data structures*; see the following sections. The main reason for operating this separation is linked with the *very different epistemological status of concepts* – which define a *generic, abstract mold* for some *compulsory notions* that must be taken into consideration in a given domain – *with respect to the individuals*, which represent only *transitory entities found out in the context of some concrete events* of the domain. In this respect, *concepts can be considered as necessary and permanent, at least in the context of a given application* – even if, in practice, customizing

HClass for an application requires the addition of several new, low-level concepts *online* (and, in some cases, their modification and withdrawal). Individuals represent, on the contrary, *unpredictable, randomly occurring entities* stored consecutively (and continuously) into an NKRL-based system, characterized by the absence of any *necessity attribute* and that can, therefore, be *eliminated without any consequence for the logical coherence of the system.*

Similar considerations could also be formulated about the reasons for distinguishing between descriptive (templates) and factual component (predicative occurrences) entities – even if, in this case, the *need* for such a differentiation is more concretely evident (the predicative occurrences constitute the formal basis for encoding our nonfictional narratives).

Note that the separation concepts/instances (individuals) can appear as an *obvious requirement today* but, in reality, recognizing that there is a need for this distinction is a *relatively recent notion.* Many "expert systems" environments in the 1970s and 1980s could not differentiate between the two. A well-known example in this context is that of KEE [Fikes and Kehler, 1985], one of the early and most powerful commercial environments for the development of complex frame-based systems. Followers of a uniform approach in which all the "units," to adopt the KEE terminology, have the same status, claim that, for many applications, this distinction *is not very useful and only adds some important logical and semantic difficulties.* From a knowledge representation point of view, the formalization of the concepts/instances distinction can be traced back to the well-known Woods [1975] paper "What's in a link: foundations for semantic networks" and to *his claim for a separation between "intension" (concepts) and "extension" (instances, e.g. the sets of entities that "materialize" the concepts).* One of the examples used by Woods concerns the classical Frege's (and Quine's) example about the two different concepts of "morning star" and "evening star" (intension) that are both materialized by the same instance (extension), the planet Venus. We note that NKRL follows Woods' conclusion of conceiving all the nodes of an ontology as *intensional entities* (i.e. as concepts), and *to add a specific predicate of existence only when necessary to introduce some instances*; see Section 2.2.1.4. A corollary of this decision concerns the fact that, in NKRL, individuals (instances) are *terminal symbols (leaves) of the HClass hierarchical structure (the NKRL "ontology" of concepts)* and that they *cannot be further specialized*, i.e. they cannot receive further instances; again, see Section 2.2.1.4 and Zarri [1997].

2.2 The Data Structures of the Four Components

The data structures proper of the four components are *systematically implemented as structured objects identified by a symbolic label.* Within this general framework, very important differences exist between the definitional/enumerative and the descriptive/factual structures.

2.2.1 Definitional/Enumerative Data Structures

The definitional and enumerative data structures that support concepts and individuals have been implemented in a relatively simple and straightforward way, given that *the most complex and intriguing aspects of the "narrative" phenomena are taken into account by the descriptive and factual data structures.* Therefore, in designing these structures, the aim has been simply that of implementing *a clean and simple semantics allowing very efficient and fast managing of operations.* These structures (basically "binary" – see the discussion in Chapter 1) have, then, been organized in a (traditional and well-known) *frame-like fashion,* i.e. as bundles of *properties (attributes, features, qualities,...)/value* relations where neither the number nor the order of the properties is fixed. This type of organization, then, concerns both the *definitions* associated with the concepts and the *descriptions* of the corresponding individuals.

NKRL "frames" conform to the general requirements of the Open Knowledge Base Connectivity (OKBC), [Chaudhri et al., 1998], *and are not very different from the object structures used in Protégé* [Noy et al., 2000; Gennari et al., 2002]. As is well known, Protégé is a sort of *standard* for the set up of frame-oriented ontologies: in a recent survey based on 627 answers to a questionnaire about the practices of the SW community [Cardoso, 2007], Protégé was the ontology editor most frequently mentioned with a "market share" of 68.2%. A prototype that extends the present Protégé system to support *collaborative ontology editing in a Web-based environment* is presented, for example, in Tudorache and Noy [2007]. Note that the NKRL software makes use of a *specific environment* – the *HclassEditor* – to set up its frame structures and to store them onto an ORACLE database; see also Appendix A. This environment is very similar to the *standard* (i.e. without additional plugins) Protégé environment, and the two can, at least in principle, *be indifferently used to introduce new concepts or individuals into HClass or to modify them.* Some of the reasons for building up a specific NKRL environment for the set up of frame-like structures are explained in the following sections. Information below refers, in general, to *concepts*: the specific problems proper to the *implementation of NKRL instances* (individuals) are examined in detail in Section 2.2.1.4.

2.2.1.1 General Principles of the HClass "Frames"

We will quickly recall here some well-known notions concerning the set up of ontologies of concepts under the form of "frames."

These ontologies are structured as *inheritance hierarchies* making use of the IsA link (also called AKindOf (Ako), SuperC, etc.). A relatively unchallenged (however, see Brachman [1983]) semantic interpretation of IsA states that this relationship among concepts, when noted as (IsA C_2 C_1), means that concept C_2

is a *specialization* of the more general concept C_1. In other terms, C_1 *subsumes* C_2. This assertion can be expressed in logical form as

$$\forall x \ (C_2(x) \ \rightarrow \ C_1(x)) \tag{2.1}$$

Equation (2.1) says that, if any elephant_ (C_2) IsA mammal_ (C_1), and if CLYDE_ is an elephant_, then CLYDE_ is also a mammal_. When Eq. (2.1) is interpreted strictly, it also implies that a given concept C_k and all its instances *must* inherit *all* the properties and their values of *all* the concepts C_i in the hierarchy that have C_k as a specialization; we speak in this case of *strict inheritance*. Note that, even under the strict inheritance hypothesis, totally new properties can be added to C_k to specialize it with respect to its parents. The problems connected with a systematic interpretation of "inheritance" as "strict inheritance" are discussed in Bertino et al. [2001: 139–147].

A "frame" is now basically *a set of properties* (normally called "slots") *with associated classes of admitted values* (the "fillers" of the slots) that is *associated with the nodes representing the concepts* (not necessarily the totality of the concepts) of a given ontology. Introducing a frame corresponds, then, to add to the fundamental IsA relationship that *necessarily concerns all the concepts C_i of an ontology* a new sort of relationship between a *specific* concept C_k to be defined and *some* of the other concepts $C_1, C_2, \ldots, C_n$ of the ontology. The relationship concerns the fact that $C_1, C_2, \ldots, C_n$ are used in the frame defining C_k to indicate the *class of fillers* that can be associated with the "slots" of this frame – the slots denoting, as already stated, the main properties (attributes, qualities, etc.) of C_k. In NKRL (HClass), no fixed number of slots exists and no particular order is imposed on them; slots can be accessed by their names.

To see how the relationships between a generic C_k and concepts $C_1, C_2, \ldots, C_n$ can be formally described, let us suppose that a specific concept C_1 (e.g. home_address) is endowed with a property R_1 (e.g. HasNecessarily) that associates it with a concept C_2 like postal_code. We can formalize this situation as

$$\forall x \ (C_1(x) \ \rightarrow \ \exists y \ (C_2(y) \ \wedge \ R_1(x, y))) \tag{2.2}$$

Equation (2.2) means, according to our example, that every home address is endowed with the property of having a postal code (the slot HasNecessarily will appear in the frame associated with the concept postal_code). As already stated, properties (slots) can be *systematically* inherited along an inheritance hierarchy only under the "strict inheritance" hypothesis. Instances ("individuals" in the NKRL terminology) inherit from the father concept.

As usual in the ontological domain, it is possible to allow an HClass concept to inherit its properties (slots) from two or more concepts by clicking on the button "Multi-Inheritance" in the *hClassEditor* environment. *The user can then choose the concepts in the ontology that they want to assume as "fathers" for the selected concept.*

We can remark now on a first, important difference with respect to the Protégé approach *in case of possible conflicts among inherited slots in a multiple inheritance context*, i.e. in the case of slots coming from different father concepts and having the *same name* but *different values*. Protégé makes use, in fact, of automatic heuristics to solve these conflicts. A *precedence list* is computed in a "mechanical" way by starting with the first leftmost concept that represents a generalization (superconcept) of the concept where the conflict has been observed; the construction of this list proceeds by visiting depth-first the nodes in the left branch, then those of the right branch, then the join, and up from there. The "conflicting" concept inherits the properties of the first element of the list. This technique depends, obviously, *on the particular arrangement adopted in the construction of the inheritance hierarchy, and can oblige one to insert a number of "dummy concepts" in order to produce a correct precedence list.* In NKRL, we have decided, on the contrary, *to have systematic recourse to the intervention of the user to solve any possible incoherence.* As stated above, the user will then be *asked to select the correct set of properties/values explicitly for the concept under examination*, i.e. to specify exactly the *superconcept from which a given conflicting property must be inherited.*

We conclude this section by noticing that, as we have seen, the use of multi-inheritance in HClass is admitted; we must now add that it is also *strongly discouraged*. We agree, in fact, with Guarino [e.g. Guarino, 1998] when he says that, in the ontological domain, *there is a tendency towards relying on multiple inheritance ("IsA overloading") to solve all the possible "polysemy" (in the most general meaning of this term) problems.* In reality, a more in-depth examination of these (supposed) multiple-inheritance situations shows that, for example, by simply duplicating the "polysemic" concepts, or by reducing to "properties" (roles) some "dubious" concept, *the need for multiple inheritance disappears.* Moreover, in NKRL, the possibility of expressing *dynamic* concepts making use of descriptive/factual structures (i.e. by expressing some of these "concepts" as templates/predicative occurrences – see Section 2.2.1.3) can help to further reduce the "IsA overloading" phenomenon and to eliminate then the need for multi-inheritance connections.

2.2.1.2 Prototype Slots

In a "frame" context, there always has been a lot of debate about the theoretical problems linked with the *arbitrariness* in the choice of the slots (in the choice of the particular properties intended to describe in a better way the "meaning" of a concept). A "classical" paper in this framework is Wilensky [1987]. Given the evident impossibility of finding a global (and shared) solution to this problem at the theoretical level, some practical solutions have been implemented. They are all based on the use of *meta-structures intended to describe in a precise way the computational behavior of a given slot* – and, therefore to give, in a certain way, also a sort of "definition" of the slot. A well-known approach in this context consists in adding *facets* to the slots, where a facet is *an annotation describing some characteristics of the slots* like, for example, type restrictions on the values of the slot (VALUE-TYPE facets) and specifications of the exact number of possible values that the slot may take on (CARDINALITY facets). An evolution of the facet approach concerns making use of full *"slot-control schemata"* – i.e. of a *structured object containing complete information about the properties of a specific slot,* not only those concerning domain, range and cardinality, but also, for example, *detailed inheritance specifications for the slot.*

To deal, at least partly, with the *arbitrariness* problem (in particular the arbitrariness of the "attribute" slots – see below), NKRL follows the "slot-control schemata" approach, giving then to the HClass slots the status of *full-fledged objects.* As in Protégé and in the OKBC requirements, slots in NKRL are then defined a priori as *"prototype slots,"* independently then from the specifications of any particular concept. Prototype slots are grouped in a list, and *attached to specific concepts when necessary.* According to a classical example, an "attribute" like "age" can, in fact, be used to describe the characteristics of both (among other things) the concepts author_ and manuscript_. The slot Age will be then defined as a *slot prototype* whose minimal value is set to "0," and which cannot be used in a situation where it is required that the slot must be capable of containing negative values. Age will then be attached, in case, to author_, manuscript_ and to many other possible concepts. Analogously, an attribute like Name will be introduced as a slot prototype that can be filled only with a value of the "string of characters" type, etc.

In NKRL, the *data types* admitted for the fillers of the HClass (prototype) slots are *strictly the following*:

- Boolean;
- (HClass) concept/individual;
- double (precision);
- integer;
- string (of characters).

Moreover, the *values* corresponding to the previous data types can be submitted, as usual, to *constraints.* The *cardinality constraint* defines the number of values that can be associated with a slot; *this number must be included between the CardMin and CardMax limits,* which respectively define the minimal and maximal number of values. If the slots are of the *integer* or *double precision* types, then their fillers must be included *within a numeric interval.* If the slots are of the *concept/individual* type, then the fillers can only be chosen among *the instances, and all the specific terms with their instances,* of the concept defined as default value, etc.

There is, however, *an important difference between our approach to the management of the prototype slots and that of Protégé* – in Protégé, the prototype slots are called *template slots.* In this last environment, the features originally associated with a prototype (template) slot can always be *overridden* when the prototype is associated with a concept. For us, *the constraints associated with a specific prototype* (type of the value, cardinality, min/max, possible default value, etc.) *are strictly enforced* to maintain the coherence of the global knowledge base, and they *cannot be changed* when a prototype is associated with a specific concept, becoming then a slot proper to this concept. This means that, when a prototype slot is concretely used and the user realizes that the constraints associated with this slot are not well tailored to her/his specific needs, *the user cannot intervene directly on the slot at the concept level* but must either (i) *edit the original prototype slots (change its constraints)* or (ii) *define a new prototype slot that fits exactly her/his specific needs*.

There is, in practice, only a possibility of *directly editing* the information already associated with the slots of a concept, and this concerns a *restriction of the domain of the admitted values*. More precisely:

- a modification of the cardinality is allowed only if *the new CardMin/Card-Max interval is included within the interval of the original prototype;*
- the same restriction applies to the *min/max numeric interval of the integer and double precision values;*
- if a default concept is associated with the slot, then this default can be changed only if the new default is *an instance, or a specific term with all its instances, of the original default.*

Figure 2.1 reproduces an *hClassEditor* screen dump, showing the use of prototype slots to associate properties with the biotechnology_company concept – a specific term of biological_company in HClass.

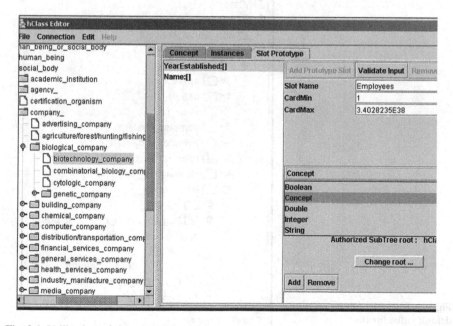

Fig. 2.1 Utilization of the prototype slots

In the situation illustrated, two slots, i.e. YearEstablished and Name, have already been associated with the concept under definition; moreover, we have selected again the "Slot Prototype" window to add a new slot, Employees, to biotechnology_company. In this window we have clicked on the "Add Prototype Slot" button, and selected Employees in the prototype slots list. Employees appears with its features, the cardinality constraints and the type, the latter being "Concept." The *default value* associated with the prototype is hClass; according to the third of the rules for editing slots introduced above, *we can "specialize" the default making use of the "Change root ..." button*. Clicking on this opens a "Select concept" window (see Fig. 2.2) where a new default for the slot will be selected, i.e. individual_person. Clicking on the "Validate Input" button (Fig. 2.1) will cause the Employees slot to be listed among the biotechnology_company slots.

2.2.1.3 Categories of Properties

From a *semantic* point of view, the properties of the concept C_k to be defined (i.e. all the possible types of relationships between C_k and some other concepts

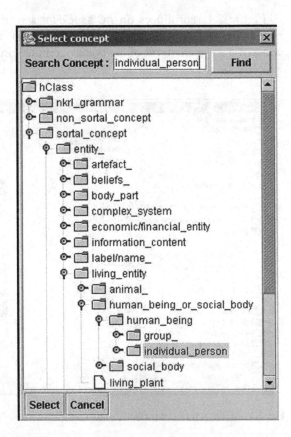

Fig. 2.2 Selecting a new default value for the Employees slot

Table 2.1 Types of properties in an NKRL frame

{OID	
[Relation	(IsA | InstanceOf:
	HasSpecialization | HasInstance:
	MemberOf | HasMember:
	PartOf | HasPart:
	UserDefined$_1$:
	...
	UserDefined$_n$:)
Attribute	(Attribute$_1$:
	...
	Attribute$_n$:)
Procedure	(Procedure$_1$:
	...
	Procedure$_n$:)]}

C_1, C_2, ..., C_n of the ontology that appear in the definition of the frame associated with C_k – see Section 2.2.1.1) can be classed in three categories: *relations, attributes*, and *procedures*; see Table 2.1.

OID (Object IDentifier) stands for the "symbolic name" of the particular concept to be defined; see, in an NKRL context, some symbolic labels like business_person, postal_code or biotechnology_company introduced in the previous paragraphs. The presence of the IsA and HasSpecialization properties is *mandatory for the concepts* – as is *mandatory the presence* of InstanceOf and HasInstance *for the individuals*; these properties define, in fact, *the general structure of the ontology*. From a practical point of view, we can note that the IsA and HasSpecialization properties do not require an implementation under the form of a "slot," given that they are *implicitly defined by the structure of the HClass hierarchy* (e.g. see Fig. 2.1); the same is true for the InstanceOf and HasInstance properties. *All the residual properties are implemented as instantiations of predefined prototype slots*, independently from their semantic category.

"Relation-type" Properties

The properties of the "relation" type are used to represent *mutual kinds of relationships between a concept or individual and other concepts or individuals of the ontology*. Eight "standard" properties of the "relation" type are used in NKRL (see Table 2.1); they are: IsA, and the inverse HasSpecialization, InstanceOf, and the inverse HasInstance, MemberOf (HasMember) and PartOf (HasPart). Some of their formal attributes (under the "strict inheritance" hypothesis) are described in Table 2.2 (also see Schiel [1989]); in Table 2.2, C_i denotes a generic concept and I_i a generic instance/individual.

An important point about these properties concerns the fact that, because of the general definitions of "concept" and "instance" and because of the characteristics of IsA, InstanceOf, PartOf and MemberOf illustrated in Table 2.2,

Table 2.2 Some formal attributes of IsA, InstanceOf, PartOf, MemberOf

$$(\text{IsA } C_1 \ C_2) \wedge (\text{IsA } C_2 \ C_1) \leftrightarrow C_1 \equiv C_2$$
$$(\text{IsA } C_1 \ C_2) \wedge (\text{IsA } C_2 \ C_3) \rightarrow (\text{IsA } C_1 \ C_3)$$
$$(\text{IsA } C_1 \ C_2) \wedge (\text{IsA } C_1 \ C_3) \rightarrow \exists C_4 (\text{IsA } C_2 \ C_4) \wedge (\text{IsA } C_3 \ C_4)$$
$$(\text{PartOf } C_1 \ C_2) \rightarrow \neg(\text{PartOf } C_2 \ C_1)$$
$$(\text{PartOf } C_1 \ C_2) \wedge (\text{PartOf } C_2 \ C_3) \rightarrow (\text{PartOf } C_1 \ C_3)$$
$$(\text{IsA } C_1 \ C_2) \wedge (\text{PartOf } C_2 \ C_3) \rightarrow (\text{PartOf } C_1 \ C_3)$$
$$(\text{IsA } C_1 \ C_2) \wedge (\text{PartOf } C_1 \ C_3) \rightarrow (\text{PartOf } C_2 \ C_3)$$
$$(\text{IsA } C_2 \ C_3) \wedge (\text{PartOf } C_1 \ C_3) \rightarrow (\text{PartOf } C_1 \ C_2)$$
$$(\text{IsA } C_1 \ C_2) \wedge \text{MemberOf } C_2 \ C_3) \rightarrow (\text{MemberOf } C_1 \ C_3)$$
$$(\text{InstanceOf } I_1 \ C_1) \wedge (\text{IsA } C_1 \ C_2) \rightarrow (\text{InstanceOf } I_1 \ C_2)$$
$$(\text{PartOf } I_1 \ I_2) \wedge (\text{InstanceOf } I_1 \ C_1) \wedge (\text{InstanceOf } I_2 \ C_2) \rightarrow (\text{PartOf } C_1 \ C_2)$$
$$(\text{PartOf } C_1 \ C_2) \wedge (\text{InstanceOf } I_2 \ C_2) \rightarrow \exists I_1 (\text{InstanceOf } I_1 \ C_1) \wedge (\text{PartOf } I_1 \ I_2)$$

a concept or an individual (instance) cannot make use of the totality of the eight "relation properties" introduced above. More exactly:

- The relations IsA, and the inverse HasSpecialization, *are reserved to concepts.*
- HasInstance can only be associated with a *concept*, InstanceOf with an *individual* (i.e., the concepts and their instances, the individuals, are linked by the InstanceOf and HasInstance relations).

Moreover, MemberOf (HasMember) and PartOf (HasPart) can only be used *to link concepts with concepts or instances with instances, but not concepts with instances*, see also [Winston et al., 1987].

We can also remark that *only two*, i.e. MemberOf and PartOf (and their inverses), of the so-called "meronymic" relations appear in the list of the "relation properties" of NKRL. Our basic criterion for differentiating between MemberOf and PartOf is likened with the homogeneity (MemberOf) or not (PartOf) of the component parts; in this way, "Cardinal Ratzinger is MemberOf the Holy College" (or "This tree is MemberOf the forest") and "a handle is PartOf a cup." PartOf is also characterized by a sort of "functional" quality (see again the "a handle is part of a cup" example) that is absent in MemberOf.

As is well known, *six different meronymic relations* are defined on the contrary in Winston et al. [1987]: component/integral object (corresponding to our PartOf), member/collection (corresponding to our MemberOf), portion/mass, stuff/object, feature/activity, place/area. Note that Winston et al. [1987] is still the *reference paper* for people interested in the practical implications of making use of meronymic concepts; for an overview of some more theoretical (and description logics-oriented) approaches, see Artale et al. [1996]. Recent work in a SW context has apparently not introduced any significant advance in this field, e.g. see Rector and Welty [2005]. The justification of our approach is twofold:

- A first point concerns the wish of keeping the HClass component of the NKRL language *as simple as possible*. In this context, the only "relation properties" that it was really necessary to introduce (in addition, of course, to IsA, InstanceOf and their inverses) were the MemberOf and HasMember relations, given that they intervene in the definition of the data structures used, for example, to represent plural situations in NKRL; see Section 2.2.2.3 and Appendix B. We have also then added, of course, the "complementary" PartOf and HasPart relation properties.

- On the other hand, dealing systematically with the examples of "non-NKRL relation properties" given by Winston and his colleagues by using only the four meronymic relations accepted in NKRL leads to results *that are not totally absurd*, even if, sometimes, some aspects of the original meaning are lost.

With respect to this last point, an example given in the Winston et al. paper is "this hunk is part of my clay," which is interpreted as an illustration of the "portion/mass" meronymic relation. We can show that, in an NKRL context, this example could also be understood as a MemberOf/HasMember relation, in the style of "this tree is MemberOf the forest." We can, in fact, interpret "my clay" as an individual, GENERIC_PORTION_OF_CLAY_1, an instance then of generic_portion_of_clay that can be considered as a (low-level) specialization of physical_entity. As we will discuss in detail in Section 3.1.2.1, we cannot, in fact, make use of a simpler individual in the CLAY_1 style that would be a *direct instance* of clay_; the latter, as a substance_, *cannot be endowed in fact with direct instances*. It is now easy to see GENERIC_PORTION_OF_CLAY_1 as formed (HasMember) by several hunks, HUNK_1, …, HUNK_n. The latter are, in turn, instances of a concept like, for example, hunk_of_clay: as the trees in the forest, they are all *homogeneous* and play *no particular functional role* with respect to the whole represented by GENERIC_PORTION_OF_CLAY_1. Passing now to other examples: "A martini is partly alcohol" (stuff/object) can be easily rendered using, for example, an "attribute property" (see below); "an oasis is a part of a desert" (place/area) can be represented using PartOf (there is no particular homogeneity between "oasis" and "desert"); etc.

"Attribute-type" Properties

The *characteristic properties* of a concept/individual are specifically represented by the slots of the "attribute" type. For example, for a concept like tax_, possible attributes (slots) are TypeOfFiscalSystem, CategoryOfTax, Territoriality, TypeOfTaxPayer, TaxationModalities, etc.; all these attributes must be defined previously, of course, as *prototype slots*. These sorts of slot represent, normally, the "core" of the definition of a given concept C_k.

For these properties, the concepts C_1, C_2, …, C_n that appear in the slots of the frame associated with C_k must be interpreted as *constraints* on the sets of legal fillers (values) that can be associated with these properties *when the concept C_k is specialized or instantiated*. An important point concerns the fact that, in NKRL, *these "constraints" can only be expressed using the data types introduced* *in Section 2.2.1.2: integer, double precision, Boolean, string of characters, HClass concept, HClass individual.* As in Protégé, additional "legal" constraints are the "*cardinality*" constraints; see also Fig. 2.1. This means, in particular, that *specific operators* proper to, for example, a description logics environment that could be used to build up *complex constraints* in the style of (INTERSECTION human_being (UNION doctor_ lawyer_) (NOT.ONE.OF fred_)) *are not admitted here.* This last formal expression can be interpreted as denoting a class of fillers that are men, can be doctors or lawyers, but cannot be Fred. This limitation is not at all disturbing for two main reasons:

- According to the NKRL philosophy, expressions like the above that, *introducing complex relationships about concepts and individuals,* can be considered as pertaining in reality *to the "narrative" and "event-specific" domains* are best described *by using the "descriptive" and "factual" tools, templates and predicative occurrences.* This means, in practice, that not only is it possible to represent expressions like the above correctly in NKRL, but also that NKRL is able to encode them in the most appropriate way.
- Avoiding making use of these complex constraints – and avoiding, then, all the theoretical and practical problems linked with the inheritance of role fillers built up in this way – allows one *to steer clear from the exponential complexity problems that affect terminological reasoning* and that, according to the different configurations, may be NP-hard, co-NP-hard, NP-complete, PSPACE-complete; see Bertino et al. [2001: 164–168] in this context.

"Procedure-type" Properties

The "procedure" slots are used in general to store information about the *dynamic characterization* of a concept or individual, e.g. by giving the description of its *typical behavior,* the *instructions for the use,* etc. Classically, this sort of content can be represented as *procedural pieces of code* in the "methods" or "demons" style. A characteristic of NKRL, however, concerns the possibility of describing this "procedural" information in a *declarative* style using, as fillers of the "procedure" slots, *descriptive (templates) or factual (occurrences) structures.* The data type of the "procedure" prototype slots is then always "string of characters."

For example, *specific complex concepts* can be defined *in detail* making use of *templates*; an example is given by the concept norms_for_indirect_transfer_of_ revenues_abroad in the legal domain, where templates have been used for supplying an *operational* description of these norms; see Section 2.3.2.2 (Table 2.20). As a second example we will see, in Appendix B, the use of "declarative" techniques making use of templates for *disambiguating complex "plural" expressions.* Note that the templates used in this context are *partially instantiated templates,* where *at least some* of the *explicit variables* have been replaced with HClass terms congruent with their constraints; we will return to this point later.

A particularly useful way of utilizing the "procedure" slots is to make use of these slots to store the so-called *HClass occurrences.* The latter take their origin from the remark that, when examining the narrative information included in news stories, for example, we find a lot of *background information* that is (i) of a *general import*, and really needed for a complete understanding of these stories, (ii) *relatively independent* from the proper "event(s)" related in a specific story, and (iii) *highly repetitive*. If we look, for example, at the news stories inserted in the "Philippine terrorism" corpus used in a recent NKRL application carried out in the context of the PARMENIDES project [Rinaldi et al., 2003; Black et al., 2004], we find – systematically repeated for each of these stories – background information in the style of: "The Abu Sayyaf group is an Islamic separatist group in the Southern Philippines," "The Abu Sayyaf group routinely performs ransom kidnapping in order to finance its activities," "The town of Isabela is located on Basilan island," "Jolo is the capital of the southern Sulu province," etc.

It is now evident that inserting information in this style *directly into the HClass records for individuals*, like ISABELA_, IOLO_, ABU_SAYYAF_GROUP, etc., *instead of coding it again and again* for each new story, can give rise to a double benefit: (i) *increasing the logical coherence* of the knowledge stored into the system; (ii) *reducing notably the global amount of NKRL code* needed for each application. The fillers of the "procedure" roles represented under the form of *HClass occurrences* are, in this case, (sequences of) *NKRL predicative occurrences*, i.e. the formal representations of the specific "narrative events." More details can be found in Zarri and Bernard [2004a].

2.2.1.4 NKRL Instances (Individuals)

In Section 2.1, we have already noticed that, in NKRL, some form of InstanceOf link must be implemented as the *necessary complement* of IsA for the construction of *well-formed HClass hierarchies* of "standard" concepts.

The difference between (IsA C_2 C_1) and (InstanceOf I_1 C_1) is normally explained in terms of the difference between the two options of (i) considering C_2 as a *subclass of* C_1 in the first case, operator "⊂," and (ii) considering I_1 (an instance) as a *member of* the class C_1 in the second, operator "ε" – see also the definitions in Table 2.2. Unfortunately, this is not sufficient to eliminate any ambiguity about the notion of instance, which is, eventually, *much more controversial than the notion of concept*. In this section we will discuss briefly the NKRL solutions for two of the main problems concerning the *practical implementation* of instances ("individuals," enumerative component), namely (i) the possibility of considering *as instances in themselves all the "intermediate" nodes of an ontology* (to the exclusion then of the root), instead of admitting that the instances can only be some "leaves" of the hierarchy; (ii) even limiting the notion of instance to this last interpretation, the possibility of having several levels of instances, i.e. instances of an instance. For simplicity's sake, we will make use for the discussion below of a fragment of the elementary, well-known ontology relating elephant_ to mammal_ and animal_; see Fig. 2.3.

With reference now to the first of the two problems stated above, if a very liberal interpretation of the notion of instance is admitted, then CLYDE_ is an

54 2 The Knowledge Representation Strategy

Fig. 2.3 Fragment of the elephant_/mammal_, etc. ontology

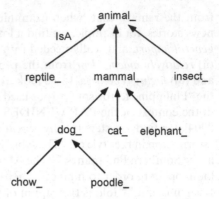

instance of elephant_ but elephant_ can also be considered, to a certain extent, as an instance of mammal_; this is accepted in many object-oriented systems, in the description logics systems, in Protégé, etc. In this latter system, for example, both individuals (instances) and classes (concepts) can be instances of classes: Protégé can then introduce *metaclasses* as classes whose instances are themselves classes. Every class (concept) has a dual identity, it is a "subclass" of another class (its "superclass") in the normal class hierarchy defined by the IsA links, and it is at the same time an "instance" of another class, its "metaclass." As a class defines a sort of "compelling mold" for its instances, *the metaclass defines a compelling mold for the associated classes*, describing, for example, which specific slots these latter can have, and the constraints for the values of these slots.

This position can be seen – along with the a priori definition of the frame slots as first class objects under the form of "template" or "prototype" slots – as a further answer to the congenital problem proper to any type of object/ property-based system (including description logics systems) that concerns *the arbitrariness in the choice of the properties* (in the choice of the slots); see the discussion in Section 2.2.1.2. A solution in this style is surely *elegant*, and can contribute to assuring the logical coherence of the resulting knowledge bases, *but it is not deprived of inconveniences*.

We can note first that, by admitting that also the concepts can be considered as "instances" of other concepts, the logical and semantic properties of the *"proper" instances* are likely to become *strongly dependent* on the particular choice of primary concepts selected to set up a given inheritance hierarchy. Under this assumption in fact, we can infer that, according to the definition given in Eq. (2.1), the InstanceOf relationship should be, like IsA, *always transitive*. With reference then to Fig. 2.3, and assuming that the relationship (InstanceOf FIDO_ poodle_) holds, the (InstanceOf FIDO_ animal_) also holds. But if, in this same figure, we substitute the root animal_ with the root species_, then we can still consider that (InstanceOf poodle_ species_) holds, *but it becomes very difficult to assert* (InstanceOf FIDO_ species_). More generally, the above assumption introduces *a considerable amount of epistemological confusion* by equating entities that, like the "concepts," are *atemporal* – at least in the context of a given application – and *not linked to a specific location* with others, like the "instances," always characterized by *very precise (even if sometimes implicit) spatio-temporal coordinates*; also see Lenat and Guha [1990: 332–339].

The solutions adopted in NKRL for the introduction of the instances and their association to the HClass hierarchy consist, then, *in adding to the set-oriented definition of an instance a sort of an "extensional" definition in the Woods style* [Woods, 1975]; see Section 2.1. According to this principle, we consider that *all the nodes of a well-formed inheritance hierarchy (ontology) like that of Fig. 2.3 must be considered only as "concepts,"* i.e. general descriptions/ definitions of generic *intensional notions*, like that of poodle_. When necessary, to each of these nodes can be added an InstanceOf link having the meaning of a *specific existence predicate*, e.g. we can declare that a specific, extensional incarnation of the "concept" poodle_ is represented by the "individual" FIDO_. In this way, the introduction of instances becomes strictly a *local operation, to be executed explicitly, when needed, for each node (concept) of the hierarchy*. A consequence of this assumption is represented by the fact that, as already stated, concepts participate in the HClass inheritance hierarchy *directly*; instances participate *indirectly* in this hierarchy *through their parent concepts*.

We can now conclude this section by examining the second of the problems evoked before, i.e. the possibility of creating *instances of instances*. The classical example [e.g. Zarri, 1997] is given by PARIS_, an individual (enumerative component) that is an *instance* of the concept city_, but that could, at least in principle, be *further specialized through the addition of proper "instances"* (i.e. viewpoints) like "Paris of the tourists," "Paris as a railway node," "Paris in the *Belle Epoque*," etc. According to what was stated above, instances in NKRL are always considered as *terminal symbols; this excludes, then, any possibility of implementing instances of instances using this language*. Viewpoints can, however, be easily realized in NKRL according to a solution that goes back to the seminal paper by Minsky [1975] about frames. This solution consists, then, in introducing in the inheritance hierarchy *specialized concepts* like tourist_city, railway_node, historical_city that all admit the individual PARIS_ as an instance; PARIS_ *inherits from each of them particular, "bundled" sets of attributes (slots)* like, for example, {TaxisBaseFare, EconomyHotels, UndergroundStations,...} from tourist_city, {TypesOfMerchandise, DailyCommutersRate,...} from railway_ node, etc.

2.2.2 Descriptive/Factual Data Structures

The data structures used for the descriptive and factual components (templates and occurrences) are more worthy of note than those utilized for the concepts and individuals of the definitional and enumerative components. They are of the *n*-ary type; see the discussion in Section 1.2.1. From a formal point of view they show, for example, some similarities with the data structures proper to the *Case Grammars* used in linguistics and computational linguistics [e.g. Fillmore, 1968; Bruce, 1975]. As already stated, however, Case Grammars deal with *linguistic/surface-level* entities, whilst the NKRL descriptive/factual data structures deal with *symbolic/deep-level* entities; see again Rosner and Somers [1980].

2.2.2.1 General Format of the Descriptive/Factual Structures

In opposition then to the *binary* (basically, "attribute-value") structures used for the frames of the definitional and enumerative component, the descriptive/ factual data structures – i.e. those used for *both the "templates" (descriptive component) and the "predicative occurrences" (factual component)*; see later Section 2.3 for the *second-order structures* – are "n-*ary*" *constructions* characterized by the association of "*quadruples*." These connect together the *symbolic name* of the whole template/occurrence, a *predicate* and the *arguments* of the predicate introduced by named relations, the *roles*; see again the discussion in Chapter 1 and Eq. (1.2), reproduced below for ease of reference. *The quadruples have in common the "name" and "predicate" components.* As already stated, we denote in Eq. (1.2) with L_i the *generic symbolic label* identifying a given template t_i or an occurrence c_i, with P_j the predicate used (like MOVE, PRODUCE, RECEIVE, etc.), with R_k the generic role (slot, case, like SUBJ(ect), OBJ(ect), SOURCE, DEST(ination)) and with a_k the corresponding argument (concepts C_i, individuals l_j, or associations of concepts or individuals):

$$(L_i(P_j(R_1a_1)(R_2\ a_2)\ldots(R_n\ a_n)))\qquad\qquad (1.2)$$

As we have seen, templates are inserted into an HTemp(lates) hierarchy, where each node represents a template object and which – at the difference of HClass that is (at least in principle) a direct acyclic graph (DAG) – *consists simply of a tree.* Predicative occurrences, i.e. the formal NKRL representations of "elementary events" represent the "leaves" of this tree. Taking into account the fact that templates are nothing else than *formal descriptions of classes of structured events*, HTemp corresponds, therefore, to a *taxonomy of events*. This enlarges the traditional interpretation of ontologies, where only "taxonomies of concepts" are usually taken into consideration.

2.2.2.2 Semantic Predicates, Roles, Templates and Occurrences

One of the main assumptions of NKRL is that, *at least for a large class of nonfictional narrative documents*, the semantic and conceptual structures that convey the narrative knowledge are *limited in number and relatively stable*, so that it is possible to denote these structures by making use of some sort of (partial) *canonical representation*. This confirms, among other things, that the NKRL representation of templates (classes of narrative events) and occurrences (specific events) is *independent of the different NL surface utterances used to describe these classes or events*; see also the discussion in Section 1.1.2.2.

Semantic Predicates as Primitives

Returning to Eq. (1.2), its central element consists of a *deep semantic predicate* identifying the *basic type of action, state, situation, etc.* that concerns a specific event (predicative occurrence) or a class of events (template) – see again Section 1.1.2.2.

Note that, in conceptual systems that share some similarities with NKRL (like Semantic Networks [Lehmann, 1992] or Conceptual Graphs [Sowa, 1984, 1999]), the semantic predicates can be chosen, *at least in principle, according to any "deep" or "surface" option*. For example, in the "Primitives and prototype" section of his 1984 book, Sowa says that: "In general, a system should allow high-level concepts to be expanded in terms of lower ones, but such expansions should be optional, not obligatory" [Sowa, 1984: 14]. In reality, in the implemented systems, *the "surface" option is largely preferred* – probably, among other things, because *choosing the "deep" option (the "primitive" option) means defining exactly the condition of use of these primitives, i.e. establishing some sort of HTemp "catalogue," and this can be long and very annoying work.* Making use, on the contrary, of a "surface" approach *can give the impression that this "defining" work is not really necessary, given that the "predicates" used (NL verbs, in practice) have an intuitive meaning in NL.* In the surface approach, however, the other side of the coin concerns *the introduction of an excessive number of degrees of freedom in the representation of complex "entities" like the nonfictional narratives*, with the negative effects, e.g. *on the possibility of securing the reproduction or the sharing of the results* already mentioned in the discussion about CGs in Section 1.2.2.2.

For the predicates, NKRL has then chosen the "deep" (primitive) option. A long experience with the conceptual representation of all sorts of multimedia, nonfictional narratives has shown that it is possible to make use, in the templates and occurrences, of *only seven "deep" (canonical) semantic predicates corresponding to very general, prototypical categories of the "behavior" of all sorts of human and nonhuman "characters"* – these predicates were five in the RESEDA project; see the Preface. Their conventional labels (along with an *intuitive description* of their "meaning") are indicated in Table 2.3: in NKRL, then, these seven predicates represent the *only "legal" entities* that can be substituted to the P_j term in Eq. (1.2).

We can note immediately – and this is true in general for all the entities mentioned in Eq. (1.2) like, for example, the "roles" – that *the actual definition of each of these predicates is strictly operational* and is supplied, in practice, by *the fact of being used within a given, exactly identified subset of the templates of the HTemp hierarchy* described in Chapter 3. This means also that (i) each of the structures derived from Eq. (1.2), i.e. the templates (and, accordingly, the

Table 2.3 Semantic predicates in NKRL

Predicate	Mnemonic description
BEHAVE	A character adopts a particular attitude, plays a particular role, or acts (concretely or intentionally) to obtain a given result
EXIST	To be present, also metaphorically, in a certain place; when associated with "temporal modulators" like begin and end, see Section 2.2.2.4, the predicative occurrences built up around this predicate can also be used to represent the "origin" or the "death" of a person, a company, etc.
EXPERIENCE	A character is affected by some sorts of good, bad or "neutral" news or events
MOVE	The displacement of a person or a physical object, the transmission of a message, a change of opinion ...
OWN	To have, to possess (also metaphorically, e.g. a given entity "has" a particular property)
PRODUCE	Execute a task or an activity, cause to exist or occur (with reference to material or immaterial entities, like the production of a service), etc.
RECEIVE	To acquire, to obtain, also abstract entities like information or advice

predicative occurrences), must be considered *as a whole* and that (ii) the templates constitute the veritable *basic units* to be taken into consideration with respect to the *definition of the entire descriptive/factual domain*.

Note, in this respect, that the reduced set of NKRL "semantic predicates" *could evoke, in effect, the well-known, reduced set of 11 "primitive acts" utilized by Schank* in the early descriptions of his "conceptual dependency" (CD) theory; see Schank and Abelson, [1977] and the discussion in the first chapter. We recall here that, in Schank's terms, the elementary event "X walked to the cafeteria" is represented roughly as "X (the 'actor') PTRANS ('physical transfer,' the primitive act) X (the 'object') to the cafeteria (the 'directive case')." This model has been criticized mainly on the basis of the *evident impossibility of reducing always, and in an unambiguous way, all the universe's complexity to 11 primitive acts*. We must add, for correctness' sake, that, in the most recent applications, Schank and his colleagues have relied more and more on high-level concepts/predicates, like DIS-PUTE, PETITION, NEED-SERVICE, AUTHORIZE, LEGAL-CONSULTATION, HAVE-MEDICAL-PROBLEM, etc., instead of expanding everything into primitives [Schank and Abelson, 1977; Schank and Carbonell, 1979; Schank, 1982; Lytinen, 1992].

From an NKRL point of view, a first, very rough reply to this type of criticism (too limited a number of primitives) could be the remark that NKRL is not at all a *universal formalism* – like CD, but also, for example, Sowa's CGs – but only *a formalism to represent correctly only the (relatively restricted) domain of nonfictional narratives*.

But a more convincing reply can be given with reference to a much more "subtle" type of criticism of the Schank approach expressed, for example, in Wilensky's [1987] report already mentioned. In this document, Wilensky does not criticize the possibility/opportunity of the decomposition in primitive terms, but the fact that *this decomposition can be of no utility in many practical situations*. Decomposing "walking" in terms of PTRANS does not exempt the CD users from the need of reconstructing, in some way, the *full concept of "walking" when inferencing is needed*, given that PTRANS has, in itself, a *very loose semantic link* with a very specific notion like that of "walking"; see Wilensky [1987: 10–14].

Wilensky's remark about *the need of going beyond the restricted conceptual scope of each single Schankian primitive acts* (of each NKRL semantic predicate) complies well with NKRL's general philosophy. As has been mentioned before, and as will appear even more clearly later when the characteristics of the NKRL's "catalogue" of HTemp templates are discussed, the *"primitive"* entities of NKRL are *not at all represented by the seven semantic predicates listed in Table 2.3 – or by the "roles" of Table 2.4. They coincide in reality with (at least) the about 150 (extensible and customizable) templates listed in HTemp and derived by the controlled combinatory of predicates, roles and arguments of the predicates (HClass concepts or combinations of these concepts) expressed according to the format represented by Eq. (1.2)*.

We can conclude about "primitives" by noticing that a *hardline support to a whole primitive approach* can be found in the work of Anna Wierzbicka; see her well-known early books [Wierzbicka, 1972, 1981] and the recent book with Cliff Goddard [Goddard and Wierzbicka, 2002]. Wierzbicka's aim – carried on through her "Natural Semantic Metalanguage" (NSM) research program – is that of finding (making use of "reductive paraphrase" tools) *the smallest set of basic concepts in terms of which all other words, concepts and grammatical constructions can be explicated, and that cannot themselves be explicated in a noncircular fashion*. The (provisional) result is a list of about 60 *semantic primes* regrouped in classes like "substantives" (I, YOU, SOMEONE/PERSON, PEOPLE), "quantifiers" (ONE, TWO, SOME, ALL, MANY/MUCH), "actions and events" (DO, HAPPEN, MOVE), "existence and possession" (THERE IS/EXIST, HAVE), "time" (WHEN/TIME, NOW, BEFORE, AFTER, A LONG TIME, A SHORT TIME, FOR SOME TIME, MOMENT), "space," "logical concepts," etc. This work is very interesting; many of these "primes" coincide in general with some "high-level" HClass concepts, and could surely be useful for the set up of all sorts of "conceptual lexica." Unfortunately, at least for the moment, Wierzbicka and colleagues are not completely clear about the way *to combine these primitives in order to give rise to a sort of "universal syntax/grammar" that could be retrieved in all the possible languages*, and this lessens, then, the interest of her work for NKRL's (present and pressing) needs.

Introducing the NKRL Roles

As stated at length in Chapter 1, the use of "roles" to link the "semantic predicate" to its (simple or complex) "arguments" (see the terms R_i in Eq. (1.2)) represents one of the *main features that allows NKRL to go beyond the limited*

Table 2.4 NKRL's roles

Role	Acronym	Mnemonic description
Subject	SUBJ	The *main protagonist* (the "agent," but also, in case, the "patient"...) of the elementary event (of the class of elementary events). The "filler" (argument of the predicate) of this role is often, but not necessarily, an animate entity or a group of animate entities (e.g. a social body)
Object	OBJ	The entity, animate or not, which is *acted upon* in the context of the event (the class of events)
Source	SOURCE	The animate entity (group of entities) who is *responsible for* the particular behavior, situation, state, etc. of the SUBJ of the elementary event (of the class of elementary events)
Beneficiary	BENF	The animate entity (group of entities) who constitutes the *addressee* (the "recipient," etc.) of the OBJ mentioned in the event or class of events (or, more generally, the addressee of the global behavior of the SUBJ of the event or class of events)
Modality	MODAL	The (often inanimate) entity (or the process) that is *instrumental* in producing the situation described in the event or class of events
Topic	TOPIC	The *theme* ("à propos of...") of the fact(s) or situation(s) that are represented in the event (in the class of events)
Context	CONTEXT	The *general context* ("in the context of...") of the fact(s) or situation(s) that are represented in the event (in the class of events)

"binary" approach used by many present knowledge representation systems. NKRL's roles are listed in Table 2.4. We can add that:

- "Role" is a *very general notion* used, among other things, both in linguistics and in knowledge representation. Making reference to the classification illustrated, e.g., in [Van Valin, 1999] – where roles are introduced at three different levels of generality, the *verb-specific* semantic roles (like runner, killer, hearer, broken, lover, etc.), the *thematic relations* (like agent, instrument, experiencer, theme, patient), and the two *generalized semantic roles* (actor, undergoer) – and in agreement with the "deep" (conceptual) nature of the language, *NKRL roles can be associated with the "thematic relation" category.*
- However (see the discussion in Section 1.1.2.3), NKRL roles represent simply a *functional/semantic relationship* that holds between a predicate and one of its (simple or complex) arguments and that is *strictly necessary in itself for the full appraisal of the "meaning" to be represented.* This means that (at the difference, for example, of what happens with Jackendoff's [1990] "thematic roles – see again the discussion mentioned above), the decision of making use of an NKRL particular role is *totally independent from any surface structure (any syntactic) consideration.* NKRL roles, then, are eventually more similar to the "correlators" of Ceccato's operational

linguistics [Ceccato, 1961, 1967] – where to each correlator corresponds a set of *mental operations* – than to the (syntactically constrained) Jackendoff's "thematic roles."

As it appears from Table 2.4, there are then *seven roles* in NKRL, that are used to identify the *participants* in a given elementary event or class of events. They, like the semantic predicates, are *primitive* – with the *caveats already expressed about the primitive character of the semantic predicates*, see also below and the next Section – and, like the predicates, are identified by means of *symbolic names*. In this respect, NKRL's position is, once again, opposed to that of Jackendoff [1990: 44–58], who refuses to attribute standard names to its thematic roles – even if, in practice, he makes use of the usual "Agent, Source, Goal . . ." terms.

An important point to emphasize is that the NL descriptions that appear in Table 2.4 are there, as well as those of Table 2.3, *only to suggest an intuitive explanation of the function of the NKRL roles, and do not constitute at all a "definition" of these roles*. Their real definition is given, once again, *operationally*: (i) by their mandatory presence/optional presence/absence in the *formal descriptions of the different templates*; (ii) by *the set of constraints* that are explicitly associated with the roles in the templates and that define the *classes of their legal fillers*. As already stated at length, the templates constitute, in a sense, the *real "primitives" of the NKRL language*. Ambiguities that can rise by examining the NL descriptions of Table 2.4 are then settled by examining the *formal definitions* of the templates of the HTemp hierarchy. For example (see Chapter 3), the "property" to be explicitly declared in templates like Own:SimpleProperty and Own:CompoundProperty is *necessarily associated as filler with the* TOPIC *role*, ruling out, then, any possible ambiguity about the use in this context of the MODAL (or CONTEXT) role.

The "fillers" of the seven roles listed in Table 2.4 – i.e. the a_i terms in Eq. (1.2), the "arguments" of the semantic predicate – are represented, in the *templates*, by *variables and constraints on the variables* (see next section) and by *HClass terms, concepts and individuals*, in the predicative occurrences. Note that these arguments can be "simple," i.e. represented by a unique variable or HClass term, or "structured." Structured arguments, called "expansions" or "complex fillers" in NKRL terms, *are built up by combining HClass terms or variables according to a precise syntax*; this topic will be discussed in detail in Section 2.2.2.3

The NKRL Templates and the "Catalogue"

The (single) "semantic predicate," the seven "roles" and the "arguments" are the three *basic building blocks that make up a template* t_i – and, therefore, a predicative occurrence (instance of template) c_j. *These three blocks cannot, separately, receive an interpretation in terms of classes of meaningful events; an (at least partial) valid interpretation will only arise after their (mandatory) assembling has been carried out.* An immediate corollary of the above is that *the presence of at least a filled role in a template is a necessary (but not sufficient) condition in order that the template be meaningfully interpreted* – note that, in NKRL, the role SUBJ(ect) must *necessarily be filled in any possible template or predicative occurrence*; see also the discussion about the "Kimian-like events" in Section 1.1.2.1.

In a template/predicative occurrence, the single arguments, simple or structured (expansions), and the template/occurrence as a whole, may be characterized by "determiners" (attributes) that introduce further details about their significant semantic aspects. Note that, in opposition to what happens with the predicates, roles, and arguments, the determiners are never strictly necessary for the interpretation of a template (of a predicative occurrence) in terms of a general description of a class of meaningful events (of an event). For example, templates and occurrences may be accompanied by "modulators" (like "nonintentional," "social," "possible") that, as their name suggests, are there to refine or modify the basic interpretation of the template or occurrence; moreover, predicative occurrences are necessarily associated with the two "temporal" attributes date-1 and date-2. Examples of determiners that, on the contrary, can only be associated (through the "external" operator ":") with the fillers (arguments of the predicate) of the SUBJ, OBJ, SOURCE and BENF roles are the "location" attributes. The determiners are described in detail in Section 2.2.2.4.

The general scheme of a template or predicative occurrence is shown in Table 2.5. In reality, the temporal attributes indicated in this table are *never associated with specific templates*, given that these latter represent *atemporal* categories of the NKRL language. On the contrary, they are *always associated with the predicative occurrences*, even if these attributes can be "empty" in some specific cases; see Chapter 3.

The format of Table 2.5 is called "external NKRL format," in contrast with the "*internal format*" concretely used to store and process the NKRL structures, see Zarri and Bernard [2004b: appendix A]. This internal format is normally called the "*Béatrice format*" in NKRL jargon. Note that, in the examples of coding inserted in the following sections, the roles will be *omitted* in the external representations of templates and occurrences, for simplicity's sake, *when the corresponding fillers (arguments of the predicate) are "empty."* In reality, all seven roles are always present in the internal format that is, fundamentally, a sort of "positional" format.

Table 2.5 External format of an NKRL template/predicative occurrence

PREDICATE	SUBJ	{<argument> : [location]}
	OBJ	{<argument> : [location]}
	SOURCE	{<argument> : [location]}
	BENF	{<argument> : [location]}
	MODAL	{<argument>}
	TOPIC	{<argument>}
	CONTEXT	{<argument>}
	[modulators]	
	[temporal attributes (missing in the templates)]	

Returning now to the three basic building blocks (*predicate*, *roles*, *arguments*) that make up a template/predicative occurrence, if we combine the *seven predicates* with the *seven predicative roles*, the *several hundred upper level concepts* of the HClass hierarchy (see Chapter 3: these high-level concepts are practically *invariable* given that they are used to define the constraints on the arguments of the templates – see Tables 2.6 and 2.7), the determiners, etc., we obtain *a (very large) solution space where all the legal templates are in principle represented*. In reality, these possible combinations are *filtered* making use of pragmatic rules like: "the OWN templates must necessarily provide for an OBJ(ect) role and, in their Own:Property variant, cannot be endowed with a BEN(e)F(iciary) role"; "all the EXIST templates of the "origin or death" sub-hierarchy require the presence

Table 2.6 Building up predicative occurrences

(a)

name: Produce:Violence
father: Produce:PerformTask/Activity
position: 6.35
NL description: "Execution of Violent Actions on the Filler of the BEN(e)F(iciary) Role"

PRODUCE		SUBJ	var1: [(var2)]
		OBJ	var3
		[SOURCE	var4: [(var5)]]
		BENF	var6: [(var7)]
		[MODAL	var8]
		[TOPIC	var9]
		[CONTEXT	var10]
		{[modulators],	+(abs)}
	var1 =	human_being_or_social_body	
	var3 =	violence_	
	var4 =	human_being_or_social_body	
	var6 =	human_being_or_social_body	
	var8 =	violence_, weapon_, criminality/violence_related_tool, machine_tool, general_characterizing_property, small_portable_equipment	
	var9 =	h_class	
	var10 =	situation_, spatio/temporal_relationship, symbolic_label	
	var2, var5, var7 =	geographical_location	

(b)

mod3.c5) PRODUCE	SUBJ	(SPECIF INDIVIDUAL_PERSON_20 weapon_wearing (SPECIF cardinality_ several_)): (VILLAGE_1)
	OBJ	kidnapping_
	BENF	ROBUSTINIANO_HABLO
	CONTEXT	#mod3.c6
	date-1:	1999-11-20
	date-2:	

Produce:Violence (6.49)

On November 20, 1999, in an unspecified village (VILLAGE_1), an armed group of people has kidnapped Robustiniano Hablo

Table 2.7 The syntax of the constraint expressions

var$_i$ = *h_class_term*

The *simplest form of constraint*, e.g. see the constraints on all the variables of Table 2.6 apart from the constraints on *var8* and *var10*. We will suppose first that *h_class_term* represents a *concept*. In this case, the constraint says simply that *in all the occurrences derived from the specific template where var$_i$ occurs*, the value bound to *var$_i$* must be a *specific term*, concept or individual (with respect to the HClass hierarchy) of the concept *h_class_term* that represents the constraint. If *h_class_term* represents an *individual*, then the value associated with *var$_i$* must be an individual *strictly identical* to the *h_class_term*

var$_i$ = *h_class_term_1, h_class_term_2, ..., h_class_term_n*

NKRL constraints are frequently expressed using this syntax, e.g. see the constraints on *var8* and *var10* of Table 2.6. The "comma" operator ",", represents here an "*exclusive or*"; i.e. in the occurrences, the value bound to *var$_i$* must be a *specific term*, concept or individual *of one of the listed concepts to the exclusion of all the others*. If some of the *h_class_term_i* constraints represent an *individual*, then the identity holds only if the value associated with *var$_i$* is an individual *strictly identical* to this constraint

var$_i$ ≠ *h_class_term_1, h_class_term_2, ..., h_class_term_n*

In this case, the "comma" operator ",", represents an "*and*"; i.e. in the occurrences derived from the template where *var$_i$* occurs, the value bound to *var$_i$ must be different from all the listed constraints h_class_term_i, including the specific terms, concepts and individuals, of all these constraints*

var$_i$ = *var1, var2, ..., var$_n$*

The "comma" operator ",", represents here an "*and*." This syntax means that the values (concepts or individuals) assumed by *var1, var2, ..., var$_n$* in the occurrences derived from the template where *var$_i$* occurs must be *strictly identical* to the value assumed by *var$_i$*. Note that, in the concrete templates/inference rules, the variables *var1, var2, ..., var$_n$* are, normally, *introduced before* the variable *var$_i$* comes into sight

var$_i$ ≠ *var1, var2, ..., var$_n$*

In this case, too, the "comma" operator ",", represents an "*and*"; the value (concept or individual) assumed by *var$_i$* must be *strictly different* from the values assumed by *all the variables var1, var2, ..., var$_n$*

var$_i$ = *symbolic_label_1, ..., symbolic_label_n*

This syntax (a variant of the second expression of the list) means that the value of *var$_i$* must be the *symbolic label of a predicative occurrence*; see the *completive construction* in Section 2.3.1. The operator ",", represents an "*exclusive or*"

var$_i$ = *h_class_term_1, ..., h_class_term_n, individual_*

This expression means that the value of *var$_i$* must be, at the same time, *an individual and a specific term, concept or individual of one of the h_class_term_1, ..., h_class_term_n* constraints. The "comma" operators ",", represent an "*exclusive or*" (see the second expression of this table), *with the exception of the last operator, which represents an "and"* (the value must be also an individual)

of a temporal modulator"; "the displacements of a person or group of persons, predicate MOVE, are always expressed in the form of a SUBJ(ect) who moves himself as an OBJ(ect)," etc. This filtering leads, eventually, to a *limited number* of templates, actually *about 150* –see Chapter 3 and the full description of the HTemp hierarchy in Zarri [2003a]. As already stated, HTemp is a *tree*; we can

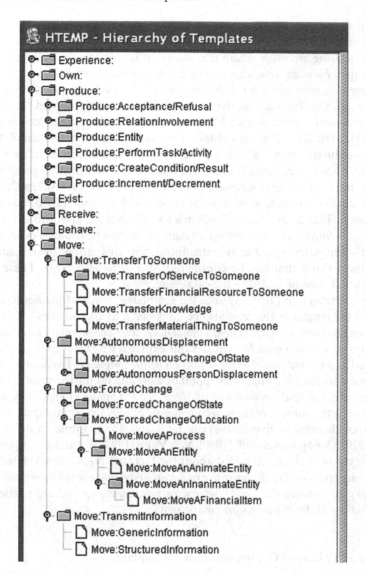

Fig. 2.4 HTemp fragment illustrating (part of) of the MOVE (and PRODUCE) branch(es)

add that it is structured into *seven branches*, where each branch corresponds to one of the *seven semantic predicates* accepted by the language and described in Table 2.3, i.e. *each branch includes only templates built up around a specific predicate*. Figure 2.4 reproduces a partial list of the templates included in the MOVE (and PRODUCE) branch(es) of Htemp; see Chapter 3. The HTemp hierarchy coincides, then, with the *catalogue of the NKRL templates*.

We must add that, when we speak of a "catalogue," this does not mean that this last must be *immutable and definitive*. The HTemp catalogue is, on the contrary, a *living structure* where it is always possible to insert new elements. For example, *by using (mainly) specialization (customization) operations concerning the classes of possible role fillers*, we can obtain, from one of the present templates, all the (specific) "derived" templates concretely needed for the different, practical applications. From a template like Move:MoveAProcess (Fig. 2.4) [Zarri, 2003a], we can obtain, for example, a "derived" template like "move an industrial process" and the predicative occurrences – e.g. "move, in a well-defined spatio-temporal framework, this particular industrial production" – that correspond to the description of events in the style of: "Sharp Corporation has shifted production of low-value personal computers from Japan to companies in Taiwan and Korea." When a specific NKRL application has been *completely defined and it is routinely running*, it is then possible to evaluate the "derived" templates specifically introduced for this application, choosing among them those that can be considered of a *general interest*. These latter templates will then be added to the catalogue.

From a formal point of view, since the templates represent the *basic defining entities* of the language, they can also be considered as the "axioms" of NKRL, identifying then *which classes of nonfictional narratives can be concretely dealt with and according to which modalities of use*; this explains why the "catalogue" *can be considered as part and parcel of the definition of the language*. Eventually, we can note (from a "theoretical linguistics" point of view and taking for granted that the templates are the *real "primitives" of the NKRL language*) that they can be interpreted in the context of those *verb semantic classes* that (making abstraction from minor theoretical divergences) can be found, for example, in the work of Cook [1979: 63–65], Jackendoff, [1990], Van Valin [1993: 39], and Levin [1993]. In this context – with the usual caveat about the fact that *NKRL is interested in the "deep" conceptual level of the narrative material taken into consideration and not in any theory concerning the syntax/semantics relationships* – we are particularly sympathetic with Beth Levin's *pragmatic* work.

Deriving a Predicative Occurrence from a Template

To represent a simple narrative like "On November 20, 1999, in an unspecified village, an armed group of people has kidnapped Robustiniano Hablo," we must first select the HTemp template corresponding to "execution of violent actions"; see Table 2.6a. The selection is realized (automatically or manually) on the basis of "deep predicate" considerations like those expounded in Section 1.1.2 (Kimian and Davidsonian analysis). In our example, the selected template is a specialization (see the "father" code in Table 2.6a) of the particular PRODUCE template corresponding to "perform some task or activity"; also see Fig. 2.4. The particular narrative to be represented is extracted from one of the (declassified) new stories dealt with, in NKRL's terms, in the context of the PARMENIDES project already mentioned; these stories have been supplied by the Greek Ministry of Defence (MoD), one of the PARMENIDES partners.

As appears clearly from Table 2.6a, in a template the *arguments of the predicate* (the a_k terms in Eq. (1.2)) are represented by *variables with associated constraints* – which are expressed as HClass concepts or combinations of HClass concepts. The syntax of the "constraint expressions" is explained in Table 2.7. When creating a predicative occurrence like mod3.c5 in Table 2.6b, *the role fillers in this occurrence must conform to the constraint of the father template.* In the occurrence mod3.c5, for example, ROBUSTINIANO_HA BLO (the "BEN(e)F(iciary)" of the kidnapping) and INDIVIDUAL_PER SON_20 (the unknown "SUBJ(ect)," actor, initiator of this action) are both instances of individual_person – a specialization of human_being_or_social_ body; see, in Table 2.6b, the constraints on variables *var1* and *var6*. kidnapping_ is a specialization of violence_; see *var3*, etc.

In a template, optional elements are in square parentheses. This means, for example, that filling the SOURCE, MODAL, TOPIC and CONTEXT roles of Table 2.6a *is not mandatory* in the predicative occurrences derived from the Produce:Violence template. Also, the presence of individuals/concepts that can replace the "location variables" (*var2*, *var5* and *var7* in Table 2.6a) is not compulsory in these occurrences: as already stated, the "location attributes" are linked with the predicate arguments by using the colon operator ":"; also see Section 2.2.2.4. Possible "forbidden" elements (e.g. a particular role that cannot exist for a given template) are marked as "+()"; for example, in Table 2.6a, the code {[modulators], +(abs)} means that several "modulators" (see Section 2.2.2.4) can be associated with the occurrences derived from the template, to the exception of the modulator abs(olute).

With respect now to the occurrences, a *conceptual label* like mod3.c5 in Table 2.6b represents the *symbolic name used to identify a specific predicative occurrence* c_i. The use of this sort of "pointed" notation is not, in principle, strictly mandatory; it is, however, *strongly recommended*, and it has been systematically used in all the later applications of the NKRL software. The first component of the "pointed" notation identifies the *original document* to be represented into NKRL format, in this case the third news story of the MoD corpus. The second component, c5, tells us that the specific predicative occurrence is the *fifth* within the set of predicative and binding (see Section 2.3) occurrences *that represent together the NKRL "image" of the complete original narrative document.* This formal image is called both the *metadocument* or (more often) the *conceptual annotation* associated with the original document; see again Section 2.3 and Chapter 3.

In the mod3.c5 predicative occurrence of Table 2.6b, the "filler" of the SUBJ(ect) role is a *structured argument* (expansion) that makes use of the "attributive operator," SPECIF(ication), one of the four operators that make up the specific *AECS sub-language* – this sub-language, and the rules for building up *well-formed expansions*, is detailed in Section 2.2.2.3. This structured argument means that the kidnapping has been realized by a group,

(SPECIF cardinality_ several_), of unknown individuals that are *collectively iden-tified* as INDIVIDUAL_PERSON_20; (SPECIF cardinality_ several_) is one of the typical "*NKRL idioms*" (see Table 3.2) that is used to represent the *cardinality of sets of totally undefined size*, like those corresponding to *generic plural referents* as "men" or "books." The unknown individuals were *armed*, weapon_wearing. weapon_wearing is a specialization of the dressing_attribute concept of HClass; this corresponds to saying that, via the generalizations dressing_attribute and physical_aspect_attribute, it also corresponds to a specialization of animate_enti-ty_property; see Section 3.1.2.1.

This particular structured argument is associated with a *location attribute*, represented by the individual VILLAGE_1 in Table 2.6b. Other attributes are the two *temporal attributes* date-1 and date-2 that materialize *the temporal interval associated with the elementary narrative event represented by the predicative occurrence*. The syntax/semantics of the attributes is explained in Section 2.2.2.4, where a detailed description of the methodology for representing tem-poral data in NKRL is also supplied.

2.2.2.3 Structured Arguments and the AECS Sub-language

The tools for representing structured arguments like the "filler" of SUBJ in Table 2.6b discussed above are of particular importance in NKRL, where they are used, among other things, for implementing a wide-ranging representation of *plural entities and expressions*; see Appendix B.

The AECS Sub-language

In NKRL, structured arguments are built up in a *principled way* making use of a *specialized sub-language*, AECS, which includes four *expansion operators*, the *disjunctive operator* (ALTERNative = A), the *distributive operator* (ENUMeration = E), the *collective operator* (COORDination = C), and the *attributive operator* (SPECIFication = S). Their definitions are given in Table 2.8.

From a formal semantics point of view, we can note, for example, that

$$(\text{SPECIF } e_i \ a \ b) = (\text{SPECIF } e_i \ b \ a) \tag{2.3}$$

$$(\text{ENUM } e_1 e_2) = (e_1 \wedge e_2 \wedge \neg(\text{COORD } e_1 e_2)) \tag{2.4}$$

Equation (2.3) says that, within a SPECIF list, the order of the properties *a*, *b*, ... associated with an entity e_i, concept or individual, is *not significant*. Equation (2.4) enunciates in a more formal way what is already stated in Table 2.8: the main characteristics of the ENUM lists are linked with the fact that the entities e_1, e_2, ... *take part necessarily* in the particular relationship between the structured argument and the predicate which is expressed by the role that introduces the arguments, but they satisfy this relationships *separately*.

Table 2.8 NKRL operators for structured arguments (expansions)

Operator	Acronym	Mnemonic description
Alternative	ALTERN	The *disjunctive operator*. It introduces a list of arguments, namely concepts, individuals or lists labeled with *different* expansion operators. *Only one* of the arguments of the list takes part in the particular relationship, with the predicate defined by the role-slot to be filled with the expansion; however, this *particular argument is not known*
Coordination	COORD	The *collective operator*. All the elements of the list (concepts, individuals or lists labeled with *different* expansion operators) take part (*necessarily together*) in the relationship with the predicate defined by the role-slot
Enumeration	ENUM	The *distributive operator*. Each element of the list (concepts, individuals or lists labeled with *different* expansion operators) satisfies the role–predicate relationship, but they do so *separately*
Specification	SPECIF	The *attributive operator*. This is used to associate a list of "attributes" (properties), under the form of concepts, individuals *or other SPECIF lists*, with the *concept or individual* that constitutes the *first term of the list*. This allows us to characterize this last element better. Note that each property appearing inside a SPECIF list can be *recursively associated, in turn*, with another SPECIF list

From a "pragmatic" point of view, it can be useful to conceive the SPECIF(ication) operator as frequently used to translate "adjectives" *that pertain to the "qualifying" and "possessive" grammatical categories.* However, as usual in NKRL – and as a confirmation of the fact that purely "linguistic" considerations are often misleading in the context of a "deep level," "conceptual" type of representation – only *the (mandatory) syntax proper to the different templates* (and, in particular, *the restrictions associated with the different roles*) must be taken into account to solve the *possible ambiguities.* For example, "John has got a civil servant employment" – where "civil servant" could be considered as a "qualification" of John's post – is translated in reality making use of the Behave:Role template (see Section 3.2.2.1) where civil_servant fills the MODAL role. In all the Own:Property templates (Section 3.2.2.5), the "qualifying, etc. properties" associated with a given "inanimate entity" fill systematically the TOPIC role, and so on.

Because of, among other things, the possibility of setting up embedded lists – see, in particular, the recursive nature of the SPECIF structures – *an unruly utilization of the AECS operators could give rise to very complex expressions, difficult to interpret and disentangle (unify).* Therefore, the definitions of Table 2.8 are used in association with the so-called *"priority rule,"* which can be visualized by using the following expression:

$$(ALTERN(ENUM(COORD(SPECIF)))) \qquad (2.5)$$

Table 2.9 An example illustrating the "priority rule"

ex.c1)	EXIST	SUBJ	(ALTERN (ENUM MR_BROWN (COORD MR_SMITH JENNIFER_SMITH)) (ENUM MR_BROWN (COORD MR_SMITH LUCY_SMITH))): (WHITE_HOUSE)
		CONTEXT	RECEPTION_15
Exist:HumanPresentAutonomously (3.2122)			

This expression is to be interpreted as follows: it is *forbidden* to use within the scope of a list introduced by the binding operator B_i a list labeled in terms of one of the binding operators *appearing on the left* of B_i in the priority expression above,, e.g. it is impossible to use a list ALTERN within the scope of a list COORD.

The *strict and mandatory* application of this rule in NKRL implies that it is sometimes necessary to *duplicate* some parts of a complex expansion expression in order to comply with Eq. (2.5). For example, a narrative elementary event like: "Mr. Brown attended the reception at the White House; Mr. Smith also there, accompanied by his daughter Jennifer (but the accompanying lady could also be his wife Lucy)," will be translated in NKRL according to the representation given in Table 2.9 (note that Mr. Brown and Mr. Smith are supposed they went separately to the reception, as shown by the use of ENUM). Of course, each of the single coding elements (MR_BROWN, etc.) within the expansions could be further specified by a proper SPECIF list.

Note that an important consequence of the priority rule is that *a SPECIF list can only be linked with a specific NKRL term, concept or individual, and not with a list*. Moreover, a location associated with an expansion formed of a SPECIF list refers, obviously, to the first element of the list, i.e. to the term that is "specified."

Sophisticated additions to the basic system of the AECS operators have been proposed in Zarri and Gilardoni [1996]: they will be discussed in Section 4.1.1.3.

2.2.2.4 Determiners (Attributes)

As already stated (see Section 2.2.2.2 and Table 2.5), *single arguments* of a template/predicative occurrence, or *templates/occurrences as a whole*, may be characterized by *determiners* (attributes) that (i) *introduce further details/precisions* about the "meaning" of these arguments or templates/occurrences, but that (ii) are *never strictly necessary for their basic semantic interpretation in NKRL terms*. We can immediately note, however, that the presence of the two *temporal determiners is mandatory* in order that we can *produce well-formed predicative occurrences* (factual component) – even if, as we will see, these temporal determiners can be "empty." NKRL determiners can be conceived, at least partly, as the "deep-level" (conceptual) counterparts of the surface "adverbials," e.g. see Austin et al. [2004] for recent research on this topic.

In this section, we will focus on three classes of determiners: *modulators, location determiners*, and *temporal attributes*). A fourth class of determiners is represented by the *validity attributes*: in the most recent NKRL applications, *only two validity attributes have been concretely used, i.e. the "contradictory validity attribute" and the "uncertainty validity attribute."*

The *contradictory attribute*, represented in external coding by the "exclamation mark," code "!," is used to make known that information expressed in a given NKRL structure (in practice, in an occurrence c_k) *contradicts* information expressed in another structure (in another occurrence c_i). In this case, the symbolic labels of the two structures (occurrences) become, respectively, $!c_k(c_i)$ and $!c_i(c_k)$, i.e. *the list including the labels of all the occurrences that are in contradiction with c_i is directly associated with the symbolic label of c_i.* The *uncertainty attribute*, code "asterisk" "*," may characterize either an occurrence c_i as a whole or single concept C_i or an individual l_i. In particular, the uncertainty attributes are *necessarily associated* with all the occurrences that describe future or possible events; see Section 2.3.2.1 and Chapter 3.

Modulators

Modulators apply to a *full template or occurrence*. This means that, to understand the meaning of a template/occurrence in the presence of modulators, we must first think about the *basic meaning* of this template/occurrence *without modulators* and then *particularize* such meaning according to the modulators used. Modulators can evoke, to a certain extent, the (*universal and standardized*) primitive "lexical functions" proper to the meaning–text theory of Igor Mel'čuk, like Magn (intensification), Loc (standard location), Bon (approval, appreciation), AntiBon (disapproval), Oper, Func, Labor, etc. and their variants [e.g. Žolkovskij and Mel'čuk, 1967; Mel'čuk, 1996]. Note once again, however, that NKRL is not a linguistic theory, but a practical tool restricted to the representation and management of nonfictional narrative information.

NKRL modulators pertain to three categories: *temporal modulators, deontic modulators* and *modal modulators*.

Temporal Modulators

The definitions for the temporal modulators are given in Table 2.10. They are used to represent the *start* or *end points* of given elementary events, or the *observation* that, at a given point in time, *a specific event is running*. Note, however, that their *operational meaning* is strictly associated with that of the *temporal determiners* (*temporal attributes*); see below.

Deontic Modulators

Deontic modulators were integrated in NKRL during the NOMOS project [Zarri, 1992b] to deal with subsets of the French "General Taxation Law" – namely the norms used to settle cases concerning the transfer of revenues

Table 2.10 Temporal modulators

Temporal modulator	Acronym	Mnemonic description
begin	begin	In the time interval associated with the elementary event described in a predicative occurrence, we distinguish a particular point, *the timestamp (date) identifying the beginning of the event*, e.g. "On April 5th, 1982, Francis Pym is appointed Foreign Secretary by the British Prime Minister"
end	end	The timestamp (date) marking the *end* of an elementary event is identified
observe	obs	We identify a *specific timestamp* where a specific event can be *observed*. obs will be used, for example, to represent the information "It is known that, in June 1903, Lev Trotsky still agreed with the Mensheviks about the strategy toward socialism." This situation is attested for June 1903, but we cannot give, at this level, any information about its duration that, in reality, *extends in time before and after the given date*

abroad. They have been systematically used afterwards for representing *"legal-oriented" narrative information*; a recent paper on this topic is by Zarri [2007]. Their definitions are given in Table 2.11.

The deontic modulators of NKRL satisfy the logical relationships of Table 2.12, which allow us to reduce all of them to the modulator perm.

This *deontic* system is very simple, for example, with respect to the formal analysis contained in Lomuscio and Nute [2005]. Associated, however, with HClass sub-trees particularly relevant from a "legal" point of view, like beliefs_, guiltiness_, innocence_, plea_, violence_, etc., it can compare favorably with the metadata system described in Gangemi et al. [2003] and describe correctly the most simple legal situations.

Table 2.11 Deontic modulators

Deontic modulator	Acronym	Mnemonic description
faculty	fac	Power of doing or not doing *by autonomous choice*
interdiction	interd	To forbid in a *formal or authoritative manner*
obligation	oblig	Someone is *obliged to do or to endure something*, e.g. by authority of law, by moral authority, or according to an autonomous need
permission	perm	*"To be authorized to …,"* i.e. having the right to do something where the right is granted by an external intervention

Table 2.12 Logical relationships among deontic modulator

$$\text{perm}\,(x)$$
$$\text{oblig}\,(x) = \neg\,(\text{perm}\,(\neg\,(x)))$$
$$\text{fac}\,(x) = \text{perm}\,(x) \wedge \text{perm}\,(\neg\,(x))$$
$$\text{interd}\,(x) = \neg\,(\text{perm}\,(x))$$

Modal Modulators

If the NKRL determiners correspond, in general, to surface adverbials, then modal modulators can be considered as the "deep-level" counterparts of some specific "modal adverbials" [e.g. Shaer, 2003]. The modal modulators actually accepted by the NKRL software are simply listed in Table 2.13. The semantic properties of the most important among them (e.g. wish, poss) will be examined in correspondence with *their utilization in the context of particular templates/ occurrences*; see Chapter 3.

Concurrent Utilization of Several Modulators

Several modulators *can be associated with the same occurrence*, as in this fictitious example: "Mr. Smith could renounce to go to Paris on the condition...." To represent correctly the first part of this narrative, two modal

Table 2.13 Modal modulators

Modulator	Acronym	Mnemonic description
absolute	abs	Used within EXIST occurrences to indicate the creation or disappearing (birth, death) of an individual or social body
agreement, opposition	for, against	E.g. "to manifest a favorable/negative attitude with respect ..."
denied event	negv	The reality of a particular event is denied ("Mary did not get the book from John")
desire, intention	wish	E.g. "Mary would like to be informed about..."
firstly	first	The event is the first of a series of events
intentional, unintentional	int, nint	E.g. "Mr. Smith has, voluntarily/involuntarily, started a fire"
leadership	lid	A character acts as a leader, e.g. "Mr. Smith took control of the demonstration for peace"
mainly	main	E.g. "the plant will mainly make high value-added products"
mental	ment	The activity of the SUBJ(ect) does not give rise to a concrete manifestation in the physical domain (e.g. a plan is only conceived, but not necessarily executed)
multiple	mult	An event takes place several times within the time period associated with the occurrence
necessary	necs	E.g. "required to fulfill something"; necs does not imply any coercion or obligation by force of law; see oblig in Table 2.11
possibility	poss	The event represented in the occurrence *could* exist, or by itself or as a consequence of another event
repeat	rep	A particular event already happened in the past (e.g. a politician has been re-elected)
secretly	krypt	The activity of the SUBJ is hidden, e.g. a clandestine meeting
social	soc	The activity of the SUBJ concerns her/his socio-professional duties
virtuality	virt	A situation, e.g. the nomination to a public function, that should be true in principle, even it is not yet realized

modulators, negv and poss (see Table 2.13), should be added to the "basic" predicative occurrence representing the displacement (MOVE) of Mr. Smith to Paris. The first one, negv (denied event), is needed to represent the "negation" of the event representing the journey; the second, poss (possibility), is needed to say that the fact of renouncing to the journey is only a possibility linked to the realization of a "condition" expressed in a second occurrence.

The possible, simultaneous presence of several modulators could introduce a problem of *scope ambiguity*, see the well-known examples in the style of "*x*{perm, negv} go to work yesterday" opposed to "*x*{negv, perm} go to work yesterday." In NKRL, *scope ambiguity is strictly forbidden*. As already stated, when only a modulator is present, it works as a *global operator that takes as its argument the whole predicative occurrence*. When a list of modulators is present, *they apply successively to the occurrence in a prefix notation (polish notation) way*. Therefore, the presence of a list {perm, negv} in the previous example means that *x* has been permitted not to go to work yesterday (negv is applied first, and then perm), while the presence of the list { negv, perm } means that *x* has not been permitted to go to work yesterday. In the "Mr. Smith" example at the beginning of this Section, the correct sequence for the two modulators is then {poss, negv}. Note that:

- NKRL *good coding practices* recommend to make use, whenever possible, of *a single modulator for each predicative occurrence* – it is normally better to duplicate a predicative occurrence than to stack up several modal modulators. However, *particular combinations of modulators, in a prearranged order, are directly imposed as mandatory by the syntax of a few templates*; see Chapter 3. As an example, we can mention here the use of EXIST templates to represent the creation or dissolution of a social body (e.g. a company), where the association {abs, begin/end} (in this order) must be *necessarily used*. Note also that the temporal modulators can be *freely associated* with the modal/deontic ones, normally as the "more external ones"; see {begin, wish} or {end, soc} – it is important to realize that *the temporal modulators are mutually exclusive*.

- As appears clearly from the above example, many of these "concurrence" problems *are linked with the presence of the modulator negv* – for some troubles and possible solutions that concern dealing with "negation" in a conceptual representation context, see, among many others, the recent paper by Mugnier and Leclère [2007]. From an NKRL point of view, we can note that negv is a "historical heritage" of the RESEDA project and that, with the growth of the number of conceptual entities present in both the HTemp and HClass hierarchies, it is used less and less, *even outside a strict "multiple modulators" context*. For example, "Bill is too busy, and he doesn't have time to exercise" will be "translated" using an Experience: NegativeHuman/Social template (see Section 3.2.2.3), where BILL_, as a SUBJ, EXPERIENCE(s) an impediment_ (OBJ) about (SPECIF finding-time gym_exercising), which represents the TOPIC; the CONTEXT is given by (SPECIF commitment_ (SPECIF cardinality_ many_)). "Mary doesn't want people watching her undress" will be represented making use of the template Behave:HumanProperty (Section 3.2.2.1), where MARY_, as a SUBJ, BEHAVE(s) MODAL unwilling_ about the TOPIC of being scrutinized, etc.; "Catia is unable to make use successfully of. . ." will make use again of the template Experience:NegativeHuman/Social, where CATIA_, the SUBJ, EXPERIENCE(s) OBJ failure_ about (TOPIC), etc. For some minor limitations on the query/inference operations imposed by the presence of negv, see Section 4.2.2.

Locations

Location determiners can only be associated, through the operator "colon" ":" (in external format), with the first *four "main" roles* of Table 2.4: SUBJ(ect), OBJ(ect), SOURCE, BEN(e)F(iciary) – see also Table 2.5. The "locations" of the fillers of the residual three roles, MODAL(ity), TOPIC and CONTEXT, can be deduced, in case, from those associated with the "main" four roles.

The *format* of the location determiners follows these two general laws:

- A location determiner is *always represented by a list of elements, concepts or individuals*. If this determiner is associated with an argument of the predicate (i.e. with a filler of a role like SUBJ, OBJ, . . .) consisting of *only one term*, then the elements of the list represent the different locations where this term is *simultaneously situated*, as in the example: "Sharp Corporation produces its personal computers in Taiwan and Korea." In this case, the two elements (individuals) of the list (TAIWAN_ KOREA_) that make up the location determiner must be interpreted as the locations where the filler of the OBJ role, personal_computer, is simultaneously produced. If the argument of the predicate (i.e. the role filler) is, in turn, composed of a list, *a biunivocal correspondence must exist among the terms of the two lists* ("Sharp Corporation makes notebooks in Taiwan and desktops in Korea").

- Particular rules are followed in the different MOVE constructions; see Section 3.2.2.4. For example, in the MOVE templates that are specializations of Move:MoveAnEntity, the location list linked with the OBJ(ect) filler is always *a two-term list where the first term represents the initial location and the second the final location*. In the example: "Sharp Corporation has shifted production from Japan to Taiwan and Korea," the location determiner linked with the OBJ filler will be the embedded list (JAPAN_ (TAIWAN_ KOREA_)). If some *stop points* along the way ought to be represented, then it would be necessary *to use a list of three terms, where the (list constituting the) middle term represents the stop(s)*. In the MOVE templates that concern the *generic displacement of a character or a social body* and that derive from Move:AutonomousDisplacement, we systematically represent this situation *by indicating that the character or social body, as a SUBJ(ect), moves himself as an OBJ(ect)*. From a practical point of view, this means that, in an occurrence concerning a trip of John, JOHN_ will be the filler of both the SUBJ and OBJ slots. In this case, the location determiner (possibly a list) associated with the SUBJ argument represents *the initial location(s) of John*, and the location determiner linked with the OBJ argument *his final location(s)*; see Section 3.2.2.4. If the stop points must be represented, then the OBJ location attribute is a list where *the first term – again a list in case of multiple stop points – corresponds to these points*.

We can note that, in some specific NKRL applications where a very precise characterization of the locations was required, the location determiners of the type "individual" had a *specific internal representation* made up of *two components*:

- A complex, alpha-numerical "zip-code-type" symbol, giving the *best possible approximation of the spatial coordinates of the location to be represented*.
- The *proper individual* (enumerative component), labeled as usual by using the place-name of the location (if this was known); see examples like KOREA_, CHAMPS_ELYSEES, SCHOOL_342, CHURCH_18, 10_DOWNING_STREET, FARM_71, etc.

Note also that, independently from the internal representation, individuals like those above (KOREA_, CHAMPS_ELYSEES, SCHOOL_342, etc.) are instances of the particular HClass concepts denoting the *category* of the given location, e.g. country_, street_, school_, church_, official_ building, farm_, etc.

Temporal Determiners (Attributes)

The problem of finding a complete and computationally efficient system of knowledge representation for temporal data has been intensely discussed in recent years, thanks mainly to the debate aroused by the publication by James Allen, at the beginning of the 1980s, of his proposals of an *Interval Algebra*; see Allen [1981, 1983, 1984]. An "interval" is a finite length of time that starts and ends at definite points; it can be visually represented as a horizontal line with time going from left to right. According to Allen, a "time specialist" dealing automatically with temporal information does not have to consider *either absolute time or the duration of intervals, but merely the relations between intervals*, i.e. it can leave unspecified the exact temporal relationship between intervals. Seven primitive relationships (predicates) between the temporal intervals i_1 and i_2 (and their inverses) are then defined in the Interval Algebra: i_1 before i_2, i_1 equal i_2, i_1 meets i_2 (i_1 is before i_2 but there is no interval between them, i.e. i_1 ends when i_2 starts), i_1 overlaps i_2 (i_1 starts before i_2, and they overlap), i_1 during i_2, i_1 starts i_2 (i_1 and i_2 share the same beginning, but i_1 ends before i_2), i_1 finishes i_2 (i_1 and i_2 share the same end, but i_1 begins before i_2). A set

of *transitive axioms* [Allen, 1983] defines the behavior of the above predicates;
two examples are

$$\text{before}(i_1, i_2) \wedge \text{before}(i_2, i_3) \Rightarrow \text{before}(i_1, i_3) \qquad (2.6)$$

$$\text{meets}(i_1, i_2) \wedge \text{during}(i_2, i_3) \Rightarrow (\text{overlaps}(i_1, i_3) \vee \text{during}(i_1, i_3)$$
$$\vee \text{ meets}(i_1, i_3)) \qquad (2.7)$$

Work that extends Allen's proposals is described, for example, by Ladkin
[1986; Ladkin and Maddux, 1987]; work that investigates the relationships
between the "Interval" and "Point" algebras can be found, for example, in
Vilain and Kautz [1986] and Tsang [1987]. A temporal logic system introduced
independently from the work of Allen, where the concept of "persistence of a
situation" is introduced (see also Section 4.1.2) is given by McDermott [1982].
Kowalski and Sergot's [1986] "Event Calculus" is an attempt to set up a general
system for reasoning about time and event in a logic programming framework;
in a way, this system can also be considered as an extension of Allen's proposals.
A "spatial" system related to Allen's interval algebra is the RCC8 Calculus
[Randell et al., 1992], which consists of eight topological base relations for
extended spatial regions.

In recent years, as a reaction to a pure "interval-based" system in Allen's
style, *we can remark a renewed interest for the "point-based" approaches*: many
recent systems described in the literature can handle both *metric (quantitative)*
and *qualitative (interval-based)* temporal information. See, in this context,
TimeGraph [Miller and Schubert, 1990], MATS (Metric/Allen Time System)
[Kautz and Ladkin, 1991], TimeGraph-II [Gerevini and Schubert, 1995],
LATER (LAyered TEmporal Reasoner) [Brusoni et al., 1997], etc.

Three recent projects can be considered as representative of the "state of the
art" in the temporal representation domain – at least with respect to the
possibility of implementing "non-toy," concrete applications in this specific
domain.

The first is the "Advanced Research and Development Activity (ARDA)
Challenge Project on Event Taxonomy" [Bolles and Nevatia, 2004], managed
by the ARDA Northwest Regional Research Center and having SRI International (SRI) and the University of Southern California (USC) as principal
partners. Centered on the automatic recognition of events in video records,
the project has created, among other things, a Video Event Representation
Language (VERL) that includes a temporal representation component. *Time
can be specified as instants and intervals.* Representation of intervals conforms
to Allen's interval algebra; three relationships, begins, inside, and ends, can
hold between an instant *t* and an interval *T*; see, in NKRL, the three temporal
modulators defined in Table 2.10. Note also the existence of the three "predicates" change, cause, and enable, where the last two have a *binding function*

similar to that of the "binding occurrences" that, in NKRL, deal with the "connectivity phenomena"; see Section 2.2.3.

The second project, linked with W3C/SW activities, is a "work on progress" about the definition of an *ontology of temporal concepts*, OWL-Time, for describing the temporal content of Web pages and the temporal properties of Web Services; see Hobbs and Pan [2006]. OWL-Time is the successor of the DAML-Time project [Hobbs and Pan, 2004]. The ontology defines two sub-classes of TemporalEntity (i.e. Instant and Interval), three relations (i.e. begins, ends and inside) for describing the relationships between instants and intervals (see begins, inside, and ends in VERL and the NKRL's temporal modulators), a relation (i.e. before) on temporal entities, and a series of "interval relations" (i.e. intervalEquals, intervalMeets, intervalOverlaps, etc. and their reverse relations) to reproduce Allen's system. All these "relations" are defined as ObjectProperty in OWL and have as range either Instant or Interval. The ontology also includes a set of specialized concepts, predicates and relations to allow the representation of durations (as properties of intervals), dates and other temporal entities: e.g. January is a subclass of DateTimeDescription, with the restrictions that the property unitType takes AllValuesFrom the class UnitMonth and the property month has a value of 1. Clumsy examples of use of these definitions in a Web Services context are described by Hobbs and Pan [2006].

The third project – the best known, and probably also the most interesting from an NKRL point of view, in spite of the big differences both with respect to the practical aims and to the general approach – concerns the Specification Language TimeML; see Pustejovsky et al., [2005]. TimeML has been developed in a *computational linguistics context* with the aim of *annotating*, from a tem-poral point of view, an NL text by *identifying and extracting events from this text* and by *establishing their temporal anchoring*. To annotate the texts, TimeML makes use of four types of *tags* that make use of a syntax in the XML style (with attributes and values): EVENT, TIMEX3, SIGNAL and LINK.

With respect to the first tag, EVENT, the modalities of identification of events in TimeML do not appear as especially original and seem to be of the "neo-Davidsonian" type (see the discussion in Section 1.1.2.2). They are then linked with the retrieval of tensed verbs, untensed verbs ("...called the first minister *to thank* him..."), nominalizations ("...a possible *attack*..."), adjectives ("...a *dormant* volcano..."), predicative clauses ("...there is no reason why they would not *be prepared*...) or prepositional phrases ("*on board*"). Attributes for the tag EVENT are of two types, i.e. EventID (the identification of the event, automatically assigned) and Class, with values like OCCURRENCE (die, crash, build, merge, sell), STATE (on board, kidnapped, love), PERCEPTION (see, hear, watch, feel), etc. The annotation of an event is completed making use of a "secondary" tag, MAKEINSTANCE, used to introduce further information about the event, like indications on the tense (PAST, PRESENT, FUTURE, etc.), the aspect (PROGRESSIVE, PERFECTIVE, ...), the modality, etc.

The TIMEX3 tag is employed to mark up *explicit temporal expressions*; it use is modeled on both the use of TIMEX2 – a set of annotations guidelines for creating normalized representations of temporal expressions ("temporal annotations") in free text originally developed under the DARPA TIDES (Translingual Information, Detection, Extraction and Summarization) program (see Ferro et al. [2005] and http://timex2.mitre.org) – and on that of Andrea Setzer's TIMEX tag [Setzer and Gaizauskas, 2000; Setzer, 2001]. Note the existence of an automatic time tagger, TEMPEX, to generate TIMEX2 tags in text documents automatically [Mani and Wilson, 2000]. The TIMEX3 tag can be associated with several types of *attributes*: some of them are listed below.

- TimexID (automatically assigned).
- type, with values like DATE, to annotate *fully specified* time expressions like September 3rd, 2007; TIME, to annotate (as in TIMEX2) *underspecified or context-dependent* expressions like "The hostages were released *that afternoon*"; DURATION, for annotating expressions like "three months" or "two years"; SET, for annotating expressions like "twice a month", "daily"; etc.
- value, where this attribute is used to introduce an instance of the ISO 8601 normalized date format [ISO, 2004], like 2007-10-26T09:15:00 that denotes "October 26, 2007, 09/15."
- mod, used to capture specific "temporal points" like BEFORE, AFTER, ON_OR_BEFORE ("no less than a year ago"), "temporal comparisons" like LESS_THAN, MORE_THAN, EQUAL_OR_THAN, "points and durations" like START, MID ("the middle of the month") or APPROX ("about three years ago").
- temporalFunction, which introduces a binary value to indicate whether all the temporal information needed is provided ("twelve o'clock September 2, 2007"), or if this is not true (e.g. "yesterday" or "next year") and it is then necessary to make use of a *temporal function*.
- FunctionInDocument (an optional attribute), with values like CREATION_-TIME, MODIFICATION_TIME, PUBLICATION_TIME, etc.

For example, the CREATION_TIME of a document can be used in the "temporal functions" mentioned above to identify a "temporal anchor" (AnchorTimeID attribute) from which to start to calculate an actual (ISO) value for "underspecified expressions" like "last week"; the anchor can then be used to locate the week of creation of the document, allowing then to find the week that precedes immediately this "creation week."

The SIGNAL tag is used to annotate sections of the text, usually function words, which can be used to show *how temporal objects are related together.* They denote then "temporal prepositions and conjunctions" (from, before, after, during, while, when, ...), "temporal modifiers" (twice, every, three times, ...), "subordinators" like "if," etc.

However, the most important innovation introduced in TimeML (following Setzer's [2001] thesis) concerns certainly the set of LINK tags (TLINK, ALINK and SLINK) that, as already signaled in Section 1.1.1.2, are particularly interesting because they can be considered as TimeML's solution to the problems posed by "connectivity phenomena." TLINK, the "temporal link," is used to represent *the temporal relationship that holds between events or between events and a specific time*. The relType attribute of this link can be used to denote simultaneous events (SIMULTANEOUS, as in the example "Jane was watching TV while Mary was cooking"), before/after events (BEFORE/AFTER), during states or events (DURING, "Mary cooked for 40 minutes on Tuesday"), etc. ALINK, the "aspectual link," is used to represent *the relationships between an "aspectual event" and its "argument event"*; in this case, the attribute relType can denote an event that INITITATES, as in "Mary started (aspectual event) to cook (argument event)," CULMINATES ("Jane finished assembling the table"), TERMINATES or CONTINUES – see, on the contrary, the NKRL use of *temporal modulators* in this context in Table 2.10. Note also that, in TimeML, the "aspectual" predicates like "start" and "finish" in the above examples *are treated as "separate events,"* independent from the specific modified event like "cook." Eventually, SLINK, the "subordination link," is used *to denote "contexts" and relationships between two events* – dealing, then, once again, with the omnipresent "connectivity phenomena" – see values for the relType attribute like FACTIVE ("Mary managed to leave the party") COUNTER_FACTIVE ("John forgot to buy some bread") or MODAL ("Mary wanted John to buy some bread").

In spite of its unquestionable richness and interest, TimeML sometimes also appears particularly "heavy" and convoluted – we have far from mentioned all the intricacies of its syntax – and not immune from certain dangers of ambiguity and underspecification.

NKRL, Timestamps and Intervals

The association of temporal attributes with temporal modulators is at the heart of the NKRL representation of the specific temporal data to be taken into account in a "narrative information" context; note, however, that a complete apprehension of this representation system cannot be obtained without examining how *it is used in a querying and inferencing context*; see Section 4.1.2. The two temporal attributes date-1 and date-2 define, in fact, the global time interval or a specific point on the time axis (when associated, in particular, with the modulators begin, end and obs; see Table 2.10) *where a predicative occurrence c_k (i.e. the corresponding elementary event) "holds."* Among other things, this implies that, for each predicative occurrence – and in contrast to what happens for the modulators and the location determiners that, with few, very precise exceptions, are in general *not mandatory* – the presence of the attributes date-1 and date-2 is absolutely *mandatory* in order to be able to assign a correct interpretation to this occurrence; e.g. see occurrence mod3.c5 in Table 2.6b.

More precisely, any predicative occurrence c_k is *necessarily associated* with the formal representation of the time interval *i* in which holds(c_k, *i*) *is true*; *i* is in turn defined by *the timestamps associated as values* with the two temporal attributes date-1 and date-2. Timestamps are composed of sequences of integers like <year-month-day-hour-minute...>, where the left and right boundaries of the sequence represent, respectively, the maximum (e.g. years) and minimum (e.g. nanoseconds) *temporal grain* chosen for a given application. In internal representation, each sequence is converted into a *single real*; the equivalence "timestamp ≡ real" preserves the order of the original timestamps on the time axis. From now onward, the term "timestamp" will denote *the real number corresponding to the original sequence*. For clarity's sake, however, we will continue to use in the following the intuitive *"external" NKRL symbolic notation for timestamps*, e.g. in the style of "2006-10-26" – which corresponds, therefore, to the sequence <year-month-day> and which is compatible with the ISO 8601 standard [ISO, 2004]. Pragmatic solutions have been adopted to deal with the problem of "lacunary dates," given that, in the historical "narrative" applications for example, not all the elements of the original sequence corresponding to a timestamp can be known simultaneously. Assuming, for example, that "maximum grain = years," *sequences with the year unknown are not permitted*. In this case, a set of possible years must be specified, automatically or by the domain specialist: a copy of the associated occurrence is created for each possible year and the set of occurrences is added to the knowledge base.

Given the above assimilation of timestamps with reals corresponding to points of the time axis, it is now possible to make use of the standard arithmetical properties to establish the relationships between timestamps, and to calculate, when necessary, the duration of the intervals (in the James Allen style). Expressing the generic timestamp as t_k, we can make use, for example, of the simple axioms described in Table 2.14; see also Miller and Schubert [1990].

To calculate concretely the "metric duration," *dt*, of an interval bounded by the timestamps t_1 and t_2, it is necessary to reconvert t_1 and t_2 into the original sequences of integers *to express these two timestamps in terms of "significant multiples" of the minimum grain*. "Significant" means that, e.g., for two timestamps t_1 and t_2 including the years 2006 and 2007 in their

Table 2.14 Relationships among timestamps	$((t_1 \leq t_2) \wedge (t_2 \leq t_3)) \Rightarrow (t_1 \leq t_3)$
	$(t_1 \leq t_2) \Leftrightarrow (t_1 < t_2) \vee (t_1 = t_2)$
	$(t_1 \leq t_2) \leftrightarrow (t_2 \geq t_1)$
	$(t_1 < t_2) \Rightarrow \neg (t_2 \leq t_1)$
	$(t_1 \geq t_2) \Rightarrow \neg (t_2 < t_1)$
	$((t_1 \leq t_2) \wedge (t_2 \leq t_1)) \Rightarrow (t_1 = t_2)$, etc.

original sequences, and assuming that "years" and "days" are, respectively, the maximum and the minimum grain, *only one year period will be added to t_2 when converting the whole sequences into days*. Denoting with $g(t_k)$ the significant multiple of the minimum grain corresponding to the generic time stamp t_k, we will then simply have

$$dt(t_1, t_2) = g(t_2) - g(t_1) \text{ and if } t_1 \leq t_2 \leq t_3, dt(t_1, t_3) = dt(t_1, t_2) + dt(t_2, t_3) \quad (2.8)$$

Categories and Perspectives

If we examine the *qualitative relationships* between the *duration* of an occurrence c_k (the duration of the corresponding event) and the *temporal information* carried by the temporal attributes date-1 and date-2, we can notice several configurations.

In the simplest case, the duration is *fully defined*, as in the representation of the elementary event "Between July 15 and September 5, 2006, John was hospitalized"; in the corresponding predicative occurrence, we do actually have two timestamps t_1 and t_2, $t_1 \equiv$ 2006-07-15 and $t_2 \equiv$ 2006-09-05, which allow us to *localize exactly the boundaries of the event*. From the point of view of temporal information, this situation can thus be schematized as in Fig. 2.5: the two timestamps t_1 and t_2 represent the values associated with the temporal attributes date-1 and date-2 respectively.

We can now introduce a first fundamental concept of the NKRL system of temporal representation, that of *category of dating*. The first temporal attribute, date-1, is said to be represented *in subsequence* – the event begins to be true at the timestamp t_1 (generalized date) that corresponds to the value associated with this attribute – and the second date-2, which denotes the upper temporal limit of the event, is said to be represented *in precedence*. The *values* of the two attributes, and the *category of dating* (subsequence or precedence) associated with these attributes, permit us to reconstruct the *temporal interval* fully (in Allen's meaning) that corresponds to the event we are taking into consideration.

It is often necessary to deal with an event in which *only one* of the two boundaries, t_1 or t_2, is to be considered – for example, when it is necessary to supply special information about the circumstances at the *beginning* or *end* of the event. Another possibility is that only an *intermediate* timestamp t_3, between t_1 and t_2, is known. In all these cases, NKRL requires that we make use only of

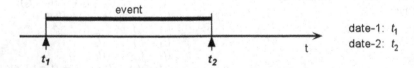

Fig. 2.5 The duration of the event is fully defined

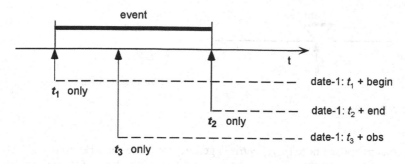

Fig. 2.6 The duration of the event is unknown

the *first* temporal attribute, date-1, i.e. *the single timestamp available is systematically associated as value with* date-1, *the second attribute,* date-2, *being "empty." The three cases are differentiated by using one of the "temporal modulators" of Table* 2.10, to be linked to the global coded event. The *beginning of an elementary event* (timestamp t_1) will be represented by making use of the modulator begin, and the "filled" temporal attribute date-1 is then represented *in subsequence.* To indicate the end of an event (timestamp t_2), the modulator end is used, and the temporal attribute, date-1, must be represented *in precedence.* If, finally, a *particular moment* within an event is to be indicated – for example, to express the information that *it appears* that British Airway's indebtedness was low on July 2, 1993, or that *it is known* that, in June 1903, Lev Trotsky still agreed with the Mensheviks about the strategy toward socialism, but *without giving any information about the beginning or end of these particular states that extends beyond the given dates* – the modulator "obs(erve)" is used. In this last case, the nonempty temporal attribute, date-1, is now said to be represented *in coincidence.* The three cases illustrated in this paragraph are summarized in Fig. 2.6.

Eventually, a last case corresponds to the *point events,* i.e. events that have a metric duration *dt* less than or equal to the minimum temporal grain considered. If, for example, we look at the narrative fragment "Brussels, July 2, 1993. British Airways Plc President Colin Marshall said in a Belgian newspaper interview the company's indebtedness was low . . .," it is likely that Colin Marshall's speech *has occupied only a relatively small slice of July 2, 1993.* This sort of event *appears, then, as concentrated in a particular "point" of the time axis;* see Fig. 2.7. The corresponding occurrences are characterized by the following format: (i) the *timestamp t_i* representing the date of the point event *is associated as a value with the temporal attribute* date-1; (ii) the temporal attribute date-2 is *empty;* (iii) *no temporal modulator is to be associated with the predicative occurrence.* The category of date-1 is the "coincidence."

Whatever the timestamp to be considered and the associated category, an important source of fuzziness is associated with the accuracy, or rather the *lack of accuracy,* with which this timestamp can be located on the time axis. The

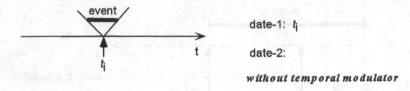

Fig. 2.7 Point event

solutions proposed here (*perspectives*) generalize some remarks that go back to Kahn and Gorry [1977]; see also Miller and Schubert [1990: 110]. Perspectives represent a *simple and elegant way for dealing with some of the "context-dependent expressions"* we have evoked, before, in the context of TimeML (e.g. see certain attributes of the TIMEX3 tag), and compare favorably with the solutions proposed in this project.

In NKRL, "perspectives" correspond to *different ways of "capturing" a timestamp*. We have defined five different perspectives:

- *direct perspective* (no fuzz, as in "July 2, 2006, at noon");
- *inclusion fork*, or simply *fork* ("between April 7 and September 2, 2006");
- *limit from which* ("after January 1, 2006": a way of *indirect dating*, as in the case of a letter A that does not bear a date but mentions having received a letter B, which is dated "January 1, 2006," this last date is thus a "limit from which" for letter A);
- *limit to which* (the symmetric case, "before December 2, 2005": letter A does not bear a date, but is mentioned in a letter C, which is dated);
- *circa perspective* (no lower or upper bounds, as in the case of a letter A which does not bear a date, but mentions the celebration of a feast day the date of which is known, without saying if the feast has passed or is to come: letter A is situated around that date, "about December 25, 2005").

We will stress here that the *type of perspective* that affects the temporal information associated as a value with a temporal attribute is *completely independent* of the *category* according to which the attribute itself is represented. In a piece of information of the type: "John has been hospitalized in 2006, over a period whose first limit is probably between June 10 and June 30, 2006, and the second between September 1 and September 15 of the same year," the corresponding predicative occurrence would have both the temporal attributes date-1 and date-2 "filled," the first "in subsequence" and the second "in precedence"; but, for both, *the perspectives associated with the timestamps "filling" these temporal attributes would be of the "fork" type. The "category" concerns the temporal attributes; the "perspective," the values (timestamps) to be associated with such attributes.*

Thus, if we exclude direct dating, these perspectives *all specify a range of possible values for the timestamp to be recorded*. The only element that distinguishes them from each other is the way in which this *range* is indicated in the

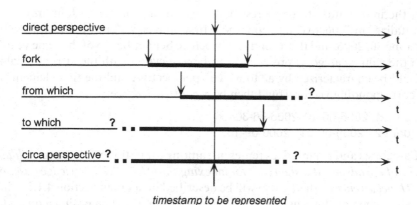

Fig. 2.8 Timestamps and perspectives

original information sources (Fig. 2.8); *we see that it can always be reduced to a "fork,"* where *both* limits can be specified, *one* only ("from which" and "to which"), or *none* of them ("circa").

When both the limits are not provided, *the missing limit(s) must be restored*: a *reconstructed date* is noted conventionally in *round brackets* in the external NKRL format. Such a reconstruction could be executed (i) *manually* by the domain expert at the moment of building up the knowledge base of occurrences, making use of the context of the event to be coded and of its personal knowledge, or (ii) *automatically by inference*, at the processing time, using some algorithm designed to calculate "so many days" or "so many months," etc. before and/or after the effective timestamp (date) known and some sort of conceptual representation of the context. See in this context, for example, the "methods" by Kahn and Gorry [1977: 95–98] and, more recently, the "temporal functions" in TimeML mentioned before.

We will conclude this section by noting that the *values* associated with the temporal attributes date-1 and date-2 are *represented, in reality, by a vector of two elements* (two timestamps). Each time we have to deal with *nondirect perspectives* (fork, from which, to which, circa; see Fig. 2.8 again), *the two elements of the vector are both explicitly expressed, giving the limits of a fork inside which is situated the (unknown) "correct" timestamp to be associated with the attribute.* On the other hand, the vector expressing *a value to be represented in direct perspective* only contains *one* explicitly expressed timestamp, e.g. see the value 1999-11-20 associated with date-1 in occurrence mod3.c5 in Table 2.6b. The temporal attributes associated with the occurrence translating the previous example, "John has been hospitalized in 2006 ...," will then be coded as

    date-1: 2006-06-10, 2006-06-30
    date-2: 2006-09-01, 2006-09-15

If the information to be represented was, on the contrary, "John has been hospitalized in 2006, over a period whose first limit is probably between June 10 and June 30, 2006, and the second surely before September 15 of the same year," then the value (category: precedence) to be associated with the attribute date-2 would be characterized by a "to which" perspective, and the first element of the corresponding vector would then be *reconstructed*; see:

date-1: 2006-06-10, 2006-06-30
date-2: (2006-09-01), 2006-09-15

Categories and perspectives represent, among other things, *the basic building blocks of the advanced system used for indexing the ORACLE knowledge bases of NKRL occurrences* – this system will be described in detail in Section 4.1.2. This indexing schema allows us to reach a twofold result: (i) when posing a query to the knowledge base, most of the (very complex) operations concerning temporal information *are directly take into account at the index level*; (ii) the real (and, once again, very complex) operations of filtering/unification between the query and the contents of the knowledge base *are executed on a very reduced subset of the knowledge base of predicative occurrences*.

2.3 Second-order Structures

In Chapter 1, we have already discussed the importance, in a general "narrative" context, of being able to deal with those *connectivity phenomena* – expressed, in NL, through syntactic/semantic constructions like causality, goal, indirect speech, coordination and subordination, etc. – that, in a narrative, cause its *global meaning to go beyond the simple addition of the information conveyed by each constitutive elementary event*. These NL connectives constitute, then, the *surface evidence* of those *deep semantic mechanisms* that assure the *logical coherence among the different components of the "stream" identifying a specific narrative*.

For concrete solutions suggested for dealing with the connectivity phenomena from a CS/AI point of view, we can evoke here, first, some "old," well-known proposals of Schankian inspirations evoking all sorts of scripts, scenarios, thematic abstraction units (TAUs), memory organization packets (MOPs), etc. [e.g. Schank and Abelson, 1977; Schank, 1980; Dyer, 1983; Kolodner, 1984] – the SnePS (Semantic Network Processing System) of Shapiro [1979; Maida and Shapiro, 1982] pertains roughly to the same period and allows us, for example, to represent "narrative" situations like "Sue thinks that Bob believes that a dog is eating a bone." Among the recent suggestions we can evoke the (already mentioned) CG mechanisms for dealing with "contexts"; see Sowa [1991] and Section 1.2.2.1. In a generic "linguistics/computational linguistics" framework, some solutions have been put forward by DRT [Kamp, 1981; Kamp and Reyle, 1993]; as already stated, DRT is a semantic theory developed for representing and computing trans-sentential anaphora and other forms of text cohesion. In the same context, see also the TimeML proposals analyzed in the previous section.

In NKRL, the connectivity phenomena are dealt with by making a (limited) use of *second-order structures*: these are obtained from the *reification of predicative occurrences* (of templates in some special cases – see Section 2.3.2.2) *based on the use of their symbolic labels* (see the L_i terms in Eq. (1.2) and, as a concrete example, mod3.c5 in Table 2.6b). "Reification" is intended here in general (as usual in a object-oriented and AI contexts) as the possibility of *making objects out of already existing complex conceptual patterns* (in our case, templates and predicative occurrences) and to *"say something" about them without making reference to the original pattern*.

2.3.1 The Completive Construction

A first example of second-order structure is given by the so-called "completive construction," which consists of using as *filler of a role in a predicative occurrence c_k the symbolic label (symbolic name) of another occurrence c_l. Only the OBJ, MODAL, TOPIC and CONTEXT roles of c_k can accept as filler a symbolic label c_l.*

Note immediately that the symbolic labels c_l used as fillers can denote *not only predicative occurrences*, as in the examples of this section, but also examples of those *binding occurrences* we will introduce in the next section. Additional constraints are:

- *only one* among the OBJ, MODAL, TOPIC and CONTEXT roles associated in the case with an occurrence c_k can be filled with a symbolic label c_l;
- c_l must correspond *strictly* to a *simple filler* (it must be, then, a *single* symbolic label), i.e. complex fillers (expansions) cannot be used in the framework of a completive construction reference.

For implementation reasons this unique label is prefixed, *in external format, by a "sharp," "#," code*. The general format of a *"completive construction filler"* actually corresponds, then, to #symbolic_label; see the tables below. Note that symbolic_label is a *regular concept of HClass* (see Section 3.1.2) that has as instances all the *concrete labels* used to denote *both predicative or binding occurrences* in the different NKRL applications.

As an example of completive construction, Table 2.15 gives the NKRL representation of a fragment of Reuters' news already mentioned in previous sections, like "Brussels, July 2, 1993. British Airways Plc President Colin Marshall said in a Belgian newspaper interview the company's indebtedness was low...." For simplicity's sake, in this example, as in the majority of the other examples of the book, the frame structures corresponding to the individuals – Colin Marshall, Brussels, etc. in this case – are not reproduced in the table.

Table 2.15 A completive construction of the "transmission of information" type

conc5.c1)	MOVE	SUBJ	(SPECIF COLIN_MARSHALL
			(SPECIF chairman_ BRITISH_AIRWAYS)):
			(BRUSSELS_)
		OBJ	#conc5.c3
		BENF	(SPECIF newspaper_ BELGIUM_)
		MODAL	interview_
		date-1:	1993-07-02
		date-2:	

Move:StructuredInformation (4.42)

conc5.c3)	EXPERIENCE	SUBJ	BRITISH_AIRWAYS
		OBJ	(SPECIF indebtedness_ (SPECIF amount_ small_))
		{obs}	
		date-1:	1993-07-02
		date-2:	

Experience:NegativeHuman/Social (3.222)

In Table 2.15, the SPECIF sub-list (SPECIF amount_ small_) in the occurrence conc5.c3 is one of the special SPECIF sub-lists *labeled in a normalized way* ("NKRL idioms") that will be examined in detail in Section 3.1.2.1; see also this last section for a discussion about an HClass quantifying_property like small_. As already stated (see Table 2.10), the presence of the temporal modulator obs(erve) leads to an interpretation of the occurrence conc5.c3 as the description of a situation that, at this particular date, *is observed to exist*.

The *completive link* is realized here by introducing the symbolic label, conc5.c3, of a "subordinate clause" (bearing the informational content to be spread out, the decrease of British Airways' indebtedness in our example) as the OBJ(ect) filler (see OBJ #conc5.c3 in occurrence conc.c1) of a MOVE predicative occurrence. In NKRL, this particular type of completive construction is largely used given that it *is the mandatory way of translating any sort of "transmission of information"*; see the discussion about the Move:TransmitInformation template and its specializations in Section 3.2.2.4. However, *the use of the completive construction is not limited to the representation of information transmission phenomena*; as already stated, fillers in the form of #symbolic_label can also be used in association with the MODAL, TOPIC and CONTEXT roles.

As a further example of completive construction, let us consider the code represented in Table 2.16, which translates this sort of complex situation (the example concerns a corporate application of NKRL for managing complex dialogue structures in the "Beauty Care" domain):

- *Occurrence skin7.c1*. On January 1st, 2002, Sarah121 sends a message to the Beauty Net Community; the content of this message is detailed in occurrence skin7.c2.

Table 2.16 Further examples of completive constructions

skin7.c1)	MOVE	SUBJ	SARAH_121
		OBJ	#skin7.c2
		BENF	BEAUTY_NET_COMMUNITY
		date-1:	2002-01-01
		date-2:	
Move:StructuredInformation (4.42)			
skin7.c2)	RECEIVE	SUBJ	SARAH_121
		OBJ	advice_
		SOURCE	BEAUTY_NET_COMMUNITY
		TOPIC	#skin7.c3
		CONTEXT	(SPECIF eyeshadowing_ SARAH_121)
		{wish}	
		date-1:	2002-01-01
		date-2:	
Receive:DesiredAdvice (7.21)			
skin7.c3)	OWN	SUBJ	(SPECIF use_ eyeshadow_powder)
		OBJ	property_
		TOPIC	(SPECIF more_effective_than
			(SPECIF use_ eyeshadow_cream))
		CONTEXT	eyeshadowing_
		{poss}	
		date-1:	2002-01-01
		date-2:	
Own:CompoundProperty (5.12)			

- *Occurrence skin7.c2.* In this message, she says she would like (modulator *wish*) to obtain their opinion, in the context of some eye shadowing operations, about (TOPIC role) what is related in occurrence skin7.c3.
- *Occurrence skin7.c3.* In particular, she would like to know whether, in the context of these eye shadowing operations, the utilization of an eye shadow powder is more effective than that of an eye powder cream.

In these predicative occurrences, the first one, skin7.c1, is an instance of the template Move:StructuredInformation, skin7.c2 is an instance of Receive:Desired Advice and skin7.c3 is an instance of the specific Own:CompoundProperty template; the Own:Property templates are largely used in NKRL to describe the properties of both entities and processes (see Section 3.2.5.5). advice_ is a specific term of information_content in HClass via its subsuming terms generic_word_ content and word_content; more_effective_than is a relational_property, i.e. a non_sortal_concept; see Section 3.1.2.1. eyeshadowing_ is a specific term of beauty_ care_process (a specialization of process_) via its subsuming term eye_related_ care_process; eyeshadow_powder and eyeshadow_cream are both specific terms of artefact_ through their subsuming terms eye_related_product/tool and beauty_ care_product terms, etc. – these last terms pertain to the specific branches of HClass added to deal with the particular terminology of the Beauty Care domain.

Table 2.17   The Move:StructuredInformation template

name: Move:StructuredInformation
father: Move:TransmitInformation
position: 4.42
NL description: "Transmit a Structured Information"

	MOVE	SUBJ	$var1$: [($var2$)]
		OBJ	$var3$
		[SOURCE	$var4$: [($var5$)]]
		[BENF	$var6$: [($var7$)]]
		[MODAL	$var8$]
		[TOPIC	$var9$]
		[CONTEXT	$var10$]
		{[modulators], $\neq$abs}

$var1$ = human_being_or_social_body
$var3$ = symbolic_label
$var4$ = human_being_or_social_body
$var6$ = human_being_or_social_body
$var8$ = electronic/media_product, information_support, service_, services_agency, transmission_medium, temporal_attribute
$var9$ = sortal_concept
$var10$ = situation_, symbolic_label
$var2$, $var5$, $var7$ = location_

To give an example of how the *mandatory use* of completive constructions for predicative occurrences is denoted in a "template" context, Table 2.17 reproduces the template Move:StructuredInformation – which is at the origin of the occurrences conc5.c1 of Table 2.15 and skin7.c1 of Table 2.16 (see also Section 3.2.2.4). The constraint on the OBJ filler shows clearly that this role *must* be necessarily filled by an instance of the symbolic_label concept.

For clarity's sake, we will now reproduce below *the totality of the syntactic rules* that govern the set up of *well-formed completive expressions*:

- The creation of an *associative relationship* of the "completive construction" type consists in introducing the symbolic label c_l of an NKRL occurrence, *predicative or binding* (see next section), as "filler" of a role of a *predicative occurrence c_k.*
- *Only the roles OBJ, MODAL, TOPIC and CONTEXT of c_k can be "filled" with the symbolic label c_l.*
- In c_k, *only one of the above four roles can be filled with c_l*, i.e. it is forbidden to make use of more than a *single* completive construction reference within the same predicative occurrence.
- The filler c_l must be a "simple" filler, i.e. expansions (structured argument) implying the use of the AECS operators *cannot be used* to set up relationships among occurrences in the completive construction style.
- In the predicative occurrence c_k, the actual format of the filler c_l is #symbolic_ label, where symbolic_label is a regular HClass concept.

- In the templates, the mandatory use of a completive construction filler in the derived predicative occurrences is denoted through the use of a symbolic_label constraint on one of the variables var_i of the template; see Table 2.17.

2.3.2 Binding Occurrences

A second, *more general* way of linking together NKRL structures to take into account the "connectivity phenomena" consists of making use of *"binding occurrences," i.e. binary structures under the form of lists labeled with specific "binding operators," whose arguments are represented (reification) by symbolic labels of (predicative or binding) occurrences.* Extensions to binding structures having "partially instantiated templates" as arguments will be introduced in Section 2.3.2.2.

Unlike templates and predicative occurrences, binding occurrences are then characterized by *the absence of any predicate or role*: they present *strong syntactic similarities* with the "expansions" (structured arguments) introduced in Section 2.2.2.3, the most important difference being that *"binding occurrences" are full-fledged, "independent" second-order objects endowed with a proper symbolic "name."*

2.3.2.1 The Binding Operators

Like the expansions, the binding occurrence lists are then characterized by the presence of an *operator* (a *"binding operator"* here) as the *first element* of the list. The binding operators are listed in Table 2.18; see also the expansion operators of Table 2.8. To enforce the syntactic coherence of the global NKRL code, the binding occurrences *must necessarily conform* to the following *mandatory* restrictions to be considered as *well formed*:

- The terms (arguments) c_i that, in a generic binding list, are associated with one of the operators of Table 2.18, *denote necessarily (single) symbolic labels of (predicative or binding) occurrences.* Therefore (in contrast to what happens when dealing with the expansion structures), these *arguments cannot denote (canned) lists labeled in turn with binding operators.* Note also that each element c_i of the binding list refers to a *different* binding or predicative occurrence.
- In the binding occurrence of the ALTERN, COORD and ENUM type, *no restriction is imposed on the cardinality of the list*, i.e. on the possible number of terms (arguments) c_i.
- In the binding occurrences labeled with CAUSE, REFER, GOAL, MOTIV and COND, in contrast, *only two arguments, c_k and c_l, are admitted*. The binding occurrence labeled with the above five binding operators are then simply of the type: (OPERATOR c_k c_l). In these lists, the arguments (symbolic

Table 2.18 Binding operators of NKRL

Operator	Acronym	Mnemonic description
Alternative	ALTERN	The *disjunctive* operator. *Only a term* of the associated list of labels of predicative/binding occurrences must be considered, but this term is not known a priori
Coordination	COORD	The *collective* operator. *All the terms* of the list must, obligatorily, be considered *together* to give rise to a valid binding relationship
Enumeration	ENUM	The *distributive* operator. *Each term* of the list must be considered to produce a valid binding relationship, but they satisfy this relationship *separately*
Cause	CAUSE	The *strict causality* operator, introducing a *necessary and sufficient causal relationship between the first and the second arguments of the list*, the latter explaining the former. Only two terms can appear in a CAUSE binding occurrence; see also Section 2.3.2.3
Reference	REFER	The *weak causality* operator, introducing a *necessary but not sufficient* causal relationship between the first and the second arguments of the list
Goal	GOAL	The *strict intentionality* operator; the first argument is *necessary* to realize the second, and the second is *sufficient* to explain the first. The predicative occurrence(s) corresponding to the second argument is/are *necessarily marked* as "uncertain," operator "*" (see Section 2.2.2.4)
Motivation	MOTIV	The *weak intentionality* operator; the first argument is *not necessary* to realize the second, but the second is *sufficient* to explain the first. The predicative occurrence(s) corresponding to the second argument is/are *necessarily marked* as "uncertain," operator "*"
Condition	COND	The *predicative occurrence* corresponding to the first argument represents an event that *could happen* if the *predicative/binding* occurrence (i.e. event or complex situation) corresponding to the second argument *could be realized.* The first argument (predicative occurrence) *is necessarily associated* with a modulator poss (see Table 2.13); the predicative occurrence(s) corresponding to the second argument is/are *necessarily marked* as "uncertain," operator "*"

labels) can denote, in general, both a predicative and a binding occurrence; an exception is represented by the COND binding occurrences, where the first argument c_k *must correspond necessarily to a predicative occurrence*; see Table 2.18.

A first example will show, among other things, how "completive constructions" and "binding occurrences" can coexist within a fragment of *conceptual annotation* (or *metadocument*); a conceptual annotation (see Zarri [2003b] and the examples of Chapter 3) is a *structured association of binding and predicative occurrences* intended to supply a *detailed representation of the "meaning" of a*

Table 2.19 Mixing completive constructions and binding occurrences

conc5.c1)	MOVE	SUBJ	(SPECIF COLIN_MARSHALL
			(SPECIF chairman_ BRITISH_AIRWAYS)):
			(BRUSSELS_)
		OBJ	#conc5.c2
		BENF	(SPECIF newspaper_ BELGIUM_)
		MODAL	interview_
		date-1:	1993-07-02
		date-2:	

Move:StructuredInformation (4.42)

conc5.c2) (CAUSE conc5.c3 conc5.c4)

conc5.c3)	EXPERIENCE	SUBJ	BRITISH_AIRWAYS
		OBJ	(SPECIF indebtedness_ (SPECIF amount_ small_))
		{obs}	
		date-1:	1993-07-02
		date-2:	

Experience:NegativeHuman/Social (3.222)

conc5.c4)	PRODUCE	SUBJ	BRITISH_AIRWAYS
		OBJ	(SPECIF capital_increase BRITISH_AIRWAYS)
		date-1:	(1993-01-01), 1993-07-02
		date-2:	

Produce:EconomicInterestActivity (6.48)

complex narrative document. Table 2.19 provides, then, the *complete NKRL image* of the example already used in Table 2.15: "Brussels, July 2, 1993. British Airways Plc President Colin Marshall said in a Belgian newspaper interview the company's indebtedness was low *following a capital increase.*"

In Table 2.19, *the content of the message is now represented by the binding occurrence* conc5.c2. This occurrence – which is labeled using the CAUSE operator defined in Table 2.18 (see also Section 2.3.2.3) and that follows the "only two arguments" rule – means that event conc5.c3, the main event, *has been caused* by event conc5.c4. The new predicative occurrence conc5.c4 translates an elementary event that has been interpreted as a *point event* (no temporal modulator) from a *category* point of view, and as a *limit to which* ("before July 2, 1993," see the date fork) from a *perspective* point of view; see the "Categories and perspectives" subsection in Section 2.2.2.4. The first term of the fork, January 1st, 1993, is a *reconstructed date*, noted in parentheses in external format.

2.3.2.2 Priority Rule and Generalization to Templates

We will now introduce two important, general remarks about the binding operators introduced in the previous section.

Correspondence between "Expansion" and "Binding" Operators

A first remark concerns the correspondence between the operators of Tables 2.8 and 2.18. The basic semantics of ALTERN, COORD and ENUM are, obviously, *the same* whether they are used within expansion lists or binding occurrence lists. This is why, to avoid any possible confusion, these three operators are denoted in the "external" NKRL notation as ALTERN1, COORD1 and ENUM1 *when they are used as expansion operators*.

Moreover, the CAUSE, REFER, GOAL, MOTIV and COND operators of Table 2.8 correspond, in a sense, to the operator SPECIF(ication) of Table 2.8. This last operator is used, in fact, to *supply further information* about the *first argument* of a SPECIF list – in a list (SPECIF e_i *a b c* ...) in fact, the properties *a*, *b*, *c*, ..., concepts or individuals, introduce additional details about the item e_i (the first argument) that follows immediately the operator SPECIF. When dealing with binding lists labeled as CAUSE, GOAL, etc., we can consider the (single; see Table 2.18) predicative or binding occurrence c_2 that represents, for example, the second argument of a list (CAUSE c_1 c_2) as an element that, once again, *supplies further information* (the cause in this case, but also the goal, the possible condition for the realization ...) about what is stated in the first argument (occurrence c_1) of the list.

However, for the binding occurrences, no strict formal constraints in the style of the "priority rule" introduced in Section 2.2.2.3 can be imposed. This depends mainly on the possibility that binding occurrences labeled with COORD can be found, within a structured list of binding and predicative occurrences, in a position that contradicts the strict sequence of the operators imposed by the priority rule. In fact:

- In a binding list of the CAUSE, REFER, GOAL, MOTIV and COND type, one of the two symbolic labels (normally the second, c_2) *can correspond to another binding occurrence, in particular to a binding occurrence of the* COORD *type*. For example, in Table 2.19, the second argument conc5.c4 (the CAUSE) in the binding occurrence conc5.c2 could, in fact, *instead of a single predicative occurrence* (a single elementary event), denote *a long narrative development represented by several occurrences grouped in a* COORD *list*. This last situation would then be equivalent to the introduction of a COORD list within a CAUSE, REFER, GOAL, etc. binding list, i.e. *within a list that, according to what is expounded above, is supposed to correspond to a* SPECIF *list*. The priority rule as expressed in Section 2.2.2.3 would then be *implicitly violated*.

- This situation is quite frequent in practice – as evidenced also by the examples of Chapter 3 – because of the decision of admitting a *liberal use* of COORD binding lists within long sequences of predicative occurrences in order to *group together ("factorize")*, for both readability and logical coherence's sake, occurrences that *are very close from a semantic content point of view*. For example, we could group together in a COORD binding occurrence (i) a PRODUCE predicative occurrence relating the creation of some artifacts and (ii) several occurrences in the style of skin7.c3 in Table 2.16 (derived then from Own:Property templates) *to specify the different properties of these artifacts.* The resulting COORD binding occurrence could, after that, correspond to the *second argument* of a CAUSE, GOAL, etc. list.

Concretely, the only restriction on the use of binding operators within binding occurrences (introducing, then, a sort of weakened form of the priority rule) concerns the impossibility of making use of arguments c_i denoting binding occurrences of the ALTERN and ENUM types within binding occurrences of the COORD type. Within these COORD binding occurrences, however, c_i labels can be freely used to denote binding occurrences of the COORD, CAUSE, REFER, GOAL, MOTIV and COND types – as already stated, the last five operators correspond (very roughly, and only from an operational point of view) to the SPECIF operator of the AECS sub-language.

Using Template Labels within Binding Structures

A second remark concerns the *generalization of the binding structures* that can be obtained by using as arguments the symbolic labels of "partially instantiated templates" t_i, instead of symbolic labels of predicative/binding occurrences. These *binding structures* are sometimes called *binding templates.* This possibility is particularly useful when *knowledge contents of a high level of abstraction and generality must be represented*; see the definitions associated with the "procedure type properties" in an HClass context, Section 2.2.1.3, and the "NKRL inference rules" in Chapter 4. We recall here that a "partially instantiated template" corresponds to a standard template (descriptive component) where *at least some of the explicit variables (var$_i$) originally associated with this template have been replaced by some of their constraints* (HClass terms) – or by specializations/instances (individuals) of these constraints.

As an example, we reproduce in Table 2.20 the "predicative" and "binding" templates included in the representation of a fragment of "normative" text, the beginning of article no. 57 of the French General Taxation Law – e.g. see Zarri [1992b] for a more complete analysis of this text. Article no. 57 is the main normative source used to settle cases concerning an "indirect transfer of revenues abroad"; as already stated in Section 2.2.1.3, the NKRL code of Table 2.20 is then part of the definition of the HClass concept norms_for_indirect_transfer_ of_revenues_abroad. The beginning of this article reads as follows, according to a rough English translation: "*To determine the income tax payable by companies in France which are under the authority of, or which exercise a control over, companies domiciled abroad*, the revenues indirectly transferred abroad must be added to the results registered in the books." For simplicity's sake, the code reproduced in Table 2.20 concerns only the fragment in italics of the above definition.

Objects like ind_trans.t4 and ind_trans.t5 are then "*binding*" templates, i.e. binding structures where the arguments of the operators are the symbolic labels

Table 2.20 "Binding" and "predicative" templates

ind_trans.t1)	(GOAL ind_trans.t2 ind_trans.t3)		
ind_trans.t3)	(ALTERN ind_trans.t4 ind_trans.t5)		
ind_trans.t4)	(COORD ind_trans.t6 ind_trans.t7)		
ind_trans.t6)	PRODUCE	SUBJ	var1
		OBJ	(SPECIF calculation_ income_tax)
		BENF	var2: (FRANCE_)

var1 = human_being_or_social_body
var2 = company_

Produce:Numerical/StatisticalProcess (6.44)

ind_trans.t7)	OWN	SUBJ	var2: (FRANCE_)
		OBJ	control_
		TOPIC	var3: (var4)

var2 = company_
var3 = company_
var2 ≠ var3
var4 ≠ FRANCE_

Own:ControlOfCompany (5.221)

ind_trans.t5)	(COORD ind_trans.t8 ind_trans.t9)		
ind_trans.t8)	PRODUCE	SUBJ	var1
		OBJ	(SPECIF calculation_ income_tax)
		BENF	var2: (FRANCE_)

var1 = human_being_or_social_body
var2 = company_

Produce:Numerical/StatisticalProcess (6.44)

ind_trans.t9)	OWN	SUBJ	var3: (var4)
		OBJ	control_
		TOPIC	var2: (FRANCE_)

var3 = company_
var2 ≠ var3
var4 = country_
var4 ≠ FRANCE_
Own:ControlOfCompany (5.221)

t_i of *partially instantiated templates*. ind_trans.t1 says that the operations *consisting of the addition of the revenues transferred abroad to the results, etc.* (see the wording of the article) – these operations (denoted by ind_trans.t2) *are not explicitly represented* in the code of Table 2.20 – are *strictly necessary* (GOAL) to allow the realization of the main task described in article no. 57 (the calculation of the income tax, ind_trans.t3); moreover, they also *precede* the execution of this task (see also the next section). ind_trans.t3 represents the *alternative* that is expressed by the textual fragment in italics. According to ind_trans.t4, the calculation of the income tax (ind_trans.t6) may concern a French company, *var2*, that controls (ind_trans.t7) a generic foreign company, *var3*;

according to ind_trans.t5, the same calculation (ind_trans.t8) may concern a French company that is controlled by a foreign company (ind_trans.t9). Note that all the binding structures conform to the *syntactic restrictions* defined above.

In Table 2.20, ind_trans.t6 and ind_trans.t8 are *partial instantiations* (see the utilization of the individual FRANCE_ and of calculation_, a specialization of the concept numerical/statistical_process) of the template Produce:Numerical/StatisticalProcess. ind_trans.t7 and ind_trans.t9 are partial instantiations of Own:ControlOfCompany; see the addition of specific locations, etc.

2.3.2.3 Binding Operators and Temporal Representation

If we consider the relationships between *temporal information* and *binding occurrences*, a first remark concerns the fact that the temporal attributes date-1 and date-2 necessarily associated with the predicative occurrences mentioned in the binding occurrences are *normally filled with explicit temporal indications* (explicit timestamps). Therefore, their *temporal arrangement* within the binding occurrence is not difficult to assess.

Moreover, the four binding operators that constitute together the NKRL *taxonomy of causality*, CAUSE, GOAL, REFER and MOTIV, are associated with *explicit temporal valences* as illustrated by the examples of Fig. 2.9. As we can see, CAUSE and GOAL respectively express a sort of *strict* causality or

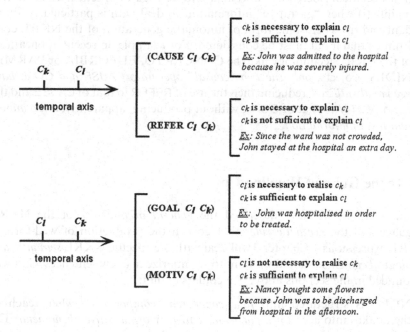

Fig. 2.9 Time and causality in NKRL

purpose; REFER and MOTIV express a *weak* causality and purpose respectively. Expressed in different terms, we can say that the use of CAUSE and GOAL is only permitted in the presence of a "material implication" $c_k \supset c_l$, where c_k and c_l denote two generic predicative occurrences (elementary events). It is evident that this last condition is not respected in the two examples of Fig. 2.9 that illustrate the use of REFER and MOTIV.

We can conclude this section with two simple remarks:

- The first is that the taxonomy outlined above looks, of course, *quite simplistic* compared with all the possible "classical" theories about causality, going back to Aristotle's work (who considers four types of cause – material causes, formal causes, efficient causes, and final causes) and continuing with Hume, Kant, Gibbon, etc. Unfortunately, many of these theories are *too complex or not specific enough* to be used within a *practical and robust computational framework*; see, in this context, the recent "Force Dynamics" causal theory (of cognitive linguistics origin) proposed by Talmy [1988, 2000] and characterized, among other things, by a sophisticated dichotomy between prototypical and nonprototypical specializations of the "causing" and "letting" categories. "Practical" proposals nearer in their basic motivation to NKRL's approach can be found, for example, in Schank and Abelson [1977: 30–32] and Lenat and Guha [1990: 240–243]; see also NKRL's treatment of "wish, will," etc. in Section 3.2.2.1.
- However, even the "causal taxonomy" proposed in this section has sometimes been considered as *too complex* to be used in practical applications, mainly (i) when "narrative" information to deal with is particularly abundant and (ii) when some form of automatic generation of the NKRL code from textual input must be considered. For example, in recent applications of the NKRL technology like the CONCERTO, EUFORBIA or PARMENIDES projects, *only the two "causal" operators CAUSE and GOAL have been really utilized*, reducing then the use of REFER to that of CAUSE and the use of MOTIV to that of GOAL, without producing, apparently, *a too important loss of information*.

2.4 In the Guise of Winding Up

In this chapter, we have described the *general architecture* of the NKRL language and the *syntactic rules* that govern the production of well-formed NKRL expressions – Chapter 3 will deal with the specific NKRL *semantic and ontological contents*. Should we want to summarize in a few sentences what was expounded in the sections above, we could say that:

- NKRL is structured into *four connected "components,"* where each of them takes into account *a particular category of narrative phenomena*. The *definitional component* concerns the formal definition of the *concepts* C_i

(according to the usual "ontological" meaning of this term), and the *enumerative component* concerns the definition of the *instances* l_i of these concepts (*individuals*). The *descriptive component* deals with the *formal representations (templates, t_i) of general classes of elementary events* like "moving a generic object," "formulate a need," "be present somewhere," and the *factual component* deals with the representation of the *specific events that correspond to particular instantiations of these general classes* (predicative occurrences, c_i). With respect to description logics terminology, the definitional component corresponds roughly to Tbox and the enumerative component to Abox. *No description logics structures correspond to the descriptive and factual structures of NKRL.*

- Concepts and individuals are inserted into an "ontology of concepts," a directed acyclic graph that, in NKRL, takes the name of HClass (hierarchy of classes). Their "binary" data structures are *relatively standard* and consist basically of *frame-like structures*, i.e. of bundles of *property/value* relationships where neither the number nor the order of the properties is fixed. The properties (i.e. the slots) of the frames describing specific concepts/individuals are obtained by specializing a set of *prototype slots*. From a semantic point of view, the properties are grouped in three categories: *relations, attributes,* and *procedures*. The latter are of particular interest, given that their (complex) values are described making use of the "*n*-ary" data structures proper to the descriptive and factual components. In NKRL, *concepts cannot be considered as instances of other concepts*; individuals are added, when necessary, as "leaves" of HClass by using *explicit local operations*.

- The *n*-ary data structures, templates and predicative occurrences, used (i) for the description of the general classes of events (*templates*) and (ii) for the description of their instances, i.e. the concrete events (*predicative occurrences*), are formed by bundles of "quadruples" connecting together the *symbolic name* of the template/occurrence, a *predicate* and the *arguments* of the predicate introduced by *named relations*, the *roles*. The quadruples have in common the "name" and "predicate" components. Predicates and roles are *primitive*; the arguments can be simple HClass elements, concepts or individuals, or well-formed structures (*structured arguments or expansions*), where *lists of HClass elements*, labeled using the four operators of the AECS sub-language, can be *interwoven* according to a *priority rule*.

- To assign a *valid semantic interpretation* (as an event or a class of events) to an NKRL descriptive/factual structure (template or predicative occurrence), the latter *must* at least consist of a predicate, a role and an argument. However, *determiners* (attributes) that (i) *introduce further details/precisions* concerning the "meaning" of these templates/occurrences but that (ii) are *never strictly necessary* for their basic semantic interpretation in NKRL terms can also be added. Determiners include *modulators (temporal, deontic and modal modulators), locations* and *temporal determiners*: the presence of two *temporal determiners,* date-1 and date-2, is mandatory in order that a *predicative occurrence* can be considered as *well formed*. Original concepts of the NKRL representation system for temporal data are the *"category of dating,"* which allows defining the relationships (*precedence, subsequence, contemporaneity*) between timestamps and events, and the "perspective," which defines the *different ways (different degrees of precisions) of "capturing" a timestamp.*

• *Second-order structures* obtained through the *reification* of templates and predicative occurrences are used to deal with those *connectivity phenomena* (in NL terms: causality, goal, indirect speech, coordination and subordination, etc.) that, in a narrative represented by a stream of elementary events, cause the *global meaning of the narrative to go beyond the simple addition of the information conveyed by each elementary event.* A first type of second-order structure is the *completive construction*, where the symbolic label of a predicative/binding occurrence can be used directly (reification) as filler of a role in (different) predicative occurrences. A second, *more general way* of linking together NKRL occurrences consists of making use of "binding occurrences," i.e. *binary structures under the form of lists labeled with specific "binding operators."* The arguments of the binding operators *are represented (reification) by symbolic labels of NKRL occurrences* – and, more in general, of NKRL *templates*. Four of these "binding operators" (CAUSE, GOAL, REFER and MOTIV) form the NKRL "taxonomy of causality."

To conclude about the four NKRL components, we present in Fig. 2.10 a graphical representation of their *main relationships*. We make use for this of a very simple narrative example where, for intelligibility's sake, the temporal information has been suppressed: "Berlex Laboratories have performed an evaluation of a given compound."

Many additional simplifications have been introduced in this figure. For example, the organization of the HTemp and HClass hierarchies is extremely simplified with respect to their real structure (see Chapter 3); the template "evaluate an artifact" that appears in the "descriptive component" layer as an offspring of the Produce:PerformTask/Activity template is an approximation of the "real" template Produce:Assessment/Trial; the "individual" (enumerative component) COMPOUND_27, which represents the specific compound mentioned in the event, is supposed here to be a direct instance of the (very high level) concept artefact_, etc. Note that, for uniformity's sake, we have considered that the proper assessment activities are well specified and that, therefore, they can be described using a particular *individual*, ASSESSMENT_1. The concept assessment_ is a specific term of activity_, and company_ is a specific term of social_body.

The arrowhead lines represent, in general, *have an instance* links. This means, for example, that the predicative occurrence "Berlex Laboratories have performed an evaluation..." of the *factual component* has been created from the corresponding "evaluate an artifact" template of the *descriptive component*, which is, in turn, a *specialization* of the generic template, Produce:Perform Task/Activity, used to describe the fact/situation/event of "performing a task

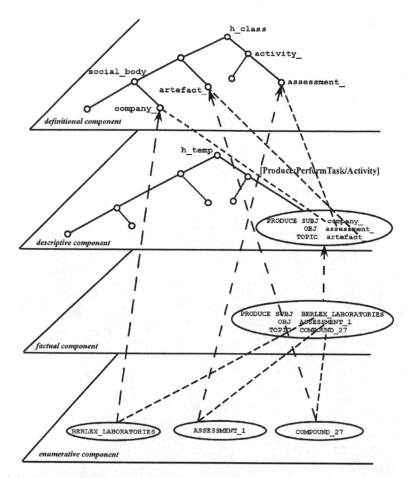

Fig. 2.10 Relationships among the NKRL components

or an activity." More precisely, the predicative occurrence has been obtained by replacing – for each role SUBJ(ect), OBJ(ect), TOPIC (à propos of...) of the original "evaluation" template – the concepts indicating the general classes of legal fillers (constraints) for these roles, e.g. company_, with (in this case) particular individuals, e.g. BERLEX_LABORATORIES.

The dotted lines without any arrow represent a sort of "coreference link." This means that, for example, in the HTemp "evaluation" template (descriptive component), company_ is a symbolic label allowing us to access, from the descriptive component environment, information stored in the frame-like structure company_ that pertains to the definitional component (HClass). Similarly, the label COMPOUND_27 in the "evaluation" occurrence (factual component) refers to the corresponding frame-like object pertaining to the enumerative component environment.

Chapter 3
The Semantic and Ontological Contents

Having introduced in Chapter 2 the main characteristics of NKRL as a *generic environment* (based on the use of *two integrated ontologies*) for the set up of conceptual descriptions of narratives, we will now supply some details about the specific *semantic "contents"* of the two ontologies, the "ontology of concepts" HClass and the "ontology of events" HTemp. Their contents can be considered, in fact, as *an integral part of the definition of the language*.

Section 3.1 will then describe the organization of the "upper level" of HClass, by emphasizing, among other things, the differences of the NKRL approach with respect to other popular ontological tools like the W3C languages, DOLCE, SUMO or CYC. In Section 3.2, we will introduce the main characteristics of each of the seven "branches" of the HTemp hierarchy. This section will then concern the description of the *specific* NKRL structures that must be *routinely used* to describe narrative features, like the amounts of money exchanged in a commercial transaction, the transmission of messages or the planning of complex activities. Section 3.3 will supply a quick synopsis of the main points expounded in the chapter.

3.1 The Organization of the HClass Hierarchy

As already stated, HClass, the NKRL "hierarchy of classes," is a *binary* structure perfectly equivalent to one of those *ontologies* of concepts that are now so popular. In this section, we will first review some important aspects of the general "ontological" domain, and we will then describe in detail the proper characteristics of HClass.

3.1.1 General Notions about Ontologies

Starting from the 1990s, *ontologies* have emerged as an important research topic investigated by several research communities (AI, computational linguistics,

G.P. Zarri, *Representation and Management of Narrative Information*,
DOI 10.1007/978-1-84800-078-0_3, © Springer-Verlag London Limited 2009

cognitive science, data engineering, etc.) and used especially in defining the *standard for data exchange, information integration, and interoperability.*

3.1.1.1 Ontologies, Taxonomies, and Concepts

The word "ontology" comes from medieval philosophy, where it was used to talk about the existence of beings in the world [Guarino and Giarretta, 1995; Zúñiga, 2001]. According to its modern, computer science technical meaning [Gruber, 1993], a well-known consensus definition says "Ontologies represent a formal and explicit specification of a shared conceptualization," where:

- *Conceptualization* refers to an *abstract model of some phenomena/situations in the world*, where the model results by the identification of the *relevant concepts* that characterize these particular phenomena/situations. From a practical point of view, the "concepts" can be understood as the *discrete, important notions* that must be necessarily utilized to describe the phenomena/situations under consideration.
- *Explicit* means that the types of concept used, and the constraints on their use, are *explicitly defined.*
- *Formal* refers to the fact that the ontology should be *machine usable.*
- *Shared* reflects the notion that an ontology captures *consensual knowledge*; that is, this knowledge is not private to some individual, but must be accepted by a group.

Apart from the requirement of being usable on a computer, there is nothing in the previous characterization of an ontology that, for example, could not also be applied to a *taxonomy* in the classical Linnaean meaning: it is obvious in fact that Carl Linnaeus's classifications for biology, etc. were intended to give an *exhaustive definition* of some phenomena/situations, and that they were intended to be *explicit and shared.* And surely, *taxa* for a notion like "mammal" is not so different from a *concept* for the same notion. Moreover, both the concepts and the taxa are organized into *hierarchies* that take the form of a tree – of a DAG if multi-inheritance is admitted. For an operational distinction between "taxonomies" and "ontologies" we must then rely on the *scope* of the definitions associated with the concepts/taxa. In taxonomies (and even in some of the simplest examples of contemporary ontologies) taxa/concepts have only an *implicit* definition deriving from the fact of *being inserted in a network of specific/generic relationships* with the other elements of the hierarchy. This means that a taxon/concept like company_ is only defined by the fact of being, at the same time, a *specific* term of a higher order taxon/concept as social_body (company_ is subsumed by social_body), and a *generic* term with respect to a specialized concept as computer_company (company_ subsumes computer_company).

To get an ontology now according to the *usual computer science meaning* of this term, we must supply some *explicit* definitions for the concepts (or at least for a majority among them) even if nothing is stated about this specific point in the "consensus" definition given above. This can be obtained, for example, by associating a *frame* (a set of properties/attributes with associated classes of admitted values – see also Sections 1.2.1.1 and 2.2.1.1) with these concepts. For example, if we consider that properties useful to better specify the concept company_ could be, among other things, DateOfCreation and DomainOfActivity, then we will associate such properties (slots) with the concept. At the same time, we will also impose that, when specific examples ("instances") of the concept company_ are created, the slot DateOfCreation will only be filled by numeric values structured according to a given format (dates) and the DomainOf Activity slot with specific terms of another concept of the hierarchy, like mar-ket_sector. From the above, it is then evident that the definition mechanisms of ontologies require the use of some sort of *knowledge representation language*, and this is *totally extraneous* to the "philosophy" of taxonomies according to their usual Linnaean meaning.

3.1.1.2 The Semantic Web Solutions

In recent years, in connection with the popularity of the SW approach, many researchers have chosen an *SW language* like OWL, the "Web Ontology Language," as the knowledge representation tool to implement their ontologies – according to Cardoso [2007: 87], 75.9% of the respondents to the questionnaire about the practices of the SW community already mentioned in Section 2.2.1 have selected OWL in this context. We can recall here that the SW vision is, in fact, deeply rooted in an "ontological" approach, and an "ontology vocabulary" constitutes one of the fundamental layers of the SW's architecture (the "cake") as proposed originally by Berners-Lee and his colleagues [Berners-Lee et al., 2001].

As is well known, on February 10, 2004, the W3C published an *official "recommendation"* concerning OWL [Bechhofer et al., 2004]; W3C – the World Wide Web Consortium, coordinated by MIT (USA), ERCIM, the European Research Consortium for Informatics and Mathematics, and Keio University (Japan) – includes all the main bodies on Earth interested in the developments of the Internet and the Web. At the beginning of this document is stated:

> The Web Ontology Language (OWL) is a semantic markup language for publishing and sharing ontologies on the World Wide Web. OWL is developed as a vocabulary extension of RDF (the Resource Description Framework) and is derived from the DAML+OIL Web Ontology Language ... An OWL ontology is an RDF graph, which is in turn a set of RDF triples.

The mention of DAML+OIL [McGuinness et al., 2002] in this statement explains the *strong logic orientation of OWL*, given that OIL (Ontology Inference Layer), the "European" component of DAML+OIL (DAML is the Darpa Agent Markup Language) was implemented in description logics (DL) terms – DL [Baader et al., 2002] was created to offer, among other things, a formal foundation for frame-based systems. OWL consists of three subsets (three specific sub-languages) characterized by an increasing level of complexity and expressiveness, OWL Lite, OWL DL and OWL Full [Bechhofer et al., 2004].

A Quick Reminder of some OWL, etc. Features

As mentioned in the above W3C statement, OWL can be considered as an extension of RDF, the "Resource Description Framework" – see Manola and Miller [2004] and, for a short introduction, the "unofficial" Swartz's primer [Swartz, 2002] – which represents another fundamental building block of the SW architecture. It is used to describe generic "things" ("resources," according to the RDF jargon) on the Web. As already mentioned in Section 1.2.1.1, an RDF document is, basically, a list of statements under the form of *triples* having the classical format: <object, property, value> – more exactly, <subject, predicate, object> according to the (misleading) RDF terminology – where the elements of the triples can be URIs (Universal Resource Identifiers), literals (mainly, free text) and variables. RDF statements are normally expressed in XML format – using the so-called "RDF/XML syntax" [Beckett, 2004]. RDF can also be seen as a specific DTD (Document Type Description) of XML specialized for the description of "resources." According to Shadbolt et al. [2006: 97], RDF represents a sort of "... minimalist knowledge representation for the Web."

RDF Schema (or RDFS) [Brickley and Guha, 2004] is a particularly important complement to RDF that provides a mechanism for constructing *specialized RDF vocabularies* making use of *application-specific classes and properties*. We can then use the constructs rdfs:Class to declare that a particular resource (denoted by a URI) is a class *representing a whole set of resources*; these resources are called the "instances" of the class. More precisely, the instances of a specific class are declared making use of the specific rdf:type property, i.e. when a resource has an rdf:type property whose value is some specific class, then we can consider that this resource is an instance of the specified class. To describe the properties that can be associated with the classes, RDFS makes use of the RDF construct rdf:Property, to be interpreted now as the class of all the RDF properties; rdf:Property is then an instance of rdfs:Class. Some specific, useful properties (instances of rdf:Property) are predefined in RDFS, like rdfs:domain and rdfs:range. For example, we could define the creator property saying that it has the resource document as *domain* (i.e. the resource document is necessarily associated with this property) and that it has the resource person as *range* (rdfs:range) – the value of the creator property is always of the person type. Moreover, one of the main functions of RDFS consists in allowing the construction of *hierarchies*, both *hierarchies of concepts* and *hierarchies of properties*. RDFS provides then the specific property rdfs:subClassOf, which allows us *to build up hierarchies of classes by relating a subclass to its superclass.* Analogously, we will make use of the construct rdfs:subPropertyOf to declare that *a property is a subproperty of another.*

OWL is more *expressive* than RDF with respect to the description of the resources and of their relationships, the core idea being that of enabling the set up of *ontologies open to the implementation of decision procedures.* Note, however, that some SW authorities *do not see OWL as a full-fledged knowledge representation language, but only as a tool for exchanging ontologies*; see http://ontolog.cim3.net/ cgi-bin/wiki.pl?ConferenceCall_2005_08_11/SessionTranscript (courtesy of Jim Schoening). To illustrate now very quickly how the OWL tools are, nevertheless, currently used for the set up of standard ontologies, we reproduce in Table 3.1 a small fragment of the OWL version of the "wine" ontology, an ontology often used for exemplification purposes in the SW milieus [McGuinness et al., 2002; Smith et al., 2004]. For simplicity's sake, we have not reproduced in this table the "housekeeping" declarations necessary to identify all the XML namespaces associated with this ontology.

In the first line of Table 3.1, the class Wine is introduced making use of an rdf:ID attribute, having as its value a "fragment identifier" (here Wine) that represents an abbreviation of the complete reference to the URI of the resource being described. This is formed by taking the base URI of the wine ontology, e.g. http://www.w3.org/TR/2004/REC-owl-guide-20040210/wine, and appending the character # (to indicate that what follows is a fragment identifier) and then Wine to it, giving then the absolute URI reference: http://www.w3.org/TR/2004/ REC-owl-guide-20040210/wine#Wine. Note that the Wine class can now be referred to by using #Wine; e.g. rdf:resource = "#Wine" is a well-formed OWL statement. As already stated, the fundamental W3C constructor for setting up ontologies is rdfs:subClassOf; the second line of the code of Table 3.1 allows, then, the insertion of the class Wine into the global ontology by asserting that it is a specialization of the class (concept) PotableLiquid (liquid suitable for drinking) – which can be defined, in turn, as a specialization of the class ConsumableThing.

The third line of the code warns that the class Wine is also a specialization of a second class; the latter is an "anonymous" class, whose definition is included

Table 3.1 A fragment of the OWL wine ontology

```
<owl:Class rdf:ID = "Wine">
 <rdfs:subClassOf rdf:resource = "#PotableLiquid"/>
 <rdfs:subClassOf>
  <owl:Restriction>
   <owl:onProperty rdf:resource = "#madeFromGrape"/>
   <owl:minCardinality rdf:datatype = "&xsd;nonNegativeInteger">1 </owl:minCardinality>
  </owl:Restriction>
 </rdfs:subClassOf>
...
</owl:Class>
```

within the opening owl:Restriction markup element in line 4 and ends with the closing /owl:Restriction markup element in line 7. In OWL, in fact, a *property restriction on a class* is a special kind of class description, that of the *anonymous class including all the individuals that satisfy the given restriction*. In line 5, the owl:onProperty constructor introduces the name of the property, madeFrom-Grape, to be associated with the class Wine; line 6 specifies that the cardinality of this property is 1. The insertion of this restriction in the definition of Wine states, globally, that every specific wine must also be characterized by at least one madeFromGrape relation. The &xsd;nonNegativeInteger datatype used to introduce the literal 1 in the owl:minCardinality restriction of line 6 is part of the built-in XML Schema datatypes [Biron and Malhotra, 2001].

Note that, in spite of the formal "external" appearances, *the "frames" and "W3C" approaches to the construction of ontologies are not totally incompatible* – as we have seen in Chapter 2, NKRL/HClass follows a "classical" frame approach. They are primarily based, in fact, on the same (binary) "property-value" approach. We can also note, in this context, that *an "OWL plugin" for Protégé* (see http://protege.stanford.edu/overview/protege_owl.html/ and Horridge [2004]) is now widely in use; as recalled in Section 2.1.1, Protégé can be considered as the "standard" tool for any frame-based approach. This plugin allows loading and saving OWL and RDF ontologies, editing and visualizing OWL classes, their properties and rules, editing OWL individuals and, mainly, supporting reasoners, such as the description logics classifiers.

Even if this topic is only indirectly related with the construction of ontologies, we would like to conclude this Section by mentioning what, in our opinion, constitutes one of the most interesting novelties introduced by the W3C activities, i.e. the SW Services (SWSs). For a general introduction to the SWSs domain, e.g. see Cardoso and Sheth [2005] and also the recent Studer et al. [2007].

A "normal" Web Service can be defined as a Web site that does not simply supply static information, but that also allows us to execute automatically some "actions" (services), like the sale of a product or the control of a physical device; an increasing number of Web Services are accessible on the Web, developed by independent operators or large companies, such as Amazon and Google. To carry out their tasks, Web Services must provide interoperability among diverse applications, using platform- and language-independent interfaces for a smooth integration of heterogeneous systems. This has led to a standardization of the Web Service descriptions, discovery and invocation, making use of XML-based standards like WSDL (a description protocol) [Christensen et al., 2001] and SOAP (a messaging protocol) [Mitra, 2003]. However, these standards, in their present form, are characterized by a *low level of semantic expressiveness*; for example, WSDL can be used to describe the interface of the different services, and how these services are deployed via SOAP, but it is very limited in its ability to express what the overall competences of this service are. SWSs, then, are Web Services that can specify not only their interfaces, but also describe in full their capabilities, and the prerequisites and consequences of their use.

OWL-S (Semantic Markup for Web Services), see Ankolekar et al. [2002] and http://www.daml.org/services/owl-s/1.1 (formerly DAML-S) is a specification, in the form of an OWL-based ontology, that should enable Web users and software agents *to automatically discover, invoke, select, compose and monitor Web-based services*. The ontology is structured into three main parts. The "profile" component *supplies a general description of a particular Web Service by specifying the input and output types, the preconditions and the effects that characterize this service*. The "process model" component describes the details of the above parameters, i.e. it describes *how the Web Service works* and the Web Service interaction protocol; note that each service is either an atomic process that can be executed directly or a combination of several processes. The "grounding" component specifies how the different components defined in the process model can be *combined together and mapped into WSDL descriptions* in order to achieve the desired results.

In an SWSs context, we can also mention the ODE SWS framework [Gómez-Pérez et al., 2004] that proposes both *an ontology* to describe SWSs and *an environment to support their graphical development*, and WSMO (Web Service Modeling Ontology) [de Bruijn et al., 2005], whose main characteristic consists of the use of several types of *mediator* for the resolution of all the types of heterogeneity that can rise in the context of an SWS.

Some General Remarks about the Semantic Web Solutions

Because of the *hype of academic origin* that, in recent years, has affected all SW activities, it is really difficult to produce a *fair and unbiased assessment* of their real value from a scientific and practical point of view.

We can, however, note that the "traditional" computer sciences milieus have often expressed *strong criticisms* towards these "semantic" solutions, given (among other things) that Berners-Lee's proposals, at least in their *original formulation* [Berners-Lee et al., 2001], seem to ignore *some fundamental components of computer science today*, from database technology (the whole world economy runs on SQL) to UML (Unified Modeling Language) – and this in spite of the fact that UML has, for example, a type hierarchy comparable to OWL. Proposals for establishing bridges between UML and the SW ontology languages can be found [e.g. Baclawski et al., 2001; Cranefield, 2002; Falkovych et al., 2003]. On the other hand, AI researchers have remarked at times that the SW seems to be nothing more than a sort of "renaming" of the traditional AI and knowledge representations challenges, without any real progresses in these fields. Some critics have even suggested that the *WWW as a whole* should simply be considered as the result of implementing the original ideas of Vannevar Bush (the "memex") – see http://www.theatlantic.com/unbound/flashbks/computer/bushf.htm – obviously also taking into account the introduction of Arpanet, the creation of GML/SGML and the innovations, including hypertext and the docuverse paradigm, proposed by Ted Nelson in the Xanadu project; see http://www.xanadu.net and the site "WEB Publishing Paradigms," http://www.faced.ufba.br/~edc708/biblioteca/interatividade/web%20paradigma/Paradigm.html.

Limiting now strictly to the SW and to its *ontological and semantic features*, it is not very difficult to point up *some very positive aspects of this endeavor*. We can mention in this context *the general emphasis on the need for a "semantic" and "content-oriented" attitude towards information management (no more "brute force" approach)*, the promotion of ontologies, the establishment of new, very interesting domains of research, like the SWSs noted above. From a more technical point of view, we can also highlight the fact that all these activities are based, ultimately, on XML, with an obvious advantage from an *interoperability point of view* – and this in spite of XML's well-known and boring verbosity. And none can challenge the fact that the SW has developed into a serious, academic research topic diffused worldwide, with its own conferences and journals. This is not to say that we adhere totally to the "SW philosophy," for at least the following reasons.

- The first concerns, obviously, the *low degree of expressiveness* of RDF/OWL originated by their "binary" nature. This limitation (and the unconvincing solutions proposed to obviate this problem) has already been discussed in Section 1.2.1.2. See also Section 4.2.1, about the weakness of the "rule" systems proposed up to now in a W3C context. As already stated in Chapter 1, all these limitations make the W3C languages an *unsatisfactory solution for dealing with complex knowledge representation situations* like (but not only) those represented by the nonfictional narratives; to give only one example, see in this context the problems encountered in using OWL for representing *generic situations in a legal reasoning context* [Hoekstra et al., 2006]. We can add that the improvements to OWL suggested in recent years, like OWL 1.1 [e.g. Cuenca Grau et al., 2006; Motik and Horrocks, 2006], *do not cope really with the concrete problems associated with the different versions of this language*. OWL 1.1 limits itself, in fact, to introducing a set of "minor" improvements; these concern, for example, an increased expressiveness of the properties (e.g. properties can be made disjoint, and it is possible to define properties that can be reflexive, irreflexive, symmetric or antisymmetric), number restrictions, and a sort of meta-modeling device called "punning" that relaxes the mandatory disjointedness of vocabularies in OWL DL when it is possible to disambiguate the exact meaning of a name (e.g. a name like **Person** can then be used as a class, an individual or a property). Note also that nothing has been said about the tangible implementation of OWL 1.1; moreover, OWL 1.1 (a DL language) is *not compatible* with both RDF and OWL Full.
- A second reason for disappointment concerns *the low degree of penetration of the SW ideas and tools (the OWL-based tools in particular) in the concrete world* – and this in spite of the considerable investments in time and money

consented in recent years to these technologies (the European Commission has been particularly liberal in financing such efforts). Even if ORACLE (see the ORACLE 11*g* RDF database), Amazon, Adobe and a few other industrial groups have shown some interest in this sort of work, the 5 to 10 years of delay commonly anticipated before the "mainstream adoption" of the W3C tools can appear *quite optimistic*. In the survey mentioned above, 66% of the respondents identified themselves in fact as in academia, with only 18% coming from industry and 16% qualifying themselves as both industry and academia [Cardoso, 2007: 85] – note also that the majority (27.9%) of the 627 respondents *do not have plans to use any type of SW system in the future*. The reasons for this slow penetration in the real world are not difficult to understand. In spite of their "expressive" limitations, it is evident in fact that the SW technologies are *conceptually very difficult to use for both developers and end users, and that they can also pose very difficult problems to the most experienced software developers*. From this point of view, to base the central version of OWL (OWL DL) on an axiomatic and highly formalized set of tools like DL has been, probably, an *unfortunate idea*. Already dismissed at the beginning of the 1990s because of their inefficiency from a practical point of view (see also Section 4.2.1), these logics have been resurrected in an SW context thanks to a *distorted interpretation of this "sound and clean semantics" exigency that leads to sacrificing representational sophistication in the name of an (abstract) conception of computational tractability* – see, in this context, the disenchanted remarks of the "heretic" DL scholar, Robert MacGregor, the "father" of the LOOM system, in a paper available at http://www.isi.edu/isd/LOOM/papers/macgregor/Loom_Retrospective.html. We can also remark that many W3C decisions concerning the *knowledge representation aspects of the SW* can be defined at least as "*hasty.*" The (too) quick endorsement of OWL as "the standard" is the best-known example; with respect now to RDF (less powerful, but surely more practically usable and used than OWL), Tim Bray's description of the way he and Ramanathan V. Guha have conceived RDF and have submitted it to the W3C is particularly edifying; see http://www.tbray.org/ongoing/When/200x/2003/05/21/RDFNet. Among other things, these conceptual and practical difficulties of use of the W3C tools *do not certainly contribute* to the diffusion in the commercial and industrial domains of a concept like that of "ontology" – that, at least in principle, seems to be *so natural and potentially useful*. In the above-mentioned survey, for example, the author remarks that: "... One surprising conclusion ... is that ontologies being developed are much smaller in size that that can be ascertained from many research papers and conference keynotes and talks" – according to the survey, in fact, *the "existing" ontologies include on average less than 1,000 concepts, and many of them have less than 100 concepts*. Of course, we must acknowledge the difficulty of introducing "ontological and semantic" principle in an industrial world where the possibility of making use of systems offering more than 10,000 Mips (millions of instructions per second) of useable throughput have given a youthful look (and a commercial legitimacy) to venerable dinosaurs like MVS and Cobol (Object Cobol).

- A last reason for perplexity concerns the present sort of headlong rush to the *never-ending introduction of new types of (Semantic) Webs*, with the consequence of blurring what was once the monolithic "SW vision" and of introducing *further doubts about the necessity and the opportunity of its accredited tools*. We have recently assisted, in fact, in the irruption of the so-called "Social Web" (or Web 2.0) on the stage, a new sort of Web that it is difficult to define exactly, beside the fact that it must be *"all about the people."* Let people create, collaborate, share and interact then, and *do not care about technology and standards*. Attention, then, is moving from the inaccessible formal peaks of OWL and DL, understandable only by machines, to *mundane, user-centric, shared and collaborative applications* like folksonomies, wikis, weblogs, podcasts, OpenAPIs and all the collaborative tagging systems in the style of Del.icio.us (http://delicious.com) and Flickr (http://www.flickr.com). And, of course, we have also the advocates of *a reconciliation between the "old" SW and the "new" Web 2.0 that should then give rise eventually to a Web 3.0, the "real" Intelligent Web* characterized by ubiquitous connectivity and open technologies, and where the "intelligent applications" (machine learning, machine reasoning, autonomous agents, NL applications) should be supported by an universal "World Wide Database." Even more interesting, *the current Web sites should be progressively transformed into (Semantic) Web Services*, offering then an API – and this, at least, confirms us the idea that SWSs are among the most appealing results of the present W3C activities, even if hampered by the low expressiveness and flexibility of the current W3C tools. We can note, however, that the bridges between SW and Web 2.0 seem to be confined, at least for the moment, to some limited use of RDF techniques in the Web 2.0 tools, e.g. see the RDF export format of GroupMe! (http://groupme.org/GroupMe/), a recent folksonomy. In this muddled context, it can also be interesting to note that Tim Berners-Lee and some colleagues have recently proposed a *wider framework* than that depicted by their traditional SW's "cake." Accordingly, the "usual" SW now becomes only one of the components of a general *Science of the Web* – the science of decentralized information systems – where Web Services, P2P approaches, social factors, NL processing techniques, Bayesian techniques, etc. are also evoked; see Berners-Lee et al. [2006] and http://webscience.org/.

SW techniques (in the most general and embracing meaning of this expression) are surely here to stay, but it is difficult to anticipate the exact form they will take. In this respect, we would like to conclude this section with a last citation from the already mentioned SW survey: "[the fact that] ...the large majority of ontology developed are rather small ... shows that the SW does not even need OWL and can achieve important objectives such as data-sharing and data-integration using just RDF alone" [Cardoso, 2007: 88].

3.1.1.3 The Search for a "Standard Upper Ontology"

Independently of the discussions about the different, concrete mechanisms for setting up ontologies, one of the targets of the "ontological community" in recent years has been that of attaining a sort of "Holy Grail" corresponding to a "Standard Upper Ontology." According to the definition given by the "Standard Upper Ontology Working Group" (SUO WG), an Institute of Electrical and Electronics Engineers (IEEE)-chartered discussion group unevenly active these last few years (see http://suo.ieee.org), "...An upper ontology is limited to concepts that are *meta, generic, abstract and philosophical*, and therefore are *general enough to address (at a high level) a broad range of domain areas*" (emphasis added). Therefore, concepts specific to given domains are excluded from the SUO domain; however, "... this standard will provide a structure and a set of general concepts upon which domain ontologies (e.g. medical, financial, engineering, etc.) could be constructed." The set up of a standard "... will enable computers to utilize it for applications such as data interoperability, information search and retrieval, automated inferencing, and natural language processing." The SUO WG has, in the course of its existence, accepted as "candidate solutions" a certain number of well-known (like OpenCYC [Matuszek et al., 2006] and SUMO, Suggested Upper Merged Ontology [Niles and Pease, 2001a, 2001b] – see below) and lesser known ontological constructions, the aim being that of comparing them to find the "ideal" solution.

The SUO WG is still operational today (November 2007) even if its original aims have been weakened because of the absence of real concrete results: *the existing "upper levels" are, in fact, extremely different both from a theoretical and an implementation point of view*, as we will see in more detail in the following sections. More modest activities of the SUO WG now concern, for example, the set up of a *person upper ontology project* (see http://idcommons.net/cgi-bin/mailman/listinfo/person-ontology) taking as its starting point the results of the so-called "Higgins project" – see also, in this last context, http://www.eclipse.org/higgins/higgins-charter.php.

Recent SUO-like and SUO-oriented Efforts

In a recent paper, Bundy and McNeill [2006: 85] wrote that:

> Attempting to build a general-purpose representation is chasing rainbows. The world is infinitely complex, so there's no end to the qualifications, ramifications, and richness of detail that you could incorporate and that you might need incorporate for a practical application.

They then continued by noting that even the most fervent partisans of an SUO approach recognize sometimes that *their goal can be unrealistic*; for example, in the above-mentioned paper about SUMO, Niles and Pease say that their goal is that of constructing a single, consistent, and comprehensive ontology, but that this goal is *perhaps unattainable*.

Goals like the set up of a real SUO, then, seem today to be replaced by more practical objectives like finding algorithms for the *mapping, merging or aligning of existing ontologies*; e.g. for some introductive papers, see Kalfoglou and Schorlemmer [2003], de Bruijn et al. [2004], and Choi et al. [2006]. NeOn (http://www.neon-project.org/) is an expensive recent project, funded by the European Commission, whose aim concerns the creation of an open infrastructure able to support the development of semantic applications based on a network of contextualized ontologies, which will exhibit local but not necessarily global consistency. The project started in March 2006 for a duration of 4 years. In this "mapping" connection, we can also mention the efforts addressing the creation of "lattices of theories" – e.g. see Sowa's (Internet) paper titled "Theories, models, reasoning, language, and thruth" at http://www.jfsowa.com/logic/theories.htm. These lattices are ordered collections, organized by generalization and specialization, of upper, middle, and domain ontologies, intended to provide *measures of similarity* useful for converting knowledge from one theoretical framework to another.

Some activities in a more "classical" SUO-like style are, however, still going on in the US Federal Government milieus. We can mention first, in this context, the release of an evaluation report about "... the Use of an Upper Ontology for U.S. Government and U.S. Military Domains" [Semy et al., 2004]. The report states from the beginning that: " ... One approach for mapping disparate ontologies is to use a standard upper ontology." The "Conclusions," however, are not very optimistic: "... it is difficult to use an upper ontology as intended today," but the authors also affirm that: "...Although there is no single best upper ontology, our current bias is to use DOLCE as a conceptual framework for mid-level and domain ontologies." This assumption is justified mainly in terms of a (supposed) better theoretical basis of DOLCE – see Masolo et al. [2002], Gangemi et al. [2002] and the next section – with respect to other candidates like SUMO and CYC. The "Semantic Interoperability Community of Practice" (SICoP, see http://colab.cim3.net/cgi-bin/wiki.pl?SICoP) has been created by individuals representing a broad range of US government organizations with the purpose of achieving "semantic interoperability" and "semantic data integration" focused on the government sector. One of its working groups was the "Common Upper Ontology WG"; this has been recently transformed into the "Cross Domain Semantic Interoperability Working Group, CDSI," see http://www.visualknowledge.com/wiki/CDSI. The CDSI's mission is that of proposing solutions for implementing data interoperability across the enterprise; among the candidate technical solutions, they take into consideration the SW approaches towards ontology mapping and linking, the existing examples of single upper ontologies (SUMO, DOLCE, CYC, etc.), and the possibility of producing sets of mapped upper ontologies; see also Schoening [2007]. On March 15, 2006, the US National Institute of Standards (NIST), SICoP and other governmental organisms organized at NIST an "Upper Ontology Summit" (UOS), focused on "...developing a method and the resources to relate existing upper ontologies to each other, and to share the information on this very important effort with the public."

Some Examples of Upper Level Ontologies

A quick examination of the organizational principles underpinning the "upper level" of some well-known ontologies – e.g. see John Bateman's portal (http://www.fb10.uni-bremen.de/anglistik/langpro/webspace/jb/info-pages/ontology/ontology-root.htm) for other "upper" ontologies not mentioned here, like GUM (The Generalized Upper Model) or BFO (Basic Formal Ontology) – should confirm the difficulty of producing a *reasonable synthesis* among them.

We have already mentioned CYC [e.g. Lenat and Guha, 1990; Lenat et al., 1990; Guha and Lenat, 1994] in Section 1.2.2.1, in the context of the discussion about "binary" and "*n*-ary" representations. CYC concerns one of the most controversial endeavors in the history of AI. Started in the early 1980, as an MCC (Microelectronics and Computer Technology Corporation, Texas, USA) project under the leadership of Douglas Lenat, it ended about 15 years later with the setting up of an enormous knowledge base containing about a million hand-entered "logical assertions," including both simple *statements of facts* (axioms) and *rules* about what conclusions can be inferred if certain statements of facts are satisfied. Cycorp, Inc., now commercializes the results of the project.

The *proper Cyc Ontology* consists actually of about 200,000 atomic terms, where each term is associated with several dozen assertions; new assertions are continually added to the knowledge base by human knowledge enterers, and millions of nonatomic terms can be automatically created by using functions. This huge knowledge base is partitioned into *modules* called "microtheories" [Guha and Lenat, 1994]. Each microtheory consists of a limited set of assertions that are linked together according to a shared set of *assumptions* on which the truth of the assertions depends, or according a *shared topic* like, for example, buying or selling, or according a *shared source* (e.g. CIA World Factbook 2006). One microtheory may inherit and extend another microtheory. CycL, the knowledge representation language of CYC, is, as already stated, an *n*-ary language [e.g. Ramachandran et al., 2005].

The "upper level" of the ontology, including 6,000 concepts and 60,000 assertions about these concepts, is now freely accessible on the Web ("Open-CYC"; see http://www.cyc.com/cyc/opencyc); an (extremely partial) reproduction of this upper level is given in Fig. 3.1. All the entities reproduced in this figure are *collections*, with Thing being the *supreme collection*.

The links of Fig. 3.1 are *generalization/specialization* links, which are encoded using the CycL constant #\$genls; all the collections of the ontology correspond, then, to *specializations* of Thing. The formula (#\$genls X Y) means that every instance of collection X is also an instance of collection Y. A characteristic of the CYC ontology concerns the fact that the relation IsA (the CycL constant #\$isa) is used in CYC to express that *a given* X *is an instance of a collection* Y, (#\$isa X Y), e.g. that the Eiffel Tower is an instance

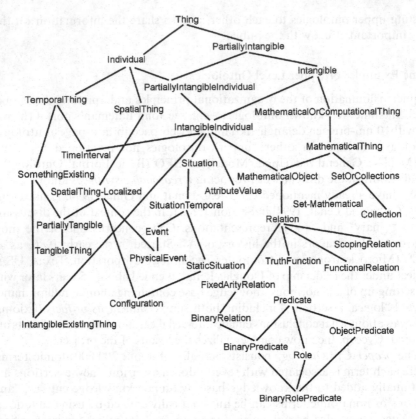

Fig. 3.1 OpenCYC upper level

of the collection of all towers. Returning now to Fig. 3.1, Intangible is the collection of all the things that cannot be touched; MathematicalOrComputatio-nalThing are then abstract entities that do not have temporal or spatial proper-ties, like an integer. On the contrary, TemporalThing is the collection of things that exist in time; the instances of the collection SpatialThing-Localized are all those things that have a location in space. Individual is defined as the collection of all the things that are not themselves sets or collections, e.g. like physical objects or numbers. CYC's documentation states that Indvidual and Collection are disjoint collections; no CYC constant can be an instance of both. An analysis of the origins, developments and motivations of CYC can be found in Bertino et al. [2001: 275–316].

CYC's ontology is a really impressive intellectual construction, with plenty of ingenious solutions and including *an immense amount of useful knowledge*. On the other hand, when examining this collection of entities, people are often struck by its complexity (i.e. the number of branches and their interrelation-ships) and wonder whether it is all really necessary.

In this context, it may be interesting to mention Lenat and Guha's reply to the criticisms about the organization of the CYC's ontology expressed in a special section of the *Artificial Intelligence* journal [Stefik and Smoliar, 1993], which included, among other things, six reviews of the Lenat and Guha's [1990] book and a response by the authors. They said, in synthesis, that the difficulties encountered by their "knowledge enterers" when setting up CYC's ontology were related mainly to *very specific, relatively low-level ontological issues* like "... buying and selling, human capabilities and preferences and desires, the weather, furniture, etc." more than to high-level representation problems like "... substances, time, types and collections" and that, eventually, "... most of the knowledge in the knowledge base does not depend crucially on the exact structure of the top level" [Guha and Lenat, 1993: 162–164]. This downgrading of the role of the upper level ontologies is not, of course, very congruent with the hypothesis of the existence of an SUO. From a more specific NKRL point of view, we can note that a *messy and tangled upper level is inconceivable from an HClass point of view*, given that, as we will emphasize afterwards, the (invariant) upper level of HClass is used to set up the *constraint expressions* that specify the *admissible values* for the variables of the (invariant) HTemp templates.

SUMO was initially developed by Ian Niles and Adam Pease at Teknowledge Corporation in an SUO framework, and is presently maintained by Adam Pease at Articulate Software, a consulting firm based in the San Francisco, California, area. SUMO was originally created by *merging different available ontological contents*, even if these sources were only starting points, and the current version of SUMO bears limited resemblance to any of the initial contributions. Ontologies that were merged included: John Sowa's upper level ontology (see below), Russell and Norvig's [1995] upper level ontology, James Allen's [1983] temporal axioms, Casati and Varzi's [1995] formal theory of holes, Barry Smith's [1996] ontology of boundaries, "mereotopology", Guarino and colleagues' logical theory of space [Borgo et al., 1996] and other ontologies coming from several "ontological" servers in the Ontolingual style (http://www.ksl.stanford.edu/software/ontolingua). The first step of the merging was a sort of "syntactic merge" of all these ontologies, realized by translating them into a variant (SUO-KIF) of KIF (Knowledge Interchange Format) [Genesereth and Fikes, 1992]. More difficult was the realization of the following step, i.e. the "semantic merge" activities intended to produce the final, unique and logically coherent structure: the strategy used was that of merging first the two higher level hierarchies, i.e. Sowa's and Russel and Norvig's ontologies, and aligning all the others on the upper level structure obtained in this way. The details are given in Niles and Pease [2001a, 2001b].

The copyright of the final SUMO ontology is owned by the IEEE, but the ontology can be freely accessed, e.g. through the Web site of Articulate Software (http://www.adampease.org/Articulate/).

SUMO is "modular," i.e. it is divided into *self-contained sub-ontologies* (ontological domains) with a *dependency structure*; see Fig. 3.2, which is slightly adapted from that reproduced on the Articulate site. In this figure, the dependencies among the most general domains are expressed as arrows; note that, in some cases, the dependency is bidirectional. In addition to the SUMO *core upper ontology*, SUMO is also associated with *lower level ontologies* (see again Fig. 3.2), including a Mid-Level Ontology (MILO) and a set of *domain ontologies* like Communications, Countries and Regions, Government, Physical Elements, Transportation, etc., all available from the Articulate Software site. Together, these ontologies now amount to some 20,000 terms and 60,000 axioms. SUMO and MILO have also been mapped to all of the WordNet 1.6 lexicon – WordNet is the well-known online lexical database containing about 120,000 English word-sense pairs ("synsets") [e.g. Miller, 1995].

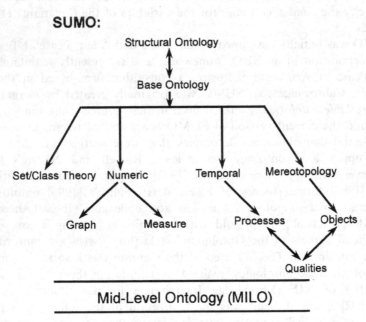

Fig. 3.2 SUMO and the associated ontologies

The Structural Ontology in Fig. 3.2 includes the specifications of the basic classes/concepts (like subclass, subrelation, instance, attribute, equal, disjoint, etc.) used to set up the different ontologies. The "real" root node (topmost concept) in SUMO is Entity, defined as "the universal class of individuals" and included in the Base Ontology. Entity is further split into Physical ("an entity that has a location in space-time") – having Object and Process as immediate specializations – and Abstract. This last concept is explained in terms of "Properties or qualities as distinguished from any particular embodiment of the properties/qualities in a physical medium. Instances of Abstract can be said to exist in the same sense as mathematical objects such as sets and relations, but they cannot exist at a particular place and time without some physical encoding or embodiment." Specializations of Abstract are SetClass, Proposition, Quantity, Attribute, etc. We will return in the following on the differentiation, in general, between "physical" and "abstract" entities.

DOLCE (Descriptive Ontology for Linguistic and Cognitive Engineering) has been developed in the framework of the European IST (Information Society Technologies) project WonderWeb [Oberle et al., 2005] as the first, "reference module" of a library of "foundational ontologies," serving as a reference module for the library. DOLCE [e.g. Gangemi et al., 2002] is based on the *fundamental distinction between "enduring" and "perduring" elements* ("endurant" and "perdurant"), where these terms correspond, at least partly, to the usual "entity" and "situation" notions respectively; see also Section 3.1.2.2. In fact, according to their customary definitions [e.g. Bittner et al., 2004], an "endurant" is an element (entity) that *is wholly present in time along with all its parts*, like the ordinary objects and artifacts, but also, for example, like a record in an information system. "Perdurants" are elements (situations) that *develop (unfold) over time in successive temporal parts or phases*; for example, "events" and "states" considered according to their temporal characteristics are "perduring" elements – see also Fig. 3.3.

Even if three upper level categories only, Abstract, Endurant and Perdurant/Occurrence, are directly associated in Gangemi et al. [2002] with the top of the DOLCE hierarchy (i.e. Entity), the "normal" architecture for the DOLCE top level seems to correspond to the *four-element structure* represented in Masolo et al. [2002] and reproduced partially in Fig. 3.3.

"Feature(s)" are "Endurant(s)" that represent "parasitic entities," like holes, bumps, surfaces or stains; normally, they depend on "Physical Object(s)" that represent their "hosts." Features may represent *relevant parts* of their hosts, like bumps or edges, or represent *places* like a hole in a piece of cheese, the underneath of a table, or the front of a house, which do not correspond to parts of their hosts. In DOLCE, "boundaries" are included among the features. "Physical Object(s)" that have *intentionality* (i.e. the capability of heading for/dealing with objects or states of the world) are called "agentive" (Agentive Physical Object, like a natural person). They are in general made up of Nonagentive Physical Object(s) (without intentionality): human persons (agentive) are composed of organisms (nonagentive), robots are composed of

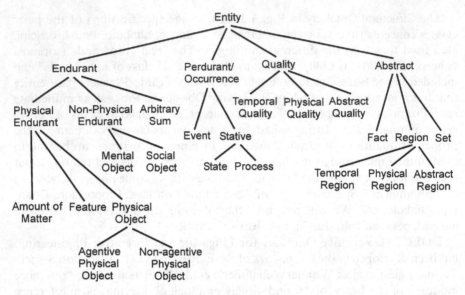

Fig. 3.3 Partial reproduction of the DOLCE's upper level

mechanisms, etc. Ordinary objects, like houses, computers, organs, scissors or pieces of woods, are a Non-agentive Physical Object. The differentiation of Mental Object from Social Object that characterizes Non-Physical Endurant – more precisely, Non-Physical Object, a specific term of Non-Physical Endurant not reproduced in Fig. 3.3 for simplicity's sake – is based on acknowledging whether the "objects" are "produced" by a single agent or recognized by a community of agents. In the first case, we have Mental Object(s); these, like an "idea," for example, are specifically dependent on Agentive Physical Object(s). In the second case, we have on the contrary Social Object(s), which can be in turn "agentive" like the president of the United States or Microsoft, and "nonagentive" like laws, shares, peace treaties, etc.

Event(s) are called Achievement(s) if they are atomic, and Accomplishment(s) in the other cases. Examples of Achievement are "reaching the summit of a mountain, a departure, a death"; examples of Accomplishment are "a conference, an ascent, a performance." Quality(ies) are seen in DOLCE as the basic entities we can perceive or measure, like shapes, colors, sizes, sounds, smells, masses, lengths, etc. Gangemi et al. [2002: 170] makes clear that:

> The term "Quality" is often used as a synonymous of "property", but this is not the case in DOLCE: qualities are particular, properties are universals. Qualities *inhere* to entities: every entity (including qualities themselves) comes with certain qualities, which exist exactly as long as the entity exists ... no two particulars can have the same quality, and each quality is *specifically constantly dependent* on the entity it inheres in: at any time, a quality cannot be present unless the entity it inheres in is also present.

A differentiation between a Quality (e.g. the color of a specific rose) and its "value" (e.g. a particular shade of red) is then introduced; this value is called a Quale.

DOLCE is based on the principles specified in the OntoClean methodology [Guarino and Welty, 2002], a *theoretical tool* used for testing the *ontological adequacy* of hierarchies of concepts. This *"methodological" bias* of the creators of DOLCE – with a background in philosophy and epistemology more than engineering and computer science – is particularly evident when examining the upper level categories of their ontology, where the differentiations are often based on very "subtle" criteria whose *necessity* is not evident at first sight. Among all the "upper level" ontologies examined in this section, *DOLCE is the one that imposes the more constraining conceptual burdens on its users*.

We will now conclude this review of some popular upper level ontologies with the reproduction (Fig. 3.4) of the lattice of top-level CG concepts proposed first by Sowa [1995] and then revised in Sowa [1999]. This is a very sophisticated and hyper-symmetrical construction that Sowa justifies making reference, amongst others, to Peirce, Aristotle, Leibniz, Heraclitus, Quine, Kant, Plato and Husserl.

In this figure, T and ⊥ respectively represent the "universal type" and the "absurd type." The alternate name for T is ENTITY; all the other concept types are specializations of ENTITY. The intuitive meaning for ⊥ can be captured if we consider that, for example, the greatest common subtype of CAT and DOG,

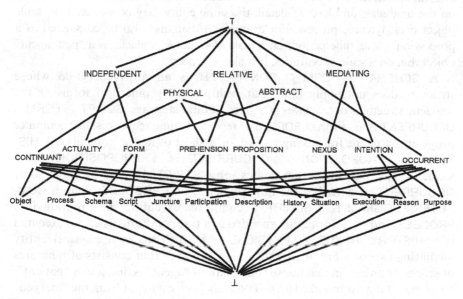

Fig. 3.4 Top-level of the CG hierarchy

written as CAT ∩ DOG, is the absurd type ⊥. More formally, ⊥ is a primitive that satisfies the following axioms:

$$\text{nothing is an instance of } \bot : \neg \, (\exists x) \, \bot \, (x) \qquad (3.1)$$

$$\text{every type is a supertype of } \bot : (\forall t : \text{TYPE}) \, \bot \leq t \qquad (3.2)$$

As for ⊥, also T, INDEPENDENT, RELATIVE, MEDIATING, PHYSICAL, ABSTRACT, CONTINUANT and OCCURRENT (see Fig. 3.4) are characterized by sets of associated axioms. We can note here that CONTINUANT, defined informally by Sowa as "An entity whose identity continues to be recognizable over some extended interval of time" bears some similarity with Guarino and colleagues' notion of Endurant, while OCCURRENT (defined by Sowa as "An entity that does not have a stable identity during any interval of time") can be related with Perdurant.

All the other types present in Fig. 3.4 are defined as the greatest common subtype, ∩, of two supertypes from which the type considered inherits the axioms; see Sowa [1999: 497–498]. In this way, for example, FORM is defined as ABSTRACT ∩ INDEPENDENT, and represents intuitively abstract information independent from any embodiment. INTENTION = ABSTRACT ∩ MEDIATING is an abstraction considering as mediating other entities. PROCESS = ACTUALITY ∩ OCCURRENT concerns an ACTUALITY, i.e. a physical entity whose existence is independent from any other entity, considered as an OCCURRENT during the interval of interest. With respect to this last definition, we can note that, depending on the time scale and level of detail, the same entity may be viewed as a stable object or a dynamic process. For example, a diamond also be considered as a process on a long time period; on a scale of minutes, a glacier is a "permanent" object, but on a scale of centuries, it is also a process.

A SCHEMA = FORM ∩ CONTINUANT is an abstract FORM whose structure does not imply time relationships, like geometrical forms or the syntactic structures of sentences in a given natural language. SCRIPT = FORM ∩ OCCURRENT is an abstract FORM that represents time sequences, like computer programs, a recipe for baking a cake, or a sheet of music to be played. HISTORY = PROPOSITION ∩ OCCURRENT is a PROPOSITION or a sequence of propositions that relates some SCRIPT(s) to the stages of some OCCURRENT. It describes the time sequence of a PROCESS; then, if COMPUTER-PROGRAM is a SCRIPT, a computer executing the program is a PROCESS, and the information encoded in a trace of the instructions executed is a HISTORY. NEXUS = PHYSICAL ∩ MEDIATING is a physical entity mediating two or more other entities, e.g. an arch that consists of junctures of stones or an action that consists of what an "agent" is doing to a "patient"; etc. Note that a notion like MEDIATING has been excluded from the "merged" SUMO described before because, according to Niles and Pease [2001]:

"Although this notion may be philosophically indispensable, it was difficult to justify its inclusion in an engineering-oriented context, and, for this reason, it was removed from the merged ontology."

3.1.2 HClass Architecture

In any given application domain, there are some *important notions* that we would like to represent; moreover, the most general among them, like "human being" or "physical object," are common to a majority of domains, and are included in the "upper levels" of the different proposed ontologies. As already stated in Section 2.1, the "definitional component" of NKRL – personified by the HClass hierarchy – supplies the tools for representing these notions that, *by convention and according to a strictly empirical/pragmatic/functional approach*, are called "concepts." For a discussion about the different theories concerning the notion of "concept," the Classical Theory versus the Prototype Theory versus the Theory-Theory versus the Neoclassical Theory versus Conceptual Atomism, see Margolis and Laurence [1999] and, in particular, Chapter 1. Note that, to give rise to well-formed *NKRL ontologies*, the original notions must be conceived in terms of "sets" and "subsets" – where, as usual, asserting that a pertains to the set A, (a: A), is equivalent to assert that a is characterized by the type A. No confusion is allowed between subsets – giving rise to standard new HClass concepts, like european_city that is a specialization of city_ – and instances (individuals), like PARIS_; instances are still associated with HClass as terminal symbols, but they are in the domain of another NKRL component, the "enumerative component"; see again Section 2.2.1.4.

In NKRL, the terms of the HClass hierarchy, concepts and individuals, carry out two fundamental missions:

- The first consists in *specifying the constraints associated with the variables of the HTemp templates*; see Section 2.2.2.2. Normally, (high-level) *concepts* are used for this function even if, at least in principle, nothing precludes *individuals* from being used for specifying constraints. Given the importance of this duty for the general economy of NKRL, *no ambiguity about the structure of HClass (and, in particular, about the structure of its upper level) can be permitted* – e.g. all the NKRL inference rules we will describe in Chapter 4 are built up using *partially instantiated templates* (see Section 2.2.2.3) where some variables have been replaced by HClass terms, concepts or individuals, compatible with their associated constraints.
- When these variables have been *replaced by actual values* (concepts or individuals) in the derived occurrences, a second essential task concerns the possibility of *checking that these values (role fillers) are really consistent with the original constraints*. This congruence control implies, then, *traversing the HClass tree* to find a path between the actual value and the constraint; see also Section 4.1.1. Note that the congruence must be checked by

all the modules of the NKRL environment that deal with the set up, retrieval and management of occurrences (see also Appendix A); executing this sort of control requires, once again, that all the layers of HClass are *exactly defined*.

The specific *data structures* used for HClass have already been described in detail in Section 2.2.1; note in this context, as already stated, that we can consider the *templates* (described in Section 3.2.2) as the *axioms* associated with the HClass ontology. With respect now to the HClass's "contents" (more than 2,700 concepts presently, by November 2007), Fig. 3.5 (see also Fig. 3.7 below) gives a general idea of the organization of the upper level of this ontology.

Three branches stem from the concept h_class that represents the top of this hierarchy: nkrl_grammar, non_sortal_concept, sortal_concept. The (very tiny)

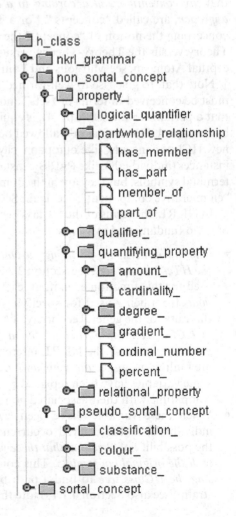

Fig. 3.5 HClass upper level (more in particular, the "non-sortal" branch)

nkrl_grammar branch consists of few "utility" concepts like numerical_value or symbolic_label; the conceptual labels (like #conc5.c3 of Table 2.15) used as fillers of the OBJ(ect), etc. role in a "completive construction" context are instances of the concept symbolic_label.

The partition between sortal_concept and non_sortal_concept constitutes the *main architectural principle of HClass*, and corresponds to the differentiation between "*(sortal) notions that can be instantiated directly into enumerable specimens*," like "chair" (a physical object), and "*(non-sortal) notions, which cannot be instantiated directly into specimens*," like "gold" (a "substance"; see Section 3.1.2.1). The specializations of sortal_concept, like chair_, city_ or european_city, can have *direct instances* (CHAIR_27, PARIS_), whereas the specializations of non_sortal_concept, like gold_, or colour_, *can admit further specializations*, see white_gold or red_, but *do not have direct instances*.

Even if the above two "founding" notions are present in some form in the most common upper level ontologies examined in the previous sections (e.g. see notions like FORM or ACTUALITY in Sowa's ontology), they are not expressed in *explicit form* in these ontologies and they do not have the central status they own in HClass. To find some concrete correspondences, it is then necessary to look at the philosophical and theoretical linguistics literature.

For example, in the first case, we can mention a paper by Guarino and his colleagues [Guarino et al., 1994] where they discuss the essence of "sortal" and "non-sortal" *predicates*: according to them, an example of the former is "apple" and an example of the latter is "red" – they note that this sort of notions goes back to Locke's work. They remark also correctly that, in Artificial Intelligence, the problems introduced by the evident need for differentiations of this type have been normally solved *by associating the sortal predicates with "concepts" and the non-sortal predicates with "properties."*

This remark is particularly important. From an NKRL point of view, in fact, solutions of this sort are *clearly unacceptable* because, among other things, they would imply that a notion like that of "gold" – a "substance" and then, in NKRL, a *non-sortal notion* – could not correspond to a concept: in HClass, all the sortal and non-sortal "notions" (see Fig. 3.5) correspond equally to *full-fledged "concepts."* This is not to say that a specific notion could not *also* be used in a *property role*. For example, in Table B.4 (Appendix B) we can find the *concept* has_part used within a predicative occurrence, ex.c12, and the *relation type properties* (see Section 2.2.1.3) HasMember and PartOf used in the enumerative component data structures that define the *individuals* associated with this occurrence.

In a linguistic context, we can find some interesting (*but partial*) correspondences between, respectively, "sortal concepts" and "count nouns" and "non-sortal concepts" and "uncount (or mass) nouns."

Count nouns refer to *things that can exist as separate and distinct individual units* (see "apple" again). *Uncount nouns* refer to things that *cannot be "counted" because they are thought of as "wholes" that it is impossible to cut into parts* (e.g. "gold"); they often refer to abstractions and often have a collective meaning (e.g. "furniture"). In this context, a first, immediate remark concerns the fact that the HClass concepts are *not limited* to the linguistic category of "nouns" but correspond also to verbs ("buy") or adjectives ("big") – conversely (see Section 1.1.2.2), nouns and adjectives can correspond to *NKRL deep predicates*. Moreover, the existence of *inconsistencies* that affect the linguistic definition of count/uncount are well known; see ambiguous count/uncount nouns or syntagms, like "difficulty," "war," "beer," "fear," "to protest against injustice," "the injustices of world poverty" [Hunston and Francis, 2000]. Making use, as in NKRL, of the *"possible existence of instances"* principle that constitutes the basis of the differentiation "sortal/non-sortal" in HClass, "war" is immediately classed as a sortal concept in HClass ("the World War II"), like "specific injustice (an action)" ("this new injustice"), "a glass of beer" or "a well-known brand of beer"; "fear," "injustice as moral principle" and "beer as a substance" correspond, on the contrary, to non-sortal concepts.

We will now illustrate briefly some important points about the non_sortal_ concept and sortal_concept branches of HClass; it is possible to find a complete description of this hierarchy in, for example, Zarri [2003a].

3.1.2.1 Non-sortal Concepts

As appears from Fig. 3.5, the non_sortal_concept component of HClass is formed of two branches: property_ (which is then, in itself, a full-fledged concept) and pseudo_sortal_concept.

The "property_" Concepts

First of all, it is important to recall here that the concepts inserted in the property_ sub-hierarchy of non_sortal_concept *cannot represent the main filler of the SUBJ(ect) role* in the different NKRL templates; see the examples in Section 3.2.2. The reasons for this have been explained in Section 1.1.2.1, "A Kimian-like analysis."

The logical_quantifier branch of property_ includes a number of "quantifying" non-sortal concepts like all_, all_except, none_, one_of_two, one_of_several, some_, etc.

As already stated, examples of use of the concepts pertaining to the part/ whole_relationship branch of property_ (has_member, has_part, etc.; see Fig. 3.5) can be found in Appendix B, in the context of the discussion about the representation of plural situations in NKRL. The criteria for differentiating between the use of the "part" and the "member" types of *concepts* are the same as already introduced for differentiating among the *properties* (slots) HasPart/ HasMember and PartOf/MemberOf (Section 2.2.1.3), the main thing being, once again, the *symmetry* ("member": "This tree is MemberOf the forest") or *asymmetry* ("part": "The handle is PartOf the cup") of the relationship of the specific item with respect to the whole. In the NKRL application about

"Terrorism in the Philippines" already mentioned, we will then use the concept member_of to encode the elementary event (predicative occurrence) relating that a *single person* pertains to the Abu Sayyaf group, while will using the concept part_of to tell that *a small group of unknown persons* that attempted a kidnap is a *subset* of the whole Abu Sayyaf group. This will allow us to emphasize the *asymmetry* of this small group with respect to the whole of Abu Sayyaf.

An interesting feature of the property_ branch of non_sortal_concept concerns the partition of relational_property into binary_relational_property and multiple_relational_property. Examples of concepts pertaining to the binary_relational... branch are all those (different_from, equal_to, greater_than, similar_to, etc.) classified as specific terms of compared_to; other binary_relational... are additional_to, developed_by, exemplified_by, suitable_for, etc. A typical multiple_relational... concept is between_. All these relational_property concepts are normally used within SPECIF(ication) lists. For example, to express the information that a given GEOGRAPHICAL_ LOCATION_1 is endowed (SPECIF) with the property of being different from another location, we will write:

(SPECIF   GEOGRAPHICAL_LOCATION_1   (SPECIF   different_from GEOGRAPHICAL_LOCATION_2))

To say, on the contrary, that this location is situated in between two other locations, we will write

(SPECIF GEOGRAPHICAL_LOCATION_1 (SPECIF between_ GEOGRAPHICAL_ LOCATION_2 GEOGRAPHICAL_LOCATION_3))

We can then note the presence of a *single* element (argument) associated with the binary_relational... concept different_from in the first example, and the (*mandatory*) presence of *two* arguments associated with the multi-ple_relational... concept between_ in the second example.

The bulk of the property_ concepts are included in the qualifier_ sub-branch: the upper level of this last sub-branch is reproduced in Fig. 3.6.

Some of the specific terms of general_characterising_property are beautiful_, current_, durable_, easy_to_use, important_, irrelevant_, painful_, popular_; see again Zarri [2003b]. Specific terms of temporal_modality are again_, always_, never_, often_, sometimes_, etc.; see also, in this context, the TIMEX3 tags of TimeML, Section 2.2.2.4.

A noteworthy specific term of animated_entity_property is the concept role_. This must be intended here as *the top of a specific structured sub-hierarchy including branches like* extended_family_role *and* professional_role, and not as an *unduly transposition under the form of a binary concept* (to keep alive the illusion of the universality of the "binary" approach) *of the general relationship that links the arguments of a predicate to this last one*; see the remarks in Sections 1.2.1, 2.2.2 and 3.2.1. The utilization of the role_ sub-hierarchy in the context of the Behave: templates is discussed in detail in Section 3.2.2.1.

Fig. 3.6 The qualifier_
sub-branch of property_
(non-sortal concepts)

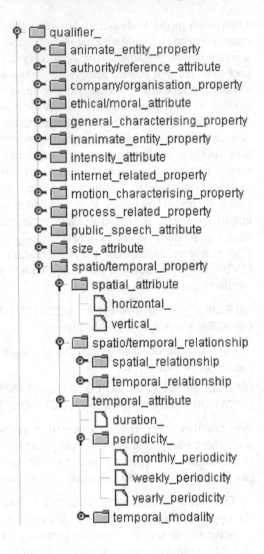

Representing the "General Quantifier" Concepts

An interesting epistemological problem that concerns several property_ concepts corresponding to "generalized quantifiers" – e.g. the concepts associated
with the size_attribute sub-branch (Fig. 3.6) of qualifier_ like large_, medium_
or small_, some of the logical_quantifier concepts such as many_, few_ or
some_, the degree_ concepts (Fig. 3.5) like most_ and totally_, etc. – is linked
with the difficulty of *representing* (*quantifying*) in a relatively precise (and
computationally satisfactory) way their "meaning."

From a formal logic point of view, this problem has been dealt with in the
context of the "generalized quantifiers and NL" theories [e.g. Peterson, 1979;

Barwise and Cooper, 1981; Partee et al., 1990; Peters and Westerståhl, 2006];
from a more pragmatic knowledge representation point of view, the (few)
solutions proposed are, often, highly empirical – see, however, Sowa [1991].
For many NKRL applications, *an exact and in-depth definition of the "meaning"
of these concepts is not really necessary*, and it is sufficient to signal correctly,
when needed, their *presence* within the role fillers of a template/occurrence, e.g.
see the use of small_ in the conc5.c3 predicative occurrence of Table 2.15.
Further precisions can be added, in case, under the form of inference rules.
For other applications (especially when the application requires *the frequent
utilization of these generalized quantifiers in many different contexts*) some sort
of a priori definition must be provided: it is, in fact, evident that, in numerical
terms, a "small amount" of ants can be very different from a "small amount" of
diamonds.

   In these cases, NKRL makes use of a very simple and pragmatic solution
that consists in trying to *parameterize* the possible numerical values to be linked
with these concepts *as a function of the type of concepts/individuals they are
associated with and of the type of application under consideration*. The solution
consists, then, in adding to the frames defining terms like few_, some_, many_,
etc. (and also small_, cheap_, etc.) a CardinalityUpperLimit property (slot) of
the "attribute" type; see Section 2.2.1.3. This will accept as value a *real number
set up in a totally empirical way*: for a concept like few_, for example, this could
be 500 if the application deals with ants, and 5 if the application deals with
diamonds. In case the application deals simultaneously with "ants" and "diamonds," *we can make use of properties (slots) in the style of the "procedure"
slots*; see again Section 2.2.1.3. In this way, it will be possible to employ, in a
definitional/enumerative context like that of HClass, *syntactic constructions
making use of those "structured arguments" (expansions) that are proper to the
descriptive/factual components of NKRL*; see, in this context, the example of
"procedure slots" reproduced in Table 2.20. The value of the CardinalityUpper-
Limit slot for few_ could then become (ALTERN (SPECIF ant_ 500) (SPECIF
diamond_ 5) ...).

The "NKRL idioms" of the property_ type

The "NKRL idioms" are *normalized* SPECIF(ication) sub-lists used to encode
in an unambiguous and regular way some *standard and recurring narrative
fragments* that can occur within a global situation/state/event. Examples of
these fragments are the wording used to express the amount a given quantity
of, for example, money, the indication that a given company is involved in a
particular type of activity, the expression of a given nationality, etc. Many of
these idioms are built up using concepts pertaining to the property_ branch of
non_sortal_concept, and can then be considered as "complex syntactic extensions" of these property_ concepts. Among these idioms of the property_ type,
some of the most commonly used are listed in Table 3.2. Other sorts of idioms
will be mentioned in the following sections.

Table 3.2 Some NKRL idioms of the property_ type

Concepts	Remarks
amount_	amount_ (see Fig. 3.5) admits further specializations like approximate_amount_, periodical_amount, zero_amount_, etc. The syntax of the corresponding idioms is:(SPECIF amount_ *n*), where *n* represents, implicitly or explicitly, a numeric value; see the examples in Tables 3.3 and 3.4. In particular, the amount *n* of a specific monetary transaction is given by the expression (SPECIF money_ currency_(SPECIF amount_ *n*)); see also Section 3.2.2.7
cardinality_	A SPECIF sub-list introduced by cardinality_ (which, like amount_, is a quantifying_property; see Fig. 3.5) is used to represent, implicitly or explicitly, the number of elements in a given set. Note that the particular idiom (SPECIF cardinality_ several_), see the example in Table 2.6, *is used to represent the cardinality of sets of totally undefined size*, like those corresponding to a generic plural referent, as in "men" or "books." several_ pertains to the logical_quantifier sub-tree of property_; see Figure 3.5
equal_to, etc.	The idioms including terms of the relational_property sub-tree appear, typically, as fillers of the TOPIC role in the predicative occurrences derived from the Own:CompoundProperty template; see Section 3.2.2.5
part_of	The general use of part_of, member_of, etc. has been discussed in the previous paragraphs. The syntax of the particular NKRL idiom corresponding to the expression "entity *x* is part of entity *y*" is: (SPECIF *x* (SPECIF part_of *y*)). Note that the coding of a fragment like: "... *x* is part of the German companies ...," to be understood as: "... part of (ALL) the German companies..." is given by: (*x* (SPECIF part_of (SPECIF company_ GERMANY_ (SPECIF cardinality_ all_))))
percent_	The SPECIF sub-list introduced by percent_ (Fig. 3.5) is typically, but not obligatorily, used within an amount_ idiom; see the detailed example illustrated by Tables 3.3 and 3.4

To illustrate the modalities of use of these sorts of normalized sub-lists (and to begin to discuss some difficulties linked with the use of complex SPECIF expressions, and the possible solutions), let us consider the NKRL representation (see Tables 3.3 and 3.4) of this fragment of financial news: "Berlin, October 15, 1993. Berliner Bank AG said it acquired a 50 percent stake in the Optimus Bank füer Finanz-Service GmbH." For simplicity's sake, we will consider here

Table 3.3 Examples of use of normalized SPECIF sub-lists

cob2.c5)	PRODUCE	SUBJ	BERLINER_BANK
		OBJ	purchase_
		TOPIC	(SPECIF stake_in OPTIMUS_BANK (SPECIF amount_ (SPECIF percent_ 50 (SPECIF share_capital OPTIMUS_BANK))))
		date-1:	(1993-10-05),1993-10-15
		date-2:	
Produce:Buy (6.481)			

Table 3.4 Use of Own:Property occurrences to reduce the complexity of the SPECIF lists

cob2.c6)	OWN	SUBJ	STAKE_IN_1
		OBJ	property_
		TOPIC	(SPECIF amount_ (SPECIF percent_ 50 (SPECIF share_capital OPTIMUS_BANK)))
		{obs}	
		date-1:	1993-10-15
		date-2:	
Own:CompoundProperty (5.12)			

that the two banks are already known by the system (they have already been mentioned in previous predicative occurrences/annotations): we can then leave out from this code details like the nationality and the type of company.

The first part of the fragment, "Berliner Bank said . . .," is translated using a "completive construction" introduced by a predicative occurrence derived from the Move:StructuredInformation template; see Sections 2.3.1 and 3.2.2.4; the message issued by Berliner Bank is represented by the occurrence cob2.c5 of Table 3.3 According to the typical NKRL modality for dealing with "actions," the purchase is represented by making use of a PRODUCE construction where the "action name" ("acquisition, purchase") that corresponds to the surface verb "acquire" is denoted by the HClass sortal concept purchase_ (or one of its specific terms) inserted in the OBJ(ect) slot; e.g. see Zarri [1992b]. Note that, as usual, if the precise identification of a specific purchase action was required, then an individual in the style of PURCHASE_1 should be used. Note also that the "argument" of the purchase must be inserted as filler in the TOPIC slot, as explicitly required by the syntax of the Produce:Buy (or Produce:Sell) template; see also Section 3.2.2.6.

The most external SPECIF list of the TOPIC filler denotes, according to the general meaning of the "attributive operator" (see Table 2.8) some properties that can be asserted about its first element, stake_in. A first property concerns the name of the company, OPTIMUS_BANK, which has sold the stake, and a second (a SPECIF list giving details about the amount_) describes the importance of this stake. The extent of this amount is defined by a percent_ SPECIF list used to say (i) that the magnitude of the percentage is 50 (i.e. 50%) and (ii) that we are speaking of a percentage of the Optimus Bank's share capital.

As the example of Table 3.3 illustrates, the SPECIF lists (and, more generally, the lists formed by making use of the AECS operators) constitute *a powerful and flexible tool for representing exactly all the details of narrative situations*. The other side of the coin is represented by the *high level of complexity* that can affect the (embedded) SPECIF constructions, and that can bother, for example, the "external" readability of these lists. NKRL suggests, then, a general strategy for simplifying, in case, the expression of the SPECIF lists; this consists of making use of *additional predicative occurrences* derived from the Own:Property template of HTemp and from its specializations; see Section

3.2.2.5 for additional information. The main function of these templates is, in fact, that of allowing the "autonomous" declaration of the properties of given, *nonhuman*, entities.

For example, returning to the occurrence of Table 3.3, we could decide to reduce the SPECIF list that fills the TOPIC slot of cob2.c5 to the simple expression (SPECIF STAKE_IN_1 OPTIMUS_BANK). In this case, the additional properties of the purchased stake will be expressed introducing the predicative occurrence cob2.c6 of Table 3.4, derived from the template Own: SimpleProperty that is a specialization of Own:Property. Note that the stake is now expressed as an "individual," STAKE_IN_1, instead of a generic "concept"; in this way, it becomes evident that the stake whose properties are illustrated in cob2.c6 of Table 3.4 is the same that appears as the filler of the TOPIC slot of cob2.c5 (coreference link). The last operation required concerns the association of cob2.c5 and cob2.c6 within a "binding occurrence" of the COORD type; see Section 2.3.2.

The "pseudo_sortal_concept" Concepts

The second branch of non_sortal_concepts, see again Fig. 3.5, is represented by the specializations of pseudo_sortal_concept, grouped into the three sub-trees of classification_, colour_ and substance_. The "pseudo-sortal" label constitutes a reference to the behavior of these concepts with respect to the "instantiation" criterion. On the contrary, in fact, of the concepts of the property_ type that are clearly impossible to conceive under any "instantiated" form, the concepts of this branch appear sometimes as *open to some form of "materialization" into instances* in expressions like "the red of that Ferrari racing car" or "this piece of wood." Note that a different definition of "pseudo-sortal," based on the notion of "rigidity," is given by Guarino et al. [1994].

With respect to particular to substance_, we will give reason for the attribution of these concepts to the non-sortal category by discussing the approach to the "substance" problem followed by the CYC team; see their well-known examples in the style of "peanut butter" [Guha and Lenat, 1990; Lenat and Guha, 1990; Lenat et al., 1990]. Lenat and colleagues start from a quite reasonable remark, which we could even accept as a first, rough and very empirical way of individuating "substances." If we consider *spatial sub-portions* of substances like "water," "wood" or "peanut butter," we still obtain water, wood or peanut butter. In spite of the strong ambiguity of the notion of "spatial sub-portion of a substance" this rule could, for example, allow us to conclude correctly that "wooden chair" is not a substance given that, when separating a wooden chair into its constituent elements, we do not get a collection of chairs. From the above, Lenat and colleagues infer, however, that those *"spatial sub-portions" really "exist,"* and that they can be considered as *instances* of the concepts of water, wood or peanut butter; this amounts, eventually, to saying that *a substance like "wood" should be interpreted as the set of all the possible enumerable pieces of wood*, and that a concept like peanut_butter must be seen as the collection of all the possible pieces of peanut butter [Lenat and Guha, 1990: 41; Guha and Lenat, 1990: 43]. And, of course, this *strongly "physicalist" position* that associates the definition of the general properties of a concept like "wood" with the fluctuating number of pieces of woods we can find in the overall universe is *at least debatable*. For a more detailed description of the "substance" theory in CYC, see also Bertino et al. [2001: 291–299].

In NKRL, the specializations of substance_, because they are non-sortal concepts, cannot be instantiated *directly* into individuals. This means that individuals like WOOD_1 or GOLD_1, derived abruptly from wood_ or gold_, *do not make sense*; note also, among other things, that concepts like timber_ or white_gold are *specializations* of wood_ and gold_, not *instances* of these individual concepts. Should we really need *"well-formed" individuals*, we must have recourse, according to the NKRL approach, to *sortal concepts* like, for example, physical_object – or artefact_, making use in the latter case of a standard HClass term. From these sortal concepts – thanks to the passage through specializations of physical_object (e.g. like piece_of_firewood*)* and specializations of artefact_ (e.g. like piece_of_gold_jewellery) – we can then obtain *fully fledged (and logically sound) individuals* as PIECE_OF_WOOD_27 or GOLD_NECKLACE_3. With respect to the specific "peanut butter" example, we will have in particular, according to the NKRL approach: (i) butter_ is, like gold_ or wood_, a substance_; (ii) peanut_butter is a specialization (not an instance) of butter_ (and, *a fortiori*, of substance_) and it is still, therefore, a *non-sortal concept without immediate instances*; (iii) piece_of_peanut_butter is not an instance of peanut_butter, nor a specialization of this concept, but a *totally new concept* derived (through a possible foodstuff_ sub-tree of artefact_) from sortal_concept – it is, in fact, possible to buy a particular instance (a pat of butter) of piece_of_peanut_butter (or of loaf_of_bread) in a supermarket.

There is, of course, a relationship between the *sortal* concept piece_of_peanut_butter (piece_of_gold), which admits now *direct instances*, and the *non-sortal* concept peanut_butter (gold_), without instances – and this can contribute to explaining, among other things, why substances are classed as pseudo_sortal_concept in NKRL. This relationship concerns some "intrinsic" properties of peanut_butter (gold_), i.e. some slots of the "attribute" type (see Section 2.2.1.3) like ColourOf, MeltingPoint, PhysicalState and so on and the corresponding values – that must also be associated with piece_of_.... Adding these slots and their values can be simply realized by copy/paste operations, or obtained dynamically by making use of specific "procedure type" properties (see again Section 2.2.1.3), e.g. like GetIntrinsicProperties. In this last case, the user must detail the inheritance semantics (i.e. the information-passing characteristics) indicating which slots and values can be inherited over that relation.

With respect now to the non-sortal concept colour_ and its pseudo-sortal aspects, we could deal in a complete way with the problem of "pseudo-instances" like "the red of Mary's coat" or "the red of that Ferrari racing car" by introducing some specializations, like colour_appearance and colour_red_appearance, of the HClass *sortal concept* physical_appearance (see Fig. 3.7

Fig. 3.7 HClass upper level, "sortal" branch

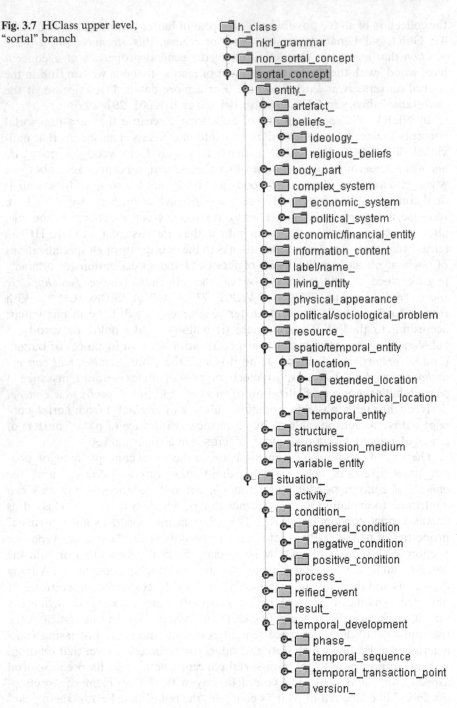

below). "The red of. . ." could then be represented as an *individual*, COLOUR_ RED_APPEARANCE_1, characterized by the presence of an attribute type slot, ReferencePhysicalObject, having as value individuals like a particular Ferrari's model or a given coat whose owner is Mary. Note, however, that we are rarely faced with the need of dealing with these "pseudoinstances" problems in a really complete way. We can, then, accept to lose some nuances of the original meaning, and *simply consider the particular color as a propriety– SPE-CIF(ication) – of the individual mentioned in the event.* Supposing now that "the red of Mary's coat" can be assimilated to a "scarlet," the NKRL representation of this fragment would be in the style of (SPECIF COAT_1 (SPECIF owner_ MARY_) (SPECIF colour_ scarlet_)) – the two properties mentioned for the coat corresponding then to (i) the designation of its owner and (ii) its color. The second SPECIF list could be coded simply as (SPECIF_ colour_ red_) if the particular shade of red cannot be determined.

We can conclude this discussion by recalling that a notion like that of "color" (and of its specializations) can be typically (and simultaneously) used in *two different functions.* For example, should we want to use the definition/description of this notion "in itself," then we must have recourse to the pseudo sortal concept colour_. If, at the same time, we are defining the notion of "rose" (the flower), and we want to utilize the notion of "color" to better define the *sortal* concept rose_, we must associate a property (an attribute slots; see Section 2.2.1.3) ColourOf to this last concept.

Examples of classification_ concepts are market_sector (building_sector, che-mical_sector, retail/trade_sector, etc.) and technology_domain (chemical_ domain, information_technology_domain, medical_domain, etc.).

3.1.2.2 Sortal Concepts

The (more than 2,700) HClass concepts pertain mainly to the category of sortal concepts; we find there, in fact, the great majority of the *domain-dependent concepts* (low levels of the HClass ontology), i.e. the concepts that have been introduced in HClass according to a specific NKRL application. Among the sortal concepts, therefore, we find all the specific terms and sub-terms of very specialized concepts like, to give only some examples, weapon_ (edged_wea-pon, biological/chemical_weapon, firearm_, . . .), beauty_care_product (hair_car-e_product, skin_care_product, . . .), racist_site (anti_jewish_site, eugenics_site, pro_white_site, . . .), etc., that correspond to particular applications in the military, beauty care, or internet filtering, etc. domains. Note that the low level of HClass can be considered, in a way, as a "library" of small ontologies specialized according to specific domains. In this section, then, we will limit ourselves to introducing some general comments about the "sortal" branch of HClass, referring the reader again to Zarri [2003a]. This branch is partitioned into two sub-hierarchies, entity_ and situation_; their present (November 2007) configuration is illustrated in Fig. 3.7.

The general criterion used to organize the "sortal" domain, therefore, is that of distinguishing the *entities* – roughly corresponding, as already noted, to "endurants" in DOLCE – from the *situations* ("perdurants") where these entities are involved. Examining now the contents of Figs. 3.5 and 3.7, we can immediately note that *no particular emphasis* is put in NKRL on notions like "Physical," "Non-physical," "Abstract," "Tangible," "Intangible," etc. that are largely utilized in Cyc, SUMO, DOLCE and Sowa's ontology; see again Section 3.1.1.3 and, in particular, the definitions given for these terms in SUMO. In NKRL, an HClass sortal concept as fire_breathing_dragon is simply a specific term of entity_ and, like any sortal_concept, can then be directly "materialized" into a "legal" (Tolkenian) instance like GLAURUNG_.

The concept human_being_or_social_body (a specialization of living_entity) is an important concept of the entity_ type that is largely used for expressing the template constraints. The corresponding sub-hierarchy is split into two branches, i.e. human_being and social_body. Specializations of human_being are individual_person and group_; specific terms of group_ are, for example, internet_community or public_opinion. The social_body branch is very "bushy" and includes many sub-branches, like academic_institution, agency_, certification_organism or company_; the upper level of company_ is illustrated in Fig. 3.8. Returning to Fig. 3.7, specific terms of extended_location are internet_site (and its specializations) and premises_ (commercial_premises,

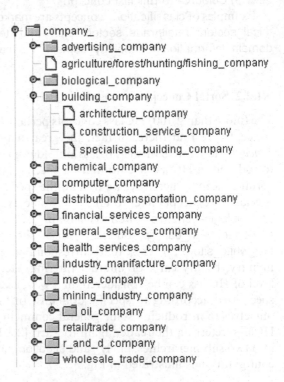

Fig. 3.8 Upper level of the sortal concept company

industrial_premises, military_premises, public_premises like hospital_, etc.). Specific terms of temporal_entity are, for example, date_ and time_period (day_, week_, month_, year_, . . .).

With respect now to the situation_ branch of sortal_concept, we can remark there the presence of a concept like reified_event; this concept represents the top level of a sub-hierarchy structured into several branches, e.g. like meeting_, company_related_event, military_event, political_event, social_event, etc. This presence stems from the fact that *the events represented by means of templates and occurrences must be "structured events,"* i.e. they must be characterized by the *explicit presence* of a *predicate*, of its *arguments* (actors, objects, instruments, etc.) introduced by *roles*, plus in case *additional information* like the temporal attributes, etc. If we do not know *the structural details of an event*, or whether such details are *uninteresting* in a given context, it is possible to represent simply the event as an *individual* (enumerative component), i.e. as an instance of one of the specific terms of the upper level concept reified_event of HClass (e.g. president_bush_interview_49). Within the predicative occurrences, we typically find such reified events as fillers of CONTEXT.

The differentiation between activity_ and process_ in Fig. 3.7 corresponds to the use of the two following criteria:

• An activity is seen as a *voluntary initiative of a particular individual* (or several individuals); see concepts like professional_activity, domestic_activity (errand_, gardening_, housework_, . . .), leisure_, etc. The processes in themselves (i.e. independently from the decision(s) that have led to their activation) are seen as a *more "passive" and "neutral" procedure* where, normally, *several entities are involved*; see manufacturing_, medical_process, management_, planning_, etc.

• The activities give the impression of *being concentrated in a relatively limited temporal interval*, even if they can extend, in reality, over a very long period of time. Processes are *necessarily formed of several steps and phases*, and this explains why they are *necessarily perceived as extended in time*.

The two main branches of condition_ (see again Fig. 3.7) are negative_condition and positive_condition. A (severely abridged) image of the negative_condition sub-hierarchy is shown in Fig. 3.9; specific terms of positive_condition are positive_feeling (alleviation_, contentment_, . . .), availability_, excellence_, etc.

3.2 The Organization of the HTemp Hierarchy

While for HClass it was relatively straightforward to find examples of systems sharing with this quite "standard" ontology *the same aims and some general options* in spite of the *architectural differences*, the same comparisons are not so easy to perform for HTemp, which seems to represent a *relatively isolated example* in the present ontological landscape. Before passing to the concrete discussion of

Fig. 3.9 An abridged representation of the negative_condition sub-hierarchy

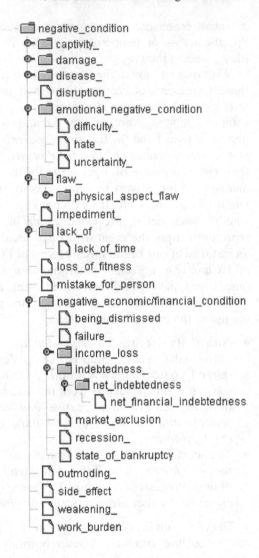

the HTemp characteristics, we will mention quickly, in the next section, some *current* systems that have been created to palliate, in some way, the need for *high-level conceptual constructions that go beyond the traditional ontological approach*, and that could then represent possible alternatives to the HTemp solutions.

3.2.1 Recent Examples of "Structured" Ontological Systems

In the real-life domain, there is an obvious need for tools able to represent on a computer those (pervasive) *high-level conceptual structures* (contexts, norms, situations, events, ...) that cannot be taken into account efficiently by the "standard" ontologies. To deal with this problem, NKRL (HTemp) tries to make use of *new knowledge representation tools* that seem to suit well, at least partly, the general characteristics of these elements. The actual trend in the ontological domain seems to consist, on the contrary, in *trying to adapt/extend in some way the traditional, "binary" tools.*

We have already discussed, in Chapter 1, the *theoretical work* done in a W3C context in order to extend RDF and OWL and allow them to deal with *n*-ary relationships [Noy and Rector, 2006]. In the same W3C context, the *practical solutions* for representing a *variety of states of affairs that can all be reduced to some sorts of dynamic, "narrative" situations* (e.g. a clinical situation with a diagnosis made by some agent, a murder reported by a witness, an accident described as a speed excess case) *seem all to follow the same common schema.* This consists, in substance, of *trying to preserve the general binary background and of dealing with the above "dynamic" phenomena by reducing in some (simple or very complex) way the notion of "role" to the status of "normal" concept/class.* This notion, as already stated several times hitherto, must be considered, on the contrary (both intuitively and on semantic and logical grounds), as a "relation," the relation in particular that links a semantic predicate to its arguments.

A first example is given by the approach called *D&S (Descriptions and Situations)* that has been implemented as a plug-in extension to DOLCE [Gangemi and Mika, 2003].

Beneath the formal apparatus, this approach amounts, in practice, to super-imposing a *relational structure suitable for the representation of situations/events* to the top level of the standard DOLCE hierarchy. This structure adds, then, to DOLCE *new classes* (concepts, unary predicates) and *new tagged relationships* (binary predicates); the new classes are subsumed by the unary predicate Description that is a specification of Non-PhysicalEndurant in basic DOLCE. In this way, FunctionalRole (then a *class/concept*) defines, using the playedBy relationship, the *"roles" that given physical entities (endurants) can play within these events.* CourseOfEvents is a class that organizes *entities temporally denoted* (perdurants, according to DOLCE's jargon) making use of the *binary relationship* sequences; the class Parameter – linked to the standard DOLCE concept Region by the valuedBy relationship – is used to *characterize roles and events.* Other inter-categorial, "transverse" binary relationships can be added, like modalityFor or hasForRequisite; see Fig. 3.10, which presents an abridged description of the top level of D&S. For example, the modalityFor links FunctionalRole to CourseOfEvents and can be used to express modalities like "willing," "hopeful," "cautious," "obliged," etc.

From the point of view of the formalization of the nonfictional narrative domain, a possible interest of the general schema shown in Fig. 3.10 concerns the fact that it can be *specialized according to several types of events/situations* (e.g. in the legal, financial, medical, commercial, technical domains), thus giving rise to sets of *general models of events, situations, etc.* that can evoke NKRL's templates. These models can then be instantiated with data proper to a specific context to produce something in the "predicative occurrences" style.

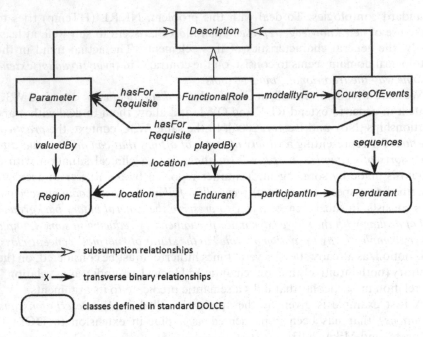

Fig. 3.10 Concise representation of the D&S hierarchy

This sort of approach is presently carried on at LOA (Laboratory for Applied Ontology), a research center of the Italian National Council for Research (CNR), e.g. under the form of work on the "Content Ontology Design Patterns (CODePs)" and, more recently, of Collaborative Ontology Design Ontologies (C-ODOs); see http://wiki.loa-cnr.it/index.php/LoaWiki:Ontologies for the details. In practice, CODePs are, for example, *fragments of ontologies* in the DOLCE style that can be used, by specializing or composing them, to build high-level domain ontologies in a modular way. Examples of CODePs are a "participation pattern" that can be used to represent situations/events like "Members themselves will PARTECIPATE in the final selection," a "plan/ execution pattern" ("The school will continue with its PROJECT to end all violence related to racism, xenophobia and intolerance"), a "collection/entity pattern" ("An ARMY of postal workers descended on my office"), etc. Few details, however, are given on how these D&Ss, CODePs, etc. are concretely set up and instantiated. The idea of making use of some sort of predefined "patterns" to add "expressiveness" and further possibilities of "structuring" to OWL can be found in several recent research efforts; to give only an example, see the work aiming at introducing in OWL some tools for expressing "ordering," e.g. for encoding and arranging into subsumption hierarchies protein "motifs," i.e. short sequences of amino acids that perform a particular function [Drummond et al., 2006].

Still in a general SW, OWL/RDF context, we can mention an interesting (even if limited) study – more practically oriented than D&S/CODePs, etc.– that has been recently carried on jointly at the Fujitsu Laboratories and the Ricoh Company with the ambition of developing an *ontology for modeling the general intellectual work activity in an office*. This ontology is called "Ontology for Knowledge Activity Resources (OKAR)" [OKAR Working Group, 2005]. OKAR defines four main classes, i.e. Agent, Role, Event and Artifact, seven derivative subclasses, i.e. Person, Organization, Equipment, Software, Action, GroupEvent, Document and two "auxiliary" classes, i.e. Location and Person-Name. The relationships among these entities are shown in Fig. 3.11, where the dotted-line arrows refer to the auxiliary classes; the subclass relationships are expressed using the standard rdfs:subClassOf. The properties of the Agent class/subclasses are expressed mainly making use of the vCard vocabulary [Iannella, 2001]; see the upper part of Table 3.5, which describes a generic Agent instance (Taro Yamada). Note the presence in this code of the rdf:parse-Type = "Resource" attribute that allows omitting the introduction of an <rdf:Description> </rdf:Description> pair.

The most interesting innovation of OKAR concerns the *introduction of a Role class*; see also the FunctionalRole class in D&S above. This class is used to connect the Agent class and other (non-Role) basic classes; see the lower part of Table 3.5, which describes the role of Taro Yamada within a given "A-Division" ("#role:TaroYamada:A"); okar:owner represents the link between the Agent and Role classes. It is assumed in general that an Agent can have more than a Role. Also, the Role properties are expressed using the vCard vocabulary; in the case of conflicts among the same properties in the Agent and Role descriptions, a *preference rule* suggests that the Role description content overwrites the Agent description content. The Event class describes the activities of a given Agent at a certain time in a certain place, using mainly the iCalendar vocabulary [Connolly and Miller, 2005] for representing the properties of this class. The Artifact class concerns the results produced by an Agent that is the subject of some actions; properties are expressed mainly making use of the well-known Dublin Core vocabulary for describing metadata [Dublin Core, 2004].

A characteristic of OKAR consists in making use as much as possible of *existing ontologies* and, in particular, of defining the *properties* only when there exists no ontology that is already in possession of defined properties suitable for OKAR's aims. A table of 20 OKAR "proper" properties (which refer mainly to the "enterprise" domain) is reproduced in OKAR Working Group [2005: 11]. Among them we can find hasRole, having Agent as rdf:domain and Role as rdf:range, leader (rdf:domain = Organization and rdf:range = Role(Person)), regularMember, groupMember, etc. Making use of the above tools, OKAR can express simple sequences of events like the fact that Taro Yamada, who was Director of the A-Division, has moved to Senior Director of the C-Division at a certain date; however, no information is given in the Draft Guide about

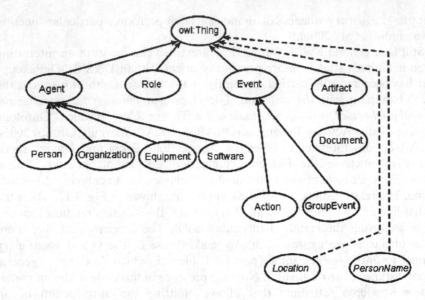

Fig. 3.11 Basic class hierarchy in OKAR

the possibility of implementing OKAR-specific querying/inferencing operations.

The OKAR OWL definition, see the appendix of the Draft Guide, consists of only six pages of code in N3 format – N3 (Notation3) is a shorthand *non*-XML serialization of RDF, designed with human readability in mind [Berners-Lee, 2006]. In spite of its limits and its experimental nature, OKAR constitutes an interesting attempt to introduce some "narrative" elements in the RDF/OWL world.

Table 3.5 Fragments of instance definitions in OKAR

```
<okar:Person rdf:about = "#person:TaroYamada">
   <vcard:FN>Taro Yamada</vcard:FN>
   <vcard:N rdf:parseType = "Resource">
      <vcard:Family>Yamada</vcard:Family>
      <vcard:Given>Taro</vcard:Given>
   </vcard:N>
</okar:Person>

<okar:Role rdf:about = "#role:TaroYamada:A">
   <okar:owner rdf:resource = "#person:TaroYamada">
   <vcard:TITLE>Director</vcard:TITLE>
</okar:Role>
```

To conclude about SW's options that seem to lead systematically to an interpretation of the notion of "role" as a "class," we can mention Rowls, a role-based service matchmaker in a healthcare context developed with the support of the CASCOM European project and of the Spanish Ministry of Education and Science [e.g. Cáceres et al., 2006; Fernández et al., 2006]. To model the interactions between a patient, the healthcare professional and external assistance organizations in an emergency situation, Rowls' developers have created a *general ontology* of "social roles and interactions." A *role-based matching algorithm* takes then as inputs a "service request" and a "service advertisement" and returns the degree of match between the two, expressed as a real number between zero and one. The interesting point of this approach is that *both the service request and the service advertisement are based on the general ontology above*. For example, the service request includes two components. The first includes the "searched provider roles," i.e. some roles of the ontology in the style of Advisor or Explainer, or more complex expressions formed by disjunctions of conjunctions of roles; the "requester capability roles" specify the roles the requester can, in case, play (e.g. Advisor or Explainer again) if an interaction with the provider is necessary.

From an NKRL point of view, the main problem with this approach is that it mixes up in the *same standard "binary" hierarchy* (i) what could be an ad hoc fragment of a "static" ontology of professional roles similar to the HClass professional_role sub-hierarchy mentioned in Section 3.1.2.1 and (ii) several "dynamic" situations/events ("interaction taxonomy") where the persons characterized by the previous roles are involved – according to an NKRL philosophy, these situations/events should, on the contrary, correspond to templates. Among the "static" elements of the hierarchy we can find, then, notions/concepts such as Advisor, MedicalAdvisor, HealthcareProfessional, Patient, Informer, Informee, etc. – and some ad hoc roles like SecondOpinionRequester or SecondOpinionExplainer. Among the "dynamic" events/actions we find notions like InformationExchange, MedicalAdvisementExplanation, MedicalRecordsInfoExchange, HospitalLogin, HealthStatusInfoExchange, etc. Moreover, all these "roles" are defined/described making use of the "semantically poor" OWL/OWL-S tools, and this explains why the result of the matching algorithm mentioned above can only be expressed by a (quite imprecise) numeric value. This work appears, eventually, both as particularly complex and subject to caution with respect to its real possibilities of generalization.

Leaving now the SW domain, we can look rapidly at the "narrative" solutions developed in the context of the ICOM-CIDOC Conceptual Reference Model (CRM, ISO/CD 21127) [Doerr, 2003; Crofts et al., 2007]. CRM constitutes a well-known piece of work implemented in a cultural heritage context – ICOM-CIDOC is the International Committee for Documentation of the International Council of Museums.

CRM derives originally from a relatively "ancient" AI proposal, TELOS [Mylopoulos et al., 1990], without making use of the specific TELOS assertional language. CRM follows a classical "binary" (class–property) approach, i.e. *its knowledge representation model is limited to the declaration of individual, classes, unary and binary relations.* It presents, however, an interest from a methodological point of view because of its *up-to-date* (see RDF) *"property centric" philosophy.* CRM considers, in fact, that properties (about 150, equivalent to "verbs" in natural language) *have priority with respect to classes (about 85) from a modeling point of view.* According to this property-centric approach, classes are admitted only if they can be accepted as "domains" (sets of classes characterized by a given property) or "ranges" (sets of classes that can be associated as values to a property) of legal properties. Examples of CRM properties are: has current location (domain: Physical Object; range: Place); has language (domain: Linguistic Object; range: Language); has number of parts (domain: Physical Object; range: Number); carried out by (domain: Activity; range: Actor); used specific technique (domain: Modification; range: Design or Procedure); etc. The complete list of the properties and associated classes (as of November 2007) can be found in Crofts et al. [2007].

From a "nonfictional narrative" point of view, the appeal of CIDOC CRM is linked mainly with its privileged domain of utilization, i.e. cultural heritage. Because of this, *CRM must be able in fact to take the historical knowledge and reasoning into account*, where "... 'Historical' must be understood in the widest sense, be it cultural, political, archaeological, medical records, managerial records of enterprises, records in scientific experiments, criminal or jurisdictional data" [Doerr, 2003: 2]. And this *narrative and "dynamic" nature of CRM* is well expressed by the presence of properties like transferred title to, custody received by, brought into existence, dissolved, was influenced by, etc. There is then an *evident parallelism* between the *general aims* of CIDOC CRM and those of NKRL, where the burden of taking charge of the representation of the "multifaceted" and "dynamic" aspects of the world is entrusted in this latter language to the "templates."

CRM's properties are, however, simply *"binary" functions.* NKRL's templates, as a form of *n*-ary representation, can, on the contrary, represent *not only single properties of classes or concepts, but also general categories of events.* To simulate this last possibility, CRM must have recourse to *kinds of (binary) semantic networks* where several properties, and the associated classes, are simultaneously employed; an example is given in Fig. 3.12.

This figure consists of a reproduction, somewhat adapted, of a slide extracted from Martin Doerr's presentation at the 13th CIDOC CRM Special Interest Group Meeting in Nürnberg, November 14–15, 2005; see http://cidoc.ics.forth.gr/docs/crm_for_nurnmberg.ppt. In this slide, a fairly complex structure, making use of nine different properties and seven classes, is used *only to model some simple activities of the "move" type that amount, basically, to move a physical object.*

In NKRL, *the whole conceptual domain of "move"* – including all sorts of forced, autonomous, physical, mental, etc. movements, the transmission of messages, the transfer of concrete (money) or abstract (knowledge) entities,

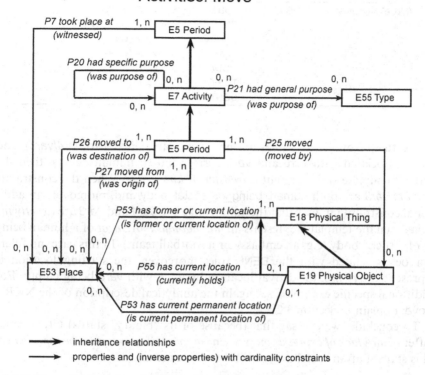

Activities: Move

Fig. 3.12 Formalization of some "move" activities in CIDOC CRM

the changes of attitudes or professions, etc. – *can be synthesized into the single general schema* of Table 3.6; see the specific details in Section 3.2.2.4.

As explained in this last section, the *different, specific templates* representing the general "move" domain are then obtained by associating with the variables of Table 3.6 *proper sets of HClass constraints*. For example, when *var1* can be bound to individuals or social bodies, *var3* to physical objects and *var4/var5* to geographical locations different from each other, and where the first represents the *starting location* and the second the *arrival location*, the derived template corresponds to the CRM *displacement of a physical object* structure of Fig. 3.12. If all the previous constraints remain unchanged – with the exception of those associated with the generalized locations *var4/var5*, which now impose some "status" or "versions" as values for the "starting" location *var4* and the "arrival" location *var5* – the corresponding template will represent a *change of status of a physical object* (e.g. moving form a solid to a liquid state). If the value associated with *var1* can be a human being or a social body, that associated with *var3* is an

Table 3.6 Schematic representation of the "MOVE" conceptual domain in NKRL

[MoveTemplates]	MOVE	SUBJ	var1: {var2}
		OBJ	var3: {var4}, {var5}
		SOURCE	var6: {var7}
		BENF	var8: {var9}
		MODAL	var10
		TOPIC	var11
		CONTEXT	var12

intellectual resource (no values are now necessarily linked to *var4/var5*), and those associated with *var6* and *var8* correspond to human beings, then the derived template will represent a *transfer of knowledge*. When the constraints on *var1/var3* are both human_being_or_social_body and, moreover, an additional constraint imposes that the values linked to *var1* and *var3* are *exactly the same*, then the template represents an *autonomous movement* of a human being or of a social body (e.g. an embassy or a football team). In this case, no fillers can be associated with the BENF role; moreover, the starting location is represented by *var3*, the arrival location by *var4*, with *var5* being empty. For additional specific examples, see again the analytical description of the NKRL move: domain in Section 3.2.2.4.

To conclude, we can say that (because of its "binary" status) CRM could suffer from a *lack of expressiveness* when *complex situations must be represented*. This state of affairs can have a twofold consequence:

- Some difficulties for expressing "deep" semantic contents arise when the description must go beyond the simple encoding of the "physical properties" and the "historical background" of a given cultural heritage item to take into account also *the mutual relationships, attitudes, behaviors, etc. of the "personages"* (in the widest meaning of this word) that, in a painting for example, represent the *focal point of interest* of this cultural heritage item.
- Because of the relatively low level of expressiveness of the CRM properties, an *unnecessary multiplication of these properties* arises whenever CRM tries to express with a certain degree of comprehensiveness *complex "dynamic" situations*.

Note that these same remarks can be expressed (in a strict W3C/OWL-RDF context) about the work recently done on the advanced representation of *still images* in the context of a subcommittee, the Multimedia Annotation in the Semantic Web Task Force, of the (now stopped) W3C Semantic Web Best Practices and Deployment Working Group (SWBPD WG). A public Working Draft produced by this subcommittee is Troncy et al. [2007], where many "cultural heritage" examples are used.

We will conclude this section with a last example of a highly structured ontological system that pertains mainly to the computational linguistics domain, namely the "Text Meaning Representation" (TMR) that is part of the OntoSem environment. OntoSem [Nirenburg and Raskin, 2004; Java et al., 2005] is an (at least partially) implemented theory of natural language processing that aims at *automatically deriving structured meaning (in TMR terms) from unstructured texts*, in a language independent way and making use of syntactic, semantic and pragmatic analysis. The central piece of the theory is a *language-independent ontology* (a "world model"), structured as a DAG (Direct Acyclic Graph) where the arcs represent IsA relationships; the ontology includes about 8,500 concepts. These are represented according to a *frame-like format*; each frame consists of a head and a list of binary relations (some of them are similar to the NKRL roles; see the example in Table 3.7) whose values can be the head of another frame, a simple value, or more complex combinations of syntactic, semantic and lexical elements. The topmost level concepts are OBJECT, EVENT and PROPERTY. A complete TMR representation is a set of six kinds of frames: one or more "propositions," one "style," one "TMR time," and zero or more "discourse relations," "modalities" and "references."

The process of derivation of the TMR representation of a textual fragment consists, then, in *"triggering" a set of concepts of the ontology*, and in *"instantiating" them* according to the specific characteristics of the text in order to produce *a network of instantiated frames*. This process makes use of an important set of computational linguistic tools; for example:

- An OntoSem lexicon for each language processed – according to OntoSem's designers, the current English lexicon includes about 30,000 "senses" including, for example, the most frequent and polysemic verbs.
- An "onomasticon," i.e. a lexicon of proper names, which should include approximately 350,000 entries.
- A syntactic–semantic analyzer, which covers preprocessing, syntactic analysis, semantic analysis, anaphora resolution, etc. and the generation of the final TMR representations.

An interesting aspect of the work done by the OntoSem's team concerns the translation into OWL format of the TMR features. Preliminary findings show, for example, that a *reasonably complete mapping* from TMR to OWL requires *using the OWL Full capabilities*, and this comes down in turn to the production of results that are too large for OWL Full reasoners to process [Java et al., 2006].

Table 3.7 reproduces the TMR coding of an example (an "event") that appears in several publications about OntoSem: "He (Colin Powell) asked the UN to authorize the war."

Apart from the "symbolic names" given in TMR to the binary relationships, we can observe other analogies with the NKRL approach, e.g. the use of the conceptual labels of individuals like WAR-73, ACCEPT-70, REQUEST-ACTION-69 as *"coreference links"* to associate together the fragments of the global representation. See the discussion about Fig. 2.10 for the corresponding NKRL techniques.

Table 3.7 Example of TMR representation of an event

REQUEST-ACTION-69	
AGENT	HUMAN-72
THEME	ACCEPT-70
BENEFICIARY	ORGANIZATION-71
SOURCE-ROOT-WORD	ask
TIME	(<(FIND-ANCHOR-TIME))
ACCEPT-70	
THEME	WAR-73
THEME-OF	REQUEST-ACTION-69
SOURCE-ROOT-WORD	authorize
ORGANIZATION-71	
HAS-NAME	United Nations
BENEFICIARY-OF	REQUESTED-ACTION-69
SOURCE-ROOT-WORD	UN
HUMAN-72	
HAS-NAME	Colin Powell
AGENT-OF	REQUEST-ACTION-69
SOURCE-ROOT-WORD	he; *reference resolution has been carried out*
WAR-73	
THEME-OF	ACCEPT-70
SOURCE-ROOT-WORD	war

The differences between the two approaches are, however, quite important, the main being, of course, the use in TMR of a (largely unstructured) *global "binary" ontology* where a neat differentiation between the *"general, static knowledge about the world" (HClass)* and the *"dynamic, temporally-conditioned succession of the events" (HTemp)* is *necessarily lacking.* See, in this context, the absence of a differentiation among general schemas of events like ACCEPT and REQUEST-ACTION in Table 3.7 – *where a general "dynamic predicate" can be isolated* – and entities like ORGANIZATION and HUMAN in the same table *that correspond to the "ordinary" concepts/notions.* This implies that the conceptual labels of Table 3.7 associated with this second category of entities (ordinary concepts/notions) are not *"roles" according to their NKRL (and standard) meaning* – i.e. relationships linking a semantic predicate to its argu-ments – *but only "slots" in a "classical" frame-like style (similar in this to the HClass slots).*

This (uniform) architectural choice can introduce *logical and practical pro-blems*, like an unnecessary multiplication of the knowledge representation items, a lack of clarity in the overall structure of the language, the loss of important, semantic aspects of the original text, etc. We can eventually remark on the lack, in TMR, of a *well-defined sub-language like AECS* to help in setting up well-formed and expressive fillers and the absence of a general mechanism in the *binding occurrences style* to take into account in a rational and general way the "connectivity phenomena" – even if we can find in Nirenburg and Raskin [2005: chapter 8] a list of five types of discourse relations.

We can conclude (see also Sowa [2005]) by noticing a certain *shortage of details* with respect to the description of the TMR features and about the way of setting up well-formed TMR expressions, and this in Niremburg and Raskin [2004] as well, the most complete description of the OntoSem environment. In contrast, all the computational linguistics details are very well developed in this latter book. And surely the main interest of the OntoSem work concerns its computational linguistics results – see, however, in this context, the (skeptical) comments of Němec [2006].

3.2.2 Main Features of Some Specific HTemp Structures

As already stated in Section 2.2.2.2, HTemp is a *tree* structured into *seven branches* where each branch corresponds to one of the seven semantic predicates described in Table 2.3, i.e. *each branch includes only templates built up around a specific predicate.*

We will now describe in some detail the most "interesting" templates included in each branch, mentioning also, in case, the *second-order constructions* that make use of these templates. For a complete description of the template "catalogue," see Zarri [2003a]. Note that:

- The HTemp status illustrated below corresponds to the status of the NKRL language/environment in November 2007. As already stated (e.g. see again Section 2.2.2.2), the HTemp hierarchy is a *"dynamic" structure* where new templates, easily modeled on the existing ones, can be entered according to the needs of new NKRL applications. The images of the HTemp branches reproduced in the figures below must not be considered, therefore, as the *"final word"* with respect to the HTemp architecture.
- In the present state of HTemp, some *very specific topics*, like "beauty care" or "violence," are *particularly in evidence*, while others (more usual and frequent) are *surely absent*. This state of affairs *depends solely on the "history" of the concrete applications of NKRL (in the financial, press and publishing, terrorism and security, beauty care, biotechnology, medical, electronic industry, etc. domains)*. Note, however, that all the templates created for a specific application have been introduced permanently into HTemp only when we have judged that their domain of application was *sufficiently wide*, and that they could then be utilized *also outside* of their original field.
- With *few exceptions*, signaled by the presence of "ex(ample)" in the left side of their symbolic labels, the occurrences used to illustrate the use of the templates *correspond to "real" occurrences* built up in the context of a given NKRL application. The corresponding original information can be, in

general, freely retrieved from the Internet and can then be considered in the
public domain. In a few cases, we have modified the name of a person or of a
product for appropriateness reasons.

3.2.2.1 Behave: Templates

The complete list of the BEHAVE templates is reproduced in Fig. 3.13. They
can be grouped in *two main classes* according to the *mandatory/forbidden
presence of the* OBJ*(ect) role*.

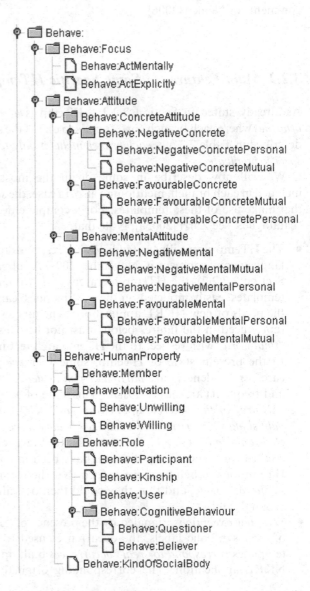

Fig. 3.13 Behave: branch of
the HTemp hierarchy

Filling the OBJ(ect) role is *forbidden*, +(OBJ), in the predicative occurrences derived from templates pertaining to the two branches **Behave:Focus** and **Behave:HumanProperty** of Fig. 3.13. The **Behave:Focus** templates are used when a character or group of characters *would like, concretely or as a desire, intention, etc., to make a given situation happen*. The **Behave:HumanProperty** templates are used in general in situations where *one or more characters perform according to a specific, proper "function," "task" or "role"*: the most important among them are those represented by **Behave:Role** and its specializations. In the two cases, *the presence in the derived occurrences of a "direct object" of the SUBJ(ect)'s behavior is logically inconsistent*.

A second class of **Behave:** templates corresponds to the **Behave:Attitude** branch of Fig. 3.13. They are used to model situations where a SUBJ(ect) manifests *directly* a given behavior, real or purely speculative, *in favor or against a person, a social body, a situation/activity, etc*. In the derived occurrences, filling the OBJ role is then *mandatory*; the BEN(e)F(iciary) role is now "forbidden," +(BENF), given that the "direct object" of the "attitude" corresponds here to the OBJ's filler.

The Behave:HumanProperty Templates

The general schema of these templates is shown in Table 3.8; the "/" symbol indicates the presence of syntactic alternatives.

Filling the MODAL role is then *mandatory* (as signaled by the absence of the "[ ]," "possible/optional," code in Table 3.8) in the *predicative occurrences derived from all the Behave:HumanProperty templates*. For generality's sake, filling the BEN(e)F(iciary) role is possible/optional for the **Behave:Member** template (being part of a group, organism, political party, etc., represented as filler of the TOPIC role), the two **Behave:Motivation** templates (willing/unwilling about the execution of a given task, represented again as filler of the TOPIC role) and the **Behave:KindOfSocialBody** template (a social body has a given type of behavior, e.g. the Abu Sayyaf group behaves as an Islamic separatist movement). Filling this role is, on the contrary, *forbidden*, +(BENF), in the **Behave:Role** occurrences – the **Behave:Role** template is fully reproduced in Table 3.9.

Table 3.8 The HumanProperty conceptual sub-domain of Behave:

[Behave:HumanProperty]	BEHAVE	SUBJ	var1: [(var2)]
		+(OBJ)	
		[SOURCE	var3: [(var4)]]
		[BENF	var5: [(var6)]] / +(BENF)
		MODAL	var7
		TOPIC	var8 / [TOPIC var8]
		[CONTEXT	var9]

Table 3.9 Examples of use of Behave:Role

(a)

name: Behave:Role

father: Behave:HumanProperty

position: 1.33

NL description: "A Human Being or a Social Body Acts in a Particular Role"

BEHAVE	SUBJ	*var1*: [(*var2*)]
	+(OBJ)	
	[SOURCE	*var3*: [(*var4*)]]
	+(BENF)	
	MODAL	*var5*
	[TOPIC	*var6*]
	[CONTEXT	*var7*]
	{[modulators], ≠(abs)}	

var1 =	human_being_or_social_body
var3 =	human_being_or_social_body
var5 =	role_
var6 =	entity_
var7 =	situation_, symbolic_label
var2, var4 =	geographical_location

(b)

mod33.c9)	BEHAVE	SUBJ	ERIC_BRACKE
		MODAL	journalist_
		{obs}	
		date-1:	1999-06-13
		date-2:	

Behave:Role (1.33)

On June 13th, 1999, we can remark (obs) that Eric Bracke is a journalist (specific term of professional_role)

(c)

mod18.c9)	BEHAVE	SUBJ	ALLA_KAHAL_ABUNDOL
		MODAL	(SPECIF leader_(SPECIF cardinality_
			one_of_several))
		TOPIC	MORO_ISLAMIC_LIBERATION_
			FRONT
		{obs}	
		date-1:	1999-08-11
		date-2:	

Behave:Role (1.33)

On August 11th, 1999, we can remark that Alla Kahal Abundol is one of the leaders of the Moro Islamic Liberation Front

Moreover, filling the TOPIC role is *possible/optional* for the occurrences derived from the Behave:Role template, but it is *necessarily required* in the occurrences derived from *all the specializations of this template*, like Behave: User or Behave:Believer. Filling this role in the Behave:Role occurrences is *compulsory* when, in agreement with the main conceptual function of the TOPIC role, it is necessary to give *additional precisions about a specific role/function/ task*. The lower part of Table 3.9 thus reproduces two examples of use of Behave:Role; the first, (b), does not imply the use of TOPIC, which is needed, on the contrary, in the second, (c).

Acting to Obtain a Given Result

The templates of the Behave:Focus type (see Fig. 3.11) can be used in a *standard way* to translate the general idea of *acting to obtain a given result* according to the following modalities:

- A predicative occurrence, *which must necessarily be an instance of a Beha-ve:Focus template*, is used to express the *"acting"* component, i.e. it allows us to identify the SUBJ(ect) of the action, the temporal coordinates, possibly the MODAL(ity) or the instigator (SOURCE), etc. In this occurrence, the OBJ role is *necessarily "empty."*
- A second occurrence (a *single predicative occurrence* or a *binding occurrence denoting several predicative occurrences*) is used to express the *"intended result"* component. This second occurrence, *which happens "in the future" with respect to the previous, Behave:Focus one*, is necessarily marked as *hypothetical*. This implies that the second occurrence itself, if this occurrence is a predicative one or, if the second occurrence is a binding, all the predicative occurrences included in this binding, *must be characterized by the presence of an uncertainty validity attribute*, code "*"; see Section 2.2.2.4.
- A third occurrence, *a "binding" one, which makes necessarily use of a GOAL operator*, is then used to link the previous two.

The general syntax of the NKRL expressions used to code the "acting to obtain a given result" situations is then given by

c_α (GOAL c_β c_γ)
c_β BEHAVE SUBJ <human_being_or_social_body>
*c_γ <predicative occurrence(s), with any syntax>

As an example, Table 3.10 translates the following narrative information: "We notice today, 10 June 1998, that British Telecom will offer its customers a pay-as-you-go (payg) Internet service." We can note that, in the coding of the occurrence conc5.c11, we have supposed that (i) *a decision about the offer has already been taken and that British Telecom will concretely take steps to imple-ment the offer*; (ii) *the new service will be activated before the end of the year 1998*.

The addition of a "ment(al)" modulator to the BEHAVE occurrence, c_β, that introduces an "acting to obtain a result" construction implies, on the contrary, that *no concrete initiative* has actually been taken by the SUBJ of BEHAVE in order to fulfill the result. This would be the case if, for example, British Tele-com's move represented above was only a project. With the addition of ment, the "result," *c_γ, reflects only the (*actual*, see below) *intentions of the SUBJ(ect)*;

Table 3.10 Acting to obtain a given result

conc5.c9)	(GOAL conc5.c10 conc5.c11)		
conc5.c10)	BEHAVE	SUBJ	BRITISH_TELECOM
		{obs}	
		date1:	1998-06-10
		date2:	
Behave:ActExplicitly (1.12)			
*conc5.c11)	MOVE	SUBJ	BRITISH_TELECOM
		OBJ	payg_internet_service
		BENF	(SPECIF customer_ BRITISH_TELECOM)
		date1:	1998-06-10, (1998-12-31)
		date2:	
Move:TransferOfServiceToSomeone (4.11)			

note that, in this last case, the template to be used for c_β now becomes Behave:ActMentally instead of Behave:ActExplicitly, as in Table 3.10.

This NKRL feature evokes some interesting knowledge representation and epistemological problems. As is well known [e.g. Cohen and Levesque, 1990; Brazier et al., 1996], a distinction is normally operated in the general domain of the *motivational attitudes* (goals, wants, desires, preferences, wishes, choices, intentions, commitments, plans) between the simple *desire* (longing, wish, …) and the real *intentions*. At the difference of a wish or desire, an intention implies, in fact, *that an agent needs to determine a way or plan to achieve it*. NKRL enforces this distinction by reserving the specific BEHAVE+{ment}+GOAL construction (where the Behave:ActMentally template is used) only to the cases where *some sort of actual "planning" is openly expressed in the formulation of the event or easily inferred from the context*. In this context, see Table 3.11, which translates this situation: "On January 1st, 2002, Sarah121 is explicitly envisaging to try a whitish silver eye shadow" – see also Table 2.16. Occurrence skin7.c13 derives from the template Behave:ActMentally, a specialization of Behave:Focus (see Fig. 3.13); skin7.c14 from Produce:Assessment/Trial (see Section 3.2.2.6). The concepts and individual used in Table 3.11, like those already used in Table 2.16, are proper to a specific NKRL application in the "beauty care" domain. EYESHADOWING_1 is then a beauty_care_ process, more precisely an instance of eyeshadowing_ that is a specific term of eye_related_care_process. EYESHADOW_LAYER_1 is an instance of eyeshadow_layer, a specific term of eye_makeup; this last concept is a specialization of artefact_ (see Fig. 3.7) through its generic terms makeup_ and body_ornament.

If, on the contrary, we are in the domain of the bare "wishes and desires," then *a simple (modal) modulator,* wish, *could be added*; see Table 2.13 and the occurrence skin7.c2 of Table 2.16. For coherency's sake, this differentiation implies that, in all the occurrences derived from Behave:ActMentally, the MODAL role *must always be explicitly filled* (see again Table 3.11) by making use of a specific term or an instance of activity_, process_ or symbolic_label.

Table 3.11 NKRL coding of explicit "intentions"

skin7.c12)	(GOAL skin7.c13 skin7.c14)		
skin7.c13)	BEHAVE	SUBJ	SARAH_121
		MODAL	planning_
		CONTEXT	(SPECIF EYESHADOWING_1 SARAH_121)
		{ment}	
		date-1:	2002-01-01
		date-2:	
Behave:ActMentally (1.11)			
*skin7.c14)	PRODUCE	SUBJ	SARAH_121
		OBJ	trial_
		TOPIC	(SPECIF EYESHADOW_LAYER_1
			(SPECIF colour_ whitish_silver))
		CONTEXT	(SPECIF EYESHADOWING_1 SARAH_121)
		date-1:	2002-01-01, (2002-01-10)
		date-2:	
Produce:Assessment/Trial (6.41)			

The Behave:Attitude Templates

The templates corresponding to the Behave:Attitude branch of Fig. 3.13 follow the general schema of Table 3.12. As already stated, filling the OBJ role is *strictly mandatory* in their derived occurrences. Also, the MODAL role is mandatory, and the constraint on the MODAL variable can be expressed in general as: *var7* = activity_, artifact_, process_, symbolic_label. Moreover, unlike the Behave:Focus occurrences discussed in the previous subsection, these predicative occurrences *cannot be included within binding occurrences of the GOAL type*. A very simple example of "positive" attitude is represented in Table 3.13; in this occurrence, commitment_ is a specific term of personal_activity.

3.2.2.2 Exist: Templates

The complete list of the Exist: templates is reproduced in Fig. 3.14.

Table 3.12 The "attitude" conceptual sub-domain of Behave:

[Behave:Attitude]	BEHAVE	SUBJ	var1: [(var2)]
		OBJ	var3: [(var4)]
		[SOURCE	var5: [(var6)]
		+(BENΓ)	
		MODAL	var7
		[TOPIC	var8]
		[CONTEXT	var9]
		{for / against}	

Table 3.13 Example of use of Behave:FavourableConcretePersonal

cob1.c1)	BEHAVE	SUBJ	(SPECIF GOVERNMENT_1 (SPECIF
			CARLO_AZEGLIO_CIAMPI prime_minister)): (ROME_)
		OBJ	(SPECIF sale_ CRDI_)
		MODAL	COMMITMENT_1
		CONTEXT	italian_privatisation_programme
		{for}	
		date-1:	(1999-08-01), 1999-09-07
		date-2:	

Behave:FavourableConcretePersonal (1.2122)

(Before September 7th, 1999), the government of Carlo Azeglio Ciampi has pledged to sell the Credito Italiano SpA (CRDI) bank as part of Italy's privatization program

From this figure, it appears that the templates of the Exist: type can be classed in two main categories:

- Templates that represent specializations of Exist:BePresent and that are used to denote *situations/events where a given entity, human or not, is present at a given location.*
- Templates that represent specializations of Exist:OriginOrDeath and that are used to model *the "birth" or the "final end" or a given entity*, human or not. They can then be employed to represent *the creation or the dismantling* of a social body, company, political party, university, etc.

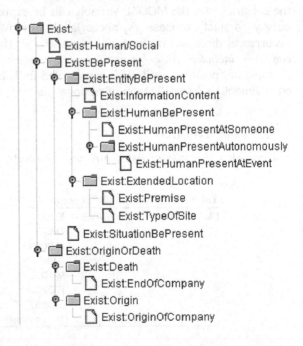

Fig. 3.14 Exist: branch of the HTemp hierarchy

The (single) template Exist:Human/Social is used to state simply that a given human being or social body is *real* (it *exists*) *independently from any possible location*.

The main characteristic of the Exist:BePresent templates is that they *all require as mandatory* the presence, in the derived occurrences, of the *location of the SUBJ(ect)*. Moreover, for the majority of them, like Exist:Human PresentAtEvent or Exist:Premise, OBJ(ect) is *forbidden* in the derived occurrences. For those obtained from the first template, SUBJ must be filled by specializations/instances of human_being_or_social_body, and the SUBJ location by specializations/instances of reified_event. For the occurrences derived from the second, SUBJ is filled with specializations/instances of premise_, and the corresponding SUBJ location will contain the specific "location" of this "premise."

For Exist:HumanPresentAtSomeone, on the contrary, the OBJ(ect) slot *must* be necessarily present in the derived occurrences. This template is used, in fact, *to represent situations where a given "human" is "co-located" with another "human" in the same location*, e.g. in her/his house. In the occurrences, the first character fills the SUBJ and the second the OBJ slot.

Simple predicative occurrences obtained from the three Exist:BePresent templates mentioned above are shown in Table 3.14.

Table 3.14 Predicative occurrences derived from specializations of Exist:BePresent

skin2.c14)	EXIST	SUBJ	SARAH_121: (EVENING_PARTY_1)
		date-1:	2002-01-15
		date-2:	

Exist:HumanPresentAtEvent (2.21221)

On January 15th, 2002 Sarah121 has taken part in an evening party

mod452.c22)	EXIST	SUBJ	LUXURY_HOTEL_1: (MANILA_)
		{obs}	
		date-1:	2000-12-30
		date-2:	

Exist:Premise (2.2131)

On December 30, 2000, we can remark that the luxury hotel (mentioned in a previous occurrence) is located in Manila

ex.c2)	EXIST	SUBJ	HEAVEN_LITTLE_ANGEL
		OBJ	MEGHAN_101: (TORONTO_ON)
		CONTEXT	BEAUTY_CARE_CONVENTION_1
		date-1:	2002-01-25
		date-2:	2002-01-27

Exist:HumanPresentAtSomeone (2.2121)

Heaven Little Angel has spent 3 days in Toronto at Meghan101's place in the framework of a Beauty Care convention

Table 3.15 Template Exist:OriginOfCompany with an example

(a)

name: Exist:OriginOfCompany

father: Exist:Origin

position: 2.321

NL description: "Creation of a Company"

EXIST	SUBJ	(SPECIF *var1* (SPECIF *var2 var3*)): (*var4*)
	+(OBJ)	
	[SOURCE	*var5*: [(*var6*)]]
	[BENF	*var7*: [(*var8*)]]
	[MODAL	*var9*]
	[TOPIC	*var10*]
	[CONTEXT	*var11*]

{[modulators], abs, begin, ≠end, ≠ment}

var1 =	company_
var1 =	individual_
var2 =	company_
var3 =	geographical_location
var3 =	individual_
var5 =	human_being_or_social_body
var7 =	human_being_or_social_body
var9 =	business_process, commercial_activity, industrial_activity, meeting_, reified_event, symbolic_label
var10 =	artefact_, center_of_interest, information_content, market_sector, resource_, sector_specific_activity, service_
var11 =	situation, symbolic_label
var4, var6, var8 =	geographical_location

(b)

conc.c5	EXIST	SUBJ	(SPECIF NEUROVASX_ (SPECIF pharmaceutical_company USA_)): (PLYMOUTH_MN)
		{abs, begin}	
		date-1:	1997-01-01, 1997-12-31
		date-2:	

Exist:OriginOfCompany (2.321)

Neurovasx was created in Plymouth, Minnesota, in 1997

Table 3.15 shows an example of use of one of the Exist:OriginOrDeath templates, Exist:OriginOfCompany; for completeness' sake, the whole template is reproduced in this table.

Two important remarks can be made.

- The first concerns the presence of the pair of modulators "abs, begin." The use of the single temporal modulator begin should have given to the occurrence conc.c5 the *simple meaning* of: "Neurovasx *has set itself* in Plymouth, Minnesota, in 1997." The addition of the modal modulator abs (see Table 2.13) *transforms this meaning* into: "Neurovasx *was created* in Plymouth, Minnesota, in 1997." Note that abs, currently, *can only be used with the templates/occurrence of the* Exist:OriginOrDeath *family*, with the specific function of indicating the creation or disappearing (birth, death) of an individual or social body.

- The second remark is not specific to the Exist: templates but concerns in general the NKRL way of *introducing a reference to a given company*. This reference is a new example of *NKRL's idiom*, and is characterized by the format shown by the filler of the SUBJ(ect) slot in the template of Table 3.15. This means that the name of the company (that refers to an individual; see the constraints) must be accompanied by the type of company (pharmaceutical_company in the example) and the nationality, the latter being expressed as an instance of geographical_location (USA_ in the example). "Type" and "nationality" can obviously be "empty." In the NKRL coding (annotation) of a narrative document dealing with a specific company, this particular format must be necessarily used *at least once*, normally when the company is introduced.

We will conclude this section by reproducing a well-known Exist: example, often used to show that the "narrative" documents dealt with by NKRL *do not consist necessarily of NL texts*. Table 3.16 represents, then, the NKRL annotation of a still image (a photograph) representing a situation that, verbalized, could be expressed as "Three nice girls are lying on the beach." The MODAL filler, lying_position, is a non-sortal concept, specific term of body/object_position (a qualifier_). The single individual GIRL_1 has been used here because we have supposed that the three girls, separately, were not sufficiently important in the context of the image to justify their explicit representation as specific individuals; see also Appendix B in this context. This is also in agreement with the NKRL basic principle already mentioned suggesting that we should try to avoid any *unnecessary proliferation of individuals*.

3.2.2.3 Experience: Templates

The Experience: templates are fully listed in Fig. 3.15.

Table 3.16 NKRL annotation of a still image

ex.c3)	EXIST	SUBJ	(SPECIF GIRL_1 beautiful_ (SPECIF cardinality_ 3)): (BEACH_1)
		MODAL	lying_position
		date-1:	
		date-2:	
Exist:HumanPresentAutonomously (2.2122)			

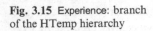
Fig. 3.15 Experience: branch of the HTemp hierarchy

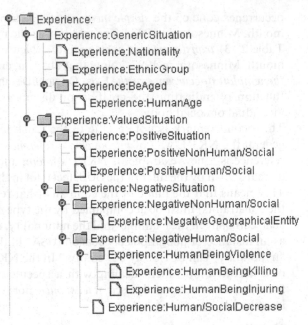

Apart from a few of them that represent specializations of Experience:GenericSituation, these templates are mainly used to represent events where a given entity, human or not, *is exposed to some sort of "experience"* (illness, richness, economical growth, starvation, success, racism, violence, ...) that can be *either "positive" or "negative."* The specific "experience" undergone is represented, in the derived predicative occurrences, by the filler of the OBJ(ect) role: this role is then *mandatory* for all the Experience: templates. On the contrary, given that all these "experiences" are strictly "personal," the BEN(e)F(iciary) role is *forbidden*, +(BENF). Table 3.17 reproduces an example of use of a "negative experience" template, Experience:HumanBeingInjuring. In this, *the SOURCE role is also forbidden, because this template must be used to encode a generic "injuring" situation where the author(s) of the negative experience is/are unknown.* A specific template of the PRODUCE type, Produce:HumanBeingInjuring (Section 3.2.2.6) should be used when an explicit action of a well-identified actor(s) is described. The same principles are valid for the "parallel" templates Experience:HumanBeingKilling and Produce:HumanBeingKilling.

Table 3.18 reproduces, on the contrary, an example of "positive experience." Note, in this occurrence, the format of the two "expansions" (structured arguments). The first, the SUBJ's filler, is an illustration of the "company format" idiom. The second, the OBJ's filler, shows an application of the standard syntax for expressing any sort of "amount of money"; see also Section 3.2.2.7. We can remark, in this syntax, the use of the "amount_ idiom" introduced in Section 3.1.2.1.

Table 3.17 An example of Experience:NegativeHuman/Social occurrence

(a)

name: Experience:HumanBeingInjuring
father: Experience:HumanBeingViolence
position: 3.22212
NL description: "A Human Being is Injured (Without an Explicit SOURCE)"

EXPERIENCE	SUBJ	SUBJ	*var1*: [(*var2*)]
		OBJ	*var3*
		+(SOURCE)	
		+(BENF)	
		[MODAL	*var4*]
		[TOPIC	*var5*]
		[CONTEXT	*var6*]
		{[modulators], ≠abs}	

var1 = human_being
var2 = location_
var3 = human_being_injuring
var4 = activity_, artefact_, degree_, process_, general_characterising_property, symbolic_label
var5 = activity_, artefact_, beliefs_, information_content, condition_, economic/financial_entity,
              body_part
var6 = situation, symbolic_label

(b)

mod61.c13)	EXPERIENCE	SUBJ	(SPECIF individual_ (SPECIF cardinality_ (SPECIF approximate_amount 8))): (ISABELA_)
		OBJ	bomb_attack_injuring
		CONTEXT	TERRORIST_BOMB_ATTACK_1
		date-1:	1999-03-15
		date-2:	

Experience:HumanBeingInjuring (3.22212)

On March 15, 1999, about eight people were injured in a terrorist bomb attack

---

Table 3.18 An example of Experience:PositiveHuman/Social occurrence

conc14.c2)	EXPERIENCE	SUBJ	(SPECIF DONNELLEYS_BOOK SPECIF book_publisher USA_)): (CINCINNATI_OH)
		OBJ	(SPECIF PROFIT_1 USA_DOLLAR (SPECIF amount_ 768,300))
		date-1:	1997-04-01
		date-2:	1998-03-31

Experience:PositiveHuman/Social (3.212)

Donnelley's One Book has made a 768,300 US dollars profit between April 1st, 1997, and March 31st, 1998

3.2.2.4 Move: Templates

The complete list of the Move: templates is reproduced in Fig. 3.16. In Section 3.2.1, we have already emphasized that the NKRL representation of the conceptual domain of all the "move" activities can be expressed in a *very concise mode*, and reduced in particular to the simple expression of Table 3.6. As already stated, the last subsumes, in fact, the formal expressions of all the Move: templates, which are then differentiated according to the *constraints associated with the 12 variables var$_i$ of Table* 3.6 and to the *conditions imposed on the different roles*. We will now discuss the "move" domain in some detail.

The templates of the Move:TransferToSomeone branch are described globally in Table 3.19. This schema is particularly simple and intuitive, and does not deserve many comments. We can note, however, that the presence of the three roles SUBJ, OBJ (the entity transferred) and BENF (the beneficiary of the transfer) is *mandatory* in all the occurrences derived from these templates. An example of use of the Move:TransferOfServiceToSomeone template is represented by the occurrence conc5.c11 in Table 3.10.

The templates of the Move:AutonomousDisplacement (*autonomous movement*) branch are described in Table 3.20. Several interesting features are present in this table. The first concerns the (obvious) *interdiction of making use of*

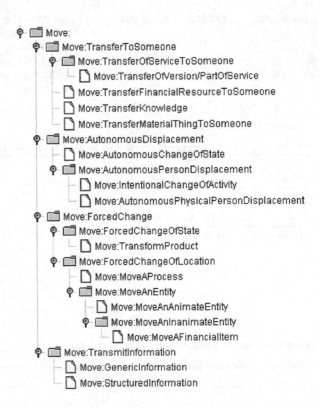

Fig. 3.16 Move: branch of the HTemp hierarchy

Table 3.19 The TransferToSomeone branch of the Move: templates

[Move:TransferToSomeone]	MOVE	SUBJ	var1: [(var2)]
		OBJ	var3
		[SOURCE	var4: [(var5)]
		BENF	var6: [(var7)]
		[MODAL	var8]
		[TOPIC	var9]
		[CONTEXT	var10]

the BEN(e)F(iciary) role in the predicative occurrences derived from all these templates: *the movement concerns solely the SUBJ(ect) of the predicative occurrences.* The second concerns the fact that an "autonomous displacement" of the SUBJ is always interpreted as "*The SUBJ moves herself/himself/itself as an OBJ*"; this explains why, see the constraints of Table 3.20, *the fillers of the SUBJ and OBJ in the occurrences must be rigorously identical.* Eventually, because of this particular interpretation of an "autonomous movement," *the location associated with the SUBJ role, var2, is interpreted as the "initial location," and the location associated with the OBJ, var4, is interpreted as the "arrival location."* Therefore, not only is the presence of the two locations *mandatory* (see the absence of the "[ ]" code), but they must also be *strictly different.*

Moreover:

- *The locations are not necessarily "geographical locations."* For example, in the template Move:IntentionalChangeOfActivity, used to represent a change of professional, etc. activity of a human being or social body (where, as usual, *var3 = var1*), *var2* and *var4* are both associated with the constraints: "market_sector, technology_domain," with *var4 ≠ var2*.
- *The SUBJ is not necessarily a human or a social body.* In the template Move:AutonomousChangeOfState, used to represent that *an inanimate entity changes of state*, *var1* (the SUBJ) and *var3* (the OBJ) are both associated with the constraints "entity_, ≠ living_entity." Locations *var2* and *var4* are specified as non_sortal_concept, with *var4 ≠ var2*.

Table 3.20 The AutonomousDisplacement branch of the Move: templates

[Move:AutonomousDisplacement]	MOVE	SUBJ	var1: (var2)
		OBJ	var3: (var4)
		[SOURCE	var5: [(var6)]
		+(BENF)	
		[MODAL	var7]
		[TOPIC	var8]
		[CONTEXT	var9]
		var3 = var1; var4 ≠ var2	

Table 3.21 supplies the full representation of the AutonomousPhysicalPersonDisplacement template, and an example.

The format of the templates of the Move:ForcedChange branch of Move: is schematized in Table 3.22. This group of templates is used *whenever an agent (SUBJ) moves an entity (OBJ = physical object, animate entity, process, ...) from the initial location of this entity, var4, to the final destination var5, with var5 ≠ var4.*

Note that a basic difference exists between these templates and the TransferToSomeone templates mentioned at the beginning of this section: the latter

---

Table 3.21 A Move:AutonomousPhysicalPersonDisplacement example

(a)

name: Move:AutonomousPhysicalPersonDisplacement
father: Move:AutonomousPersonDisplacement
position: 4.222
NL description: "Autonomous Movement of a Person or Social Body"

MOVE   SUBJ   var1: (var2)
       OBJ   var3: (var4)
       [SOURCE   var5: [(var6)]
       +(BENF)
       [MODAL   var7]
       [TOPIC   var8]
       [CONTEXT   var9]
       {[modulators], ≠abs }

var1 = human_being_or_social_body
var2 = location_
var3 = human_being_or_social_body
var3 = var1
var4 = location_
var4 ≠ var2
var5 = human_being_or_social_body
var6 = location
var7 = transportation_activity, transportation_means, use_
var8 = sortal_concept
var9 = situation_, symbolic_label

(b)

mod312.c12)   MOVE   SUBJ   JOSEPH_ESTRADA: (MANILA_)
                      OBJ   JOSEPH_ESTRADA: (JOLO_)
                      MODAL   air_transportation
                      CONTEXT   HOSTAGE_RELEASE_NEGOTIATION_1
                      date-1:   1993-12-07
                      date-2:

Move:AutonomousPhysicalPersonDisplacement (4.222)
On December 7, 1993, Joseph Estrada moves from Manila to Jolo in the context of the negotiations for the liberation of the hostages

Table 3.22 The ForcedChange branch of the Move: templates

[Move:ForcedChange]	MOVE	SUBJ	var1: [(var2)]
		OBJ	var3: [(var4, var5)]
		[SOURCE	var6: [(var7)]]
		+(BENF)	
		[MODAL	var8]
		[TOPIC	var9]
		[CONTEXT	var10]
		var5 ≠ var4	

require *necessarily* the presence of a BENF role, which is *forbidden in the present case (the movement does not imply a specific "recipient")*. Note also that:

- The location of the SUBJ, *var2, does not coincide necessarily* with the initial location of the entity moved. The entity, e.g. a missile, can be moved from a distance.
- None of the three locations *var2, var4* or *var5* is *necessarily filled* in the predicative occurrences derived from these templates. An event telling simply that a physical object has been moved, without giving any precisions about the spatial coordinates of all the entities involved, is fully plausible.

The Move:GenericInformation and Move:StructuredInformation templates that are specific terms of Move:TransmitInformation, see the last branch of Fig. 3.16, *are differentiated only by the kind of entity that can fill the (mandatory) OBJ slot* in the associated predicative occurrences. In the first case, this filler will be simply a *specific term or an instance* of one of the two HClass concepts information_content or label/name_. In the second, the filler must be an instance of symbolic_label (a specific term of nkrl_grammar, see Section 3.1.2 above), indicating then that *the content of the transmitted message is represented by one or more predicative occurrences*. In this last case, we are then in the domain of those "completive constructions" described in Section 2.3.1.

An instance of Move:StructuredInformation, coupled with instances of one of the templates of the Move:ForcedChange branch, i.e. Move:MoveAProcess, is reproduced in Table 3.23. This corresponds to the "conceptual annotation" of this nonfictional narrative: "Tokyo, March 31, 1993. Sharp Corp said it has shifted production of low-cost computers from Japan to companies in Taiwan and Korea. Taiwan's Twinhead International Corp will make notebook PCs while Korea's Hyundai Electronic Industry Ltd makes desktop types, a Sharp spokesman said."

We can note, in the occurrence cob27.c3, the use of the construction (SPECIF computer_hardware ... SHARP_CORP) to indicate that Sharp Corporation will move the production of *its own* computers.

We can conclude the section by noting that the completive construction introduced by a Move:StructuredInformation template can be used in general to represent any form of complex "enunciative situation," both *explicit*, as in the "Sharp Corp." example above, or *implicit*.

Table 3.23 Use of TransmitInformation and ForcedChange templates

cob27.c1)	MOVE	SUBJ	(SPECIF SPOKESMAN_1 (SPECIF SHARP_CORP (SPECIF electronic_company JAPAN_)))
		OBJ	#cob27.c2
		date1:	1993-03-31
		date2:	

Move:StructuredInformation (4.42)

cob27.c2   (COORD cob27.c3 cob27.c4 cob27.c5)

cob27.c3)	MOVE	SUBJ	SHARP_CORP
		OBJ	(SPECIF manufacturing_ (SPECIF computer_hardware cheap_ SHARP_CORP)): (JAPAN_ (TAIWAN_ KOREA_))
		BENF	(COORD1 (SPECIF TWINHEAD_INT (SPECIF electronic_company TAIWAN_)) (SPECIF HYUNDAI_ELECTRONIC (SPECIF electronic_company SOUTH_KOREA)))
		date1:	(1993-03-15), 1993-03-1993
		date2:	

Move:MoveAProcess (4.321)

cob27.c4)	PRODUCE	SUBJ	TWINHEAD_INT: (TAIWAN_)
		OBJ	(SPECIF notebook_pc SHARP_CORP)
		[begin]	
		date_1:	1993-03-31, (1993-06-30)
		date_2:	

Produce:Hardware (6.21)

cob27.c5)	PRODUCE	SUBJ	HYUNDAI_ELECTRONIC: (SOUTH_KOREA)
		OBJ	(SPECIF desktop_computer SHARP_CORP)
		[begin]	
		date_1:	1993-03-31, (1993-06-30)
		date_2:	

Produce:Hardware (6.21)

Let us consider, for example, an interesting problem originally raised by Nazarenko in a CGs context and concerning the *correct rendering of particular "causal" statements implying the existence of an (implicit) speech situation* [Nazarenko-Perrin, 1992; Nazarenko, 1993]. If we take, for example, one of the Nazarenko's examples: "Peter has a fever since he is flushed" [Nazarenko-Perrin, 1992: 881], it is well evident that, in this particular connotation of a "since" clause, "being flushed" is certainly not the "cause" of "having a fever." The situations expressed by the two previous syntagms are, moreover, contemporary, which is in contradiction with one of the fundamental characteristics of

Table 3.24 Use of a Move: completive construction to represent an implicit enunciative situation

ex.c4)	(CAUSE ex.c5 ex.c6)		
ex.c5)	MOVE	SUBJ	human_being_or_social_body
		OBJ	#ex.c7
		MODAL	implicit_speech_act
		date-1:	[*same date as in c6 and c7*]
		date-2:	
Move:StructuredInformation (4.42)			
ex.c7)	EXPERIENCE	SUBJ	PETER_
		OBJ	fevered_state
		date-1:	[*same date as in c5 and c6*]
		date-2:	
Experience:NegativeSituation (3.22)			
ex.c6)	EXPERIENCE	SUBJ	PETER_
		OBJ	flushing_state
		{obs}	
		date-1:	[*same date as in c5 and c7*]
		date-2:	
Experience:GenericSituation (3.1)			

a "causal" clause asking that *the "cause" occurs before the "consequence"*; see also Section 2.3.2.3.

According to Nazarenko, modeling in a complete and accurate way the previous example requires the introduction of an *implicit enunciative situation* where the flushing state of Peter is seen as the "cause" (in the ordinary meaning of this word) of an *implicit speaker action* where this unknown speaker claims (affirms, asserts, etc.) that Peter has a fever. Using the completive construction, this interpretation of the above example is easily translated in NKRL by using the four occurrences of Table 3.24.

3.2.2.5 Own: Templates

The complete list of the Own: templates is reproduced in Fig. 3.17. The first three branches of this figure, Own:Property, Own:Control and Own:AvailabilityOf, correspond to different nuances of the customary "own" meaning that stands for "being in possession of something."

Table 3.25 shows an example of use of the Own:ConcreteResource template. This particular predicative occurrence, cob3.c10, is the counterpart of the occurrence cob2.c5 used in Section 3.1.2.1, Table 3.3, to illustrate the use of the NKRL "property idioms": after having bought a stake in the share capital of the Optimus Bank, the Berliner Bank is now in possession of this share. Once again, for simplicity's sake, we will consider here that the two banks are already

Fig. 3.17 Own: branch of the
HTemp hierarchy

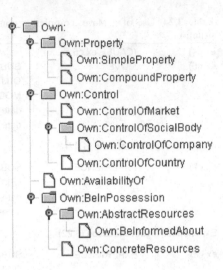

Table 3.25 An example of use of the Own:ConcreteResource template

cob3.c10)	OWN	SUBJ	BERLINER_BANK: (BERLIN_)
		OBJ	(SPECIF stake_in OPTIMUS_BANK (SPECIF amount_ (SPECIF percent_ 50 (SPECIF share_capital OPTIMUS_BANK))))
		{obs}	
		date-1:	1993-10-15
		date-2:	

Own:ConcreteResource (5.42)

On October 15th, 1993, we can remark that the Berliner Bank has a 50% stake in the Optimus Bank share capital

known by the system, thus leaving out from the code details like the nationality and the type of company. Moreover, the same simplifications of the SPECIF lists already discussed for cob2.c5 can be also implemented for cob3.c10.

Some modalities of use of the Own:Property templates have already been introduced in Section 3.1.2.1; we can now add some further details. They are then employed *to specify the "properties" of NKRL (sortal) entities to the exclusion of human being and social bodies*, especially when: (i) these properties are particularly abundant and, for clarity's sake, it is more appropriate *to distribute them onto several predicative occurrences*; (ii) the accumulation of a multiplicity of entities *within the same SPECIF list* blurs the understanding of the predicative occurrence where this list appears; (iii) it is *formally impossible* to add properties to a given item, e.g. when the latter is included within a "location" list (see Table 3.27 below). The exclusion of *human beings and social bodies* from the domain of application of these templates corresponds to a coherency's

Table 3.26 The Property branch of the Own: templates

[Own:Property]	OWN	SUBJ	var1: [(var2)]
		OBJ	var3
		[SOURCE	var4: [(var5)]]
		+(BENF)	
		[MODAL	var6]
		TOPIC	var7 / (SPECIF var7 var8)
		[CONTEXT	var9]
		var1 ≠ human_being_or_social_body	
		var1 ≠ property	
		var3 = property_	

concern: the "properties" of these two categories of sortal concepts are, in fact, *already taken fully into account by the Behave: templates.*

A general schema that subsumes the two Own:Property templates is reproduced in Table 3.26. In the occurrences derived from these templates, *the OBJ filler must be necessarily the (non sortal) concept property_;* for generality's sake, the specific terms of property_ (quantifying_property, relational_property, etc.) are also admitted. The alternative about the fillers of the TOPIC role allows us to differentiate the template Own:CompoundProperty from Own:SimpleProperty. In the first case, the "property" is *necessarily* represented by a SPECIF list where the first argument (*var7*) must be *a specific term of the (non-sortal) concepts part/whole_relationship, relational_property and spatio/temporal_relationship,* and the second (*var8*) may be any specialization or instance of sortal_concept. In the second, the "property" is *directly represented by the main filler(s) of the TOPIC slot* – which can also be, for example, the first argument of a SPECIF operator in an "expansion" list apart from the heads and the specific terms of the three "relational" sub-trees of HClass mentioned before; see the occurrence mod452.c4 in Table 3.27.

Table 3.27 reproduces first an example of connected "simple" properties represented as independent predicative occurrences, and then an example of a "compound" property. In the first example, concurrent_ is a specific term of the (non-sortal) temporal_relationship concept. In the second example, more_effective_than is a specific term of compared_to, which is in turn a specific term of the (non-sortal) binary_relational_property.

3.2.2.6 Produce: Templates

The Produce: branch is the "bushiest" one of the HTemp hierarchy; a partial image of this branch is reproduced in Fig. 3.18. The templates of the type Produce:Entity, not shown in Fig. 3.18, include items like Produce:Hardware, Produce:Software, Produce:Pharmaceutical/Medical/Bio, etc.

The syntax of the Produce: templates does not deserve any particular comment. In the derived occurrences, *the filling of the SUBJ and OBJ slots is always*

Table 3.27 Example of use of the Own:Property templates

(a)

mod452.c1)   (COORD mod452.c3 mod452.c4 ...)

The properties illustrated in the occurrences mod452.c3, mod452.c4, *etc. are logically related.*

mod452.c3)	OWN	SUBJ	(COORD1 TERRORIST_BOMB_ATTACK_4
			TERRORIST_BOMB_ATTACK_5):
			(QUEZON_CITY)
	OBJ	property_	
	TOPIC	concurrent_	
	{obs}		
	date-1:	2000-12-30	
	date-2:		

Own:SimpleProperty (5.11)

On December 30, 2000, we can remark that the two (already known) bomb attacks have been executed simultaneously

mod452.c4)	OWN	SUBJ	QUEZON_CITY: (PHILIPPINES_)
		OBJ	property_
		TOPIC	(SPECIF suburb_of MANILA_)
		{ obs }	
		date-1:	2000-12-30
		date-2:	

Own:SimpleProperty (5.11)

Quezon City is a suburb of Manila

(b)

skin1.c15)	OWN	SUBJ	baby_oil
		OBJ	property_
		TOPIC	(SPECIF more_effective_than
			NOVA_UNDEREYE_CREAM)
		CONTEXT	(SPECIF therapy_ undereye_dry_skin)
		date-1:	
		date-2:	

Own:CompoundProperty (5.12)

(One of the statements issued by a member of the Beauty Care community is that) baby oil is more effective in the therapy of under eye dry skin than the Nova Undereye Cream

---

mandatory. The OBJ slot is filled, in particular, with the "result" of the specific "production"; see also the comments about the use of the "action names" as OBJ's fillers in the discussion of Table 3.3. The other roles are not submitted to constraints of the "forbidden" type; they can be "mandatory" in some specific templates.

We will supply in the following pages some simple examples of use of **Produce:** templates. Other examples of predicative occurrences derived from these templates have been met in previous sections: a **Produce:Violence**

Fig. 3.18 Partial image of the Produce: branch of the HTemp hierarchy

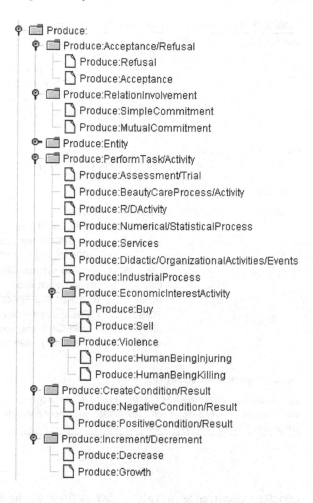

occurrence (mod3.c5 in Table 2.6), a Produce:EconomicInterest Activity occurrence (conc5.c4 in Table 2.19), a Produce:Assessment/Trial occurrence (skin7.c14 in Table 3.11), a Produce:Buy occurrence, two Produce:Hardaware occurrences, etc. Table 3.28 presents two examples of use of templates pertaining to the Produce:Acceptance/Refusal and Produce:RelationInvolvement subbranches of Fig. 3.18.

A general characteristic of the Produce:Acceptance/Refusal templates concerns the *mandatory nature of the TOPIC role*. With respect now to the Produce:MutualCommittment template (which pertains to the Produce:Relation Involvement sub-hierarchy) we can note that: (i) the filler of the SUBJ role in the derived occurrences is necessarily a *COORD(ination) list* where all the participants in the agreement are mentioned; (ii) this list is *duplicated* (in a complete or abridged form, i.e. without SPECIF list; see the

Table 3.28 Produce:Acceptance/Refusal and Produce:RelationInvolvement occurrences

mod26.c12)	PRODUCE	SUBJ	(SPECIF family_ AGAPITO_ANTONIO_JR)
		OBJ	payment_refusal
		BENF	(SPECIF INDIVIDUAL_PERSON_69
			(SPECIF cardinality_ several_))
		TOPIC	(SPECIF hostage_release AGAPITO_ ANTONIO_JR)
		date-1:	(1999-05-01), (1999-07-31)
		date-2:	

Produce:Refusal (6.11)

*At an unknown date between May and August 1999, Agapito Antonio Jr.'s family refused to pay the ransom to the kidnappers (*INDIVIDUAL_PERSON_69 *has been introduced in a previous occurrence)*

conc9.c1)	PRODUCE	SUBJ	(COORD1
			(SPECIF FREEPAGES_
			(SPECIF telecom_inquiries_company UK_))
			(SPECIF CENDANT_ (SPECIF
			internet_marketing_company USA_)))
		OBJ	marketing_alliance
		BENF	(COORD1 FREEPAGES_ CENDANT_)
		TOPIC	(SPECIF commercialisation_
			(SPECIF home_shopping_service CENDANT_))
		date-1:	(1998-06-01), 1998-06-23
		date-2:	

Produce:MutualCommittment (6.22)

Beginning June 1998 (June 23rd, 1998, is the date of the official announcement), Freepage (UK) and Cendant (USA) have signed a marketing agreement concerning the commercialization of the home shopping services of Cendant

conc9.c1 occurrence in Table 3.28) as filler of the BEN(e)F(iciary) role. The global meaning of this particular syntactic construction amounts, then, *to saying that the participants in the agreement have "produced" this particular agreement for the benefit of themselves.*

Table 3.29 reproduces an example of use of one of the Produce:Entity templates; screening_tool is a specific term of diagnostic_tool/system, which derives in turn from artefact_ through medical/tool_product.

Table 3.30 reproduces two examples of use of specific templates included in two sub-hierarchies, Produce:EconomicInterestActivity and Produce:Violence, of the tree Produce:PerformTask/Activity.

In the occurrences derived from the Produce:Buy and Produce:Sell templates (pertaining to the sub-tree Produce:EconomicInterestActivity), *the fillers of the OBJ slots are respectively (and necessarily) the terms* purchase_ *and* sale_ *or some of their specific terms/instances*; see also the occurrence cob2.c5 in Table 3.3. purchase_ and sale_ are sorts of business_process. *The "object" of the sale/*

Table 3.29 A Produce:Pharmaceutical/Medical/Bio occurrence

conc40.c17)	PRODUCE	SUBJ	(SPECIF TRIPATH_IMAGING
			(SPECIF medical_imaging_company USA_)):
			(BURLINGTON_NC)
		OBJ	(SPECIF screening_tool (SPECIF cardinality_ several_))
		TOPIC	cervical_cancer
		{ obs }	
		date-1:	1999-10-11
		date-2:	

Produce:Pharmaceutical/Medical/Bio (6.33)

Today (October 11th, 1999), we can remark that the Tripath Imaging company is manufacturing several screening tools in the cervical cancer domain

purchase action fills the TOPIC slot; filling this slot is then *mandatory* in the "purchase/sale" occurrences.

A specific term/instance of human_being_killing (which is a specific term of activity_ through violence_, etc.) is required as filler of the OBJ slots

Table 3.30 Produce:Buy and Produce:HumanBeingKilling occurrences

conc8.c6)	PRODUCE	SUBJ	(SPECIF AMERICAN_ONLINE
			(SPECIF internet_company USA_))
		OBJ	PURCHASE_47
		MODAL	(SPECIF cash_transaction USA_DOLLAR
			(SPECIF amount_ 287,000,000))
		TOPIC	(SPECIF MIRABILIS_ (SPECIF software_company
			ISRAELI_))
		date-1:	(1999-06-01), 1999-06-09
		date-2:	

Produce:Buy (6.481)

Beginning of June, 1999, American Online has acquired the Israeli Mirabilis company through a cash transaction of $287 million

mod131.c7)	PRODUCE	SUBJ	(SPECIF INDIVIDUAL_PERSON_40
			(SPECIF cardinality_ several_)): (SULU_PROVINCE)
		OBJ	human_being_killing
		BENF	(SPECIF individual_
			(SPECIF cardinality_ (SPECIF approximate_amount
			11)))
		CONTEXT	(SPECIF terrorist_bomb_attack (SPECIF cardinality_ 2))
		date-1:	(26/12/1998)
		date-2:	

Produce:HumanBeingKilling (6.492)

On December 26, 1998 (reconstructed), about 11 people died in two bomb attacks triggered by a group of people of unknown size

in the predicative occurrences derived from Produce:HumanBeingKilling
(a specialization of Produce:Violence); see also the "Brutus stabbing Caesar"
example in Section 1.1.2. As already stated in Section 3.2.2.3, the choice of a
Produce: template implies that the SOURCE of the killing *is clearly expressed in
the original formulation of this action/event*.

Two examples of use of Produce:CreateCondition/Result and Produce:Incre-
ment/Decrement templates are reproduced in Table 3.31. In conc13.c4, the
individual FOOD_AND_DRUG_ADMINISTRATION_USA is an instance of certi-
fication_organism (a social_body); therapy_ is a specific term of medical_process.
In the predicative occurrences derived from Produce:Decrease/ Produce:Growth
templates, *the TOPIC slots must be necessarily filled*. Occurrence conc47.12 is
marked as *uncertain*, given that the expenses increase will happen *in the future*
with respect to the date (February 24th, 1998) of the announcement (introduced
in previous occurrences) that German publishers will take steps (BEHAVE, see
Section 3.2.2.1) in order to raise their expenses for training.

3.2.2.7 Receive: Templates

The few Receive: templates presently included in HTemp are fully reproduced
in Fig. 3.19.

Table 3.31 Produce:PositiveCondition/Result and Produce:Growth occurrences

conc13.c4)	PRODUCE	SUBJ	FOOD_AND_DRUG_ADMINISTRATION_USA
		OBJ	(SPECIF approval_
			FOOD_AND_DRUG_ADMINISTRATION_USA)
		BENF	(SPECIF CYBERONICS_
			(SPECIF medical_company USA_))
		TOPIC	(SPECIF EXPERIMENT_1 CYBERONICS_)
		CONTEXT	(SPECIF therapy_ depression_)
		date-1:	(1999-10-01), 1999-10-11
		date-2:	

Produce:PositiveCondition/Result (6.52)

*Beginning of October, 1999, the Food and Drug USA Administration has notified to Cyberonics its
approval concerning the experiment about the therapy for depression*

*conc47.12)	PRODUCE	SUBJ	(SPECIF publisher_ GERMANY_): (GERMANY_)
		OBJ	growth_
		TOPIC	(SPECIF training_expenditure
			(SPECIF publisher_ GERMANY_))
		date-1:	1998-02-24
		date-2:	1998-12-31

Produce:Growth (6.62)

*(On February 24, 1998, the German publishers have made known they will take steps in order) to
increase their expenses for training in 1998*

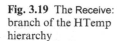

Fig. 3.19 The Receive:
branch of the HTemp
hierarchy

The Receive:BodyOrnament template has been introduced to take into account some specific applications in the "Beauty Care" style, e.g. to represent information like "receiving, by micro-pigmentation process, a permanent (tattooed) cosmetic eyebrow to obviate a severe eyebrow default." An example of use of Receive:MedicalProcess is given in Table 3.32.

In Table 3.32, medical_course_of is a specific term of medical_process; severe_acne_medicament is a specific term of acne_medicament, which is in turn a specific term of artefact_ through medicament_ and medical_tool/

Table 3.32 A Receive:MedicalProcess occurrence

skin3.c20)   (COORD skin3.c21 skin3.c22)

The two predicative occurrences skin3.c21 *and* skin3.c22 *are logically related.*

skin3.c21)   RECEIVE   SUBJ   HEAVEN_LITTLE_ANGEL: (TORONTO_ON)
                         OBJ   (SPECIF MEDICAL_COURSE_OF_1 (SPECIF cardinality_
                                        2))
                         TOPIC   (SPECIF ACCUTANE_ severe_acne_ medicament)
                         CONTEXT   (SPECIF therapy_
                                        (SPECIF teenager_acne HEAVEN_LITTLE_ANGEL))
                         date-1:   1999-01-01
                         date-2:   2001-12-31

Receive:MedicalProcess (7.13)

Over the last two years, Heaven's Little Angel has been on two courses of Accutane, a drug to be used for severe acne problems

skin3.c22)   OWN   SUBJ   MEDICAL_COURSE_OF_1
                         OBJ   property_
                         TOPIC   (SPECIF duration_ (SPECIF month_ (SPECIF cardinality_
                                        6)))
                         date-1:
                         date-2:

Own:SimpleProperty (5.11)

The courses of Accutane were semestrial courses

product. Making reference to the logical/semantic links between the two predicative occurrences of this table, we can note that, *in internal format* (Béatrice format, see Section 2.2.2.2), *all the predicative occurrences hold a list of all the*

Table 3.33 The Receive:GetMoney template with an example

(a)

name: Receive:GetMoney
father: Receive:TangibleThing/Process
position: 7.13
NL description: "Raise, Get, Receive Money (Transfer Already Realized)"

RECEIVE	SUBJ	*var1*: [(*var2*)]
	OBJ	(SPECIF *var3 var4* (SPECIF *var5 var6*))
	SOURCE	*var7*: [(*var8*)]
	[BENF	*var9*: [*var10*]]
	[MODAL	*var11*]
	[TOPIC	*var12*]
	[CONTEXT	*var13*]
	{[modulators], ≠abs}	

var1 =	human_being_or_social_body
var3 =	money_
var4 =	currency_
var5 =	amount_
var6 =	numerical_value, qualifier_
var7 =	human_being_or_social_body
var9 =	human_being_or_social_body
var11 =	symbolic_label, temporal_sequence, transaction_
var12 =	sortal_concept
var13 =	situation_, symbolic_label
var2, var8, var10 =	location_

(b)

mod2.c12)	RECEIVE	SUBJ	ABU_SAYYAF_GROUP
		OBJ	(SPECIF money_ currency_ (SPECIF amount_ large_))
		SOURCE	PHILIPPINE_GOVERNMENT
		TOPIC	(COORD1
			(SPECIF hostage_release TONG_KET_MING)
			(SPECIF hostage_release LAO_CHUNG_LAW)
			(SPECIF hostage_release SO_CHI_MING))
		date-1:	(1999-06-01), 1999-11-27
		date-2:	

Receive:GetMoney (7.13)

The Abu Sayyaf Group has received an important amount of money from the Philippine Government for the release of the three hostages binding occurrences where they appear – in our case, both skin3.c21 and skin3.c22 can then quickly refer to the binding occurrence skin3.c20.

An example of the Receive:GetMoney template is given in Table 3.33.

The Receive:GetMoney templates are characterized by the *mandatory use*, in the OBJ role fillers, of the *"amount of money" formal structure* introduced in Table 3.2 (NKRL's idioms) and already met in some examples of the previous sections: see Table 3.18 (conc14.c2) and Table 3.30 (conc8.c6). This structure can be considered as an example of a *complex NKRL idiom*. We can note, in the occurrence mod2.c12 of Table 3.33, the use of the generic concept currency_ given that, in the original document, this particular currency is not specified; large_ is a non_sortal_concept, specific term of property_ through size_attribute and qualifier_.

The predicative occurrences derived from the Receive:DesiredAdvice template are characterized by the *mandatory presence* of the modal modulator wish; see Table 2.13 and the discussion of Section 3.2.2.1. In these occurrences, *the filler of the OBJ slot is necessarily a specific term or instance of advice_*, which is in turn a specific term of information_content through weigthy_statement, etc. An example of use of this template is shown in Table 3.34. Note, in this example, the use of the "priority rule" (see Section 2.2.2.3) in the "structured argument" (expansion) used to fill the TOPIC role.

3.3 In the Guise of Winding Up

In Chapter 2, we described NKRL as a generic computer science environment that supplies tools for building up conceptual structures suitable to encode the "meaning" of (nonfictional) narrative situations. The aim of the present chapter is twofold:

Table 3.34 An example of Receive:DesiredAdvice occurrence

skin1.c8)	RECEIVE	SUBJ	CRYSTAL_EYES: (KANATA_ON)
		OBJ	advice_
		SOURCE	BEAUTYNET_COMMUNITY
		TOPIC	(ALTERN1
			(SPECIF use_
			NOVA_UNDEREYE_CREAM)
			(SPECIF use_ baby_oil))
		CONTEXT	(SPECIF therapy_ (SPECIF undereye_dry_skin
			CRYSTAL_EYES))
		{wish}	
		date-1:	2001-12-28
		date-2:	

Receive:DesiredAdvice (7.311)

On December 28, 2001, Crystal Eyes wishes to receive an advice from the Beauty Net community about the utilization of baby oil or of a commercial product (Nova Undereye Cream) in the context of her eye dry skin problem.

- on the one hand, supplying the NKRL's user with a *rich set of examples* that illustrate the *practical use of the above tools*;
- on the other hand, and more important, introducing a set of *predefined conceptual structures, "ready to use,"* that can be considered as part and parcel of the NKRL language/environment.

These "ready-to-use" structures compose *two complete ontologies*: an *ontology of concepts* (HClass) and an *ontology of events* (HTemp); these ontologies (which can be, in case, augmented and modified in a very easy way) already cover a *vast portion of the narrative domain*, and facilitate then the task of the user dealing with the representation/exploitation of "narrative" material.

The main characteristics of HClass are the following:

- From a purely formal point of view, this ontology can be considered as a *"normal" ontology of concepts* like those that can be set up using, for example, the Protégé tools. Note, in this context, that even if specific NKRL tools have been created to modify and augment HClass (see Section 2.2.1 and Appendix A), successful experiments have been carried out in the past for reconstructing significant fragments of this ontology using the standard environments in the Protégé style. From the point of view of its *conceptual organization*, HClass introduces, however, *some significant novelties* that make it *quite different* from well-known "upper level" ontologies like those proper, for example, to the CYC, SUMO, DOLCE or CG projects.
- The *main architectural principle of HClass*, then, concerns the *differentiation between* sortal_concept *and* non_sortal_concept; the two main branches of HClass stem from these two upper level concepts. The sortal_concept(s) correspond to general notions that, like the notion of "chair" (a physical object), *can be directly embodied into enumerable specimens (instances)*. The non_sortal_concept, like "gold" (a substance), can admit further specializations (see white_gold or red_), *but cannot be directly embodied into enumerable specimens*, like a hypothetical GOLD_1.
- The non_sortal_concept component of HClass is formed of *two branches*, i.e. property_ and pseudo_sortal_concept. The second branch deals with *very controversial notions* like those of colour_ and substance_. With respect to substance_, for example, we *refute the "physicalist" thesis* supported by Douglas Lenat and his colleagues according to which substances like "wood," "gold" or "peanut butter" should be interpreted as *the collection of all the possible enumerable "pieces" of wood, gold and peanut butter in the world*. In our interpretation, when it is really needed to deal with *individuals* in a "substance" context, we must have recourse to *high-level sortal concepts* as physical_object or artefact_ and from these (thanks to the passage through further specializations) then obtain *individuals* (i.e. instances of sortal concepts) like PIECE_OF_WOOD_27 or GOLD_NECKLACE_7. Sortal concepts like piece_of_gold_jewellery (which admits *direct instances*) and *non-sortal* concept like gold_ share, however, some *"intrinsic"*

properties, i.e. some slots of the "attribute" type (see Section 2.2.1.3), like ColourOf, MeltingPoint, PhysicalState and the corresponding values.

- The greatest fraction of the HClass concepts is included in the "sortal" branch of HClass. This branch is partitioned into two sub-hierarchies, i.e. entity_ and situation_. The *main criterion* used to organize the "sortal" domain, therefore, is that of distinguishing the *entities* (roughly corresponding to "endurants" in DOLCE) from the *situations* ("perdurants") where these entities are involved.

- Speaking of sortal concepts, we can immediately note that NKRL is *scarcely interested* in emphasizing the differences among notions like "Physical," "Non-physical," "Abstract," "Tangible," "Intangible," etc. that are largely utilized in other ontologies (see Section 3.1.1.3). In NKRL, an HClass sortal concept such as fire_breathing_dragon is simply a specific term of entity_ and, like any sortal_concept, can then be directly "materialized" into a "legal" instance like GLAURUNG_. Another interesting point concerns the presence of a *sortal concept like* reified_event. This is justified by the fact that the *events represented by means of templates and occurrences* must be *"structured events,"* i.e. they must be characterized by the *explicit presence* of a predicate, of its arguments (actors, objects, instruments, etc.) introduced by roles, plus additional information in case. If we do not know the structural details of an event, or if such details are uninteresting, then it is possible to represent simply the event as an *individual* instance of one of the specific terms of reified_event (e.g. president_bush_interview_49).

- From a strict *"functional"* point of view, the HClass hierarchy fulfils *two main tasks*. The first consists in using its terms *to specify the constraints associated with the variables of the HTemp templates*. Normally, (high-level) *concepts* are used for this function even if, at least in principle, nothing precludes *individuals* to be used for specifying constraints. The second task concerns *checking*, when these variables have been replaced by actual values in the derived occurrences, that *these values (role fillers) are really consistent with the original constraints*; this congruence check implies traversing the HClass tree to find a legal path between the actual value and the constraint. Given the importance of these duties for the general economy of NKRL, *no ambiguity* about the general structure of HClass (and, in particular, of its upper level) can be allowed.

While HClass can be likened to a *quite standard* ontology of concepts, HTemp seems to represent a *relatively isolated example* in the present ontological landscape (see Section 3.2.1). Some important characteristics of HTemp are the following:

- The HTemp hierarchy is a tree structured into seven branches where each branch corresponds to one of the seven semantic predicates described in Table 2.3, i.e. each branch includes only templates built up around a specific predicate.

- The Behave: branch of HTemp contains some interesting conceptual constructions. For example, the templates of the type Behave:HumanProperty are used in situations where one or more personages perform according to a given "function," "task" or "role"; see the Behave:Role template and its specializations. The Behave:Attitude templates are used when a SUBJ(ect) manifests directly a given behavior, real or purely speculative, in favor or against, a given person, social body, situation/activity, etc. The Behave: templates are also used to translate the general idea of "acting to obtain a given result." In this case, a complex conceptual construction must be used where a predicative occurrence, which must necessarily be an instance of a Behave:Focus template, is used to express the "acting" component (i.e. it allows us to identify the SUBJ(ect) of the action, the temporal coordinates, possibly the MODAL(ity) or the instigator (SOURCE), etc.), a second predicative occurrence is used to express the "intended result" component, and a third occurrence, a "binding" one, necessarily labeled making use of the GOAL operator, is then used to link the previous two.
- The Exist: templates can be classed in two main categories. The specializations of Exist:BePresent are used to represent situations/events where a given entity, human or not, is present at a given location. The specializations of Exist: OriginOrDeath are used to represent the "birth" or the "final end" or a given entity, e.g., the creation or the dismantling of a social body, company, political party, university etc. The bulk of the Experience: templates are used to represent situations where a given entity, human or not, is subject to some sort of "experience" (illness, richness, economical growth, starvation, success, racism, violence...) that can be either "positive" or "negative."
- The Move: templates are distributed into four branches: Move:TransferTo-Someone, Move:ForcedChange, Move:TransmitInformation and Move: AutonomousDisplacement. These templates present some interesting syntactic variants linked, at least partly, to the different possible arrangements of the "location" lists. For example, an "autonomous movement" of the SUBJ (Move:AutonomousDisplacement templates) is always interpreted as "The SUBJ moves herself/himself/itself as an OBJ"; the location associated with the SUBJ is then interpreted as the "initial location," and the location associated with the OBJ as the "arrival location." They must be strictly different. The Move:ForcedChange templates are used whenever an agent (SUBJ) moves an entity (OBJ = physical object, animate entity, process, ...) from the "initial location" of this entity to its "arrival location": the "initial" and "final" destination are now represented, respectively, by the initial and final term of the location list associated with the filler of the OBJ role. The Move: StructuredInformation template is typically used in the framework of second-order "completive constructions"; see Section 2.3.1.
- Apart from representing the different nuances of the notion of "possessing some sort of entity," the Own: templates, under the Own:Property form, are employed to specify the "properties" of NKRL (sortal) entities (to the exclusion of human being and social bodies) when: (i) these properties are

particularly numerous and it is then more appropriate to distribute them onto several predicative occurrences; (ii) the accumulation of a multiplicity of "properties" within the same SPECIF list blurs the understanding of the predicative occurrence where the SPECIF list appears; (iii) it is formally impossible to add properties to a given item, e.g. when the latter is included within a "location" list. The exclusion of human beings and social bodies is linked with the fact that their "properties" must be described making use of the Behave: templates.

- There are several sorts of Produce: templates, which can then be used to represent a number of conceptual domains. Some examples are mentioned here; see Section 3.2.2.6 for more details. The meaning of the Produce:Entity templates (e.g. Produce:Hardware) is self-evident. Examples of the Produce: PerformTask/Activity templates are, for example, Produce:Buy and Produce:-Sell (in the predicative occurrences derived from these two templates, the filler of the OBJ role is necessarily purchase_ or sale_ or specializations/instances of these two last concepts). Another Produce:PerformTask/Activity template is Produce:Violence; a specialization of this last template is, for example, Pro-duce:HumanBeingKilling. The templates of the Produce:Acceptance/Refusal type can be used to represent, for example, a refusal to pay a given ransom. An important specialization of Produce:RelationInvolvement is Produce:Mutual-Committment, to be used to represent all forms of "agreement" among several participants. They are mentioned in a COORD(ination) list that fills the SUBJ role and that is duplicated as filler of the BEN(e)F(iciary) role. Produce:PositiveCondition/Result is an example of the Produce:CreateCondition/Result templates; it can be used to express, for example, an official approval with respect to a given action/situation. An occurrence derived from the Produce:-Growth specialization of the Produce:Increment/Decrement template can be employed to represent the increase/acceleration/intensification/amplification, etc. of a given process/action.
- Important Receive: templates are Receive:GetMoney (the format of the OBJ fillers follows the standard NKRL format for "amount of money") and Receive:DesiredAdvice. In the occurrences derived from this last template, the use of the modal modulator wish is mandatory.

Chapter 4
The Query and Inference Procedures

We will describe in this chapter the (*implemented*) tools that will allow a user to utilize concretely the *conceptual structures* and the *actual contents* introduced in the two previous chapters. These tools can be grouped in two categories:

- Tools that, in an *information retrieval style,* allow one to recover from a knowledge base of NKRL occurrences all the predicative occurrences that correspond to a user's request for specific information. Some elementary inference procedures of the "subsumption" type that make use of the generic/ specific organization of the HClass elements will be used in this context.
- *Advanced inference tools* that, using as basic building blocks the unification/ filtering procedures developed for the previous task, allow the system, among other things to: (i) answer in some way to a direct query that failed by supplying the user with information that is *logically/semantically related* with the information originally searched for; (ii) search for *all the "implicit" relationships* (e.g. the "causal" ones) that can exist among the pieces of information registered in the knowledge base and that, to be disclosed, require the use of specific procedures composed of sequences of logically-related steps of reasoning.

4.1 "Search Patterns" and Low-level Inferences

The *basic building block* for all the NKRL querying and inference procedures is represented by *Fum*, the "filtering unification module." It takes as input specific NKRL data structures called "*search patterns.*"

Search patterns (which can be considered as the NKRL counterparts of NL queries) are NKRL data structures that supply the *general framework of informa-tion to be searched for*, in an information retrieval style, within a knowledge base of conceptual annotations ("metadocuments"). They offer, then, the possibility of querying this base *directly*.

Formally, a search pattern can be assimilated to *specialized/partially instan-tiated templates* where all the "*explicit variables*" – identified by conceptual labels in the *var$_i$* style in their external coding, (see the templates introduced in

Chapter 3) have been *replaced by concepts/individuals compatible with the original constraints* imposed on these variables. The correspondence between search patterns and the predicative occurrences of the knowledge base follows then a sort of "positional approach" [Bailey et al., 2005], where the *pattern mimics the predicative occurrences to be queried by specifying the positions of the data that must be retrieved, by pattern-matching techniques, within these predicative occurrences.*

During a (successful) retrieval operation, any *HClass concept* (to be assimilated now to an *implicit variable*) that occurs in a search pattern can *match/unify* (in the corresponding predicative occurrences of the knowledge base) *all the "identical" concepts, but also all the "subsumed" concepts* (i.e. all the specifications of this concept compatible with the structure of HClass) *and all the individuals representing its own instances and all the instances of the subsumed concepts.* This way of operating corresponds to a sort of *semantic/conceptual expansion* of the original pattern; we can then define the process of search patterns unification as a *first level of inferencing* of NKRL.

The set of predicative occurrences that globally correspond to (are unified by) a given search pattern constitutes the *answer* to the query represented by the pattern.

The upper part of Table 4.1 represents a (fictitious) predicative occurrence, ex.c8, corresponding to the narrative fragment "On June 12, 2006, John and Peter were admitted (*together*) to hospital" – note that adding the indication "together" forces the introduction of JOHN_ and PETER_ as arguments of a COORD(ination) list; see Section 2.2.2.3. A simple example of search pattern, translating the query "Was John at the hospital in July/August 2006?" is then

Table 4.1 A simple example of search pattern

(a)

```
ex.c8)   EXIST    SUBJ    (COORD1 JOHN_ PETER_): (HOSPITAL_1)
                  {begin}
                  date-1:  2006-06-12
                  date-2:
Exist:HumanPresentAutonomously (2.2122)
```

On June 12, 2006, John and Peter were admitted (together) to hospital

(b)

```
EXIST
SUBJ:   JOHN_: (hospital_)
{}
date1:   2006-07-01
date2:   2006-08-31
```

Is there any information in the system concerning the presence of John at the hospital in July/August 2006?

presented in the lower part of Table 4.1 We note that this pattern derives from the template Exist:HumanPresentAutonomously (Section 3.2.2.2) that is also at the origin of occurrence ex.c8. The "mandatory" component of this template corresponds simply to EXIST SUBJ *var1: (var2)*, where the constraint on *var1* is human_being_or_social_body and the constraint on *var2* is location_. In the pattern, these two variables have then been replaced, respectively, by JOHN_, an individual instance of individual_person (a specific term of human_ being_... in HClass), and by hospital_, a concept that is a specific term of location_ through one of its specializations, public_premises. The two temporal attributes associated with the pattern, *date1* and *date2, constitute the "search interval" used to limit the search for unification to the slice of time that it is considered appropriate to explore*; see the technical details in Zarri [1998] and in Section 4.1.2.

In this example, the search pattern of Table 4.1b can successfully unify occurrence ex.c8, which then constitutes (one of) the answer(s) to the query represented by the pattern; see the next section for the technical details. *In the absence, in fact, of explicit, negative evidence, a given situation is assumed to "persist" within the immediate temporal environment of the originating event*; see again Zarri [1998] and Section 4.1.2.

We also note that (apart from the usual obligation of respecting the syntactic rules of NKRL) no *specific constraints* are required for building up the search pattern besides those, evident, that consist in specifying *directly within the pattern* the *essential elements* to be retrieved in the occurrences of the base. Therefore, we are not bothered, as in OWL-QL for example [Fikes et al., 2004], by the need of declaring "Must-Bind Variables," "May-Bind Variables," "Don't-Bind Variables," "Answer Patterns," etc.

We can note, more generally, that the NKRL approach to querying has very few elements in common with the approaches usually followed by the XML/RDF/OWL query languages. The latter normally make use of some sort of SQL-like syntax; moreover, they are mainly based on a strict "pattern-matching" vision where few "semantic" elements are taken into account, e.g. see the recent deliverable of the "RDF Data Access Working Group" about SPARQL [Prud'hommeaux and Seaborne, 2007]. An exception is represented by Xcerpt [Bry and Schaffert, 2003; Berger et al., 2004], whose deductive, rule-based nature seems to be particularly suitable for reasoning. With respect, now, to the specific OWL query languages, it is well known [Bailey et al., 2005], for example, that they "...are still in their infancy."

4.1.1 The Algorithmic Structure of Fum

As already stated, verifying the "semantic congruence" between a search pattern and some predicative occurrences is carried out by a specific module of the NKRL software called *Fum*. From a *strict query/answering point of view*, this matching process could be better defined as a simple *"filtering" process*, giving that all the variables, under the form of "implicit variables" (see above) *are only present on the search pattern side*. However, as we will see in the following when dealing with the high-level inference procedures of NKRL, the *Fum* procedures are also used *to compare source/target structures that both contain (explicit) variables*. This is why we will speak, in this section, of "unification" and "filtering" as they were synonymous.

4.1.1.1 Basic Principles

The fundamental principle underpinning the unification/filtering operations executed by *Fum* can be expressed informally in this way: *all the terms* (predicate, roles, simple arguments, expansions with their proper operators, locations, modulators) *used to build up a search pattern must be retrieved in the same order in the matched occurrences*, either in an *identical form* (e.g. the predicate and the roles), or as *subsumed concepts or instances of the implicit variables (concepts) used in the expansions and the locations of the pattern*. *Additional terms* – (roles, role fillers or elements of these fillers) with respect to those included in the pattern can be *freely retrieved in the matched occurrences without affecting the unification's result*. Special rules must be followed for the unification of the temporal data (see next section). We can express the above principle in other terms by saying that, for a successful unification, (i) the search pattern must be *fully included* within the matched occurrences (the unification is then *oriented*, from the pattern, the "query," towards the occurrences, the "targets") and (ii) the implicit variables (concepts) of the pattern must all find *a correspondence with some of their subsumed HClass terms*, concepts or individuals, within the matched occurrences. Making reference to the (successful) example of matching of Table 4.1, we can see that (ignoring temporal information for the moment):

- The predicate EXIST, declared in the pattern, is identical to the predicate used in occurrence ex.c8.
- The (unique) role used in both the pattern and the occurrence, SUBJ, is identical in the two structures. The possible presence of *additional roles* (with their fillers) *in the occurrence*, e.g. a MODAL role, should have *no influence* on the successful result of the unification. On the contrary, the presence of *additional roles in pattern (b)* would lead to a *failure*.
- No "implicit variables" (concepts) are present in the SUBJ filler of the pattern. In this case, it is intuitively easy to see that the structure of this filler is *congruent* with that of the SUBJ filler of the occurrence, which is represented by an "expansion" – *the precise rules for unification in the presence of expansions will be detailed below*. The term JOHN_ declared in the pattern's filler can be retrieved within the COORD1 list of the occurrence's filler: the filler of (b), i.e. the pattern, is then *"fully included"* within the filler of (a), i.e. the occurrence.

- An *implicit variable*, hospital_, is present in the pattern in the "subject location" position. An individual, HOSPITAL_1, an *instance of this implicit variable*, is present in the same location of the occurrence.
- No modulators are declared in the pattern. The presence of a modulator in the occurrence does not affect the result of the unification.

From the above, the *ordered sequence* of the unification operations between a query search pattern p_i and a target predicative occurrence c_j (ignoring the temporal data) is then the following:

- Check if the predicate is *the same* in p_i and c_j. If not, unification fails.
- Check if the list of all the roles used to set up p_i is *totally included* in the analogous list of c_j. If not, unification fails.
- Check if the list of all the modulators utilized in p_i is *totally included* in the analogous list of c_j. If not, unification fails.
- For *each role* utilized in p_i, check the *congruence* (i.e. the successful matching) of its *filler* with the *filler of the corresponding role* of c_j. If the two are *not congruent, then unification fails*. In case one of the two fillers, or both, are represented by *expansions* (i.e. if they are *structured fillers*), *the matching operations are particularly complex and are detailed in the next section*. In case the fillers are *both simple fillers*, the congruence is verified when (i) the two represent the *same individual* or (ii) the c_j filler, concept or individual, is *subsumed* by the p_i filler.
- For each *successful p_i filler*, *check if a location determiner exists*. If this is true, and if *no location determiner* is associated with the corresponding c_j filler, then *unification fails*. Otherwise, the *location congruence* is verified if *the list of terms* (often, only one term) representing the p_i location is *totally included* in the list of terms of the c_j location. Given that one or more of the p_i location terms can be represented by implicit variables (e.g. see the example of Table 4.1), the inclusion check is *successful* iff, for each one of these p_i location variables, *at least one subsumed term* can be found among the c_j location terms.

4.1.1.2 Unification/Filtering of Expansions

According to the above description, the unification operations executed by *Fum* can appear as particularly simple. This is not true when "expansions" appear among the fillers of p_i, c_j or both.

All the expansions (structured arguments) – independently of the fact of taking place within a search pattern or a predicative occurrence – must *necessarily conform* to the "priority rule" introduced in Section 2.2.2.3 and reproduced here for clarity's sake:

$$(\text{ALTERN}(\text{ENUM}(\text{COORD}(\text{SPECIF})))) \qquad (2.5)$$

The meaning of Eq. (2.5) is that it is *forbidden* to use within the scope of a list introduced by the binding operator B_j a list labeled in terms of one of the binding operators *appearing on the left* of B_j in the priority rule – e.g. it is impossible to use a list ALTERN within the scope of a list COORD. The practical result of the application of Eq. (2.5) is that *every expansion can be conceived as a tree-like structure that can have three sorts of different branches*: coord-branch, enum-branch and altern-branch, assembled into *three sorts of sub-trees*: coord-tree, enum-tree and altern-tree.

The *basic building blocks* of these tree-like structures are then the coord-branches, composed of a *single HClass entity*, concept or individual (the *head* of the coord-branch), possibly *specialized* through the association with a SPECIF list (the *tail* of the coord-branch):

< coord-branch > ::= < entity > | (SPECIF < entity > { < coord-branch > } +) (4.1)

An example of coord-branch could then be the following:

(SPECIF purchase_EYELINER_1 (SPECIF BOOK_17 (SPECIF cardinality_
    several_)))

describing a purchase of two sorts of items: an eyeliner and several books. According to the semantics of the SPECIF(ication) operator, the individuals EYELINER_1 and BOOK_17 denote the *main properties* of the "head" of the *global* coord-branch, purchase_. The internal SPECIF form supplies *additional information* about one of the two properties, BOOK_17, by saying that the books purchased are more than one. The representation under tree format of this example of coord-branch is given in Fig. 4.1, using the convention of *replacing* the SPECIF operators *by edges that comply with the logical structure of the global expansion*; the "tail" of the *global* coord-branch is formed of two *subordinates* coord-branches, etc.; see Eq. (4.1).

Note that each coord-branch in the form (SPECIF < entity > (SPECIF ...)) is *subsumed* by any other coord-branch obtained by cutting this branch at any level (i.e. the original branch is *more specific* than the new one): the two are then *congruent* from a unification point of view. Returning to the previous example, the global expansion is, in fact, *subsumed by more general structures* like, for example, (SPECIF purchase_ EYELINER_1 BOOK_17), (SPECIF purchase_ EYELINER_1), purchase_.

The coord-trees are *built upon* the coord-branches *by associating several of these branches*; the general definition of a coord-tree, therefore, is

< coord-tree > ::= (COORD1 { < coord-branch > } +)

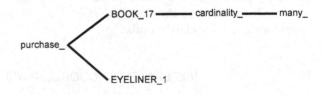

Fig. 4.1 Representation under tree-format of a coord-branch example

Fig. 4.2 An example of
coord-tree

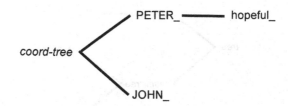

For example, the simple AECS expression

(COORD1 JOHN_ (SPECIF PETER_ hopeful_))

means, according to the definition of the COORD(ination) operator, that John and Peter take part, *in a coordinated and concomitant manner*, in a given event, e.g. hospital admission. The representation in tree format of this expression is given in Fig. 4.2. Note that the coord-trees *subsume* each of their coord-branches – two in Fig. 4.2 – i.e. *they carry the same information augmented*.

According to the priority rule, the enum-trees are *built upon* the coord-trees; they *subsume their branches*, i.e. their coord-trees:

< enum-branch > ::= < coord-branch > | < coord-tree >

< enum-tree > ::= (ENUM1 { < enum-branch > }+)

Figure 4.3 shows the tree-format representation of the following example:

(ENUM1 MARY_ (COORD1 JOHN_ (SPECIF PETER_ hopeful_)))

which, according to the semantics of the ENUM(eration) operator, means that Mary, John and Peter take part in a given event, with John and Peter *acting together*, while Mary gets involved in this event *independently*.

Eventually, the altern-trees are characterized by this syntax:

< altern-branch > ::= < enum-branch > | < enum-tree >

< altern-tree > ::= (ALTERN1 { < altern-branch > }+)

Accordingly, the tree-format representation of the example

(ALTERN1 (SPECIF JANE_ tired_) (ENUM1 MARY_ (COORD1 JOHN_
(SPECIF PETER_ hopeful_))))

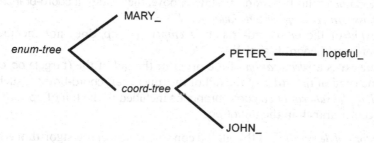

Fig. 4.3 An example of enum-tree

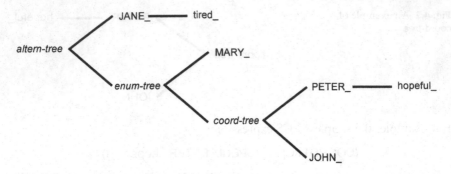

Fig. 4.4 An example of altern-tree

is shown in Fig. 4.4 ALTERN(ative)'s semantics *coincide* with that of an *exclusive OR*, stating that one and only one of its arguments – Jane on the one hand, and Mary *independently* from John *and* Peter on the other hand – takes part in the event.

Verifying the congruence of a *search pattern expansion* ep_i with a *predicative occurrence expansion* ec_j amounts, then, to making use of a *recursive algorithm* based on the following principles:

- *Unification fails* when the *priority level*, according to Eq. (2.5), of the ep_i tree is *higher* than that of the ec_j tree. For example, if the ep_i tree is an altern-tree and the ec_j tree is an enum-tree, then unification fails.
- When the priority level of the two trees is identical, or if the priority level of the ep_i tree is lower than that of the ec_j tree, then ep_i and ec_j are recursively decomposed into lower priority level trees until attaining, in case, the coord-branch level.
- The congruence is then verified iff, for every comparable priority level of ep_i and ec_j, *all* the ep_i coord-branches *can find a match* with the ec_j coord-branches.

Taking into account, now, the definition of coord-branch provided by Eq. (4.1), an ep_i coord-branch *unifies* an ec_j coord-branch iff:

- The *head* of the ep_i coord-branch is *identical to the head* of the ec_j coord-branch, or it *subsumes* this last head. As stated above, the head of a coord-branch is an *HClass term, concept or individual – AND*
- The *tail* of the ep_i coord-branch is *empty* (i.e. ep_i does not include any subordinated coord-branches) – *OR*
- There exists a *permutation* of the order of the tail of the (target) ec_j coord-branch and of the order of the tail of the (query) ep_i coord-branch, such that *each of the subordinated* coord-branches included in the tail of ep_i *unifies* an ec_j coord-branch in the tail of ec_j.

The *formal description* of this global congruence-checking algorithm is given, for example, in Zarri and Gilardoni [1996]. From a strictly programming point

Table 4.2 Congruence checking algorithm between ep_i and ec_j

ep_i/ec_j	coord-branch	coord-tree	enum-tree	altern-tree
coord-branch	succeeds/fails according to the success/ failure of the coord-branch unification process as detailed above	succeeds iff exists a successful match against one of the coord-branches of the target ec_j	succeeds iff exists a successful match against one of the coord-trees of the target ec_j	succeeds iff exists a successful match against one of the enum-trees of the target ec_j
coord-tree	fails	succeeds iff each ep_i coord-branch can find a successful match against one of the coord-branches of the target ec_j	succeeds iff the ep_i coord-tree can find a successful match against one of the coord-trees of the target ec_j	succeeds iff the ep_i coord-tree can find a successful match against one of the enum-trees of the target ec_j
enum-tree	fails	fails	succeeds iff each ep_i coord-tree can find a successful match against one of the coord-trees of the target ec_j	succeeds iff the ep_i enum-tree can find a successful match against one of the enum-trees of the target ec_j
altern-tree	fails	fails	fails	succeeds iff each ep_i enum-tree can find a successful match against one of the enum-trees of the target ec_j

of view, *this algorithm can be implemented according to the schema of Table* 4.2, where the first column represents all the possible tree formats of ep_i (the query) and the first line all the possible tree formats of ec_j (the target). Making use of this table, and supposing that ec_j corresponds to the expansion used to draw the altern-tree of Fig. 4.4, we will have:

- ep_i = JOHN_ succeeds;
- ep_i = (SPECIF JOHN_ hopeful_) fails;
- ep_i = (ENUM1 MARY_ JOHN_) succeeds;

- ep_i = (COORD1 PETER_ JOHN_) succeeds;
- ep_i = (COORD1 MARY_ JOHN_) fails;
- ep_i = (COORD1 JOHN_ (SPECIF PETER_ tired_)) fails;
- etc.

4.1.1.3 A Possible Extension of the AECS Query Language

An extension, from a "query" point of view, of the "standard" AECS sub-language has been proposed in several NKRL papers of the mid-1990s [e.g. Zarri and Gilardoni, 1996; Zarri and Azzam, 1997]. This proposal originates from the remark that, while (in general) a query about an AECS expansion must obviously be able to *exploit completely* the information carried by this structure, there exist situations in which *only a part of this information is really useful* and where supplying the user with all the retrieved information can be considered as *redundant and potentially disturbing*.

Let us consider, for example, the first of the above examples of ep_i/ec_j unification. According to the algorithm of Table 4.2, ep_i = JOHN_ unifies ec_j = (ALTERN1 ... (COORD1 JOHN_ (SPECIF PETER_ hopeful_)))) given that, at the end all the successive recursive decompositions, the ep_i coord-branch JOHN_ unifies the ec_j coord-branch JOHN_ included in the (COORD1 JOHN_ (SPECIF PETER_ hopeful_)) coord-tree. This means that, while the information we wanted to obtain *was simply whether* JOHN_ *takes part in a given event*, the answer we have obtained can be considered as potentially *redundant* because it states, among other things, that the presence of JOHN_ in the event is *necessarily linked* with the presence of another individual, PETER_.

We can then assume that a query language operating on the AECS structures must be able to *express a wide range of query modalities* and to *obtain constantly an unambiguous result*. Keeping always in mind the modalities for expressing these structures in term of trees, we can now state the basic requirements for a generalized unification of AECS expansions:

- It must be possible to specify a *perfect match*, defined as a match that succeeds iff the *tree representations* of the query (ep_i) and of the target (ec_j) AECS expression have *strictly identical structures*. Under these conditions, we can say that ep_i = (ENUM electronic_company bank_) succeeds against ec_j = (ENUM SHARP_CORP MEDIOBANCA_) – electronic_company and bank_ act as implicit variables, linked respectively to SHARP_CORP and MEDIOBANCA_ – but it fails in general against (ALTERN NEURO-VASX_ (ENUM SHARP_CORP MEDIOBANCA_)), against (ENUM NEUROVASX_ SHARP_CORP MEDIOBANCA_) and against (ENUM SHARP_-CORP (SPECIF MEDIOBANCA_ (SPECIF merchant_bank ITALY_)).
- It must be possible to specify a perfect match apart from "cardinality," i.e. a match that succeeds iff the query and the target AECS expression have identical structures without, moreover, taking into account the cardinality of the AECS lists. In this case, ep_i = (ENUM electronic_company bank_) can

succeed against (ENUM NEUROVASX_ SHARP_CORP MEDIOBANCA_), but still fails, obviously, against (ALTERN NEUROVASX_ (ENUM SHARP_CORP MEDIOBANCA_)).

- It must be possible to specify a *"subsumed" match*, i.e. a match that succeeds iff the query ep_i and the target ec_j expansion *carry information that can be considered as globally congruent from a semantic point of view*, e.g. we admit here the presence, in the target ec_j expansions, of additional SPECIF lists. This is the hypothesis underpinning the algorithm of Table 4.2 According to this paradigm, all the previous examples of ep_i/ec_j match succeed.
- It must also be possible to mix the above kinds of queries in such a way that, for example, *a perfect match is required for the top-level structure of the query and target trees but not for the constituent parts*. In this way, for example, ep_i = (ENUM electronic_company bank_) still fails against (ALTERN NEUROVASX_ (ENUM SHARP_CORP MEDIOBANCA_)), but it succeeds now against (ENUM SHARP_CORP (SPECIF MEDIOBANCA_ (SPECIF merchant_bank ITALY_)).

The implementation of this new, very complex strategy entails *augmenting the AECS sub-language with two new operators*, a STRICT-SUBSUMPTION operator and a STRICT-CARDINALITY operator, which take as argument an *HClass entity* (concept or individual) or an *expansion*; this latter, represented under the form of a tree, may consist of a coord-branch, a coord-tree, an enum-tree, or an altern-tree.

STRICT-CARDINALITY and STRICT-SUBSUMPTION have the following operational meaning:

- The presence of a STRICT-SUBSUMPTION operator forces the interpretation of the argument according to a stringent *"no-subsumption" principle*, thus requiring a match (*perfect match* – see the above definition) that complies strictly with the *type* (HClass entity, coord-branch, coord-tree, enum-tree, altern-tree)) of its argument.
- The presence of a STRICT-CARDINALITY operator forces the interpretation of the argument according to a stringent *"fixed-cardinality" principle*, thus requiring a match that complies strictly with the *cardinality* of its argument.
- The absence of any of the two special operators implies *a fully "subsuming" strategy*, implying then the fully validity of the algorithm of Table 4.2

A formal definition of the new operators and a formal description of the algorithm of Table 4.2, augmented in order to take this generalized unification strategy into account, are described, for example, in Zarri and Gilardoni [1996]. Some examples of use of the augmented algorithm are given below, assuming that the target ec_j expansion corresponds to (ENUM CHASE_MANHATTAN (COORD BNP_ (SPECIF MEDIOBANCA_ (SPECIF merchant_bank ITALY_) CITY_BANK))).

- The ep_i: (ENUM bank_ (STRICT-SUBSUMPTION (COORD BNP_ MEDIO-BANCA_ CITY_BANK))) succeeds. Note that the position of STRICT-SUB-SUMPTION within ep_i shows that this operator *concerns only the general structure of the* coord-trees, and not the structure of the single coord-branches.
- The ep_i: (ENUM bank_ (COORD BNP_ (STRICT-SUBSUMPTION MEDIO-BANCA_) CITY_BANK)) fails, because the STRICT-SUBSUMPTION restriction prevents now MEDIOBANCA_, a coord-tree, from matching a coord-branch.
- The ep_i: (ENUM bank_ (STRICT-CARDINALITY (COORD BNP_ MEDIOBANCA_))) fails, because of the STRICT-CARDINALITY restriction.
- The ep_i: (STRICT-SUBSUMPTION (ENUM bank_ (COORD credit_lyonnais mediobanca_))) succeeds. The STRICT-SUBSUMPTION restriction concerns only the *top-level structure* of the enum-trees.
- The ep_i: (STRICT-SUBSUMPTION (ENUM bank_ (STRICT-SUBSUMPTION BNP_))) fails, due to the internal (STRICT-SUBSUMP-TION BNP_) restriction.
- Etc.

The reasons that have led us to suggest the introduction of the two new AECS operators are, of course, *still very actual*. However, at least for the time being, the extended unification algorithm for expansions expounded above *has not been implemented in Fum*, which makes use, then, of the recursive matching algorithm as presented in Table 4.2 The reasons for this decision come down mainly to the following points:

- Some *difficulties* of the "average" NKRL operators *for dealing correctly with the two new operators*, linked mainly to the fact that these operators can be inserted at *any level* of the ep_i structures.
- Some difficulties in *foreseeing all the consequences of the use of the two new operators when dealing with the high-level inference procedures* – which, as already stated, are based on the use of *Fum*. These difficulties can be particularly embarrassing when these high-level inference procedures are used in an *integrated way*; see Section 4.2.4.
- The perception that, from a practical point of view, the *real benefits* of using the two new operators are not so important with respect to the *impact of the difficulties* evoked above.

4.1.2 Temporal Information and Indexing

As we have already stated (see Table 4.1), the presence in a search pattern p_i of a temporal interval delimited by the two temporal attributes *date1* and *date2* is now used to *limit the search for unification* between the search pattern and the occurrences of the knowledge base to the *particular time segment* that it is considered as appropriate to explore.

To make use of this facility implies, however, that the knowledge base *must be opportunely "indexed" from a temporal point of view*; this temporal indexing will utilize, then, *the temporal information associated with the original narrative documents* and echoed in NKRL format (see Section 2.2.2.4) in the *corresponding predicative occurrences*. The superimposition of indexes on the knowledge base allows us, in particular, *to speed up considerably all the retrieval operations*, given that the full unification/filtering operations between search patterns and knowledge base described in the previous sections will be executed only on *a small fragment of the original knowledge base* that already contains the "good" answers.

4.1.2.1 The Three Indexing Levels

In NKRL, we make use of a general indexing mechanism composed of *three different levels*, where the third one, the "temporal level," is the most complex and interesting one. More precisely:

- The first level of the indexing mechanism is very simple and corresponds to the *"predicate level" indexing*. This means that, during the unification operations, *Fum* will only take into account the predicative occurrences characterized by a semantic predicate that *coincides* with the predicate of the search pattern p_i.

- The second level of indexing is the *"main fillers level"*. For each of the four *"main roles"* (SUBJ, OBJ, SOURCE, BENF) of p_i, *Fum* will compare their *fillers* with *indexes corresponding to "main roles" fillers of each predicative occurrence* c_j. For efficiency's sake, the fillers *concretely considered in the predicative occurrences* c_j for setting up this level of indexing are only (i) *simple arguments*, i.e. concepts or individuals, or (ii) the *heads* (concepts or individuals) of all the possible coord-branches that it is possible to extract from a (complete) c_j filler. Data concerning this "main fillers level" indexing is "physically" associated with each occurrence c_j *at the time of its insertion within the knowledge base*. Note that, as usual, the correspondence *among p_i fillers and c_j indexing terms* is verified when (i) the two represent the same individual or (ii) the c_j indexing term, concept or individual, is subsumed by the p_i filler. Only the predicative occurrences that pass the "main fillers" test are taken into account by *Fum*.

- The third level of indexing is the *"temporal level"* – the main characteristics if this sort of indexing are illustrated below; see also Zarri [1998] for more details.

Implementing the third level of indexing implies, in practice, *superimposing on the knowledge base* of annotations/occurrences *a grid of nine lists*, organized according to the schema of Fig. 4.5 – see Section 2.2.2.4 for a complete definition of the notions of *temporal category* and *temporal perspective*. Each list is

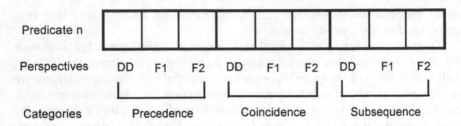

Fig. 4.5 Structuring the first and third levels of indexing

composed of *pairs* {*lc$_j$, dc$_j$*}, where *lc$_j$* corresponds to the *symbolic label of a particular predicative occurrence* c$_j$, and *dc$_j$* to one of the *four possible dates* (two for each temporal attributes, date-1 and date-2, see the examples of predicative occurrences in the previous two chapters) associated with c$_j$. The construction of the pairs, and their insertion in one of the nine lists, is carried out according to *two main criteria*:

- The first one consists of assuming that the nine lists *are arranged into three groups*, corresponding to the *three temporal categories, "precedence," "coincidence," "subsequence."* The labels and dates of all the predicative occurrences included in the knowledge base are then used to set up the pairs *associated with one of the three groups* according to the following rules:

  - The group corresponding to the category *precedence* consists of the {*lc$_j$, dc$_j$*} pairs derived from the predicative occurrences characterized by the presence of a *dc$_j$* such as *the event represented by this occurrence occurs before this dc$_j$*. For example, an occurrence c$_j$ translating the information "On September 5, 2006, John left the hospital," will involve the presence in the equivalent NKRL code of the *temporal modulator* end and of a *filled temporal attribute* date-1: 2006-09-05, the second temporal attribute date-2 being *empty*. Occurrence c$_j$ will then be represented *in precedence* with respect to the *dc$_j$* corresponding to date-1. As a consequence, its symbolic label *lc$_j$*, linked with *dc$_j$* = 2006-09-05, will form *one of the pairs to be inserted in the lists of the precedence group*.

  - The *subsequence* group is used to store the {*lc$_j$, dc$_j$*} pairs derived from predicative occurrences characterized by the presence of a *dc$_j$* such as *the event represented by the occurrence occurs after this particular date*. For example, an occurrence c$_j$ translating the information "On July 15, 2006, John was admitted to the hospital," will involve the presence of the *temporal modulator* begin and of a *filled temporal attribute* date-1: 2006-07-15, the second temporal attribute date-2 being *empty*. Occurrence c$_j$ is then represented *in subsequence* with respect to the *dc$_j$* corresponding to date-1. The label *lc$_j$*, linked with *dc$_j$* = 2006-07-15, will form *one of the pairs to be inserted in the lists of the subsequence group*.

- The *coincidence* group is used to store the $\{lc_j, dc_j\}$ pairs derived from the predicative occurrences characterized by the presence of a dc_j such as *the event represented by this occurrence occurs at that particular date*. For example, an occurrence c_j translating the information "On August 20, 2006, we can note that John was still at the hospital," will involve the presence of the *temporal modulator* obs(erve) and of a *filled temporal attribute* date-1: 2006-08-20, the second temporal attribute date-2 being *empty*. Occurrence c_j is then represented *in coincidence* with respect to the dc_j corresponding to date-1. The label lc_j, linked with dc_j = 2006-08-20, will form *one of the pairs to be inserted in the lists pertaining to the coincidence group*.

- The *coincidence* group is also used to store the pairs derived from the predicative occurrences of the "point event" type; see the example "On July 15, 2002, John went to the hospital to see a friend" (assuming here that the minimum temporal grain considered is the day). In this case, only the temporal attribute date-1 of the corresponding predicative occurrence c_j will be filled with 2006-07-15, the second temporal attribute date-2 being empty. Occurrence c_j is represented *in coincidence* with respect to the dc_j corresponding to date-1; *no temporal modulator is used*. The label lc_j, linked with dc_j = 2006-07-15, will then form *one of the pairs to be inserted in the lists of the coincidence group*.

- A last possibility can concern an original event that is *perfectly delimited from a temporal point of view*; see the example "Between July 15 and September 5, 2006, John was hospitalized." In this case, the corresponding occurrence c_j will be characterized by the fact that *both the temporal attributes* date-1 *and* date-2 *are filled*, date-1 being 2006-07-15 and date-2 being 2006-09-05; *no temporal modulator is used*. Occurrence c_j is then represented *in subsequence* with respect to date-1 and *in precedence* with respect to date-2. As a consequence, its symbolic label lc_j linked with a dc_j = 2006-07-15 *will form one of the pairs to be inserted in the lists of the subsequence group*, and the *same label* lc_j associated now with a dc_j = 2006-09-05 *will form another pair to be inserted in the lists of the precedence group*.

- The second criterion to be used for the implementation of the "temporal level" indexing consists in making use of the notion of *temporal perspective* (see Section 2.2.2.4) to choose, within each one of the three blocks, the *specific file* where to insert the $\{lc_j, dc_j\}$ pairs. More exactly:

  - The lists marked as DD in Fig. 4.5 are used to store the pairs where dc_j is *characterized by a "direct date" perspective*. No sort of fuzziness is then associated with this date, which is completely defined, as in "July 2, 2006, at noon."
  - The lists marked as F1 in Fig. 4.5 are used to store the $\{lc_j, dc_j\}$ pairs, where dc_j is *characterized by the fact of being a "first bound of a data fork."* We recall here that the "data fork" is the technique used in NKRL to

encode all *the four nondirect perspectives*, i.e. *"inclusion fork," "limit from which," "limit to which," "circa perspective."* To differentiate among them, it is then necessary to check whether the two terms of the fork correspond to "real" dates (*fork* perspective), to a real date and a "reconstructed" one (*from which* and *to which* perspectives), or to two reconstructed dates (*circa* perspective). In external format, reconstructed dates are included within round brackets; see the previous examples.

–   The lists marked as F2 in Fig. 4.5 are then used to store the $\{lc_j, dc_j\}$ pairs where dc_j *is characterized by the fact of being a "second bound of a data fork."*

4.1.2.2 The Selection Algorithm

Returning now to the *Fum* operations, when a search pattern p_i tries to unify a knowledge base, it extracts initially from this base a *first subset of predicative occurrences* that is coherent with the *two first selection criteria*, i.e. those we have called "predicate level" and "main fillers level" at the beginning of this section. Then the routines corresponding to the *"temporal level" indexing* are executed. For the most usual search patterns, i.e. the search patterns *without temporal modulators*, the selection algorithm that corresponds to the temporal level indexing is visualized graphically in Fig. 4.6; see Zarri [1998] for more details.

First, *Fum* separates each list into *three sections* that correspond to period1, etc., where the separators bound1 and bound2 represent the *two dates* included,

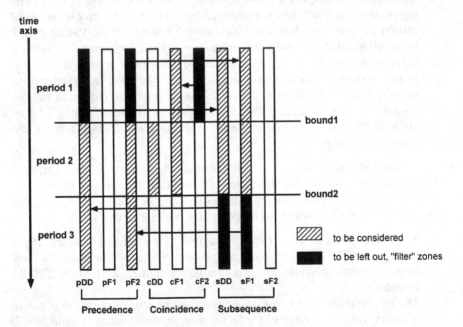

Fig. 4.6 The temporal index algorithm

respectively, in the first (*date1*) and second (*date2*) components of the *search interval associated with the search pattern* p_i. If only *date1* is filled in the search interval, then each list is split into two sections by the bound1 limit. In this way, 27 sub-lists are produced (or 18 if only one date appears in the search interval of p_i).

- The section of the list cDD corresponding to period2 is *definitely* to be selected. The occurrences c_i characterized by a temporal attribute date-1 represented *in coincidence* (point events, or occurrences associated with the modulator obs) and associated with a unique {lc_j, dc_j} pair located within this period take place in fact, at least partly, *within the search interval* bound1–bound2.
- The section of the list pDD corresponding to period2 is also to be selected: the corresponding occurrences *definitely end* (precedence = *until to* ...) *after* bound1 and *before* bound2 and, therefore, are located, at least partly, *within the search interval*. The section of the list sDD corresponding to the same period is also to be considered, since the corresponding events *definitely begin* (subsequence = *starting from*...) *within the search interval*.
- The section of the list pDD corresponding to period1 is *to be excluded*, since it refers to occurrences that *definitely end before* bound1; similarly, occurrences in the list sDD corresponding to period3 are to be excluded, since they *definitely begin after* bound2.

Occurrences mentioned in the {lc_j, dc_j} pairs located within the list pDD in period3 (occurrences that *end* after bound2) are *potentially* to be selected. However, before accepting one of these events, one must check that the same occurrence c_j (the same label lc_j) *does not also appear* in the pairs of the list sDD in period3 (this event would then *begin* and *end after* bound2). A situation of this type could be that of an event like "John has been hospitalized between September and December 2006" with respect to a search interval like 2006-07-01 (bound1)–2006-08-31 (bound2). The corresponding occurrence c_j (to be discarded) would in effect be classed *twice* in period3, both "in subsequence," date-1 = 2006-09-01 (associated with the pair {lc_j, 2006-09-01}), as well as "in precedence," date-2 = 2006-12-31 (associated with the pair {lc_j, 2006-12-31}). The section of the list sDD in period3, therefore, acts as an *exclusion filter* for the *corresponding part* of the list pDD (the occurrences that appear in both these two sections must not be selected); the same follows for the part of the list pDD in period1 with respect to the corresponding part of sDD.

A graphical example is shown in Fig. 4.7, where we have supposed that the search interval associated with a pattern p_i has given rise to the two limits bound1 (date1) = 2006-08-01 and bound2 (date2) = 2006-09-15. If we suppose now to consider a hypothetical predicative occurrence c_j having 2006-07-15 as filler of date-1 and 2006-09-05 as filler of date-2, then this will gives rise to two pairs: {lc_j, 2006-07-15} originated from date-1 and located on the sDD list, and {lc_j, 2006-09-05} originated from date-2 and located on the pDD list.

Fig. 4.7 An example of use
of the algorithm of Fig. 4.6

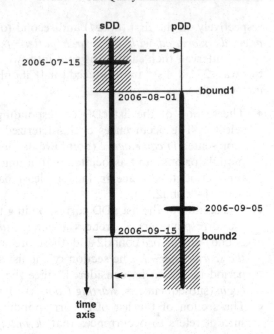

According to the above considerations, this occurrence *must be selected*. The corresponding event, in fact, *begins before the first search limit* as indicated by its sDD pair and *ends within the search interval* as indicated by its pDD pair. The two exclusion filters signaled in Fig. 4.7 are not activated for this specific occurrence.

To extend the above selection algorithm to the general case (the lists relative to the nondirect perspectives are now *nonempty*), the following considerations must be added:

- The *same group of occurrence labels* lc_j appears in the pairs associated with the lists pF1 and pF2 (the same is true for the lists cF1–cF2 and sF1–sF2). Supposing, for example, that an occurrence c_j is characterized by a date fork filling its second temporal attribute, date-2 (classed in precedence), its label lc_j will appear in a pair of the list pF1, linked with the date dc_{j1} representing the *first component* of this fork, as well as in the list pF2, linked with the date dc_{j2} representing the *second component* of the fork.
- We can then *avoid considering the lists pF1 and sF2*. The *"deciding conditions" for precedence* will be tested in fact on the *unique list pF2*, where the dates are *"lower down in the list"* in comparison with those contained *in the corresponding pairs of the list pF1*. Analogously, the *deciding conditions for subsequence* will be tested on the list sF1, where the dates are *"higher up."* If we then take into account an occurrence carrying the temporal information (forks) date-1: (2006-06-10, 2006-06-30), date-2: (2006-09-01, 2006-09-15), then the dc_j that will eventually be examined for the selection will be 2006-06-10 (dc_{j1}) on the list sF1 for the "subsequence" and 2006-09-15 (dc_{j2}) on the list pF2 for the "precedence."

- If we take the same argument for the lists pF2 and sF1 as we did for the corresponding DD lists, then we see that the portions to be *selected* are those of the list pF2 *that belong to* period2 *and* period3, and those of the list sF1 that *belong to* period1 *and* period2. The section of the list pF2 in period1 and that of the list sF1 in period3 are *definitely to be excluded*; they act, however, as *exclusion filters* with regard to the section of the list sF1 in period1 and to that of the list pF2 in period3 respectively.
- As for coincidence, it can easily be shown that the sections *to be selected* are those of the list cF1 in period1 and period2; the section of the list cF2 in period1 acts as an *exclusion filter* with respect to the section of the list cF1 in the same period.

The selection algorithms dealing with cases where a *temporal modulator*, i.e. begin, end, obs(erve), are associated with the search pattern are immediate extensions of the algorithm illustrated above. A detailed description of these algorithms, and a *formal definition*, can be found, for example, in Zarri [1998].

4.2 High-level Inference Procedures

The high-level inference procedures implemented in NKRL are characterized by the following general properties:

- All the NKRL high-level inference rules can be conceived as *implications* of the type

$$X \text{ iff } Y_1 \text{ and } Y_2 \ldots \text{ and } Y_n \tag{4.2}$$

where X is a *predicative occurrence or a search pattern*, according to the type of rule, see below, and $Y_1 \ldots Y_n$ – the NKRL translation of the successive *reasoning steps* that make up the rule – correspond to *partially instantiated templates*.
- According to the usual conventions of logic/rule programming, the different versions of the NKRL *InferenceEngine* understand, then, each implication as a *procedure* that reduces *problems* of the form X to a *succession of "sub-problems"* of the form Y_1 and $\ldots Y_n$.
- Each Y_i is interpreted in turn as a *procedure call* that tries to convert – using, in case, *backtracking procedures* – this reasoning step into (at least) a *successful search pattern* p_i able to unify one or several of the predicative occurrences c_j of the NKRL knowledge base.
- The *success of the unification operations* of the pattern p_i derived from Y_i means that *the reasoning step represented by Y_i has been validated*. *InferenceEngine* continues its work trying to validate the reasoning step corresponding to the sub-problem Y_{i+1}.

- In line with the presence of the operator "*and*" in Eq. (4.2), the implication represented by Eq. (4.2) is *fully validated* iff *all* the reasoning steps Y_1, Y_2 ... Y_n *are validated*.
- All the *unification operations* p_i/c_j make use only of the *matching/unification functions* supplied by the *Fum* discussed in the previous sections. *Fum* constitutes then the "*inner core*" of all the different versions of the *InferenceEngine* general environment included in the NKRL software.

From an operational point of view, NKRL high-level inference procedures concern *mainly* two classes of rules:

- *Hypothesis rules*. These rules allow building up automatically a sort of *causal explanation* – or, more modestly, a sort of "plausible context" – for a *narrative information (a predicative occurrence c_j) that has been retrieved within an NKRL knowledge base* (e.g. using *Fum* in a querying–answering mode). In a hypothesis context, the "head" X of Eq. (4.2) is represented by a *predicative occurrence*, c_j. Accordingly, the "reasoning steps" Y_i of Eq. (4.2) *must all be satisfied* (for each of them, at least one of the corresponding search patterns p_i must find a successful unification with the predicative occurrences of the base) in order that the set of c_1, c_2, ..., c_n predicative occurrences retrieved in this way *can be interpreted as a context/causal explanation of the original occurrence c_j*.
- *Transformation rules*. These rules try to *adapt*, from a *semantic* point of view, a search pattern p_i that *failed* (was unable to find a unification within the knowledge base) to the *real contents* of this base making use of a sort of *analogical reasoning*. In a transformation context, the "*head*" X of Eq. (4.2) is represented by a search pattern, p_i. The principle employed consists, then, in trying to *automatically "transform"* p_i into one or more *different $p_1, p_2, ..., p_n$ that are not strictly "equivalent" but only "semantically close"* (see Section 4.2.3) to the original one.

As we will see in the following, hypothesis and transformation rules are *very similar* from an *operational* point of view (the software modules used for their processing are identical or quite similar): their "heads" X, see again Eq. (4.2), are *different*, however – as already stated, they consist of a predicative occurrence c_j in a hypothesis context and of a pattern p_i in a transformation context – and their *semantics are also totally different*. For both, the processing requires the use of the *full power* of the NKRL *InferenceEngine* general environment. After some general considerations in the next section, these two classes of rules will be introduced, respectively, in Sections 4.2.2 and 4.2.3 Section 4.2.4 will explain, on the contrary, how they can be used in an "integrated" way – more exactly, how it is possible to use the transformation rules within a hypothesis context. This allows one both (i) to get rid of the strictly predefined logical schema that characterizes a hypothesis rule and, consequently, (ii) to enlarge considerably the range of possible results. Finally, Section 4.2.5 will supply some information about an additional class of simple NKRL inference rules, the "filtering" rules.

4.2.1 General Remarks about Some Reasoning Paradigms

According to what was expounded before, the NKRL inference procedures follow the *"rule/logic programming"* reasoning paradigm based on the so-called *resolution principle* [e.g. Bertino et al., 2001: 105–135]. This paradigm has given rise to *powerful logic programming languages* like Prolog and Datalog – in these, the implication rules are in the form of "Horn clauses" where, as in Eq. (4.2), at most one conclusion X is admitted – and to *successful rule programming tools* like the *forward-chaining/backward-chaining* systems used, among other things, in the Mycin-like expert systems. It still represents the basic paradigms for building up "business rules," e.g. see commercial products like Ilog's Jrules, FairIsaac's Blaze Advisor, Oracle's Business Rule Language, RuleBurst's Rules Based Engine Solution (supported by SAP), etc.; see also the Web site of the Business Rules Community at http://www.brcommunity.com.

The W3C languages in the OWL style follow, on the contrary, a *DL approach*, i.e. a form of knowledge representation that makes use for *reasoning*, basically, of *inference by inheritance*, a reasoning paradigm *orthogonal with respect to the rule/logic programming paradigm based on the resolution principle (and definitely less "expressive" than this last one)*. We can note that a form of *inference by inheritance* is used, as already seen, to implement the (*limited*) reasoning and inferencing capabilities of *Fum*. Because, then, of the *reduced "expressiveness" of the DL main inferencing component* – i.e. the automatic, *inheritance-based*, classification mechanism – *the reasoning mechanisms of the OWL-like languages are quite limited*. They are reduced in practice to offering some form of support for building up "standard" ontologies like (i) checking the *consistency* of classes/concepts (i.e. determining whether a class can have any instances) and (ii) calculating the *subsumption hierarchy* (i.e. arranging the classes according to their generic/specific relationships). To do this, the W3C scholars have at their disposal several OWL-compatible reasoning tools like RACER [Haarslev and Möller, 2003], Pellet [Sirin et al., 2006], FaCT++ [Tsarkov and Horrocks, 2006], etc. Extensions to FaCT++ to offer reasoning support for the new version of OWL, i.e. OWL 1.1, are described, for example, in Horridge et al. [2006].

The interest of being able to make use of *"rules" in the "resolution principle" style to go beyond the limitations of the reasoning tools in a strict DL framework* has been long since recognized. A pioneering and well-known work in this context is CARIN [Levy and Rousset, 1998; Goasdoue et al., 2000], a system that *integrates rules with a description logic model in a sound and complete way* by introducing some syntactic restrictions on the occurrence of DL terms in the head of the rules. Note that, *in a strict W3C languages context*, building up rule systems is a really complex problem given that (i) the *lack of the notion of "variable" in OWL* makes it impossible to rely on this language in its "native" form to build up "real" inference engines for rule processing and (ii) *no support for rules and rule processing* was introduced in the standard descriptions of these languages at the time of their conception. The consequence is that the whole *SW rule domain* seems to be in a *very early state of development*. Languages like RuleML [Boley et al., 2001], TRIPLE [Sintek and Decker, 2002)], and SWRL [Horrocks et al., 2004, 2005] – all based, roughly, on extensions of the inferential properties of Horn clauses and Datalog to deal with OWL-like data structures; see also [Rosati, 2005] in this context – appear to be, for the time being, *as quite limited with respect to the range of their possible applications and particularly complicated to be used in practice.*

Let us consider, for example, SWRL (the "Semantic Web Rule Language") that seems to represent now a sort of "standard" in the SW rule domain. This rule language "augments" OWL by allowing a user to create if–then rules written in terms of OWL classes, properties and individuals. Making use of the "open world" assumption, it does not support "negation by failure"; additionally, it does not support nonmonotonicity. Moreover, being based on a combination of OWL Lite and OWL DL sub-languages, it cannot support OWL Full and RDF/RDFS. It can, however, make use of user-defined "built-ins": built-ins are predicates in the style of "equal," "greater-than," "absolute-value," etc. that take one or more arguments and evaluate to true if these arguments satisfy the predicate. However, in spite of all these limitations, being more "expressive" than OWL DL, SWRL is not completely "decidable" (more precisely, it is "semi-decidable"); according, then, to the well-known fascination of the DL scholars for "safety," rules are often written in a decidable subset of SWRL, "DL-Safe SWRL" [e.g. Motik et al., 2005]. The practical result is that *DL-Safe SWRL variables can only be bound to known individuals in a knowledge base (in an OWL ontology)*; this is incompatible with NKRL's philosophy, where variables in the rules can also be bound, for generality's sake, to *any sort of concept* of the HClass hierarchy.

From a practical point of view anyway, an *operational* inference engine able to make *directly a full use of SWRL* seems not yet to exist. For example, users can directly load the SWRL files into Pellet and have their rules parsed and processed; however, only the DL-Safe Rules subset of SWRL can be presently used with Pellet. The "normal" strategy for executing the SWRL rules seems, then, at least for the moment, that of making use of "external" rule engines like Jess (http://herzberg.ca.sandia.gov/jess/) or Algernon (http://algernon-j. sourceforge.net/). This can be done through, for example, the SWRLJessTab, a plug-in of the Protégé-OWL plug-in [e.g. O'Connor et al., 2005] – and after having previously downloaded separately the Jess rule engine. Note that Jess (a rule engine based on the Rete algorithm) –see Bertino et al. [2001: 131–135] for a functional description of this algorithm – is, basically a re-implementation in Java terms of tools like CLIPS that go back to OPS5, the 1970s and the expert-systems era.

We conclude this section by mentioning the existence, in a W3C context, of a Rule Interchange Format (RIF) Working Group (see http://www.w3.org/2005/ rules), which is in charge of producing W3C recommendations for interoperability on the Web among a variety of rule-based formats. It should then be able to make propositions for allowing the interchange of formalisms as different as Horn-clause logics, higher order logics, production systems, etc.

4.2.2 Hypothesis Rules

To describe the functioning of *InferenceEngine* in a "hypothesis" environment we will make use of a very simple example that, unlike the complex hypotheses used in some NKRL applications – e.g. see the use of NKRL inference rules in a "terrorism" context [Zarri, 2005] – implies only the presence of *two steps of reasoning* and can then be described informally in (some) detail making use of a limited number of sentences.

Let us then suppose we have *directly retrieved*, thanks to an appropriate search pattern p_j, the occurrence conc2.c34 (see Table 4.3), which corresponds to the information: "Pharmacopeia, a USA biotechnology company, has received 64,000,000 US dollars from the German company Schering in connection with an R&D activity." We will suppose, moreover, that this occurrence is not *explicitly* related with other occurrences in the base by second-order elements (e.g. binding occurrences). Under these conditions, we can activate the modules of the "hypothesis" version of *InferenceEngine*, asking them to try to *link up automatically the above information with other information present in the base*. If this is possible, then this latter information will represent, in a way, a sort of "causal explanation" of the information originally retrieved – i.e., in our example, an "explanation" of the money paid to Pharmacopeia by Schering. A rule that can fit our case is hypothesis *h1* reproduced in Table 4.3, where the payment is related to the successful fulfillment by Pharmacopeia of an order placed by Schering.

Of course, this is *only one of the possible explanations* for the transfer of money from an individual or a company to another company: sometimes a company gets money because, for example, it is a nonprofit organization, or there are some charity aspects in the transfer, etc. Hypothesis *h1* must, then, be conceived as a *member of a "family" of inference rules, all related to the "transfer of money" theme* that, in a real context, should all be tried to find the most "*plausible*" one.

From an algorithmic point of view, all the *InferenceEngine* versions work according to a *backward chaining approach with (at least at the moment, see also the "Conclusion") chronological backtracking* [Clocksin and Mellish, 1981]. The differences with respect to other applications of this well-known approach (Mycin, Prolog, ...) are mainly linked with the *unusual complexity proper of the NKRL data structures*; this implies, after a deadlock, carrying out particularly difficult operations of restoration of the program environment to be able to return to the previous choice point. For a correct execution of the backtracking operations, four "environment variables" are used.

Table 4.3 An example of hypothesis rule

(a)

conc2.c34)	RECEIVE	SUBJ	(SPECIF PHARMACOPEIA_(SPECIF biotechnology_company USA_))
		OBJ	(SPECIF money_ usa_dollar (SPECIF amount_ 64,000,000))
		SOURCE	(SPECIF SCHERING_(SPECIF pharmaceutical_company GERMANY_))
		TOPIC	r_and_d_activity
		date-1:	
		date-2:	

(b)

Hypothesis _h1_

premise:

RECEIVE	SUBJ	var1
	OBJ	money_
	SOURCE	var2

_var1 = company__

_var2 = human_being, company__

A company has received some money from another company or a physical person

first condition schema (_cond1_):

PRODUCE	SUBJ	(COORD var1 var2)
	OBJ	var3
	BENF	(COORD var1 var2)
	TOPIC	(SPECIF process_var4)

_var3 = mutual_relationship, business_agreement_

_var4 = artefact__

The two parties mentioned in the premise have concluded an agreement about the creation of some sort of "product"

second condition schema (cond2):

PRODUCE	SUBJ	var1
	OBJ	var4
	MODAL	var5
	CONTEXT	var3

_var5 = industrial_process_

The company that received the money has actually created the product mentioned in the first condition schema

- VALAFF ("*valeurs affectables*" in French), holds the *values provisionally affected to the variables var$_i$ of the three schemata of Table 4.3 (*premise*, cond1* and *cond2*) that implement the reasoning steps of the hypothesis; these values can be *deleted*, in case, after a backtracking operation.
- DESVAR holds the *final values associated with the variables var$_i$ when the successful processing* of one of the reasoning steps (reasoning schemata) has been *completed*.
- RESTRICT holds all the *constraints* (HClass terms) associated with the variables *var$_i$ of the different reasoning schemata; these constraints will be used to *build up systematically all the search patterns* that can be derived from these schemata; see below.
- OCCUR holds the list of the *symbolic names of all the occurrences retrieved by the search patterns* derived from the reasoning schemata; the values bound to *var$_i$ that have been retrieved in these occurrences are used to build up the VALAFF lists.

The first set of inference operations is carried out by the *Exeprem* module of *InferenceEngine*, and consists in trying to unify, *using Fum*, the *premise* of the hypothesis (see Table 4.3b) and the *event* (the payment in our case, see conc2.c34) *to be "explained"* – more exactly, in trying to unify (using *Fum*) *this event and the different search patterns derived from the premise by systematically substituting to the variables var1 and var2 (see Table 4.3b) the associated constraints*. As already stated, a search pattern processed by *Fum* can only include implicit variables (concepts). In this way, this first step allows us:

- to verify that the hypothesis tested is, in principle, suitable to "explain" the particular event at hand;
- to *obtain* in case, from the external environment (the event, i.e. conc2.c34), *some values for the premise variables var1, var2*.

Note that, in an *inference context*, the unification of a search pattern with an occurrence c_i of the base *is not tried at all* if this occurrence includes a negv modulator, *with the exception of the specific case where* negv *is explicitly mentioned in the search pattern*. See also, in this context, the remarks about negv in Section 2.2.2.4 (Table 2.13). Note also that this modus operandi is valid for all the unifications executed by *Fum* within the different *InferenceEngine* versions, *independently, then, from the type of rule examined and from the type of "reasoning step" processed*.

In the present case (see Table 4.3b), the premise variable *var1* can only be substituted by the constraint company_; on the contrary, two substitutions, *var1* = human_being and *var2* = company_, are possible for the variable *var2*; see the two patterns (a) and (b) in Table 4.4. A first search pattern will then be built up by substituting, according to the *chronological approach*, the first constraint, human_being, for *var2* (i.e. a value human_being is *provisionally associated* with var2 in VALAFF). This means that *Fum* will *try to execute*

Table 4.4 Two search patterns can be derived from the premise

event to be "explained":

conc2.c34)	RECEIVE	SUBJ	(SPECIF PHARMACOPEIA_(SPECIF biotechnology_company USA_))
		OBJ	(SPECIF money_ usa_dollar (SPECIF amount_ 64,000,000))
		SOURCE	(SPECIF SCHERING_(SPECIF pharmaceutical_company GERMANY_))
		TOPIC	r_and_d_activity
		date-1:	
		date-2:	

(a) *first search pattern derived from the premise: unification with* conc2.c34 *fails*

RECEIVE
SUBJ: company_
OBJ: money_
SOURCE: human_being

(b) *second search pattern derived from the premise: unification with* conc2.c34 *succeeds*

RECEIVE
SUBJ: company_
OBJ: money_
SOURCE: company_

a first unification with the event to explain by using a search pattern corresponding to a payment done by an individual person (SOURCE: human_being) *instead of a company*; see pattern (a) in Table 4.4. This unification obviously *fails*.

The engine then "backtracks" making use of a *second module* of *InferenceEngine*, *Reexec*. *Reexec* is *systematically used* during the execution of a hypothesis rule in order to:

- carry out the *backtracking operations* when a deadlock occurs;
- *reconstruct*, making use of the *environment variables*, the data structures (environment) proper to the *previous choice point*.

The association *var2* = human_being is *removed* from VALAFF and, using the constraints stored in RESTRICT, the engine builds up a *new pattern* (see pattern (b) of Table 4.4) making use now of the value *var2* = company_. This time, *Fum* will succeed in unifying pattern (b) with conc2.c34. SCHERING_ is, in fact, stored in HClass as an individual instance of pharmaceutical_company; the latter is obviously a company_ (see Section 4.1.1.2 for the procedures concerning the unification, using *Fum*, of a pattern expansion ep_i and an occurrence expansion ec_j). *InferenceEngine* can then continue the processing of *h1*; the two values *var1* = PHARMACOPEIA_ and *var2* = SCHERING_ *will be stored in DESVAR and passed to the first condition schema* (cond1); see Table 4.3b.

The search patterns derived from *cond1* – by taking into account the values already bound in DESVAR to *var1* and *var2* and by *replacing all the other variables with the associated constraints* – will be tested making use of a *third module* of *InferenceEngine, Execond*. The latter is called *whenever conditions exist that are favorable for advancing in the hypothesis*; in other words, to be able to *process a new condition schema*. *Exeprem* and *Execond* perform then the *forward traversal of the choice tree*, with *Reexec* being called whenever the *conditions for a backtracking exist*. The difference between *Exeprem* and *Execond* consists mainly in the fact that, in an *Execond* context, *we unify the patterns derived from the condition schemata with the general base of predicative occurrences* while, in an *Exeprem* context, *unification concerns only the patterns obtained from the premise and the (single) starting occurrence*.

Further deadlocks are generated in the course of the *Execond* operations, often originated, as in the premise case, from the *chronological utilization* of the constraints. For example, when trying to make use of a pattern derived from *cond1* where the variable *var3* has been substituted by its *first constraint* mutual_relationship (see Table 4.3b), a *failure will be generated* and *Reexec* will be invoked again. mutual_relationship, a specific term of activity_, is used in fact in NKRL to denote all sorts of *private* arrangements/relationships (approval_, companionship_, endorsement_, dating_, praise_, ...) among individuals/social bodies. According to the general context of hypothesis *h1*, on the contrary, the occurrences to be retrieved that relate the relationships between Pharmacopeia and Schering *must concern possible sorts of commercial agreements*, i.e. specific terms or instances of the *second* constraint on variable *var3*, business_agreement. A new search pattern where *var3* has been replaced by business_agreement will then succeed, finding in the base an instantiation of *cond1* corresponding to an event of the form "Pharmacopeia and Schering have signed two agreements, a sale_agreement and an r_and_d_agreement, concerning the production by Pharmacopeia of a new compound, COMPOUND_1"; see Table 4.5, which shows the final results produced by running hypothesis *h1*. sale_agreement and r_and_d_agreement are both specific terms of business_agreement in HClass.

The values eventually associated with *var3* (r_and_d_agreement and sale_agreement) and *var4* (COMPOUND_1) in *cond1* will then be used to create the *search patterns derived from cond2* – note, incidentally, that variables in NKRL (at the difference of what happens in DL-Safe SWRL; see the previous section) *can be bound to any sorts of values, individuals like concepts*. It will then be possible to retrieve an occurrence corresponding to the information "In the framework of an R&D agreement, Pharmacopeia has actually produced (MODAL biotechnology_process) the new compound" see again Table 4.5 The global information retrieved through the execution of the hypothesis can then supply a sort of *plausible explanation* of Schering's payment: Pharmacopiea and Schering have concluded some agreements for the production of a given compound, and this compound has been effectively produced by Pharmacopeia.

Table 4.5 Final results for hypothesis *h1*

The start occurrence:

conc2.c34)	RECEIVE	SUBJ	(SPECIF PHARMACOPEIA_(SPECIF biotechnology_company USA_))
		OBJ	(SPECIF money_ usa_dollar (SPECIF amount_ 64,000,000))
		SOURCE	(SPECIF SCHERING_ (SPECIF pharmaceutical_company GERMANY_))
		TOPIC	r_and_d_activity
		date-1:	
		date-2:	

Pharmacopeia, a USA biotechnology company, has received 64,000,000 dollars by Schering, a German pharmaceutical company, in relation to R&D activities.

The result for level 1:

conc13.c3)	PRODUCE	SUBJ	(COORD PHARMACOPEIA_ SCHERING_)
		OBJ	(COORD sale_agreement r_and_d_agreement)
		BENF	(COORD PHARMACOPEIA_ SCHERING_)
		TOPIC	(SPECIF synthesis_ (SPECIF COMPOUND_1 new_))
		date-1:	
		date-2:	

Pharmacopeia and Schering have signed two agreements (have produced two agreements having themselves as beneficiaries) concerning the production of a new compound

The result for level 2:

conc13.c7)	PRODUCE	SUBJ	PHARMACOPEIA_
		OBJ	COMPOUND_1
		MODAL	biotechnology_process
		CONTEXT	r_and_d_agreement
		date-1:	
		date-2:	

In the framework of an R&D agreement, Pharmacopeia has actually produced the new compound

Figure 4.8 reproduces a screen dump created by *InferenceEngine* that shows the execution tree for *h1* taking as starting point conc2.c34; *to obtain a readable result, we have used a knowledge base formed by a very reduced number of predicative occurrences to produce this dump.* If we traverse the execution tree in a *depth-first mode*, the first *deadlock* we come across (deadlocks are denoted as "!match" in Fig. 4.8) corresponds to the failure of pattern (a) in Table 4.4 Pattern (b) in the same table *succeeds*, and the conceptual label conc2.c34 is stored in the OCCUR environment variable – the addition of the symbolic names of the "matched" occurrences into OCCUR is denoted as "occur" in Fig. 4.8. As already stated, *the values bound to the variables of a successful reasoning schema* that are retrieved within these *"matched" occurrences* are used to build up the (provisional) VALAFF lists and to set up the *new patterns*

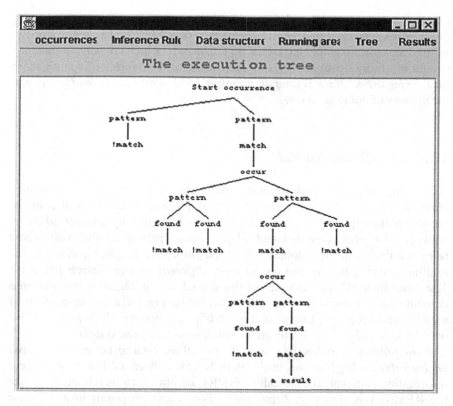

Fig. 4.8 The execution tree for hypothesis *h1* starting from occurrence conc2.c34

that allow us to *continue with the execution of h1*. In our case, the values *var1* = PHARMACOPEIA_ and *var2* = SCHERING_ are the *"final" ones with respect to the processing of the premise*, and will be used to build up the *two possible patterns* that can be derived from the first condition schema (*cond1*); see Table 4.2b and the branching after the first occur in Fig. 4.8.

In Fig. 4.8, "found" refers to the *preselection operations* executed by *Fum before* the actual unification, making use of information corresponding to the three-level indexing illustrated in Section 4.1.2.1– these preselection operations are *extremely simple* in this example, given that, for simplicity's sake, we have not introduced any temporal information in the starting occurrence conc2.c34; they are in general, however, *very useful to prune ingeniously the execution tree*. From Fig. 4.8, we see that the two *cond1* patterns are *both able to preselect two predicative occurrences* in the (very reduced) knowledge base used, but that *only one of the four* matches is successful – the match that unifies the search pattern where *var3* has been replaced by business_agreement with the predicative occurrence conc13.c3 reproduced in Table 4.5 The label conc13.c3 is stored in OCCUR and the two values associated with *var3*, i.e. sale_agreement and r_and_d_agreement, are used *to construct two new search patterns*, etc., leading eventually to the final match with occurrence conc13.c7 of Table 4.5. For this simple example, no global backtracking is essayed – which anyway, in this case, should not bring up any new result. According to the *InferenceEngine*'s structure, *trying to backtrack beyond the premises' level will definitely lead to stopping the InferenceEngine processing*.

4.2.3 Transformation Rules

As already stated, "transformation rules" are used, basically, to obtain a *plausible answer* from a knowledge base of NKRL occurrences also in the *absence* of the explicitly requested information, by searching *semantic affinities* between what was requested and what is really present in the base. These rules are then able to automatically *"transform" the original query* (i.e. the original search pattern) into *one or more different queries* (search patterns). The "transformed" queries – unlike those used for *optimization purposes* in a *database context* that return the *same results of the original query* in less time or with less resources [e.g. Lumpkin et al., 2005] – are not *strictly "equivalent" but only "semantically close"* to the query initially posed to the system.

Conceptual rules in this style based, as we will see, on a sort of common-sense *analogical reasoning* [Gentner et al., 2000], have long been used in an "intelligent information retrieval (IIR)" mode in NKRL and in previous related work like the RESEDA project [e.g. Zarri, 1986]. For recent proposals in a database context that seem to go in the same direction, see Necib and Freytag [2005a; 2005b] for example. In these last papers, however, "transformations" make use only of *"standard"* ontologies. As a consequence, they are restricted to *changing some terms in the SELECT conditions of the DB queries* by taking into account *"standard" relationships* like synonymy, SynOf ("computer" versus "calculator" versus "data processor"), IsA and InstanceOf, PartOf (a PC is composed of a "desktop," a "monitor" and a "keyboard"), etc. Their "inferencing power" is then equivalent, basically, to that of *Fum*.

To give some very simple and informal examples of the *"deep" conceptual modifications* that are, on the contrary, typical of the NKRL transformation rules, suppose first that, working in the context of a hypothetical knowledge base of NKRL occurrences about university professors, we want to ask a query like "Who has lived in the United States," even without an explicit representation of this fact in the base. If the latter contains some information about the degrees obtained by professors, then we can tell the user that, *although we do not explicitly know who lived in the United States, we can nevertheless look for people having an American degree*. This last piece of information, obtained by transformation of the original query, would indeed *normally imply* that some time was spent by the professors in the country, the United States, which issued their degree. To pass now to a "Terrorism in the Southern Philippines" example, suppose we ask "Search for the existence of some links between ObL (a well-known "terrorist") and Abubakar Abdurajak Janjalani, the leader of the Abu Sayyaf group" – as already stated, the Abu Sayyaf group is one of the Muslim independence movements in the Southern Philippines. In the *absence of a direct answer*, the corresponding search pattern can be transformed into "Search for the attestation of the transfer of economic/financial items between the two," which could lead to retrieving this information: "During 1998/1999, Abubakar Abdurajak Janjalani has received an undetermined amount of money from ObL through an intermediate agent."

For clarity's sake, it can be useful to conceive the transformation rules as made up of a *left-hand side*, the *antecedent* (i.e. the formulation, in search pattern format, of the "query" to be transformed) and one or more *right-hand sides*, the *consequent(s)* (i.e. the NKRL representation(s) of one or more queries (search patterns) that must be substituted for the given one). Denoting then with *A* the antecedent and with *Cs* all the possible consequents, a transformation rule can be expressed as

$$A(Var_i) \Rightarrow Cs(Var_j), var_i \subseteq var_j \tag{4.3}$$

With respect then to Eq. (4.2), *X* coincides now with *A* (operationally, a *search pattern*) while the reasoning steps $Y_1, Y_2, \ldots, Y_n$ are used to produce the *search pattern(s) Cs to be used in place of A*.

The restriction $var_i \subseteq var_j$ (all the variables declared in the antecedent *A* *must also appear* in *Cs* accompanied, in case, by *additional variables* – see the examples below) has been introduced to assure the logical congruence of the transformation rules. We can also note that the same restriction is valid in a hypothesis context: in this last case, *the variables declared in the premise must necessarily be retrieved within the set of variables introduced by the different "condition" schemata.*

The "transformation arrow" of Eq. (4.3), "$\Rightarrow$," has a *double meaning*:

- *Operationally speaking*, the arrow indicates the *direction* of the transformation: the original search pattern (which is a specialization of left-hand side *A* of the transformation rule) is *removed* and *replaced* by one or several new search patterns obtained through the updating, using the parameters of the original pattern, of the right-hand side *Cs*.
- From a *logical/semantic point of view*, we assume that between the information retrieved through the use of *Cs* and the information we wanted to obtain through a specialization of *A* there is a sort of *implication relationship* that, *normally* (see below), denotes solely a *possible* (a weak) implication.

In reality, *"always true" implications* (noted as $Cs \rightarrow A$, where the symbol "$\rightarrow$" represents the "normal" *implication arrow*) can be easily found, even if usually they *are not very useful in practice* (they are not very *expressive*). A straightforward example of these "always true" implications could be "If someone goes from one place to another, then he certainly has left his starting point." An implication like this should authorize replacing a search pattern in the style "Try to check whether a given *var1* has left location *var2*" with another one like "Check to see whether *var1* has moved from *var2* to *var3*." Most transformations found in *real-world applications* (like the two informal examples supplied above) represent in reality what we could call *modalized implications*. We will denote them as $\Diamond(C \to A)$, which means: "it is possible that C implies A." $\Diamond$ is the usual *modal operator for "possibility,"* which then satisfies the relation $\Diamond p = \neg \blacklozenge \neg p$ with respect to a *second modal operator*, "$\blacklozenge$" = *necessity*.

Table 4.6 Coded examples of simple transformations

t1: "delivery of official document" transformation

antecedent:
```
EXIST    SUBJ    var1: (var2)
var1 =   human_being
var2 =   location_
```

consequent:
```
RECEIVE  SUBJ       var1
         OBJ        var3
         SOURCE     var4: (var2)
         MODAL      var5

var3 =   title_
var4 =   authority_
var5 =   official_document
```

If someone (var1) receives a title from an authority by means of an official document, then it is possible they have been physically present where (var2) the authority is located.

t2: "economic/financial transfer" transformation

antecedent:
```
BEHAVE   SUBJ       (COORD1 var1 var2)
         OBJ        (COORD1 var1 var2)

var1 =   human_being_or_social_body
var2 =   human_being_or_social_body
```

consequent:
```
RECEIVE  SUBJ       var2
         OBJ        var4
         SOURCE     var1
         MODAL      var5

var4 =   economic/financial_entity
var5 =   business_agreement, mutual_relationship
```

To verify the existence of a relationship between two (or more) persons, try to verify if one of these persons has received a "financial entity" (e.g. money) from the other

A *classification of transformations* into "always true," "modalized," "reversible," etc. can be found in Zarri [1986].

The coding of the two previous (*modalized*) "delivery of official document" and "economic/financial transfer" rules is given in Table 4.6

The *modalized nature* of transformation *t1* (which allows us to deal with the informal example above about "university professors") is well evident; this rule cannot *be considered as "always valid," among other things, given that a university degree can be easily obtained through the Internet or in a correspondence school.* Nevertheless, it is possible to see that, in this case, the *semantic distance between an "always true" implication and a "modalized" one is not too important*, as it is always possible, at least in principle, to change *t1* into an *"always true" transformation* by the addition of a few constraints on the variable *var3*, e.g. *var3* ≠ obtainable_by_correspondence_degree. We can also note that the *formal* expressions of both the "antecedent" and "consequent" sides of *t1* and *t2* correspond (as in the case of the "condition schemata" in a hypothesis context) to the *partial instantiations of standard templates.* For example, the *left-hand side (antecedent)* of *t2* is the *partial instantiation* of the template Behave:FavourableConcreteMutual; see Section 3.2.2.1.

With respect to the implementation details, the *InferenceEngine* version to be used for transformations is *quite identical* to that used for processing the hypothesis rules. The module *Antexec* (execution of the antecedent) corresponds to the *Exeprem* module; *Consexec* (execution of the consequent(s)) corresponds to *Execond. Reexec* is the same in the two versions.

We can conclude about transformations by noticing that many of the transformation rules used in NKRL are characterized by the very simply format of *t1* and *t2* in Table 4.6 that implies the use of *only one "consequent" schema*. An example of *"multi-consequent" transformation* is given by this specific "terrorism in the Philippines" rule (see Table 4.7): "In a context of ransom kidnapping, the certification that a given character is wealthy or has a professional role can be substituted by the certification that (i) this character has a kinship link with another person (first consequent schema, *conseq1*) and (ii) this second person is a wealthy person or a professional person (second consequent schema, *conseq2*)."

Let us suppose that, during the search for all the possible information associated with the Robustiniano Hablo kidnapping (see occurrence mod3.c5 in Table 2.6 of Section 2.2.2.2), we ask the system whether Robustiniano Hablo is wealthy. This particular search pattern (a *partial instantiation* of template Behave:HumanProperty – see Section 3.2.2.1) is represented in the first part of Table 4.8 In the absence of a direct answer, the "transformation" version of *InferenceEngine* will *automatically modify this query* using transformation *t3* of Table 4.7 Note, in this table, that *conseq1* is a partial instantiation of the template Behave:Kinship and that *conseq2* is a partial instantiation of the template Behave:Role; see again Section 3.2.2.1.

Table 4.7 An example of "multi-consequent" transformation

t3: "kinship" transformation

antecedent:

BEHAVE	SUBJ	*var1*
	MODAL	*var2*

var1 = human_being
var2 = wealthy_, professional_role

first consequent schema (*conseq1*):

BEHAVE	SUBJ	*var1*
	MODAL	*var3*
	TOPIC	*var4*

var3 = extended_family_role
var4 = individual_person

second consequent schema (*conseq2*):

BEHAVE	SUBJ	*var4*
	MODAL	*var2*

In a context of ransom kidnapping, the certification that a character is wealthy or has a professional role can be substituted by the certification that (i) there is a kinship link with another person, and (ii) this second person is wealthy or is a professional people

---

The final result – after having activated the transformation *t3* of Table 4.7 through the unification, via *Antexec*, of the original search pattern with the antecedent of *t3*, and after the processing of the two consequent schemata using *Consexec* and *Reexec* – is shown in Table 4.8: *we do not know if Robustiniano Hablo is wealthy, but we can say that his father is a wealthy businessperson.*

4.2.4 Integrating the Two Main Inferencing Modes of NKRL

As it appears from hypothesis *h1* of Table 4.3 (see Section 4.2.2), a hypothesis rule corresponds to a *fixed scenario formed by a given number of reasoning steps*. Since these steps are represented as *partially instantiated (standard) templates* and can then make use of *variables and constraints*, their formulation is rather *flexible* and *relatively easy to generalize*. For example, thanks to the variable *var2* introduced in the premise of hypothesis *h1* (and characterized by the two constraints human_being and company_), hypothesis *h1* is valid in the context of money received either from a *company* or from *private individuals*; by adding further variables and constraints, generalization can even be improved. The reasoning steps to be executed are, however, *still rigidly predefined*.

To (i) introduce a certain degree of *fuzziness* in the execution of hypotheses and (ii) increase the probability of discovering *implicit information* during this

Table 4.8 Application of the multi-consequent transformation of Table 4.7

the original search pattern:

BEHAVE
SUBJ :   ROBUSTINIANO_HABLO
MODAL :   wealthy_
{}
date1 :
date2 :

the result for the first consequent schema (*conseq1*):

BEHAVE   SUBJ   ROBUSTINIANO_HABLO
                      MODAL   son_
                      TOPIC   INDIVIDUAL_PERSON_21
                      {obs}
                      date-1:   1999-11-21
                      date-2:

Behave:Kinship (1.332)
On November 21, 1999, wa can remark that Robustiniano Hablo is a son of an unknown individual INDIVIDUAL_PERSON_21

the result for the second consequent schema (*conseq2*):

BEHAVE   SUBJ   INDIVIDUAL_PERSON_21
                      MODAL   (SPECIF business_person wealthy_)
                      {obs}
                      date-1:   1999-11-21
                      date-2:
Behave:Role (1.33)

On November 21, 1999, we can remark that the individual denoted as father of Robustiniano Hablo is a wealthy businessman

execution, *we can make use of the concept of "transformation."* To be concretely executed, the reasoning steps of a hypothesis must, in fact, be *reduced to search patterns* and, at least in principle, *any NKRL search pattern can be automatically (and then semi-randomly) converted into a new search pattern by means of transformation rules.* For this, it is sufficient that the original pattern *unifies the antecedent* of one of the transformation rules present in the rule base of a given application.

This means, in practice, modifying *InferenceEngine* to have the possibility of *making use of the modules of the transformation version during the execution of those of the hypothesis version.* This possibility has recently been (fully) implemented thanks to the work accomplished in the framework of the PARMENIDES project; see the Preface.

4.2.4.1 Strategies for the Coordinated Inference Processing

Executing transformations in a hypothesis context means then taking a search pattern built up by *Execond* during the processing of a hypothesis rule and *transforming* it by executing the following operations:

- After having created *a list of all the transformation rules* stored in the rule base of the system whose left-hand side (antecedent) *A* is *congruent in principle* with the general format of the *current search pattern*, find in this list *one or more transformation rules*, if any, whose antecedents *can actually unify* the original pattern.
- In this case, *execute the transformation* by substituting to the original search pattern those formed using the right-hand side (consequent) *Cs* of the transformation; see Section 4.2.3.
- If the new search pattern(s) is/are *successful*, store in VALAFF (in the hypothesis environment) some *new values for the variables var$_i$ of the condition schema under execution*.

Several strategies can be adopted with respect to (i) the *"number" of transformations to be executed* and (ii) the *"conditions" of their execution*; see Zarri and Bernard [2004a] for the details. In the present versions of the NKRL software, the user is allowed to select a *specific transformation strategy*; see Fig. 4.9.

After having answered "Yes" to the question about the permission of executing "internal" transformations (i.e. the execution of transformation processes in a hypothesis context), on the left, she/he is asked, below, whether she/he wants to carry out *"positive" or "negative" transformations*. Executing *"negative" transformations* means that the transformation process is activated *only after the failure of a search pattern derived directly from a hypothesis condition schema* (this means, in practice, that a pattern able to find a unification in the knowledge base *cannot be transformed*); executing *"positive" transformations* means that *all the search patterns* derived directly from a hypothesis condition schema *can be transformed, whether they have been successful or not*. The last query on the right of Fig. 4.9 asks for the *"depth" of the transformation*, i.e. it asks if a

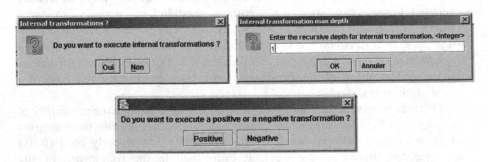

Fig. 4.9 Parameters for the internal transformations

pattern resulting from an internal transformation *can be transformed in turn,* and how many *"transformation steps"* are allowed.

4.2.4.2 The Correspondence among Variables

The main problem concerning the integration hypotheses/transformations concerns the way of finding a *correspondence* between (i) the variables, var_h, originally present in the *(hypothesis) condition schema* from which the search pattern to transform has been derived and (ii) those, *totally disjoint*, var_t, that appear in the *transformation rules to be used.* We recall in fact that the *values* found by *Fum* for the variables var_h of a given condition schema, and stored in VALAFF and DESVAR, *will be utilized to build up new search patterns* from the subsequent condition schemata to continue with the processing of the hypothesis. Making use of a transformation must allow us to *find new sets of values for* var_h; the problem is represented by the fact that these new values *will not refer directly to* var_h *but to* var_t, the set of variables proper to a *transformation rule* that, *applied to one of the search patterns derived from the original condition schemata, has been successful.* A *correspondence* among var_h and var_t should then, in general, *be found.*

We must now operate a distinction between *global* and *local* variables. In the context of the "integration" problem, a *"local" variable* is a variable that is used in *only one* condition schema, $cond_i$, *without appearing explicitly in any of the subsequent condition schemata* $cond_{i+1}, \ldots, cond_n$. A *global* variable, on the contrary, is a variable that, *after having been introduced in* $cond_i$, *is utilized again in at least one of the following n − i condition schemata.* Note that the variables introduced by the premise are *not interested* by this distinction, *given that the search patterns derived from the premise are never submitted to the transformation operations*: if these search patterns cannot unify the starting occurrence, this means, in fact, that *the hypothesis is not suitable for explaining this occurrence.* To give an example, variables *var3* and *var4* introduced in the *cond1* scheme of *h1* in Table 4.3 are *global*, because they are reutilized in the *cond2* scheme; *var5* in *cond2* is *local*, given that *cond2* is the last condition scheme of the hypothesis. We can now say that:

- If, independently from the fact that the search patterns derived from a condition schema $cond_i$ were *successful or not*, the *new variables* var_h introduced by $cond_i$ are *all local* (i.e. none of them *appear in the subsequent n − i condition schemata*), this means that, after having transformed the search patterns derived from $cond_i$, the *(possible) new values for* var_h *obtained through the transformation process are not explicitly required for the processing of the subsequent schemata of the hypothesis.* In this case, if all the original $cond_i$ search patterns *failed*, then a *successful transformation is nevertheless necessary to allow the hypothesis to continue.* If the $cond_i$ search patterns were *successful* – and the transformation operations were nevertheless admitted (*positive transformations*, see above) – then the success of the transformation *can only be useful* (i) to guarantee, in an indirect way, that $cond_i$ is *really congruent with the data of the knowledge base* and, more important, (ii) to introduce in the hypothesis's answer *some new information (occurrences) that confirms/expands the "normal" results*.

- If some of the *new variables var_h* introduced by $cond_i$ are *global* (i.e. they appear in at least one of the subsequent $n - i$ condition schemata), then the possibility of associating *new values with the global var_h* through a successful transformation process *becomes absolutely mandatory, in case of failure of the original $cond_i$ search patterns, to allow the hypothesis to continue*. In case of *success of the original $cond_i$ search patterns*, the success of the transformation process (positive transformations) will *increase the possibility of constructing new search patterns from the subsequent condition schemata making use of the new values for the global var_h*. This will *enlarge considerably the search space* and will then *augment the probability of obtaining new interesting results*. In *both these cases*, a *correspondence* between var_h (the variables of the original condition schema) and var_t (the variables used in the transformation) *must necessarily be found*.

To find the correspondence, the following procedure must be used:

- In order to build up a *generic search pattern p_h from a hypothesis condition schema $cond_i$*, the variables var_h of this schema must be replaced (see Section 4.2.2) by some values val_h, *concepts or individuals*, corresponding to (i) *values obtained from the previous steps of the hypothesis* or to (ii) *constraints originally associated with var_h* (these constraints are stored and managed in RESTRICT$_{hypo}$). *The association $var_h \equiv val_h$ is stored in VALAFF$_{hypo}$.*
- When trying to use a transformation rule to modify p_h, *the transformation variables var_t included in the antecedent A of the transformation must be replaced (according to the "chronological" strategy) by some of the constraints stored in RESTRICT$_{transfo}$ to create a (transformation) search pattern p_t;* the values val_t provisionally associated with var_t are *stored in* VALAFF$_{transfo}$. *Fum* can now be called to (try to) *unify p_t, the search pattern derived from the antecedent A, with p_h, the search pattern (derived from a condition schema $cond_i$) to be transformed. The unification is oriented from p_t towards p_h,* i.e. p_h plays the role normally associated with a "predicative occurrence" in the "standard" *Fum* unification; see Section 4.1.2.
- If the unification succeeds, *new values val_t are associated with var_t in the transformation environment, $var_t \equiv val_t$, and stored in* VALAFF$_{transfo}$. *Since the unification is successful* (the data structures of p_h and p_t are fully congruent), *the values val_t, retrieved on p_h, correspond necessarily to the values val_h previously substituted to var_h to create p_h:* these values have been stored in VALAFF$_{hypo}$. *The equality $val_t = val_h$ determined through the comparison of the values stored in VALAFF$_{transfo}$ and VALAFF$_{hypo}$ implies the correspondence $var_t = var_h$* that we wanted to retrieve. It will then be possible (i) *to transfer back to the original hypothesis environment* the values bound to var_t through the unification of the patterns derived from the consequent Cs

of the transformation with the occurrences of the base, and (ii) *to associate these values with var$_h$ to continue with the processing of the original hypothesis.*

4.2.4.3 Some Examples

In Table 4.9, we summarize informally, in NL, the *four reasoning steps* to be performed in the context of a typical "terrorism" hypothesis proper to the PARMENIDES project. This hypothesis, which we will call *h2*, can be used, in particular, *to check whether a particular "kidnapping" event can be classed in the specific category of the "kidnappings for ransom."* The detailed NKRL code that represents this hypothesis is reproduced fully in Table 4.10.

In particular, *h2* can be used to "explain" the kidnapping of Robustiniano Hablo – see Table 4.11, where we have reproduced, for clarity's sake, the occurrence mod3.c5 of Table 2.6.

A first remark we can make is that, to process the last reasoning step of hypothesis *h2* of Table 4.10, *cond4* – i.e. to try to demonstrate that Robustiniano is an "upper class" person, see also Table 4.9 – *we are obliged to use, in a hypothesis context, the "two steps" (multi-consequent) "kinship" transformation* mentioned in Section 4.2.3; see Table 4.7.

We will now make use of hypothesis *h2* to better clarify the difference introduced in the previous section between "local" and "global" variables.

If we examine *cond2* in Table 4.10 (which formalizes the second reasoning step of hypothesis *h2*, i.e. "this group carries out (currently) kidnapping for ransom" – see again Table 4.9), then we can see that the *new variables* introduced by this condition schema are *var4* and *var5* (*var3* has been introduced in *cond1*). We will focalize now our attention on *var4*, which is *local*, in the sense that it will not be used in the subsequent condition schemata – *var4*, the OBJ filler of *cond2*, has been introduced here under *"variable" form* to allow future, possible generalizations. We suppose now that *h2 fails when cond2* (see the upper part of Table 4.12) *is processed* by *InferenceEngine*. This means that it is *impossible to derive from the condition schema cond2 a search pattern able to find a successful unification within the information in the knowledge base.*

We will now suppose to have, among the transformations of the system, the rule reproduced in the lower part of Table 4.12.

Table 4.9 Reasoning steps for the *h2* hypothesis

Cond1	The kidnappers are part of a separatist movement or of a terrorist organization
Cond2	This separatist movement or terrorist organization currently practices "ransom kidnapping" of particular categories of people
Cond3	This type of kidnapping implies that the kidnapped persons are either wealthy or can be considered as "upper class" persons, i.e. executives or assimilated categories
Cond4	It can be proved that the victim is wealthy or is an upper class person

Table 4.10 The "kidnapping for ransom" hypothesis rule (*h2*)

Hypothesis *h2*

premise:

PRODUCE	SUBJ	*var1*
	OBJ	kidnapping_
	BENF	*var2*

var1	=	human_being_or_social_body
var2	=	individual_person

A human being has been kidnapped.

first condition schema (*cond1*):

BEHAVE	SUBJ	*var1*
	MODAL	member_of
	TOPIC	*var3*

var3	=	separatist_movement, terrorist_organization

The kidnappers are member of a separatist movement or of a terrorist organization.

second condition schema (*cond2*):

PRODUCE	SUBJ	*var3*
	OBJ	*var4*
	BENF	*var5*

var5	=	ransom_kidnapping
var5	=	human_being
var5	≠	*var2*

This organization performs (in general, see var₅ ≠ var₂) ransom kidnapping.

third condition schema (*cond3*):

BEHAVE	SUBJ	*var5*
	MODAL	*var6*

var6	=	artistic/performing_role, business_person, company_staff_role, consultant_,physician_, …, wealthy_
var6	≠	employee_, temporary_worker, …

The persons kidnapped in a "ransom kidnapping" context are wealthy or they can be regarded as "upper class" people. Ransom kidnappinsg do not (normally) concern simple employees, temporary workers, etc.

fourth condition schema (*cond4*):

BEHAVE	SUBJ	*var2*
	MODAL	*var6*

The victim must then be wealthy or can be regarded as an "upper class" people

Using the standard version of *InferenceEngine* for transformations, the p_t *pattern derived from the antecedent A of this rule will unify the p_h pattern obtained from cond2* in Table 4.10 (see Table 4.12 and the upper part of Table 4.13). In this last p_h pattern, *var3* has been replaced by ABU_SAYYAF_GROUP – we can suppose that this value has been obtained during the processing of *cond1* – and

Table 4.11 Robustiniano Hablo's kidnapping

mod3.c5)	PRODUCE	SUBJ	(INDIVIDUAL_PERSON_20 weapon_wearing (SPECIF cardinality_ several_)): (VILLAGE_1)
		OBJ	kidnapping_
		BENF	ROBUSTINIANO_HABLO
		CONTEXT	#mod3.c6
		date-1:	1999-11-20
		date-2:	

Produce:Violence (6.35)

On November 20, 1999, in an unspecified village (VILLAGE_1), an armed group of people has kidnapped Robustiniano Hablo

Table 4.12 A possible transformation rule for *cond2* of *h2*

search pattern p_h derived from cond2 of Table 4.9

PRODUCE
SUBJ: ABU_SAYYAF_GROUP:
OBJ: ransom_kidnapping:
BENF: human_being:
{}
date1:
date2:

The Abu Sayyaf group performs ransom kidnapping

t4: "money for ransom" transformation

antecedent:

PRODUCE	SUBJ	var1
	OBJ	var2
	BENF	var3

var1 = separatist_mouvement, terrorist_organization
var2 = ransom_kidnapping
var3 = human_being

consequent:

RECEIVE	SUBJ	var1
	OBJ	money_
	SOURCE	var4
	TOPIC	(SPECIF captivity_freeing var3)
	CONTEXT	var2

var4 = human_being_or_social_body

To verify if a given organization performs ransom kidnapping, try to see if this organization has received some money for freeing from captivity one or more human beings

Table 4.13 The original search pattern p_h derived from *cond2* and the final p_f obtained from the consequent of transformation *t4*

PRODUCE	
SUBJ:	ABU_SAYYAF_GROUP:
OBJ:	ransom_kidnapping:
BENF:	human_being:
{}	
date1:	
date2:	
RECEIVE	
SUBJ:	ABU_SAYYAF_GROUP:
OBJ:	money_:
SOURCE :	human_being_or_social_body:
TOPIC:	(SPECIF captivity_freeing human_being)
CONTEXT	ransom_kidnapping
{}	
date1:	
date2:	

var4 and *var5* have been replaced, respectively, by the constraints ransom_kidnapping and human_being.

The execution of transformation *t4* will eventually produce, *from the consequent Cs of the transformation*, the *search pattern* reproduced in the lower part of Table 4.13: we will call this type of pattern p_f, "*final pattern*," given that it will be used *to search for unifications within the knowledge base as in the "normal" processing of hypotheses.*

If this p_f pattern *can unify some information in the knowledge base*, the reasoning step *cond2* of *h2* is *now satisfied*, and the hypothesis can continue with the processing of *cond3*. With respect to *var4*, it is *not necessary* to make use of the occurrences unified by the consequent of transformation *t4 to find specific values for this variable*, given that *var4 will no more be used in the following steps of the hypothesis*. No new values will then be introduced for *var4* in the VALAFF and DESVAR repositories of the *h2* hypothesis. From this specific point of view, *the success of the transformation is only equivalent to the generation of "variants" of the "normal" results*: the evidence of the fact that the Abu Sayyaf Group carries out ransom kidnapping will be *reinforced by a specific information* telling us that the Abu Sayyaf Group has received some money for freeing people from captivity in a "ransom kidnapping" context.

If we now consider the *cond1* condition schema of hypothesis *h2* (see Table 4.10), then we can see that the *(unique) new variable* introduced in this schema is *var3*; this one is now "*global*" given that it will be used in *cond2*. The (possible) transformations operating on the patterns p_h derived from *cond1* must now be able to produce "*new*" values for *var3*. These will be stored in VALAFF/DESVAR of *h2* and *used as if they had been obtained through the "normal" hypothesis operations* – "new" means values that can be different with respect to those obtained via the usual procedures. Unlike the previous *local* case – where the execution of successful transformations in a hypothesis context *could only lead to produce "locally"* (i.e. for the cond$_i$ transformed) *some "variants" of the standard outcomes* – the success of the internal transformations *could now give rise to wholly new branches of the choice tree*, likely to produce *unforeseen results* for each of the cond$_i$ included between the transformation point and the end of the hypothesis.

A problem of *"variable correspondence"* occurs now, to be solved according to the procedure illustrated in the previous section. Let us suppose running hypothesis *h2* to explain Robustiniano Hablo's kidnapping (i.e. the starting occurrence is represented by mod3.c5 of Table 4.11) and to *"transform"* – *independently from the experience of a possible failure* – at the cond1 level. We can then make use of the transformation *t5* of Table 4.14: *the membership (even if provisional) in an organization, political group, etc. can also be verified by checking if the "member" receives some sort of permanent or occasional "salary" from the organization.*

In this case, after having entered the *specific transformation environment* and having activated the sub-module Antexec (see Section 4.2.3) to execute, using *Fum*, the *unification between the search pattern p$_t$ derived from the antecedent A of t5* in Table 4.14 and the p$_h$ *pattern corresponding to cond1 of h2*, we are confronted with the situation globally represented in Table 4.15. The top search pattern, p$_h$, is the pattern derived from cond1 in a "Robustiniano Hablo" context. Returning, in fact, to Tables 4.10 and 4.11, we can see that – because of the unification (in the original hypothesis environment and using *Exeprem*)

Table 4.14 A possible transformation rule for cond1 of h2

t5: "permanent or occasional salary" transformation

antecedent:

BEHAVE	SUBJ	var1
	MODAL	member_of
	TOPIC	var2

var1 = human_being
var2 = political_group/party

consequent:

RECEIVE	SUBJ	var1
	OBJ	var3
	SOURCE	var2

var3 = irregular_payment, salary_

To verify if a person is a member of a given organization, try to see if, among other things, this person receives a permanent or occasional salary from this organization of the premise of *h2* with the starting occurrence mod3.c5 – the variables *var1*$_{hypo}$ and *var2*$_{hypo}$ introduced by the premise have taken, respectively, the values INDIVIDUAL_PERSON_20 and ROBUSTINIANO_HABLO, as reflected by the state of VALAFF$_{hypo}$ in Table 4.15. The value separatist _movement associated with *var3*$_{hypo}$ in VALAFF$_{hypo}$, see Table 4.15, derives from the operations performed by *Exeprem* (in the hypothesis environment) to build up the search pattern *p*$_h$ from *cond1*. The pattern *sp*$_t$ has been built up by *Antexec* (in the transformation environment) from the antecedent of *t3* (Table 4.14); after the unification of *p*$_t$ and *p*$_h$ – this unification, executed by *Fum*, as already stated, is "oriented," in the sense that *p*$_h$ has a "predicative occurrence" role – the variables *var1*$_{transfo}$ and *var2*$_{transfo}$ of *t3* have, respectively, the values INDIVIDUAL_PERSON_20 and separatist_movement; see the status of VALAFF for the transformation environment in Table 4.15.

According to the procedure expounded in the previous section, *from the comparison of the values affected by the variables in the two versions of* VALAFF, for hypotheses (VALAFF$_{hypo}$) and transformations (VALAFF$_{transfo}$) – this comparison is entrusted to *Fum* – we can deduce that there *is a correspondence between var3*$_{hypo}$ *and var2*$_{transfo}$. This fact will be then registered into a CORRE-SP(ondence) table (see Table 4.16); *only var3*$_{hypo}$ *is of interest for the continuation of the hypothesis*. After the (successful) unification of *sp*$_t$/*sp*$_h$, *the processing of the transformation in its proper environment will continue*, and the *Consexec* sub-module will then build up the *"final" search pattern p*$_f$ of Table 4.15 from the consequent *Cs* of *t3* of Table 4.14.

Let us suppose now that *p*$_f$ of Table 4.15 is *able to unify* (at least) a predicative occurrence in the NKRL knowledge base. In this case, *a value will be bound to var2*$_{transfo}$; according to the information stored in CORRESP (see Table 4.16), *this value will also be bound to var3*$_{hypo}$ *and inserted into the VALAFF/DESVAR repositories of the original hypothesis (h2) environment*. If we assume now for generality's sake (see Section 4.2.4.1) that the strategy chosen for the execution of the "internal" transformations is a *"positive"* one – i.e. *all the search patterns* built up by *Execond* from a condition schema *can be transformed independently from their success or failure* – four different cases can be envisaged.

- In the first one, we suppose that *var3*$_{hypo}$, before the execution of the transformation, *was already linked with* ABU_SAYYAF_GROUP – i.e. during the "normal" execution of the hypothesis *h2*, a search pattern directly derived from the condition schema *cond1* had already retrieved the information that INDIVIDUAL_PERSON_20 (representing collectively the group of person that has realized the kidnapping) was part of the Abu Sayyaf group. We suppose now that the *final transformed search pattern p*$_f$ of Table 4.15 can retrieve information telling us that INDIVIDUAL_PER-SON_20 *receives some form of occasional salary from the Abu Sayyaf group*; *var2*$_{transfo}$ is bound to ABU_SAYYAF_GROUP as well, and passing this value to *var3*$_{hypo}$ *will add nothing from the point of view of an "augmented" development of the hypothesis*. As in the previous case of "local" variables,

Table 4.15 Data structures and environment variables after the unification of the patterns derived from *cond1* and *t5*

p_h BEHAVE
      SUBJ :   INDIVIDUAL_PERSON_20:
      MODAL :   member_of:
      TOPIC :   separatist_movement
      {}
      date1 :
      date2 :

VALAFF$_{hypo}$ (h2)
      $var1_{hypo}$ =   INDIVIDUAL_PERSON_20
      $var2_{hypo}$ =   ROBUSTINIANO_HABLO
      $var3_{hypo}$ =   separatist_movement

p_t BEHAVE
      SUBJ: human_being:
      MODAL: member_of:
      TOPIC: political_group/party
      {}
      date1:
      date2:

VALAFF$_{transfo}$ (t5)
      $var1_{transfo}$ =   INDIVIDUAL_PERSON_20
      $var2_{transfo}$ =   separatist_movement

p_f RECEIVE
      SUBJ: INDIVIDUAL_PERSON_20:
      OBJ: irregular_payment:
      SOURCE: separatist_movement:
      {}
      date1:
      date2:

Table 4.16 The CORRESP table for the example

Original condition schema: variable name	Value	Internal transformation: variable name
var3	separatist_movement	var2

the only real benefit linked with the execution of the transformation will be *a confirmation of the links between INDIVIDUAL_PERSON_20 and the Abu Sayyaf group through the discovery that the kidnappers receive some money from this group.*

- If we suppose now that, during the "normal" execution of *h2*, *all the search patterns directly derived from the condition schema cond1 failed*, then the possibility of obtaining the value ABU_SAYYAF_GROUP for *var3 $_{hypo}$* via the transformation and the passage through *var2$_{transfo}$* permits one, on the contrary, *to continue with the processing of hypothesis h2 otherwise irremediably destined to fail.*

- We can suppose now that pattern p_f of Table 4.15 is able to find a unification within the knowledge base *telling us that INDIVIDUAL_PERSON_20 receives some form of occasional salary from another group*, e.g. from a (fully hypothetical) Southern Philippines Liberation Front. SOUTHERN_PHILIPPINES_LIBERATION_FRONT will be then, in this case, *the final value bound to* $var2_{transfo}$ *after the unification with the occurrences of the base.* If, as in the previous case, $var3_{hypo}$ was *unbound* before the execution of the transformation, activating the process of internal transformation *will allow continuing with the processing of a hypothesis h2 otherwise destined to fail.*

- Eventually, let us suppose that $var2_{transfo}$ takes up the value SOUTHERN_PHILIPPINES_LIBERATION_FRONT *while* $var3_{hypo}$ *is already bound to ABU_SAYYAF_GROUP via the "normal" hypothesis processing.* This means, in practice, that the group of kidnappers is linked in some way *to both the Abu Sayyaf and Southern Philippines Liberation Front groups.* According to the correspondence between $var2_{transfo}$ and $var3_{hypo}$ registered in CORRESP, SOUTHERN_PHILIPPINES_LIBERATION_FRONT *must also be bound to* $var3_{hypo}$ and stored, accordingly, *in the VALAFF/DESVAR repositories of the h2 environment.* This new value will be used in the further processing of the hypothesis *in parallel with the original one* (ABU_SAYYAF_GROUP), leading then (possibly) to *a totally new and potentially interesting set of results.*

4.2.4.4 Additional Examples

From a practical point of view, *the "positive," very general strategy* evoked at the end of the previous section is *not often employed*, because it can be *particularly exciting* in terms of results, but can also be *very computationally expensive.*

This can be easily understood if we examine Table 4.17, derived from Table 4.9, where we have represented a sort of *expanded* hypothesis h2, i.e. h2 as it would appear in practice *by taking systematically into account the possibility of transforming each of the original four steps of reasoning.*

The transformation rules shown in this table are some of the rules (mono- or multi-consequent) commonly used in a *"terrorism in Southern Philippines" context.* All of these are, of course, *"standard" transformation rules* that can be used for *"standard" querying purposes* independently from any hypothesis context. We can remark that there is a *whole family of transformations* (see the rules *t4, t7, t8, t9, . . .* in this table) corresponding to the condition schema *cond2* of *h2.* They represent variants of this *general scheme*: the separatist movement or the terrorist organization, or some group or single persons affiliated with them, have requested/received money for the ransom of the kidnapped.

Confronted with the "cost," in computer time, of the "positive" strategy, the usual strategy is then the *"negative"* one – where transformations are used

Table 4.17 Rule *h2* in the presence of transformations concerning the intermediary inference steps

Cond1	*The kidnappers are part of a separatist movement or of a terrorist organization.*
	(Rule t5, Consequent) Try to verify whether the kidnappers receive a permanent or occasional salary from this organization.
	(Rule t6, Consequent1) Try to verify whether a given separatist movement or terrorist organization is in strict control of a specific subgroup and, in this case,
	(Rule t6, Consequent2) check if the kidnappers are members of this subgroup. We will then assimilate the kidnappers to "members" of the movement or organization.
Cond2	*This movement or organization currently practices ransom kidnapping of given categories of people.*
	(Rule t4, Consequent) Try to verify whether this movement or organization has received some money for freeing from captivity one or more persons.
	(Rule t7, Consequent) Try to verify whether the family of the victim has received a ransom request from the separatist movement or terrorist organization.
	(Rule t8, Consequent1) Try to verify whether the family of the kidnapped has received a ransom request from a group or an individual person and, in this case,
	(Rule t8, Consequent2) check whether this second group or individual person is part of the separatist movement or terrorist organization.
	(Rule t9, Consequent1) Try to verify whether a particular subgroup of the separatist movement or terrorist organization exists and, in this case,
	(Rule t9, Consequent2) check whether this particular subgroup practices ransom kidnapping of particular categories of people.
	. . .
Cond3	*In particular, wealthy persons or executives or assimilated categories ("upper class" persons) are concerned.*
	(Rule t3, Consequent1) In a "ransom kidnapping" context, we can check whether the kidnapped person has a kinship relationship with a second person and, in this case,
	(Rule t3, Consequent2) we can check if this second person is wealthy or is an "upper class" person.
Cond4	*It must then be proved that the kidnapped person is wealthy or is an upper class person.*
	(Rule t10, Consequent) In a "Southern Philippines" context, generic "personalities" like consultants, journalists, artists, teachers etc. can be assimilated to "upper class" persons.

exclusively *in case of failure* of the "standard" procedure during the processing of a specific condition schema. *The "positive" strategy is employed only when an in-depth visualization of all the possible results is strictly required.*

To give a concrete example, let us suppose *systematically adopting a "positive" strategy for hypothesis h2*: the screen dump fragment of Fig. 4.10 shows what happens at the level of the condition schema *cond2* when, *after having directly found in a hypothesis context that a given terrorist group/ separatist movement practices ransom kidnapping,* we ask the system *to never-theless transform the corresponding (successful) search pattern to retrieve the*

```
********** the result for condition 2  ****************
*************************************************************************
***Entering an internal transformation module : internal level 1 ***********************
*************************************************************************
***                      The model to transform
***
***:
***      ] PRODUCE
***      SUBJ(ect)   : ABU_SAYYAF_GROUP :
***      OBJ(ect)    : ransom_kidnapping :
***      BENF        : human_being :
***      {}
***      date-1      :null
***      date-2      :null
***      is instance of:rule1.Produce:Cond2
***
***          ********** the result for consequent 1  ****************
***mod11.c4:
***      ] RECEIVE
***      SUBJ(ect)   : ( COORD ( SPECIF family_ HADJI_ABDUL_BASIT_DIMAPORO ) ( SPECIF family_
HADJI_SAMAD_TUTUNG ) ) :
***      OBJ(ect)    : ( SPECIF ransom_demand ( SPECIF cardinality_ none_ ) ) :
***      SOUR(ce)    : ( SPECIF INDIVIDUAL_PERSON_60 ( SPECIF cardinality_ 4 ) ) :
***      TOPIC       : ( COORD ( SPECIF hostage_release HADJI_ABDUL_BASIT_DIMAPORO ) ( SPECIF
hostage_release HADJI_SAMAD_TUTUNG ) )
***      { }
***      date-1      :13/10/1999
***      date-2      :null
***      is instance of:Receive:Information
***Natural language description :
***Since the kidnapping's day (13/11/1999), the families of the two hostages did not received
any request for ransom.
***
***          ********** the result for consequent 2  ****************
***mod11.c8:
***      ] BEHAVE
***      SUBJ(ect)   : ( SPECIF INDIVIDUAL_PERSON_60 ( SPECIF cardinality_ 4 ) ) :
***      MODAL(ity) : part_of
***      TOPIC       : ABU_SAYYAF_GROUP
***      {poss }
***      date-1      :13/10/1999
***      date-2      :null
***      is instance of:Behave:Member
***Natural language description :
***It is possible that the kidnappers are member of the Abu Sayyaf Group.
*************************************************************************
```

Fig. 4.10 Members of the Abu Sayyaf's group practice ransom kidnapping

same notion in an indirect way. Note that the transformation used to obtain the screen dump of Fig. 4.10 is now a *"two-step" (multi-consequent) rule*, namely rule *t8* of Table 4.17; to demonstrate that a given terrorist/separatist group practices ransom kidnapping, we will try to find evidence that members of this group are involved in actions related to this type of kidnapping. Thanks to this rule, we can then find *additional (indirect) evidence of the fact that Abu Sayyaf performs ransom kidnapping.* This consists of two logically linked "narrative events," where the first states that the families of two hostages, Hadji Abdul Basit Dimaporo and Hadji Samad Tutung, had not received so far a request for ransom from the four individuals that have kidnapped their relatives; and the second adds that the four kidnappers are known to be members of the Abu Sayyaf group.

As a last example of use of transformations in a hypothesis context, let us suppose that, after having accepted the possibility of making use of transformations in a hypothesis context and after having chosen the *"negative"* *strategy* (see Fig. 4.9), we introduce "2" as an answer to the request about the transformation's depth (Fig. 4.9 right). This means we accept that, *after having obtained a new search pattern by transformation, this last can pass in turn through the transformation procedures.*

By using a specific hypothesis rule, *h3*, proper to the "terrorism in the Southern Philippines" application (very easy indeed to generalize), we want now to retrieve the reasons that can have led a given INDIVIDUAL_PERSON_59 to be injured by members of the Abu Sayyaf group. Hypothesis *h3* suggests checking, among other things, *whether the injured/killed person was a member of the Christian community in the Southern Philippines:* members of this community have, in fact, often been *the targets of attacks performed by the separatists.* This rule is a very simple one and implies three reasoning steps, where the last, *cond3*, consists of verifying *the Christian community membership of the offended person;* according to the state of the specific knowledge base built up for the "terrorism" application, *this fact cannot be demonstrated directly for* INDIVIDUAL_PERSON_59.

A first transformation to be used corresponds, then, to the following *common sense argument:* "A given person can be considered as a 'member at large' of a given (e.g. Christian) community whether (i) it can be proved that he has a *very strict employment relationship* (e.g. a domestic_role) with a *second person* (first consequent schema) and (ii) *this second person* (the employer) is known to be *part of this community* (second consequent schema)." The first step of this transformation can be directly satisfied by retrieving that INDIVIDUAL_PERSON_59 is the chauffeur of a Catholic priest, Fr. Benjamin Inocencio (Fig. 4.11); the second step requires, however, to find out an *explicit proof of the fact that this second person is a member of the Christian community.* Proving the membership is obtained by passing through a further one-step transformation; this will specify that being a Roman Catholic priest is equivalent to being part of the (larger) Christian community (see Fig. 4.12).

4.2.4.5 Some Remarks about the Software Solutions

Integrating the two versions, for hypotheses and transformations, of *InferenceEngine* corresponds to solving a *complex "coroutine" problem,* where the main difficulty is generated, as usual in NKRL, by the existence of *complex data structures to be managed, stored and reloaded.* The integration can be implemented according to two approaches:

```
*********  the result for condition 3   ***************
********************************************************************************
***Entering an internal transformation module : internal level 1 ************************
********************************************************************************
***                           The model to transform
***
***:
***      ] BEHAVE
***        SUBJ(ect)  : INDIVIDUAL_PERSON_59 :
***        MODAL(ity) : member_of
***        TOPIC      : christian_community
***        {}
***        date-1     :null
***        date-2     :null
***        is instance of:
***
***              *********  the result for consequent 1   ***************
***mod483.c16:
***      ] BEHAVE
***        SUBJ(ect)  : INDIVIDUAL_PERSON_59 :
***        MODAL(ity) : ( SPECIF chauffeur_ FR_BENJAMIN_INOCENCIO )
***        {obs }
***        date-1     :28/12/2000
***        date-2     :null
***        is instance of:Behave:Role
***Natural language description :
***On December 28, 2000, we can remark that the (wounded) INDIVIDUAL_PERSON_59 mentioned in
occurrences mod483.c10 and mod483.c17 was the personal driver of Fr. Benjamin Inocencio.
***
```

Fig. 4.11 First level of transformation for the wounding of INDIVIDUAL_PERSON_59

```
***                  *********  the result for consequent 2   ***************
********************************************************************************
******Entering an internal transformation module : internal level 2 ************************
********************************************************************************
******                        The model to transform
******
******:
******      ] BEHAVE
******        SUBJ(ect)  : FR_BENJAMIN_INOCENCIO :
******        MODAL(ity) : member_of
******        TOPIC      : christian_community
******        {}
******        date-1     :null
******        date-2     :null
******        is instance of:
******
******              *********  the result for consequent 1   ***************
******mod483.c14:
******      ] BEHAVE
******        SUBJ(ect)  : FR_BENJAMIN_INOCENCIO :
******        MODAL(ity) : roman_catholic_priest
******        {obs }
******        date-1     :28/12/2000
******        date-2     :null
******        is instance of:Behave:Role
******Natural language description :
******On December 28, 2000, we can remark that Fr. Benjamin Inocencio was a Roman Catholic
priest.
********************************************************************************
```

Fig. 4.12 Second level of transformation for the wounding of INDIVIDUAL_PERSON_59

- The first one is the *classical "coroutine" solution*, where the "transformation" version of the engine has the *same priority* as the "hypothesis" version, and then it starts its execution, as the latter one, from the main (Java) method of *InferenceEngine*. The most important difficulty linked with this solution concerns the fact that *it should imply the complete execution of the transformation version (the "internal" version) until a result had been obtained*, requiring then an *efficient way* (Java's threads could be used in this context) *to return to the hypothesis version (the "external" one)*. On the other hand, this solution should also imply the fact of having a separate display (text output) for the results of the "internal" execution, with some difficulties, then, in coordinating them with the displaying of the "external" (hypothesis) results.

- The second approach, which is *more manageable and simpler to implement*, consists in just *integrating the InferenceEngine Java object corresponding to the "internal" (transformation) version in the execution of the "external" (hypothesis) version*. This allows the external hypothesis version of *InferenceEngine* (which works now as the "main" program) *to run the internal version until it has a result and to get back this result simply as a function execution return*. This approach allows implementing a "transparent" running of the internal module, and implies the advantage of having the results of the "internal" execution naturally integrated with those displayed by the interface of the main (hypothesis) version.

We have then chosen the second approach. Given (i) that during the functioning of *InferenceEngine*, *Reexec* is the only module invoked in order to reconstruct the environment proper to a previous choice point and to allow then *Execond* to build up a new search pattern, and (ii) that executing transformation operations (in our case, within a hypothesis context) amounts exactly to build up new search patterns, we can conclude that only *Reexec* must be modified to implement the "integration" operations.

In practice, during the execution of an internal transformation, *Reexec* will run the "internal" (transformation) Java object *until a result has been found and returned*; the internal object is then *stopped*, and it will *wait for a new Reexec call*, producing *other results* if these are possible for the current transformation. For each call to *Reexec*, there will be then one internal module pending and waiting for further results – each main program execution level will potentially have an internal module object reference pointing to such object.

From a Java programming point of view, *InferenceEngine* includes *three different objects*: *Hypothesis*, *Transformation* and *InternalTransformation*. The first two are *practically unchanged* with respect to the "standard" working of *InferenceEngine*. The *InternalTransformation object is modeled on the Transformation* one; as already stated, it will run trying to find a result and then, if successful, it will return this result; if this is not possible, then it will throw a NoMoreResultsException(). *Reexec* now executes first the *InternalTransformation* code to get the next result and, if this is not possible, catches the exception and continues its execution trying to build a new model for this level. See Zarri and Bernard [2004a] for more information and a detailed example.

4.2.5 Inference Rules and Internet Filtering

Hypotheses and transformations are the *most well-known inference procedures of NKRL*, and they have been *systematically used* in all the applications of this language – for example, they are actually (November 2007) used, in their "integrated" version, in an important project in the "defense" domain. However, the logical principles and the practical tools underpinning these procedures can be very well adapted to other inferencing scenarios. To show this, we will illustrate briefly in this section a (simple) application of the NKRL inference rules *to filter "questionable" Web sites according to a semantic-rich approach*. This application has been carried out in the context of a European project, EUFORBIA (IAP P26505) [e.g. Zarri et al., 2002, 2003; Bertino et al., 2005].

NKRL is used in EUFORBIA to *associate with a Web site* – when it is first inserted on the Web or at the time of a major restructuring – *a "semantic annotation" called "EUFORBIA label" that represents the semantic content of the whole site* as defined by its home page and the associated pages. A EUFORBIA label includes *three sections*, where only the first is strictly mandatory:

- the "aim" section, i.e. a description of the main objectives of the site;
- *the "properties" section*, i.e. a description of *some characteristics of the site that could be interesting to note* (as the fact that the site is free or paying, the increment or decrement in the number of hints, etc.);
- the "sub-sites" section, i.e. a list of the associated sites with a short description of the main functions of each of them.

Table 4.18 reproduces a (very simplified) image of the *"aim" section* of the EUFORBIA label associated with the (fictitious) site Snoog Dopp; the meaning of this code is "The site is devoted to a (fictitious) individual named Snoog Dopp (c76); this individual is a rap star (c77)." The first syntactic expression of Table 4.18 (a "binding occurrence"), labeled c73, expresses the fact that this aim section is formed of two predicative occurrences, c76 and c77, that must take place together, COORD(ination). Note that, in EUFORBIA, the URL (Uniform Resource Locator) identifying a specific Internet site *is dealt with as an individual* instance of the HClass concept url_; the latter is a concept of the entity_ type that is classed among the specific terms of label/name_. *These particular individuals are handled by NKRL/EUFORBIA as sorts of location determiners*.

The *filtering functions* of EUFORBIA are supplied by the modules of a *specific WebBrowser/WebFilter software* (installed on a proxy server or on the user's machine) that has been built up for the project (Fig. 4.13).

Table 4.18 An example of EUFORBIA label

c73)	(COORD c76 c77)		
c76)	OWN	SUBJ	SNOOG_DOPP_internet_site: (WWW.SNOOG-DOPP. COM)
		OBJ	property_
		TOPIC	(SPECIF dedicated_to SNOOG_DOPP)

Own:CompoundProperty (5.12)

c77)	BEHAVE	SUBJ	SNOOP_DOGG: (WWW.SNOOG-DOPP.COM)
		MODAL	rap_star

Behave:Role (1.33)

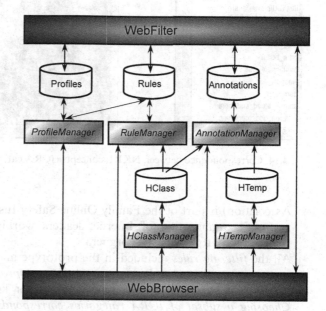

Fig. 4.13 WebBrowser/ WebFilter modules of the NKRL-based filtering prototype

The principles of functioning of the architecture of Fig. 4.13 can be summarized in the following way:

- The *ProfileManager* module allows the user to specify their "user profile," i.e. to define the categories of Web sites they do not want to see/ download. The categories proposed to the user coincide with the standard categories defined by the ICRA Association, like "explicit sexual acts" or "killing of fantasy characters." These are automatically converted into the corresponding NKRL concepts, introduced (permanently) into HClass to allow the running of the EUFORBIA project, like explicit_sexual_activity or fantasy_character_killing (see Fig. 4.14). The user profile is then stored in the "Profiles" repository. ICRA (formerly the Internet Content Rating

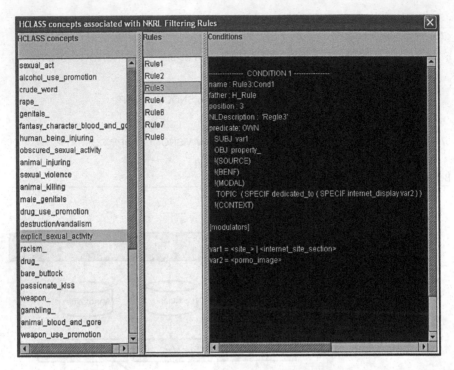

Fig. 4.14 Correspondence between NKRL concepts (ICRA categories) and filtering rules

Association) is part of the Family Online Safety Institute, an international, nonprofit organization of Internet leaders working to develop a safer Internet; see http://www.fosi.org/icra/.

- All the *filtering rules* included in the prototype and stored in the "Rules" repository *are associated with (one or more) appropriate HClass concepts*, like explicit_sexual_activity or fantasy_character_killing mentioned above. *Choosing a subset of ICRA categories corresponds then*, via the passage through the NKRL concepts, *to (implicitly) choosing a particular subset of filtering rules*; see again Fig. 4.14.

When a particular site is required, its *EUFORBIA label* (see the example of Table 4.18) – associated with the site thanks to previous, off-line operations – *is unified with the activated filtering rules*. If the unification with one of these rules *succeeds* – i.e. if *all the "conditions" (see below) for refusing the site that are included in the rule are verified by the information stored in the label* – then the site is *negated*. This means that the result of a *successful unification* between the EUFORBIA label of a requested site and a filtering rule *corresponds to the activation of the command "downloading the site is not allowed."* Thanks to the *high level of precision in the description of the sites obtained through the use of NKRL labels*, it is *very easy to perform filtering operations with a high degree of precision*, e.g. to filter out *specific subsections of a given site where "questionable" information can been found* (e.g. the subsection "lyrics" of the global Snoog Dopp site) while still allowing to *download the main site or other subsections*.

With respect now to the format of these filtering rules, see (4.4), they can be considered as a *particular case* of implication (4.2) above where *the "head" of the rules is now a constant* K *that corresponds systematically to the command "downloading the site is not allowed"*:

$$K \text{ iff } Y_1 \text{ and } Y_2 \ldots \text{ and } Y_n \tag{4.4}$$

$Y_1, \ldots, Y_n$, the NKRL translation of the "*conditions*" that must all be satisfied to activate the command, correspond, as usual, to *partially instantiated templates*. Using now, for simplicity's sake, the *usual "IF/THEN" format* – where the left-hand side corresponds to the Y_i of Eq. (4.4), which must all be satisfied, and the right-hand side to the execution of the command K – Table 4.19 gives the NL transcription of some simple filtering rules and Table 4.20 presents the actual NKRL code of RULE4 of Table 4.19.

From an *InferenceEngine* point of view, taking into account Eq. (4.4) and the format illustrated in Tables 4.19 and 4.20, it appears clearly that *the EUFORBIA filtering rules can be likened to hypothesis/transformation rules where the premise/the antecedent is missing* – or better, where the premise/antecedent is replaced by the constant K introduced above, and the main logical/algorithmic characteristics of *InferenceEngine*, like the sharing of

Table 4.19 Some simple EUFORBIA (NKRL) filtering rules

Only one condition (IF *cond1* $\Rightarrow$ *deny access*):

RULE3:   IF *a given site/site section praises topics like racism, violence, sexuality, etc.*
           THEN *the site/site section must be refused*

(e.g. see the sub-section "lyrics" of "www.snoog-dopp.com" site that advocates sexuality, violence and drug legalization)

Two conditions (IF *cond1* AND *cond2* $\Rightarrow$ *deny access*):

RULE4:   IF *a given site/section is devoted to spreading information over Internet*
           AND *this information concerns sexuality, violence, racism, etc.*
           THEN *the site/section must be refused*

(e.g. see Fig. 4.15, the unification with a site devoted to the diffusion of short stories about homosexuality, etc.)

Three conditions (IF *cond1* AND *cond2* AND *cond3* $\Rightarrow$ *deny access*):

RULE5:   IF *a site does not contain explicit nudity*
           AND *this site includes sections*
           AND *some of these show photos of women/teenagers dressed in bras or underwear*
           THEN *these sections must be denied*

(e.g. sections like "mixed-sheer-bras" and "mixed-teen-bras" of a "bra-dedicated" site)

Table 4.20 NKRL coding of RULE4 of Table 4.19

RULE4:COND1)	OWN	SUBJ	var1
		OBJ	property_
		TOPIC	(SPECIF dedicated_to (SPECIF internet_publishing var2))
RULE4:COND2)	OWN	SUBJ	var2
		OBJ	property_
		TOPIC	var3

var1 = site_, internet_site_section
var2 = information_item
var3 = sexuality_, violence_, racism_

values among variables, the backtracking or the management of the environment variables, remain *totally untouched*. The filtering rules can then be considered as reduced to a sequence of condition/consequent schemata that represent together (AND) the "reasoning" part of the rule and *that make use only of the Execond and Reexec modules*. More technical details can be found, for example, in Zarri et al. [2002].

Figures 4.15 and 4.16 concern the (*successful*) unification of RULE4 of Tables 4.19 and 4.20 with the EUFORBIA label associated with a possibly inappropriate site. If unification is found, *all the URLs* (e.g. see Fig. 4.16) *mentioned within the unified predicative occurrences will be returned to the WebBrowser*. If a URL

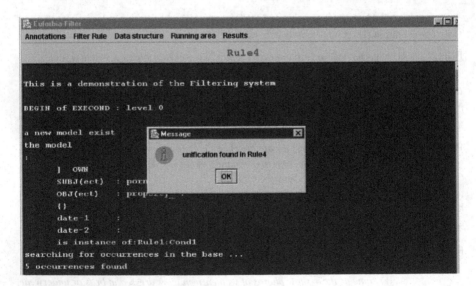

Fig. 4.15 Unification rule/label performed by Execond

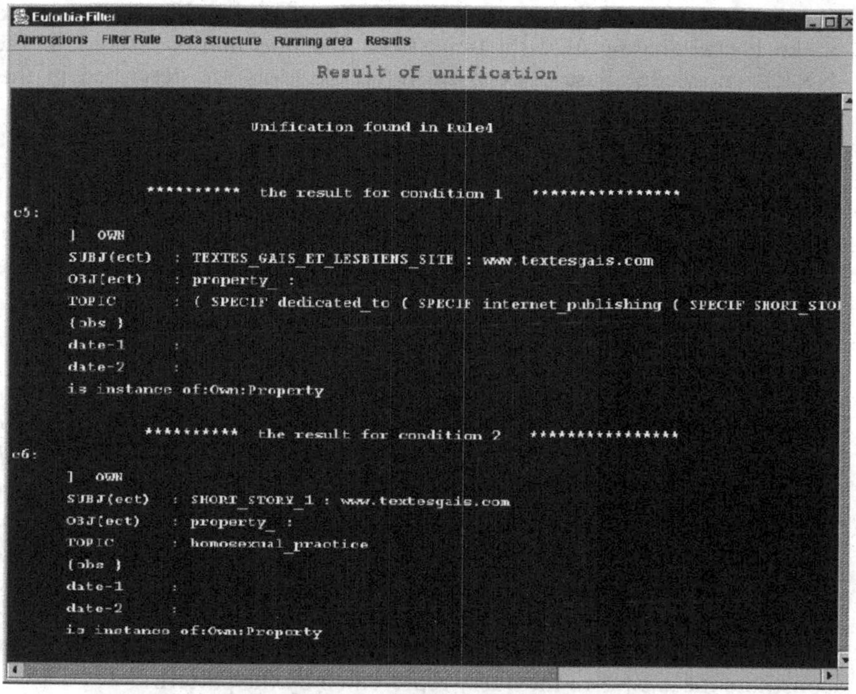

Fig. 4.16 Results of the unification rule/label for RULE4 of Tables 4.19/4.20

corresponds to a *site, the whole site will be refused.* If a URL corresponds to a *part of a site* (e.g. www.snoog-dopp.com/lyrics.shtml), then *only this part is refused.* At the user's level, this unification (i.e. the filtering) *is translated by the display of an empty screen* with the message "access denied." If no filtering rule succeeds, then the WebBrowser can freely show the required Web page to the user.

4.3 In the Guise of Winding Up

We have described in this chapter the set of (implemented) tools that allow the user *to exploit concretely the data structures and the conceptual contents introduced in the two previous chapters.* These tools can be arranged in two categories.

- *Querying tools* that (making use of some elementary inference procedures of the "subsumption" type) allow the user to *recover information from a knowledge base of NKRL annotations ("metadocuments") in an (advanced) information retrieval style.* These tools are based on the concept of "search pattern" and are embodied within the *Fum* component of the NKRL software.

- *Advanced inference tools* that, using *Fum* as basic building block, allow us to make logical/analogical deductions from the information stored in the NKRL knowledge base. Two main inference tools are described in this chapter:
  - – *transformation rules* that allow the system to answer in some way to a direct query that failed *by supplying the user with information logically/ semantically related with the information originally searched for*;
  - – *hypothesis rules* that allow the user to search for the *"implicit" relationships* (e.g. the "causal" ones) that can exist among the pieces of information registered in the knowledge base.

The main characteristics of the *query tools* are:

- The users can query directly the knowledge base making use of *"search patterns,"* i.e. *NKRL data structures that supply the general framework of information to be searched for*. The search patterns correspond to *specialized/ partially instantiated templates* where all the "explicit variables" *var$_i$* have been replaced by concepts/individuals compatible with the original constraints imposed on these variables. The patterns mimic the predicative occurrences to be queried *by specifying the positions of the data that must be retrieved, by pattern-matching techniques, within these predicative occurrences*. The set of predicative occurrences unified by a given search pattern constitute the *answer* to the query represented by the pattern.
- The unification/filtering operations between a search pattern and the occurrences carried out by *Fum* are *oriented*, which means that *all the terms* used to build up a search pattern must be *explicitly found in the matched occurrences*, either in an *identical form* (e.g. predicate and roles) or as *subsumed concepts or instances* of the implicit variables. *Additional terms* (roles, fillers and part of fillers) with respect to those explicitly declared in the pattern *can be freely found in the occurrences*.
- During the *Fum* processing, the *unification of complex fillers (expansions) must take into account the constraints imposed by NKRL for the creation of well-formed expansions*. This implies that, during the unification, the complex fillers of the search pattern and the occurrences *must be decomposed into tree structures labeled with the four AECS operators* introduced in Section 2.2.2.3, and that *the unification of these tree structures must follow the constraints defined by the "priority rule"* defined in this same section.
- Search patterns are normally associated with a *"search interval"* *date1–date2* that is used to limit the search for unification *to the slice of time that it is considered appropriate to explore*. This means, however, that the knowledge base *must be opportunely "indexed" from a temporal point of view*, making use of the temporal information associated with the original narrative documents and echoed, in NKRL format, in the corresponding predicative occurrences.
- The *indexing mechanism* of NKRL is composed of *three different levels: predicate level, main elements level* and *temporal level*. The latter is the most

complex and interesting one. Implementing the "temporal level" indexing implies *superimposing* on the knowledge base of NKRL occurrences *a grid of nine lists composed of pairs* $\{lc_j, dc_j\}$, where lc_j corresponds to the *symbolic label of a particular predicative occurrence* c_j, and dc_j to one of the *four possible dates* associated with c_j. The lists are structured according to notions of *temporal category* and *temporal perspective* defined in Section 2.2.2.4.

- The superimposition of indexes on the knowledge base allows the system *to speed up all the unification/filtering operations between search pattern and occurrences*, given that the real and complete matching operations *are executed only on a small fragment of the base that already contains the "good" answers*, "preselected" making use only of the indexing mechanisms.

The main characteristics of the hypothesis/transformation inference rules are:

- These high-level inference rules can be defined as *implications* of the type

$$X \text{ iff } Y_1 \text{ and } Y_2 \ldots \text{ and } Y_n \tag{4.2}$$

- where X, the "head" of the rule, is a *predicative occurrence* in a hypothesis context *or a search pattern* in a transformation context. $Y_1, \ldots, Y_n$ represent the successive *reasoning steps* (implemented as *partially instantiated templates*) that must all be successively validated in order to satisfy the implication. Validation is performed by finding *successful unifications* (using *Fum*) between a search pattern p_i derived from a Y_i and the occurrences of the knowledge base.
- The construction of the search patterns, the unification operations, and the transfer of the values assumed by the variables proper to a given "condition schema" *cond_i* (translation into NKRL terms of an Y_i) to the level *cond_{i+1}* (Y_{i+1}), *are executed by an InferenceEngine that works according to a backward chaining approach with (at the moment, see also the next chapter) chronological backtracking.* Four *environment variables* are used to allow the engine *to reconstruct correctly the previous choice point in a backtracking context.*
- The "hypothesis" version of *InferenceEngine* consists of *three main modules*. *Exeprem* is used to *unify the "premise" X of the hypothesis rule with the predicative occurrence to be "explained"*; a successful unification denotes, among other things, that the rule is, in principle, suitable for constructing a reasonable form of explication. *Execond* is used for deriving *appropriate search patterns from a cond_i and for finding* unifications within the knowledge base. *Reexec* is used for the *backtracking operations. Exeprem* and *Execond* perform the *forward traversal of the choice tree*, with *Reexec* being called *whenever a failure occurs.*
- The *"transformation" version* of *InferenceEngine* is *quite identical to that for the hypotheses.* In particular, the module *Antexec* (execution of the antecedent) corresponds to the *Exeprem* module, *Consexec* (execution of the consequent(s)) corresponds to *Execond*, and *Reexec* is the same in the

two versions. We recall here that, in a transformation context, the "head" X of Eq. (4.2) is represented by a *search pattern*, p_i, and that the principle employed consists then in trying to *automatically "transform" p_i into one or more different p_1, p_2, ..., p_n that are not strictly "equivalent" but only "semantically close to the original one.*

- *Transformations and hypotheses can work in an integrated way, i.e. the (standard) search patterns derived from the condition schemata condᵢ during* the execution of a hypothesis *can be "transformed" making use of the InferenceEngine version for transformations.* Integrating these two inferencing modes corresponds to:

  – From a *very practical point of view*, transformations can now be used to *try to find some useful answers when the search patterns derived directly from a condition schema of a hypothesis fail*; a hypothesis deemed to fall short can, on the contrary, *continue successfully until its normal end.*

  – From a *more general point of view*, transformations can be used to *modify in an a priori unpredictable way* the reasoning steps (condition schemata) to be executed within a "hypothesis" context, *independently from the fact that these steps have been successful or not.* This is equivalent to *"unlock" the predefined scenarios* proper to the hypothesis rules, and to augment then the possibility of discovering "implicit information" within the knowledge base.

- Integration can be performed according to *several strategies*, which come down practically to (i) *transforming systematically all the search patterns* generated during the execution of a hypothesis, *even if these patterns have been successful*, or (ii) *executing the transformation only when a failure occurred.* The first strategy is particularly useful to discover all the possible "implicit" information associated with a knowledge base of NKRL occurrences; it is, however, computationally expensive. The second is then the usual one.

- From a strict *software* point of view, integrating the two versions, for hypotheses and transformations, of *InferenceEngine, corresponds to solving a complex "coroutine" problem.* This has been worked out by *integrating the InferenceEngine Java object corresponding to the "internal" (transformation) version in the execution of the "external" (hypothesis) version.*

- From a *logical* point of view, on the contrary, the main difficulty consists in *finding a correspondence among the variables proper to the transformation rules* used to modify the search patterns created in a hypothesis context *and the original variables included in the condition schemata at the root of these patterns.* The values recovered by the transformation variables must, in fact, be passed on to the hypothesis variables to allow the original hypothesis to continue. In its integrated version, *InferenceEngine* must then build up a CORRESP(ondence) table *where the equivalence among transformation and hypothesis variables* is registered.

The chapter ends with the evocation of another category of NKRL rules, some simple *filtering rules* that have been used in the context of a European project devoted to find ways of *filtering "questionable" Web sites according to a semantic-rich approach.* The rules used in this context can be considered as a *downgraded version* of Eq. (4.2), *where the head X of the rule is replaced by a constant K corresponding to the command: "downloading this site is not allowed."* Satisfying, in fact, the reasoning steps Y_i that make up the "body" of the rules corresponds, in this case, *to verifying that all the "conditions" for considering the site as "questionable" stated in a given rule are really present in the "EUFORBIA label" associated with the site.* A *"EUFORBIA label"* is a *semantic annotation expressed in NKRL terms that describes in short the "content" of the site.*

Chapter 5
Conclusion

NKRL is a fully implemented language/environment (see Appendix A), in the sense that *all of its main conceptual principles* detailed in the previous chapters *correspond to fully implemented and running computer science modules.*

This does not mean, of course, that work on NKRL is definitively ended and that no further improvements/additions are necessary. Some of these improvements are simply of a *"cosmetic" nature.* For example, many of the visualization features – in particular those concerning the visualization of the results of the inference rules, see the figures of the last sections in Chapter 4 – are inherited from "old" software developed in old European projects and not yet re-implemented; they are somewhat "ugly" and do not do justice to the complexity and interest of the results. More substantial improvements can be classed in two main categories:

- *technological enhancements*, which mainly concern the setting up of an improved and unified software environment able to support extensive commercial applications directly;
- *theoretical enhancements*, susceptible to introduce possible new developments in the conceptual bases of the language and intended, in particular, *to establish bridges with other popular conceptual approaches.*

We will then conclude this book with some information about what could constitute *the future of NKRL's work.*

5.1 Technological Enhancements

These will concern, first of all, *the merging of the two separate environments* (file-oriented and ORACLE-supported) described in Appendix A into a single one, installed on top of *relational database systems* for generality's sake (MSSQL, ORACLE, DB2, MySQL, etc.), but *independent of the software of a particular manufacturer* (e.g. ORACLE). We can note, in this context, that *all the main conceptual problems* concerning efficient *storing and retrieval* of NKRL structures in and from relational databases have already been solved in the present ORACLE-based version [e.g. Zarri and Bernard, 2004b].

G.P. Zarri, *Representation and Management of Narrative Information*,   245
DOI 10.1007/978-1-84800-078-0_5, © Springer-Verlag London Limited 2009

Moreover, a certain number of improvements and optimization operations must be obligatorily associated with the new environment. Among them:

- The introduction of *optimization techniques* with respect to the present *chronological backtracking* used by the NKRL inference engine(s) (see Section 4.2): we plan to make use, in this context, of *more efficient pruning strategies* inspired from those (well known and dependable) developed in a logic programming framework [e.g. Clark and Tärnlund 1982]. The aim here is to reduce considerably – even in the case where *DB-based versions of the software are used* – the time of processing associated with the *most complex inference procedures*, i.e. those that imply the integrated exploitation of different types of rules; see Section 4.2.4. For example, in the "integrated" scenario, the present ORACLE version of the NKRL software takes up to some minutes to get a result when extended knowledge bases of rules and occurrences are used, whereas a few seconds are needed in the file-oriented version of the software; see also Zarri [2005].

- The use of *packaging, configuring, reformatting, etc.* techniques to improve the *"usability"* of the system; see also the "cosmetic" improvements mentioned above. This will probably imply *an in-depth redesign of all the user interfaces*, not only those devoted to the usual "querying" of the system, but also those to be used to create the "knowledge context" – ontologies, rule base(s), background knowledge base, etc. – of a given application; see again Appendix A. Work in this context is already under development (November 2007), in the context of an application of the NKRL techniques in the "defense" domain.

We can add here that the set up of a *complete and detailed documentation of the NKRL software*, the creation of updated "user's manuals," etc. will also be necessary. This work will constitute, among other things, a *preliminary and necessary step* before the submission of NKRL as an ISO Standard for the representation and management of nonfictional narratives; see also below. Another important aspect of the "technological enhancement" will concern the precise *specification of the metrics and evaluation procedures*. A starting point in this respect could be represented by the evaluation framework developed as part of the EC/NSF-sponsored EAGLES/ISLE (IST–1999–10647) initiative on standards for language engineering. We will also examine the possibility of adapting to an NKRL context other computer science standards, e.g. like the Lehigh University benchmark [Guo et al., 2007], a standard benchmark used in the context of large Semantic Web knowledge-based systems.

But the most important aspect of these "technological enhancement" activities will probably be represented by the implementation of an efficient and robust solution to the *"NL problem."* We have already discussed at length, in Chapter 1, the argument stating that *a complete and efficient knowledge representation system for nonfictional narratives can be set up without having recourse to any specific "linguistic" theory*. However, the "practical" problem concerning the possibility of speeding up the creation of large knowledge bases of NKRL-coded narrative documents starting directly from their *original formulation in an NL* (English as a first approach) still exists. Note that:

- Solving this problem is particularly important even when the original nonfictional narrative documents are *not* textual documents. Any sort of multimedia document can be, in fact, *"linguistically annotated"* by associating with it *an NL description of its "semantic content"*; see the legend "The US President is addressing the Congress" that can be added to the corresponding visual documents (photographs, videos, etc.). A quick way of annotating multimedia documents in an NL consists of making use of automatic dictation systems (ADSs) – like Dragon Naturally Speaking Professional, for example. If an NL annotation exists, *the problem of "translating" the content of a multimedia document into NKRL terms is reduced to that of "translating" the existing NL annotation into NKRL*. This last problem can be considered as "easier" than the general NL/NKRL "translation" problem, given that these sorts of (usually short) annotations are typically *strongly relevant* with respect to the "semantic content" of the corresponding multimedia documents, avoiding then the problem of first discovering the "pertinent sections" to be converted into NKRL format in the case of (very) long nonfictional texts.
- Solving this problem corresponds also to *being able to question an NKRL knowledge base in an NL*, given that a user's query is nothing more than a *short NL text* that, moreover, does not usually entail all the semantic/syntactic difficulties proper to long NL documents.

In this last context – querying NKRL knowledge bases in an NL – very encouraging results have been obtained in the framework of a recent corporate application, thanks to the use of simple techniques that implement the "translation" of NL queries into NKRL "search patterns" (Section 4.1) using *shallow parsing techniques* like the AGFL grammar and lexicon [Koster, 2004] and the *standard NKRL inference capabilities.*

To deal with the NL/NKRL "translation" problem *on a more general basis*, we plan to make use – at least as a first hypothesis – of the (partial) *results already obtained in the context of the PARMENIDES* project thanks to the use of the syntactic/semantic *Cafetière tools* provided by one of the PARMENIDES' partners, the University of Manchester [Black et al., 2003, 2004]. In short, the PARMENIDES approach to mapping from NL into NKRL was based on the use of Cafetière to (i) perform the usual *morpho-syntactic analysis* of the input texts and (ii) to identify some *"basic semantic elements"* from these texts, like the "named entities," their conceptual roles (agent, patient, beneficiary, ...) and their mutual relationships (RolePlayed, WorksFor, DefinedAs, ProducedBy, IsLocated, ...). Rules were then used to map *fragments of the morpho-syntactic analysis, enriched with the retrieved basic semantic elements, into "predicative occurrences"-like NKRL structures.* In this context, the technological enhancements to NKRL to be realized in a "linguistic" context could then include:

- Realize an *optimized and improved version of the already existing core of a "PARMENIDES-like" NL/NKRL translator* taking advantage of the improvements made to Cafetière since 2004 in the context of the UK National Centre for Text Mining, with respect in particular to scalability, efficiency and modularity. The National Centre for Text Mining is hosted by the University of Manchester.
- Otherwise, reproduce the functions of this "inner core" making use of one of the several NL syntactic/semantic analyzers developed in recent years in an academic/commercial environment.
- Add progressively to this first nucleus all the missing functionalities, like: (i) the possibility of *automatically constructing "complex fillers" for the NKRL roles*; (ii) the possibility of *generating* the temporal information code to be systematically associated with the NKRL "predicative occurrences" – Cafetière already implements some of the TimeML (see Section 2.2.2.4) features (tense, aspects), but it cannot at present generate *full temporal information*, as this possibility depends precisely on the capacity of accessing ontological event information of the HTemp type; (iii) the possibility of *generating the "binding relationships"* (CAUSE, GOAL, COORD, COND, etc.) used to link together the NKRL representation of elementary events into *wider "story trees" or "episodes"*; etc.
- Testing in depth the final software in the context of some specific, practical application.

For previous, partial experiments for implementing the "translation" NL/ NKRL in a Common Lisp context, e.g. see Zarri [1992b].

5.2 Theoretical Enhancements

The work to be done in this context is probably *less urgent* than that described in the previous section, since the "technological enhancements" introduced above should already be sufficient to allow NKRL's derivatives *to come definitively onto the market*. The "theoretical" work is, however, of a real importance because:

- It must allow validating *definitively the theoretical background of NKRL*, improving this last, if needed, with contributions from other advanced knowledge representation schemata.
- It must establish *solid bridges* with technologies, like the Semantic Web, that share with NKRL its ambition to supply a computer-understandable description of the "semantic content" of multimedia documents – even if, as already stated several times in the previous chapters, *the W3C languages are far from providing complete (and convincing) solutions, at least with respect to the "nonfictional narratives problem."*

Regarding the first point, the work will then concern mainly an *in-depth re-examination of the characteristics of the existing, high-level conceptual models, n*-ary and not – Topic Maps, Conceptual Graphs, CYC, W3C languages, F-logic, Hans Kamp's discourse representation theory (DRT), Allen's interval algebra, RCC8 spatial calculus, FrameNet, etc.; see also Chapters 1 and 2 – to see if *they include knowledge representation structures that could be useful to better describe the nonfictional narrative domain* and that are *presently missing* in the current definition of NKRL. Obvious examples in this domain can be the addition of some unification and inference techniques derived from the Conceptual Graphs domain, of new temporal primitives in the Allen, Kamp or RCC8 style, some sorts of "microtheories" modeled on CYC or new conceptual structures inspired by FrameNets' "semantic frames." However, in order to provide some *practical boundaries* to these types of "theoretical" activity, the possible addition of "theoretical enhancements" should be mainly *piloted by the needs for extensions that could derive from specific requirements of concrete applications* – for example, *needs for new multimedia-oriented primitive structures* (like new NKRL "templates") that could be required *to take even better into account the specific multimedia aspects of nonfictional narrative information.*

Work on the second point will prove particularly important with respect to the *insertion of the NKRL technology within the XML/RDF, etc. mainstream*: even if the most inflated expectations about the Semantic Web approach seem now to be over, at least some Semantic Web techniques are probably here to stay, in their present or in a more advanced form. We have identified two main fields where "cooperation" between NKRL and a Semantic Web language can be mutually useful:

- Definition and implementation of *bridges and interfaces between NKRL and RDF/OWL*. The aim here is that of implementing a sort of *interoperability* between the two categories of languages in order to allow (at least partial) possibilities of *making use of resources and reasoning tools defined for one of the two approaches in the context of the other*. We note that "translators" for passing from NKRL to RDF format and vice versa have long since existed [e.g. Zarri, 2000]. However, given the differences between RDF and NKRL with respect to their respective "expressive power," *nonstandard operators* have been defined to make the translation possible. For example, operators based on ad hoc interpretations of the RDF "containers" – RDF tools for describing collections of resources [Beckett, 2004] – have been used for taking fully into account the AECS sub-language of NKRL. *More general solutions must, however, be found*, and this work must be extended, in case, to build up bridges with OWL as well. However, it is important to understand that the conversion NKRL/W3C languages can only be a *partial one, given the difference in expressive power mentioned above*. This means that complete interoperability can only be implemented between RDF/OWL and a *downgraded version (a binary version) of NKRL*, sufficient however to make use of OWL-compatible reasoning tools within an NKRL environment. When high-level querying/reasoning operations must be accomplished, *inferencing tools in the style of those actually associated with NKRL must necessarily be used to take fully into account the "nonfictional narrative" n-ary formats.*

- *Integration of the NKRL inference procedures into a Semantic Web Services architecture.* As already stated we consider, in fact, that this last type of service constitutes *one of the most interesting outcomes* of the whole Semantic Web activities. More precisely, we are interested here in two possible uses of our technology in a Semantic Web Services context: (i) making use of *high-level, NKRL-based semantic annotations* – see also [Farrel and Lausen, 2007] – to describe *even richer services and resources* that can then be used in deploying "*context-aware Web services*"; see Maamar et al. [2006] for this last notion; (ii) relying on these semantic annotations and on the NKRL inference rules to *describe powerful selection and composition policies and to commute automatically ("transformation rule") among them.* In this last case, what we propose corresponds, in a way and by replacing UML with NKRL, to the suggestions described in Gašević et al. [2006]. In this paper, they define the use of UML-based "event–condition–action" rules that consist of a triggering event, a list of conditions, a performed action and an optional post-condition formalizing of the state change after the execution of the action. According to them, these types of rule can be considered as a *dynamic description of Web Service interactions.*

A last point to be considered about the "theoretical enhancement" consists of the *formal description of the NKRL syntax/semantics* to be conceived as a starting point for the submission of NKRL as a *proposed ISO Standard for the Conceptual Annotation and Management of multimedia, nonfictional narratives of an "economic" interest.* Examples to be followed in this domain can be John Sowa's work to define a conceptual graph standard or the recent Common Logic proposed standard, ISO/IEC FDIS 24707:2006(E).

Appendix A

NKRL Software

This appendix describes, in a very concise way, some important aspects of the NKRL software after the improvements introduced from 2003 to 2005 in the framework of the EC PARMENIDES project already mentioned; this project was coordinated by the "School of Informatics" of the University of Manchester (UK) and included partners from Germany, Greece, Switzerland and The Netherlands. A general description of PARMENIDES can be found, for example, in Rinaldi et al. [2003] and Black et al. [2004]; an important aspect of the project has concerned the implementation of a "multi-level" process of semantic/conceptual annotations intended to give rise, as a final result, to the representation of the "deep meaning" of textual documents into NKRL format. For simplicity's sake, we will not mention here some very recent developments of the software (not yet fully "certified") implemented in the framework of current projects; anyway, the "demonstration" version of NKRL still corresponds to the "file-oriented," PARMENIDES-based version of the software described below.

From a specific NKRL point of view, two important results have been obtained in the framework of PARMENIDES: (i) the implementation of two complete Java prototypes of the NKRL software, illustrated in brief in this appendix and, more in detail, in Zarri [2005/2006]; (ii) the use of this software for an in-depth exploitation of a corpus of (declassified) narrative news supplied by the Greek Ministry of Defence (MoD) – one of PARMENIDES' partners – and related to terrorism in the Southern Philippines between 1993 and 2000; e.g. see Zarri [2005]. As we have seen in the previous chapters, several of the concrete examples used in this book refer to this application.

The Two Versions of the Software

All the practical details concerning the installation of the two versions (file-oriented and ORACLE-based) of the NKRL software from the NKRL.zip file – including the description of the directories, of the .bat files, of the

251

particular instruction for installing the ORACLE version, etc. – are detailed in Zarri [2005/2006: section 2.1]. The reasons that have led to the creation of a file-oriented version are mainly the following:

- The possibility of running a *quite-complete, "demonstration" version of the NKRL software* on machines unable to support a full-fledged version of ORACLE, e.g. low-range portable computers.
- Several procedures (e.g. the most complex inference operations involving a coordinated running of "hypothesis" and "transformation" rules – see Section 4.2.4) are *considerably accelerated in the file version*, and this can be useful for those situations, e.g. (but not only) demos, where an *immediate answer* can be valuable.

Note, however, that a certain "sluggishness" of the most complex inference procedures in the standard ORACLE version is not a default in itself, given that *these rules must be conceived more as a powerful tool for discovering all the possible implicit relationships among the data in the knowledge base than as a standard question-answering system*; see again Chapter 4.

Apart from the obvious, general limitations concerning the amounts of data/knowledge that it is possible to store in the file-oriented system, the present version of this last system has some *specific limitations* – which could also be easily amended in the case of the set up of a next version. These concern mainly the specific *HClass environment*. In the ORACLE version, the tools for setting up and managing the HClass hierarchy of concepts correspond to a standard OKBC module in the Protégé style; as such, they allow, among other things, to associate complex "frames" with the concepts – see also Section 2.2.1.2. Presently this is not allowed in the file-oriented version, where only some basic functions (insert, delete, move, display,...) operating on the bare tree-structure of the ontology represented into file format *(sons.txt)* can be used.

The Main Interface

Figure A.1 illustrates the interface that appears – independently of the fact that the file-oriented or the ORACLE-based version is used – after double clicking on the *mainInterface.bat* icon included in the NKRL software package. This interface has been specifically developed in a PARMENIDES context, and it represents a major advance in the process of "rationalization" of the NKRL software, allowing us, for example, to use a *unique data/knowledge repository* for all the basic functions of this software.

Three different sorts of buttons appear in Fig. A.1:

- The "visualization" buttons, in the lower-right corner of the interface. Their function is to allow a quick inspection, both *off-line* and *on-line*, of the main *data structures* of the software, namely the event hierarchy (HTemp), the

Fig. A.1 Main interface of
the NKRL software

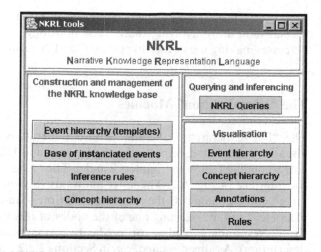

Fig. A.2 Visualization of
annotations/predicative
occurrences

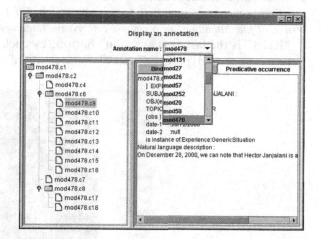

concept hierarchy (HClass), and the sections of the knowledge base devoted
to the annotations (occurrences) and to the hypothesis and transformation
rules.

- The "construction and management" buttons, on the left. Their function
  concerns the setting up and updating of the previous data structures. Note
  that the ORACLE version of the "concept hierarchy" environment is a
  *stand-alone, complete environment for the set up and use of conceptual hier-
  archies*. It could then be used in place of, for example, Protégé, independently of the other NKRL tools, by people making use of knowledge bases
  in the form of "standard" ontologies.
- The "NKRL Queries" button. This button triggers *the main processing
  activities of the environment*, i.e. the "simple" queries – in reality, as stated

in Section 4.1.1, these queries already imply a first level of inferencing (subsumption) involving the HClass ontology – and the inferencing processes making use of the "hypothesis" and "transformation" rules.

The "Visualization" Modules

The "Event hierarchy" and the "Concept hierarchy" buttons allow one to visualize and browse, respectively, the HTemp and HClass hierarchies; see the corresponding figures in Chapters 2 and 4. The "Annotations" button activates the interface of Fig. A.2. The latter allows us to visualize, in the left side, the "tree" corresponding to the whole annotation – annotation mod478 in our example – and, by selecting one of the nodes of this tree, to show on the right the corresponding binding or predicative occurrence (including their NL description). As already stated, e.g. in Sections 2.2.2.2 and 2.3.2.1, a conceptual annotation (a "metadocument") is a *structured association of binding and predicative occurrences* intended to supply a *detailed representation, in NKRL terms, of the "meaning" of a complex narrative document.*

"Rules" is the last "visualization" button; by clicking on this, two further buttons appear: "Hypothesis" and "Transformation"; see Fig. A.3.

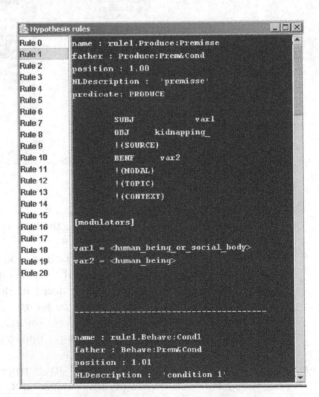

Fig. A.3 Partial visualization of a "hypothesis" rule

The "Construction and Management" Modules

The "Event hierarchy" and "Rules" buttons of Fig. A.1 respectively start the *Templates2002* and *ruleBuilder2004* modules. The first is used to set up, or to modify, the hierarchy of templates, HTemp, and consists of a Java2 update of an old CONCERTO module. *ruleBuilder2004* is a sort of "copy" of *Templates2002*, slightly adapted in a PARMENIDES context to allow the set up or the modification of the rule bases, hypotheses or transformations; see Zarri [2005/2006; Zarri and Bernard, 2004b] for additional details.

In the *file-oriented version of the NKRL software*, the "Concept hierarchy" button of Fig. A.1 starts the (very simple) *HclassEditor2002*, built up in the framework of the CONCERTO project and described in detail in Zarri and Bernard [2004b]. As already stated, it allows us to execute quickly, making use of the *sons.txt* text file, some simple operations concerning the creation/browsing/update of the basic hierarchical skeleton of an HClass ontology; the changes can be, if needed, transferred under ORACLE by making use of a specific *SonsToBDD2003* tool, also described in Zarri and Bernard [2004b].

In the ORACLE-supported version, the "Concept hierarchy" button activates the *HclassManager2004* module, which has been built up in the framework of the EUFORBIA project. The only PARMENIDES operations affecting this module have concerned the creation of a full ORACLE version starting from the original MySQL version. The "general philosophy" of this module (use of the "prototype slots," etc.) has already been described in Section 2.2.1.2; for additional details, see again Zarri and Bernard [2004b: 36–47].

Clicking the "Base of instantiated events" button of Fig. A.1 – and answering "new occurrence" to a question asking whether we want to build up a completely new occurrence or modify an existing one – causes the window of Fig. A.4 to appear; the latter is used to select one of the *three possible methods* to set up annotations/occurrences in NKRL. In the present state of the software, only the "Word/RTF file procedure" and the "stepwise procedure" can be activated. It will be possible to make use of the "NL procedure" button when some software for (semi-)automatically "translating" from NL into NKRL format

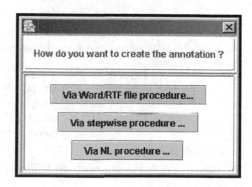

Fig. A.4 Options for building up annotations/occurrences

(see "Conclusion," Chapter 5) will be concretely integrated within the existing NKRL software.

The module activated by the "... Word/RTF procedure..." button, *DocTo-ChaineOcc2004*, has been created in a PARMENIDES context. It allows an expert NKRL operator to accelerate the set up of an NKRL database *by directly "parsing" a Word/RTF file where annotations and occurrences are written down in NKRL "external" format*, i.e. the format used thorough this book in Chapters 2–4 to describe the NKRL templates and occurrences – see, to give only an example, Table 2.6. The output is the *chaineOcc.txt* file of the *data* repository of the NKRL environment; this file is in "internal" format ("Béatrice format" in NKRL jargon), a "linear" and "positional" version of the external NKRL format that has been described in detail in Zarri and Bernard [2004b: appendix A]. When the ORACLE version is used, the content of *chaineOcc.txt* is automatically transferred into the tables of the ORACLE knowledge base, thus replacing the annotations/occurrences already stored there.

The module activated by the "... stepwise procedure..." button has been created in a PARMENIDES context to replace the old modules for the "manual" construction of annotations/occurrences inherited from the CONCERTO and EUFORBIA projects. We will now illustrate some characteristics of this new module by reproducing the main steps of the construction of the very simple NKRL annotation reproduced in Table A.1, which corresponds in

Table A.1 An example of very simple NKRL annotation

News Story t002005 – name of the annotation: *mod2005*

Original text (fragment): "ZAMBOANGA CITY (DPA) - ... Wilmarie Ira Furigay ... who is a granddaughter of Lamitan mayor Wilfredo Furigay ...." Title: 27Aug1999 PHILIPPINES: Troops kill 3 kidnap gang men

mod20.c1)   (COORD mod20.c2 mod20.c3)

The NKRL annotation for this fragment is formed of two predicative occurrences.

mod20.c2)	BEHAVE	SUBJ	WILMARIE_IRA_FURIGAY
		MODAL	granddaughter_
		TOPIC	WILFREDO_FURIGAY
		{obs}	
		date-1:	27/8/1999
		date-2:	

Behave:Kinship (1.332)

On August 27, 1999, we can remark that Wilmarie Ira Furigay is a granddaughter of Wilfredo Furigay

mod20.c3)	BEHAVE	SUBJ	WILFREDO_FURIGAY
		MODAL	(SPECIF mayor_ LAMITAN_)
		{obs}	
		date-1:	27/8/1999
		date-2:	

Behave:Role (1.33)

On August 27, 1999, we can remark that Wilfredo Furigay is the mayor of Lamitan.

turn to an NL fragment extracted from the MoD knowledge base on terrorism in the Philippines.

Clicking on the "Via stepwise procedure..." button opens a first window (see Fig. A.5), which is used for the set up of the general framework of the annotation. In our case, this consists simply of the creation of the *top binding occurrence and in the declaration of its two "sons" (two predicative occurrences)*. After having entered the name of the global annotation, mod2005, and having validated it, the system automatically inserts the name of the top binding occurrence, mod2005.c1 – and, in the same way, it will attribute a name to all the occurrences to be built up successively according to their position in the global annotation tree. The binding operator COORD is then selected and the system asks to add the first "son" of the top binding, which it will name mod2005.c2; clicking on the "Validate" button, the label of this son will be associated with the binding in the bottom right position of the window. Clicking again the "Add sons" button, and validating the label mod2005.c3 of the second son, will allow us to complete the declaration of the global annotation (see Fig. A.5).

Passing now to the actual construction of the two predicative occurrences, and after having selected the mod2005.c2 label in the global tree of the annotation (see the left-hand side of Fig. A.5), *we can declare this as a predicative occurrence by clicking the "Predicative occurrence" button in the upper right position of the "annotation" window*. An "empty skeleton" of mod2005.c2 appears in the right-hand side of the annotation window (see the upper part of the Fig. A.6), along with a "Create, modify" button. Clicking the latter opens a new window reserved for the actual construction of the predicative occurrences; see the lower part of Fig. A.6. In this "predicative occurrence" window we must now select the predicate of the father template – in our case, BEHAVE – by clicking on the "Chose one ..." button. After having selected a template – Behave:Kinship for the occurrence mod2005.c2 – and having answered "No" to the question "Do you want to modify an existing occurrence?," *a menu allows us*

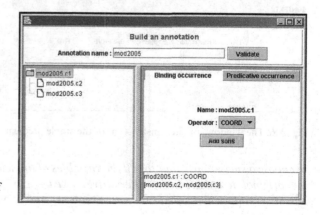

Fig. A.5 Setting up the upper binding occurrence of the annotation

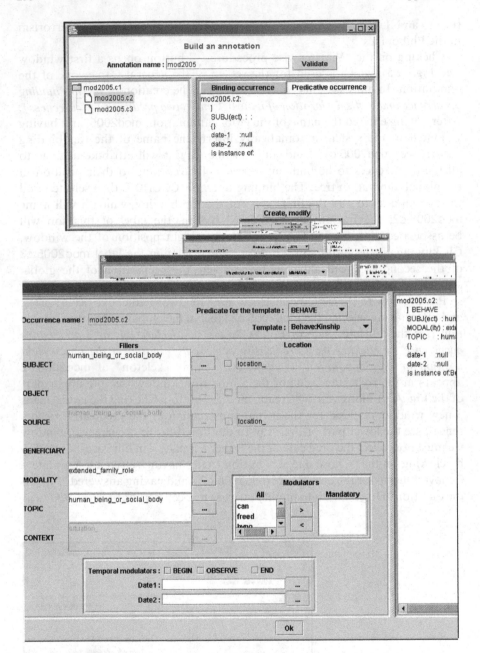

Fig. A.6 The window for the construction of the single predicative occurrences

to choose a single constraint for all the variables of the selected template in case, in the original template, some alternatives exist – e.g. *var7* of Behave:Kinship admits two possible constraints, i.e. situation_ and symbolic_label.

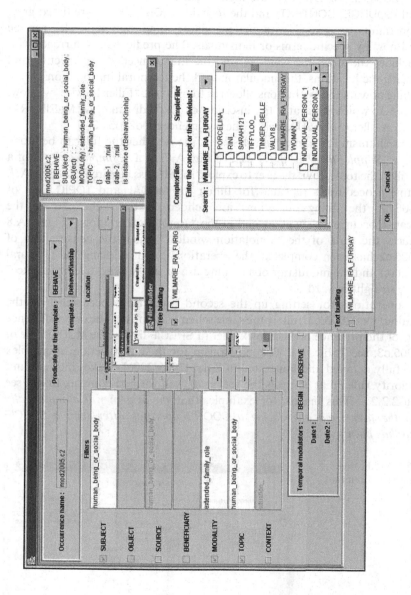

Fig. A.7 Insertion of a simple filler

The final situation is represented in the lower part of Fig. A.6. A first outline of mod2005.c2 is reproduced in the right part of the window under the form of a partially instantiated template; in the left part, the mandatory roles of Behave:-Kinship (SUBJ, MODAL, TOPIC) are highlighted (white background), while the optional (SOURCE, CONTEXT) and the forbidden (OBJ, BENF) are tinted grey. The constraints associated with the mandatory and optional roles can be replaced now by specific terms or individuals. The predicative occurrence window includes the slots, the windows and the menus needed for selecting and introducing the locations, the modulators and the temporal information.

Clicking now on the ▛▀▜ buttons allows us to open the "Filler Builder" window; see Fig. A.7, which illustrates the insertion of the individual WILMARIE_IRA_FURIGAY as filler of the SUBJ role in the occurrence mod2005.c2.

The mechanism for filling the roles asks first whether the filler to be introduced is a "*SimpleFiller*," as in the case of Fig. A.7, or a "*ComplexFiller*": for a simple filler, the tool allows the user to explore the HClass hierarchy; see Fig. A.7. The same procedure is repeated for filling the MODAL and TOPIC roles of mod2005.c2; the filling operations are echoed in the right part of the "predicative occurrence" window and in the "annotation window." Figure A.8 reproduces the state of the "annotation window" when the construction of mod2005.c2 has been completed; the operation for introducing the temporal information and the modulator obs making use of the "predicative occurrence" tools are straightforward.

The operations for setting up the second predicative occurrence of the annotation, mod2005.c3, follow the same schema as above. The only difference consists of the presence of a complex filler (a SPECIF list) in the MODAL role of mod2005.c3; see Table A.1. The mechanism for the construction of complex fillers – fully detailed and illustrated in Zarri [2005/2006] – takes into account the "priority rule" that controls the set up of well-formed complex fillers; see Section 2.2.2.3. This means, for example, that *the system will automatically prevent the user from introducing a COORD operator after than a SPECIF operator has been used.*

Fig. A.8 A predicative occurrence has been fully built up

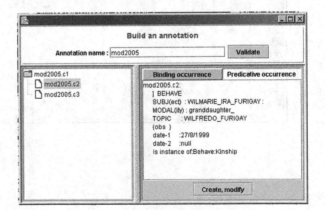

The "Querying and Inferencing" Modules

We will limit ourselves here to supplying some additional information with respect to what is already expounded in detail in Chapter 4. As usual, additional information and several additional graphical examples can be found in Zarri [2005/2006].

Clicking on the "NKRL Queries" button of the main interface of Fig. A.1 opens the window, inherited from the "old" CONCERTO project, allowing the users to build up a formal query according to the NKRL format (a "search pattern"). If the user, instead of posing a query to the system themselves, only wants to run standard examples of NKRL inference rules, transformations and hypotheses, they can click on the "DemoTrans" and "DemoHyp" buttons that appears as tinted grey in Fig. A.9. These examples include the well-known hypothesis rule about "companies that receive money from another company" that has been commented on in some detail in Section 4.2.2.

Figure A.9 shows the query window after the construction of the pattern corresponding to the question "Give me all the information inserted in the system that corresponds to some kidnapping actions in the period between the beginning of 1998 and end of 2000." The possibility of exploiting in depth the "temporal search interval" associated with a search pattern is an important

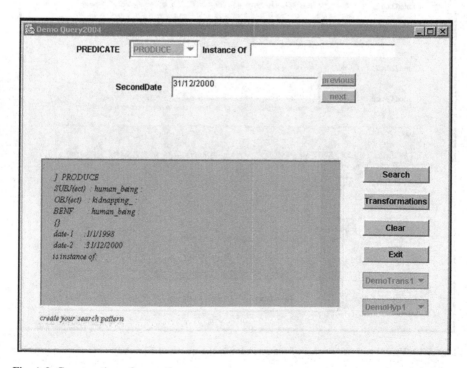

Fig. A.9 Construction of a search pattern

result obtained in a PARMENIDES context; for the theory of the temporal indexing in NKRL, see Section 4.1.2.

Sixteen answers are returned by the system. Figure A.10 shows four of them, with the answer corresponding to the kidnapping of Luis Toh highlighted. Note that an answer like "On November 14, 1993, this group of people has kidnapped Charles Walton. . ." *has been eliminated by the system given that "November 14, 1993" is outside the chosen temporal interval.* Using the "Annotation" button in the upper left corner of the answer window *allows visualizing the "context" of the answer, i.e. the whole annotation (binding occurrences included)* (mod57 in our case) *or part of it;* see Fig. A.11.

Clicking now on the "Hypotheses" button of Fig. A.10 allows us to test the hypothesis rules associated with the system; for flexibility's sake, these may be tested *in cascade* (i.e. all the premises of all the hypothesis rules inserted in the system are all tested against the "triggering occurrence"), or *separately;* see the screen dump of Fig. A.12, which concerns trying to construct a plausible

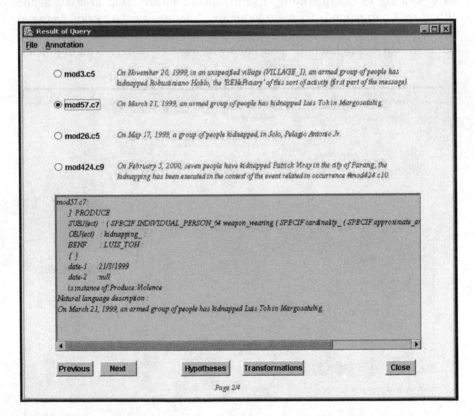

Fig. A.10 Visualization of some of the answers to the query of Fig. A.9

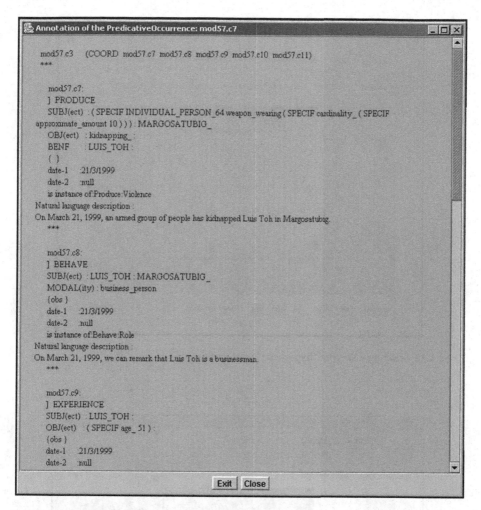

Fig. A.11 Visualization of the context (of the full annotation)

explanation about the kidnapping of Luis Toh. It could then be possible, for example, to make use of a rule like hypothesis *h2* reproduced in Table 4.10, Section 4.2.4.3; see also Table 4.9 in the same section.

The theoretical mechanisms corresponding to the different possibilities of making use of "transformations" in a "hypothesis" context have already been introduced in Section 4.2.4.1; see also Figure 4.9. Some concrete examples of these possibilities, and the screen dumps illustrating the corresponding results, can be found again in Chapter 4; see Figs. 4.10–4.12.

With respect now to the transformation rules, we will limit ourselves to reproduce, in Fig. A.13, the *"starting point" (the failure of a direct query) of the transformation process* that, making use of "multi-consequent" transformation

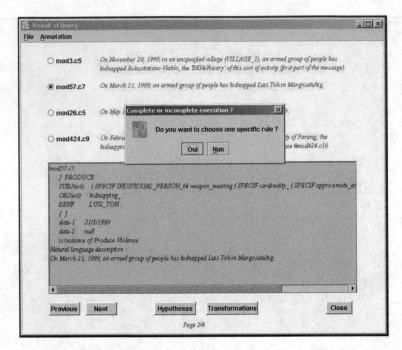

Fig. A.12 Selecting a specific "hypothesis" inference rule

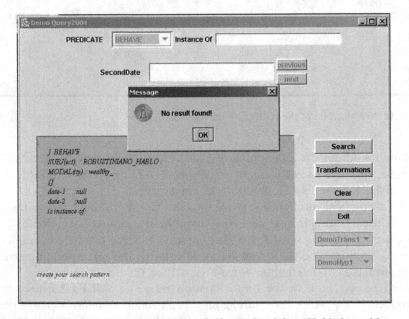

Fig. A.13 Failure of the direct query asking whether Robustiniano Hablo is wealthy

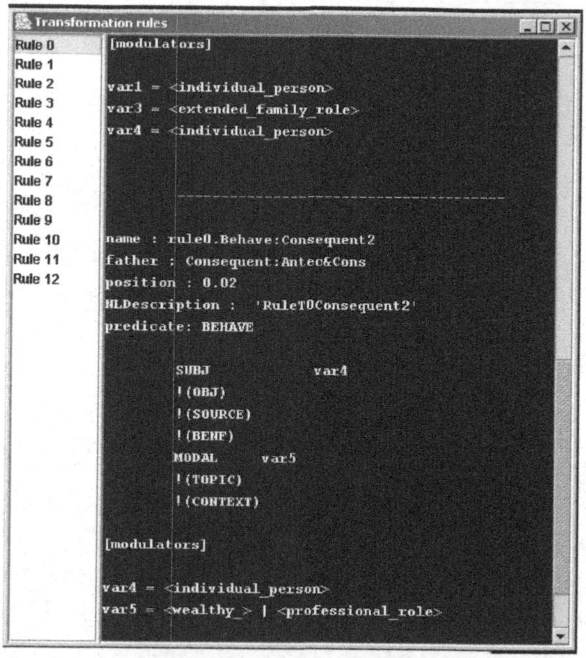

Fig. A.14 Partial screen dump of a "multi-conse-quent" transformation rule

rule like that reproduced in Table 4.7, leads to the result illustrated in Table 4.8: we do not know if Robustiano Hablo is wealthy, but we can say that his father is a wealthy businessperson. See, once again, Zarri [2005/2006] for additional information and further examples.

The screen dump of a fragment (Consequent2) of the transformation (Rule0) corresponding to the rule illustrated in Table 4.7 is reproduced in Fig. A.14; we recall here that the meaning of the full rule is "In a context of ransom kidnapping, the certification of the fact that a given character is wealthy or has a professional role can be substituted by the certification that this character has (i) a kinship link with another person (first consequent schema, Consequent1) and (ii) this person is a wealthy person or a professional person (second consequent schema, Consequent2)."

Appendix B

Plural Entities in NKRL

The NKRL mode of representation of plural entities and expressions corresponds to an interesting application of the *AECS sub-language principles* illustrated in Section 2.2.2.3. We can immediately note, in this respect, that the definitions given in Table 2.8 for the operators of this sub-language show clearly that they *must* intervene in the representation of plural entities. For example, the COORD(ination) and ENUM(eration) operators correspond *explicitly* to two of the "plural quantifiers" normally used to represent the reading variants of plural noun phrases: COORD allows us, in fact, to represent a *"collective reading,"* and ENUM a *"distributive reading."*

Researchers working on the formal treatment of plurals and plural expressions have largely focused their efforts on the correct representation, usually according to a *strict logical approach*, of the ambiguities that affect quantification of plural sentences like "Three boys bought five roses." We can mention, in this context, seminal papers like Link [1983], Webber [1983], and Scha and Stallard [1988]; recent work dealing with "plurals" is represented, for example, by Gawron and Kehler [2004] and Fast [2005]. See also the "Lecture Four" and "Lecture Five" in Landman [2000]. A partial exception to the quite-standard "predicate calculus extensions" approach to the management of these sorts of ambiguity is represented by the Allgayer and Franconi's work [Allgayer and Franconi, 1992; Franconi, 1993]. This work aims, mainly, to find a way of taking into account collections and collective relations making use of a description logics language, chosen as a general representation formalism to illustrate the semantics of sentences.

All the researches mentioned above are *essentially theoretical*; therefore, their direct transposition into the "practical" environment proper to NKRL is not at all evident. In the following, *we will thus often make reference to the solutions proposed by Sowa for the "plural" problem,* [Sowa, 1984, 1991], given that his approach looks more pragmatic and more useful from an "implementation" point of view than a pure "formal linguistics" approach.

A General Survey of the NKRL Solution

NKRL's approach to the "plural problem" *does not require the introduction of extra operators*, but relies only on the standard tools used in NKRL for the representation of sets, namely:

- at the level of the *descriptive and factual components*, the expansion operators of the AECS sub-language discussed in Section 2.2.2.3;
- at the level of the *definitional and enumerative components*, the relation slots, MemberOf and HasMember, introduced in Section 2.2.1.3.

For clarity's sake, let us start, first, with the representation of plural expressions that correspond to *predicative occurrences of the factual component*. In this context, the basic NKRL way of translating plural expressions consists of:

- the construction, within the occurrence, of a *structured argument* (expansion) where the *symbolic labels* of the concepts and/or individuals that make up the plural set evoked by the narrative expression are *explicitly represented*;
- the creation, *at the definitional and/or enumerative component level*, of the conceptual structures (*frames*) that correspond to the entities, concepts or individuals, denoted by these labels.

For example, the narrative expression "Mary has bought three books" will cause the creation of the four structures of Table B.1: an occurrence, i.e. ex.c9, and three individuals (enumerative component), i.e. BOOK_1, BOOK_2, and BOOK_3. For simplicity's sake, temporal determiners are not represented in ex.c9; we suppose, moreover, that the individual MARY_ is already known in the context of the application under examination. We suppose also that the details of the purchase act are of no interest in the context of the narrative situation examined; we then use a concept, purchase_, instead of an individual (e.g. PURCHASE_27) as the main filler of the OBJ(ect) role, thus avoiding the introduction of a specific new frame for representing this individual. According to the syntax/semantics of SPECIF (see Section 2.2.2.3), purchase_ is "specified"

Table B.1 A simple example of NKRL plural representation

ex.c9)	PRODUCE	SUBJ	MARY_
		OBJ	(SPECIF purchase_ BOOK_1 BOOK_2 BOOK_3)

[BOOK_1
InstanceOf: book_
HasMember:]

[BOOK_2
InstanceOf: book_
HasMember:]

[BOOK_3
InstanceOf: book_
HasMember:]

by detailing the three purchased items, BOOK_1, BOOK_2 and BOOK_3. The empty HasMember slot in the three individuals of Table B.1 makes it clear that each of them represents a *singleton*, i.e. a specific, unique instance of the concept book_. Eventually, we can remark that, if the titles of the three books were known, the expansion could be something in the style of, for example, (SPECIF purchase_ PICKWICK_PAPERS LORD_JIM GONE_WITH_THE_WIND).

However, this *basic model* of knowledge representation cannot be utilized all the time, especially when:

- The plural expression to be represented requires the use of *general quantifiers* like "some, many, all, ...," as in "Mary has bought some books." In this case, the elements of the plural set *cannot be explicitly enumerated* and associated with specific individuals.
- The elements of the set could be explicitly enumerated, but they are *too numerous and, at the same time, "uninteresting,"* so that the explicit construction of an individual for each of them is both *uneconomic and uninformative*. An example of this situation could be "Mary has bought thirty-two books."

In all these cases, the NKRL representation of an NL plural expression consists of a *generalization* of the above basic representation; more precisely:

- In the predicative occurrence, we make use of a *unique* individual (i.e. of its conceptual label) to represent the set *in its entirety* (e.g. the set including the three books in the example before). The individual will be accompanied by one of the *normalized SPECIF sub-lists* (NKRL idioms) that have been discussed in detail in Section 3.1.2.1, namely a cardinality_ sub-list that will include the quantifier, or the numeral, *expressing the cardinality of the set*.
- The same numeral or quantifier must be inserted in the HasMember slot of the frame describing the (unique) individual introduced in the predicative occurrence.

In this way, an example such as "Mary has bought many books" will have the representation of Table B.2. The nonempty HasMember slot in the individual, BOOK_17, of Table B.2 makes it clear that this individual makes reference, now, to several instances of the concept book_. As we have shown in Section 3.1.2.1, few_, some_, several_, many_, etc. are all labels of concepts C_i that

Table B.2 Representation of a plural expression by using a general quantifier

ex.c10)	PRODUCE	SUBJ	MARY_
		OBJ	(SPECIF purchase_ (SPECIF DOOK_17 (SPECIF cardinality_many_)))
[BOOK_17			
	InstanceOf: book_		
	HasMember: many_]		

pertain to the logical_quantifier sub-tree of property_ in the HClass hierarchy and that represent together the NKRL system of general quantifiers – see also Zarri [2003a] in this context.

We will now emphasize once more the fact that one of the main *"practical" principles* used in NKRL for the construction of large knowledge bases involves *limiting, as much as possible, any uncontrolled proliferation of individuals*. This is not only due to memory occupation and managing reasons, but mainly to the difficulty of dealing correctly with the *accumulation of symbolic labels that results from the necessity of identifying correctly all these individuals* – taking into account the fact that their names are often "meaningless" and simply formed by associating a number with the name of the concept-father, e.g. see BOOK_17 in Table B.2. This principle has been used, for example, to introduce the *concept* purchase_ instead of an individual in the previous examples.

Therefore, in the concrete NKRL applications, the presence of plural entities and expressions in a predicative occurrence is (normally) simply indicated by the insertion, in the occurrence (see again Tables B.1 and B.2), *of a SPECIF list having* cardinality_ *as its first argument*. In Table B.2, for example, an individual like BOOK_17 *does not require to be explicitly created* unless its presence is strictly necessary for other (other than "plural") reasons: its *father-concept*, book_ in our case, *can be used in its place*. The OBJ filler of occurrence ex.c10 in Table B.2 *could then be expressed simply as* (SPECIF PURCHASE_27 (SPECIF book_ (SPECIF cardinality_ many_))). We can recall here (see again Table 3.2), that several_ is conventionally used to represent the *cardinality of sets of totally undefined size*, like those corresponding to a generic plural referent, as in "men" or "books." In the (simplified or not) representation of a simple elementary event like "Mary has bought books," the most internal SPECIF list of the OBJ filler would then be (SPECIF cardinality_ several_).

It is now evident that we can represent the previous event, "Mary has bought three book," as in Table B.3, i.e. by using, instead of the representation of Table B.1, the "generalized" representation introduced in Table B.2. In Table B.3 we have used, for completeness' sake, an "extended" representation including also the explicit creation of "individuals."

Table B.3 Generalized NKRL representation of a generic plurals expression

ex.c11)	PRODUCE	SUBJ	MARY_
		OBJ	(SPECIF purchase_ (SPECIF BOOK_99 (SPECIF cardinality_ 3)))
	[BOOK_99		
		InstanceOf: book_	
		HasMember: BOOK_1 BOOK_2 BOOK_3]	
	[BOOK_1		
		InstanceOf: book_	
		MemberOf: BOOK_99]	
...			

In Table B.3, we thus make use of a *unique individual*, BOOK_99, to characterize the purchase act, and we make explicit, at the level of the enumerative component, that this individual represents, in reality, *multiple instances of the concept book_*. As explained above, the *explicit definitions* of the three individuals BOOK_1, BOOK_2 and BOOK_3 *are not strictly necessary if these definitions are of little interest with respect to the particular application carried out*: in this last case, the HasMember slot of BOOK_99 will only contain the numeral, "3," expressing the cardinality of the set: (SPECIF purchase_ (SPECIF book_ (SPECIF cardinality_ 3))). In the AECS syntax, items corresponding to integers and reals can be freely used as "properties" within a cardinality_ list.

Table B.4 NKRL representation of a "partitive" plural expression

ex.c12) PRODUCE	SUBJ	MARY_
	OBJ	(SPECIF purchase_
		(SPECIF PENCIL_11
		(SPECIF cardinality_ 10)
		(SPECIF has_part (SPECIF PENCIL_12 blue_
		(SPECIF cardinality_ 5)))
		(SPECIF has_part (SPECIF PENCIL_13 jellow_
		(SPECIF cardinality_ 4)))
		(SPECIF has_part (SPECIF PENCIL_14 green_
		(SPECIF cardinality_ 1)))))

```
[PENCIL_11
        InstanceOf:  pencil_
        HasMember: 10
        HasParts:    PENCIL_12 PENCIL_13 PENCIL_14]

[PENCIL_12
        InstanceOf:  pencil_
        HasMember: 5
        PartOf:      PENCIL_11
        Colour:      blue_]

[PENCIL_13
        InstanceOf:  pencil_
        HasMember: 4
        PartOf:      PENCIL_11
        Colour:      yellow_]

[PENCIL_14
        InstanceOf:  pencil_
        HasMember: 1
        PartOf:      PENCIL_11
        Colour:      green_]
```

Note that, strictly speaking, individuals like BOOK_99 in Table B.3 are "collections" rather then "sets" (all the HClass elements are interpreted as sets – see Zarri [1997]) given that the *extensionality axiom* (two sets are equal iff they have the same elements) *does not hold here*. In an NKRL framework, two collections, say BOOK_99 and BOOK_100, can be *co-extensional*, i.e. they can include exactly the same elements, without being necessarily considered as *identical* if created at different moments in time in the context of totally different events; see also Franconi [1993].

Let us also remark that the *slots* HasMember and MemberOf in the tables above should not be confused with the *concepts* has_member, member_of, etc. of the sub-tree part/whole_relationship; this latter, like logical_quantifier (many_, several_, ...), pertains to the property_ branch of HClass – see Section 3.1.2.1 and Fig. 3.5. However, concepts like has_member, etc. can be effectively used in the representation of particular forms of plural expressions. To give only an example, in Table B.4 see the NKRL coding of a "*partitive*" NL expression like "Mary has bought ten pencils: five of them are blue, four are yellow, the last one is green." This example is also an illustration of the criterion given in Section 2.2.1.3 for differentiating between the "relation" slots HasMember and HasParts, and which is based on the *homogeneity* of the component parts. Let us consider, in fact, the individuals mentioned in Table B.4. In each of the three sets PENCIL_12, PENCIL_13, PENCIL_14, the elements of the set are identical (or they can be considered as such) from the point of view of their semantic category and of their color; this is not true of the three sets themselves that "are part" of PENCIL_11, and which are different in color and size (number of pencils). As usual, we could also introduce in Table B.4 the explicit definition of the individuals, PENCIL_1, ..., PENCIL_10, corresponding to the single pencils.

Quantification of Plural Sentences

We can deal now with the representation of the ambiguities affecting the *quantification of plural sentences*; as already stated, this is the touchstone of all the theories concerning the formal representation of plural expressions. We will start with the classical Webber example, "Three boys bought five roses" [Webber, 1983: 346].

According to Webber, a statement like this can be used to convey a "*distributive*" meaning (each one of the three boys bought five roses), a "*collective*" reading (the three boys, formed into a consortium, bought five roses), or a "*conjunctive*" reading (the total of rose-buying boys is three, the total number of roses, each of which was bought by some boys, is five, *but the speaker either does not know or does not care to tell the listener how boys match up with roses*).

Webber gives a formal representation for the three cases by extending standard logic with the introduction of the operators "set," "cardinality" and "equality" [Webber, 1983: 350–353].

Sowa [1991: 178] calls explicitly "*Default*" the "conjunctive" reading. From a formal point of view, the "generic plural" referent – represented, in NKRL, by the HClass concept several_ – is translated, in Sowa's CGs theory, with "{*}," where the symbol "{}" is used for sets and the asterisk for the undefined referent. The symbol "{*}" alone represents, then, a "*Default*" interpretation (the least commitment, consistent with either the collective or the distributive interpretations); the distributive and collective readings are represented by making use of explicit prefixes, which gives rise to complex symbols like "Dist{*}" and "Coll{*}." Franconi [1993: 456–459] maintains an explicit denomination for Webber's conjunctive reading, which is now called "*cumulative*." He makes use of special operators, called "plural quantifiers," to represent the cumulative and distributive readings, and leaves the collective expressions nonquantified.

In NKRL, we follow Sowa's option; this consists of assuming the conjunctive/cumulative reading as the "default" interpretation, which does not require the use of any particular symbol/operator. For representing the remaining two readings, introducing new ad hoc entities is not necessary; according to the definitions given in Table 2.8 (Section 2.2.2.3), *the ENUM operator corresponds, in fact, to the "distributive reading," and COORD to the "collective reading."* The NKRL coding of Webber's example is then given in Table B.5: occurrence

Table B.5 NKRL representation of Webber's example about "boys" and "roses"

ex.c13)	PRODUCE	SUBJ	(ENUM (SPECIF BOY_42 (SPECIF cardinality_ 3)))
		OBJ	(SPECIF purchase_
			(SPECIF ROSE_97
			(SPECIF cardinality_ 5)))
ex.c14)	PRODUCE	SUBJ	(COORD (SPECIF BOY_42 (SPECIF cardinality_ 3)))
		OBJ	(SPECIF purchase_
			(SPECIF ROSE_97
			(SPECIF cardinality_ 5)))
ex.c15)	PRODUCE	SUBJ	(SPECIF BOY_42 (SPECIF cardinality_ 3))
		OBJ	(SPECIF purchase_
			(SPECIF ROSE_97
			(SPECIF cardinality_ 5)))

[BOY_42
    InstanceOf: boy_
    HasMember: 3]

[ROSE_97
    InstanceOf: rose_
    HasMember: 5]

ex.c13 represents the distributive reading, ex.c14 the collective reading, ex.c15 the default. BOY_42 and ROSE_97 represent, respectively, the "collection" of the three boys and the "collection" of the five roses; these two individuals are implicitly assimilated to "lists" for respecting the congruence with the definitions of Table 2.8.

The NKRL representation of the Sowa's examples, "nine ladies are dancing" (default interpretation), "nine ladies are each dancing" (ENUM) and "nine ladies are dancing together" (COORD) [Sowa, 1991: 178] follows the same pattern – the extension, using the ALTERN operator, see again Table 2.8, to a possible natural language formulations in terms of "one of nine ladies is dancing," is straightforward. It is well evident that, following this type of representation, *the operators ENUM and COORD are added only when it becomes absolutely necessary, for a correct interpretation of the event examined, to indicate explicitly the type of reading which has been favored.*

Let us now consider a very puzzling example proposed by Sowa concerning the correct interpretation of the sentence "five blocks are supported by three pyramids." Sowa remarks that the common sense could suggest the pyramids are to be used *collectively* to support the blocks; nothing is implied, however, *about the number of blocks supported by each group of three pyramids.* He proposes, therefore, the default interpretation given by the first CG, (a), of Table B.6; this graph says that five blocks are the "patient" of SUPPORT and three pyramids collectively are the "instrument" of SUPPORT. As already stated, the symbol "{*}" is used in the CG theory to designate the "generic plural" referent; a second operator, a "qualifier," "@," is used to indicate the cardinality of the set (it has, therefore, the same function of the HClass concept cardinality_).

The distributive interpretation requires a unique instance of supporting and a set of pyramids for each block; it could be represented by the sentence "five blocks are *each* supported by three pyramids." The corresponding CG is graph (b) of Table B.6. Eventually, the collective interpretation implies that all the blocks collectively are supported by one set of three pyramids, also acting collectively: "five blocks are *all* supported by three pyramids"; see graph (c) of Table B.6. Sowa adds that the distributive interpretation, which implies 15 pyramids, is inconsistent with the collective interpretation, which implies three pyramids. Both of them, however, are consistent with the

Table B.6 Default, collective and distributive interpretation in CGs

(a)   [BLOCK: {*}@5] ← (PTNT) ← [SUPPORT] → (INST) →[PYRAMID: Coll{*}@3]

(b)   [BLOCK: Dist{*}@5] ← (PTNT) ← [SUPPORT] → (INST)→ [PYRAMID: Coll{*}@3]

(c)   [BLOCK: Col{*}@5] ← (PTNT) ← [SUPPORT] → (INST)→ [PYRAMID: Coll{*}@3]

Table B.7 NKRL representation of Sowa's example about"pyramids"

ex.c16)	PRODUCE	SUBJ	(COORD (SPECIF PYRAMID_421 (SPECIF cardinality_ 3)))
		OBJ	supporting_action
		BENF	(SPECIF BLOCK_991 (SPECIF cardinality_ 5))
ex.c17)	PRODUCE	SUBJ	(COORD (SPECIF PYRAMID_421 (SPECIF cardinality_ 3)))
		OBJ	supporting_action
		BENF	(ENUM (SPECIF BLOCK_991 (SPECIF cardinality_ 5)))
ex.c18)	PRODUCE	SUBJ	(COORD (SPECIF PYRAMID_421 (SPECIF cardinality_ 3)))
		OBJ	supporting_action
		BENF	(COORD (SPECIF BLOCK_991 (SPECIF cardinality_ 5)))

[PYRAMID_421
    InstanceOf: pyramid_
    HasMember: 3]

....

default, which allows 3, 9, 12, or 15 pyramids [Sowa, 1991: 179–181]. In CGs as well as in NKRL (but not in Franconi, see above), *the default makes the weakest assumption*: it is implied by either the distributive or the collective assumptions.

The NKRL representation of the above example is given in Table B.7, where we have preserved Sowa's interpretation. Note that, for simplicity's sake, we have extended here to a situation where the SUBJ(ect), PYRAMID_421, and the beneficiary (BENF), BLOCK_918, are both *inanimate protagonists*, a PRODUCE template (Produce:PerformTask/Activity; see Chapter 3) where "subject" and "beneficiary" are normally human beings or social bodies.

Final Remarks

When we take into consideration Sowa's examples in the style of "many elephants that perform in a circus carn money" [Sowa, 1991: 175], or "every trailer truck has 18 wheels" [Sowa, 1991: 177] – or, in the same vein, "some cotton T-shirt is expensive" [Webber, 1983: 348] – we are confronted with quantified plural expressions that, at the difference of the plural expressions we have considered until now, *do not refer explicitly to any concrete elementary events characterized by precise spatial and temporal coordinates*, and thus that do not concern the domain of the *factual component*. Given their appearance of "general wisdom," and the lack of references to any particular character(s) operating in a defined spatio-temporal framework, they pertain rather to the

Table B.8 CGs examples of plural referents using the quantifiers "many" and "all"

[(λx) [ELEPHANT: *x] ← (AGENT) ← [PERFORM] → (IN)→ [CIRCUS]: {*}@many] -
        (BENF) ← [EARN] → (PTNT) →[MONEY]
[TRAILER-TRUCK: ∀] → (PART) → [WHEEL:{*}@18]

definitional component domain and concerns, more precisely, the definition of concepts (HClass terms) like circus_elephant and trailer_truck (or cotton_t_shirt).

The CGs coding of the expressions "many elephants ..." and "every trailer truck ..." in "linear form" (see Chapter 1) is reproduced in Table B.8. In the upper part of this table, the hyphen, "-," only means that the graph is too long to fit on one line.

In the upper graph, the first line is fully devoted to the representation of the concept node "elephant that performs in a circus"; the BENF relation indicates that such elephants are the beneficiaries of the earnings (PTNT = "patient relation"). In CG theory [Sowa, 1984, 1999], the square brackets box that represents a "concept node" can be split into two fields separated by a colon, ":," i.e. the "type field" and the "referent field" – in NKRL terms, a "type" *corresponds strongly to a concept* (HClass element) of the definitional component, while "referents" are *individuals of the enumerative component*, i.e. instances of the HClass element representing the concept. For the complex concept "elephant that performs ...," the type field (before the colon following [CIRCUS]) is filled with a "λ-expression": λ-expressions are, in the CG theory, the standard way of introducing new definitions, in this case the subtype of elephants defined in the relative clause. The "referent field" (following the colon – see also Table B.6), is formed by a plural referent with a "quantifier" (many). The "scope" of the quantification is the entire, original sentence. In sentences such as "every elephant that performs in a circus ...," "some elephants that perform in a circus," etc., the referent field should be filled with the universal, ∀, or existential, ∃, quantifier. The representation of "every trailer ...," see the second graph in Table B.8, follows the same principle.

From an NKRL point of view, and according to the representational principles proper to the definitional component (see Section 2.2.1), all we need to represent the NL sentence "every trailer truck ..." is to add, to the frame corresponding to the concept trailer_truck, an "*attribute slot*" like NumberOfWheels, having "18" as default value. For circus_elephant, if, on the one hand, a solution in terms of an attribute slot EarnsMoney seems too trivial and, on the other hand, *we want to preserve the possibility of explicitly expressing the alternatives among "every elephant," "some elephants" and "many elephants,"* then an elegant and complete solution consists of adding a particular "*declarative procedure*," e.g. procedure_121 (see Table B.9), in the defining frame for circus_elephant. As already stated (see the general schema for a definitional/enumerative entity in Table 2.1 and Section 2.2.1.3), the

Table B.9 Using declarative procedures to define an NKRL concept

[circus_elephant
IsA : elephant_
...
procedure_121: circus_elephant.t1
...]

circus_elephant.t1)	(ALTERN circus_elephant.t2 circus_elephant.t3 circus_elephant.t4)		
circus_elephant.t2)	RECEIVE	SUBJ	(SPECIF circus_elephant (SPECIF cardinality_ all_))
		OBJ	money_
		MODAL	earnings_
circus_elephant.t3)	RECEIVE	SUBJ	(SPECIF circus_elephant (SPECIF cardinality_ some_))
		OBJ	money_
		MODAL	earnings_
circus_elephant.t4)	RECEIVE	SUBJ	(SPECIF circus_elephant (SPECIF cardinality_ many_))
		OBJ	money_
		MODAL	earnings_

NKRL "procedures" are descriptions of the proper "behavior," in the widest meaning of this term, of particular concepts/individuals, *expressed in a declarative way by making use of predicative occurrences or partially instantiated templates*. In a *partially instantiated template*, as already stated, *at least some* of the *explicit variables var$_i$* of the original template are *replaced by HClass terms, concepts or individuals*, that *coincide* with the constraints associated with these variables or that represent *specializations or instances* of these constraints.

In Table B.9, the slot procedure_121 is filled with the symbolic label, circus_elephant.t1, corresponding to the "head" of the declarative procedure. This head is a *binding structure* (a "binding template" – see Section 2.3.2.2). The core of the declarative procedure is represented by three *partially instantiated* templates identified as circus_elephant.t2, circus_elephant.t3 and circus_elephant.t4, all derived from the template Receive:GetMoney; their meanings are self-evident.

To conclude about the formal representation of plural expressions, we can point up the *completeness* and the *simplicity of use* of the NKRL conceptual structures, able to differentiate efficiently between the status of NL utterances like "Mary has bought many books" (*assertion of a fact*) and that of utterances like "many elephants that perform in a circus earn money" (*assertion of a property*) without having recourse to extra operators or complex predicate calculus-inspired formalisms.

References

Allen, J.F. (1981). An interval-based representation of temporal knowledge. In: *Proceedings of the 7th International Joint Conference on Artificial Intelligence – IJCAI/81*. San Francisco: Morgan Kaufmann.

Allen, J.F. (1983). Maintaining knowledge about temporal intervals. *Communications of the ACM* **26**: 823–843.

Allen, J.F. (1984). Towards a general theory of action and time. *Artificial Intelligence* **23**: 123–154.

Allgayer, J., and Franconi, E. (1992). A semantic account of plural entities within a hybrid representation system. In: *Proceedings of the 5th International Symposium on Knowledge Engineering*. Seville: Rank Xerox Spain.

Anderson, J.M. (2006). *Modern Grammars of Case*. Oxford: Oxford University Press.

Ankolekar, A., Burstein, M., Hobbs, J., Lassila, O., Martin, D., McDermott, D., McIlraith, S., Narayanan, S., Paolucci, M., Payne, T., and Sycara, K. (2002). DAML-S: Web Service description for the Semantic Web. In: *Proceedings of the First International Semantic Web Conference – ISWC 2002* (LNCS 2342), Horrocks, I., and Hendler, J.A., eds. Berlin: Springer.

Arpírez, J.C., Corcho, O., Fernández-López, M., and Gómez-Pérez, A. (2003). WebODE in a nutshell. *AI Magazine* **24**(3): 37–47.

Artale, A., Franconi, E., Guarino, N., and Pazzi, L. (1996). Part–Whole relations in object-centered systems: an overview. *Data & Knowledge Engineering* **20**: 347–383.

Austin, J.R., Engelberg, S., and Rauh, G., eds. (2004). *Adverbials – The Interplay between Meaning, Context, and Syntactic Structures*. Amsterdam/Philadelphia: Benjamins.

Baader, F., Calvanese, D., McGuinness, D., Nardi, D., and Patel-Schneider, P.F., eds. (2002). *The Description Logic Handbook*. Cambridge: Cambridge University Press.

Baclawski, K., Kokar, M.K., Kogut, P.A., Hart, L., Smith, J., Holmes, W.S., Letkowski, J., and Aronson, M.L. (2001). Extending UML to support ontology engineering for the Semantic Web. In: *UML 2001 – The Unified Modeling Language: Languages, Concepts and Tools* (LNCS 2185), Gogolla, M., and Kobryn, C., eds. Berlin: Springer.

Bailey, J., Bry, F., Furche, T., and Schaffert, S. (2005). Web and Semantic Web query languages: a survey. In: *Reasoning Web, First International Summer School 2005* (LNCS 3564), Eisinger, N., and Mauszynski, J, eds. Berlin: Springer.

Bakhtin, M.M. (1982). Forms of time and of chronotope in the novel. In: *The Dialogic Imagination: Four Essays*, Holquist, M., and Liapunov, V., eds.; translated from Russian by Bronstom, K., and Liaponov, V. Austin (TX): University of Texas Press.

Bal, M. (1997). *Narratology: Introduction to the Theory of Narrative*, 2 nd edn. Toronto: University of Toronto Press.

Barker, K., Copeck, T., Szpakowicz, S., and Delisle, S. (1997). Systematic construction of a versatile case system. *Natural Language Engineering* **3**: 279–315.

Barwise, J., and Cooper, R. (1981). Generalized quantifiers in natural language. *Linguistics and Philosophy* **4**: 159–219.

Bechhofer, S., van Harmelen, F., Hendler, J., Horrocks, I., McGuinness, D.L., Patel-Schneider, P.F., and Stein, L.A., eds. (2004). *OWL Web Ontology Language Reference – W3C Recommendation 10 February 2004*. W3C (http://www.w3.org/TR/owl-ref/).

Beckett, D., ed. (2004). *RDF/XML Syntax Specification (Revised) – W3C Recommendation 10 February 2004*. W3C (http://www.w3.org/TR/rdf-syntax-grammar/).

Bennet, J.F. (1988). *Events and Their Names*. Indianapolis (IN): Hackett Publishing Co.

Berardi, D., Calvanese, D., and De Giacomo, G. (2001). Reasoning on UML class diagrams using description logic based systems. In: *Proceedings of the 2001 Workshop on Applications of Description Logics, ADL-2001* (CEUR vol. 44). Aachen: CEUR Publications (http://ftp.infomatik.rwth-aachen.de/Publications/CEUR-WS/Vol-44/).

Berger, S., Bry, F., Bolzer, O., Furche, T., Schaffert, S., and Wieser, C. (2004). Xcerpt and visXcerpt: twin query languages for the Semantic Web. In: *Proceedings of the Third International Semantic Web Conference, ISWC 2004* (LNCS 3298), McIlraith, S.A., Plexousakis, D., and van Harmelin, F., eds. Berlin: Springer.

Berners-Lee, T., ed. (2006). *Notation 3, A Readable Language for Data on the Web – Last Change: 9 March 2006*. W3C (http://www.w3.org/DesignIssues/Notation3.html).

Berners-Lee, T., Hendler, J, and Lassila, O. (2001). The Semantic Web. *Scientific American* **284**(5): 34–43.

Berners-Lee, T., Hall, W., Hendler, J.A., O'Hara, K., Shadbolt, N., and Weitzner, D.J. (2006). A framework for Web science. *Foundations and Trends in Web Science* **1**: 1–130.

Bertino, E., Catania, B., and Zarri, G.P. (2001). *Intelligent Database Systems*. London: Addison-Wesley and ACM Press.

Bertino, E., Ferrari, E., Perego, A., and Zarri, G.P. (2005). A multi-strategy approach to rating and filtering online resources. In: *Database and Expert Systems Applications – Proceedings of the 16th International Conference, DEXA'05*. Los Alamitos (CA): IEEE Computer Society Press.

Birnbaum, L., and Selfridge, M. (1981). Conceptual analysis of natural language. In: *Inside Computer Understanding: Five Programs Plus Miniatures*, Schank, R.C., and Riesbeck, C.K., eds. Hillsdale (NJ): Lawrence Erlbaum Associates.

Biron, P.V., and Malhotra, A., eds. (2001). *XML Schema Part 2: Datatypes – W3C Recommendation 02 May 2001*. W3C (http://www.w3.org/TR/xmlschema-2/).

Bittner, T., Donnelly, M., and Smith, B. (2004). Endurants and perdurants in directly depicting ontologies. *AI Communications* **17**: 247–258.

Black, W.J., Jowett, S., Mavroudakis, T., McNaught, J., Theodoulidis, B., Vasilakopoulos, A., Zarri, G.P., and Zervanou, K. (2004). Ontology-enablement of a system for semantic annotation of digital documents. In: *Proceedings of the 4th International Workshop on Knowledge Markup and Semantic Annotation (SemAnnot 2004) – Third International Semantic Web Conference* (November 8, 2004, Hiroshima, Japan).

Black, W.J., McNaught, J., Vasilakopoulos, A., Zervanou, K., Rinaldi, F., and Theodoulidis, B. (2003). *CAFETIERE: Conceptual Annotations for Facts, Events, Individual Entities, and Relations* (Technical Report TR-U4.3.1). Manchester: UMIST Department of Computation.

Boley, H., Tabet, S., and Wagner, G. (2001). Design rationale of RuleML: a markup language for Semantic Web rules. In: *Proceedings of SWWS'01, The First Semantic Web Working Symposium*, Cruz, I.F., Decker, S., Euzenat, J., and McGuinness, D., eds. Stanford (CA): Stanford University and W3C.

Bolles, B., and Nevatia, R. (2004). *ARDA Event Taxonomy Challenge Project – Final Report*. Richland (WA): ARDA Northwest Regional Research Center.

Borgo, S., Guarino, N., and Masolo, C. (1996). A pointless theory of space based on strong connection and congruence. In: *Principles of Knowledge Representation and Reasoning, KR'96*, Carlucci Aiello, L., Doyle, J., and Shapiro, S., eds. San Francisco (CA): Morgan Kaufmann.

Brachman, R.J. (1983). What IS-A Is and Isn't: an analysis of taxonomic links in semantic network. *IEEE Computer* **16**(10): 30–36.

Brand, M. (1997). Identity conditions for events. *American Philosophical Quarterly* **4**: 329–337.

Brazier, F., Dunin-Keplicz, B., Treur, J., and Verbrugge, R. (1996). Beliefs, intentions and DESIRE. In: *Proceedings of the 1996 Banff Knowledge Acquisition for Knowledge-Based Systems Workshop*. Calgary: Department of Computer Science of the University.

Brickley, D, and Guha, R.V., eds. (2004). *RDF Vocabulary Description Language 1.0: RDF Schema – W3C Recommendation 10 February 2004*. W3C (http://www.w3.org/TR/rdf-schema/).

Bruce, B. (1975). Case systems for natural language. *Artificial Intelligence* **6**: 327–360.

Brusoni, V., Console, L., Terenziani, P., and Pernici, B. (1997). LATER: managing temporal information efficiently. *Intelligent Systems and Their Applications* **12**(4): 56–63.

Bry, F., and Schaffert, S. (2003). The XML query language Xcerpt: design principles, examples, and semantics. In: *Web, Web-Services, and Database Systems: Proceedings of the NODe 2002 Workshop, Revised Papers* (LNCS 2593). Berlin: Springer.

Bundy, A., and McNeill, F. (2006). Representation as a fluent: an AI challenge for the next half century. *IEEE Intelligent Systems* **21**(3): 85–87.

Cáceres, C., Fernández, A., Ossowski, S., and Vasirani, M. (2006). Agent-based service discovery for healthcare: an organizational approach. *IEEE Intelligent Systems* **21**(6): 11–20.

Callaway, C.B., and Lester, J.C. (2002). Narrative prose generation. *Artificial Intelligence* **139**: 213–252.

Cardoso, J. (2007). The Semantic Web vision: where are we? *IEEE Intelligent Systems* **22**(5): 84–88.

Cardoso, J., and Sheth, A. (2005). Introduction to Semantic Web Services and Web Process Composition. In: *Semantic Web Services and Web Process Composition – Revised Selected Papers from the First International Workshop, SWSWPC 2004* (LNCS 3387), Cardoso, J., and Sheth, A., eds. Berlin: Springer.

Casati, R., and Varzi, A. (1995). *Holes and Other Superficialities*. Cambridge (MA): MIT Press/Bradford Books.

Casati, R., Varzi, A. C., eds. (1996). *Events* (International Research Library of Philosophy, 15). Aldershot: Dartmouth Publishing.

Ceccato, S., ed. (1961). *Linguistic Analysis and Programming for Mechanical Translation* (technical report RADC-TR-60–18). Milano: Feltrinelli.

Ceccato, S. (1966). Automatic translation of languages. In: *Automatic Translation of Languages: Papers Presented at NATO Summer School held in Venice, July 1962*. Oxford: Pergamon Press.

Ceccato, S. (1967). Correlational analysis and mechanical translation. In: *Machine Translation*, Booth, A.D., ed. Amsterdam: North-Holland.

Chafe, W. L. (1970). *Meaning and the Structure of Language*. Chicago: Chicago University Press.

Chaudhri, V.K., Farquhar, A., Fikes, R., Karp, P.D., and Rice, J.P. (1998). OKBC: a programmatic foundation for knowledge base interoperability. In: *Proceedings of the 1998 National Conference on Artificial Intelligence – AAAI/98*. Cambridge (MA): MIT Press/AAAI Press.

Chein, M., and Mugnier, M.-L. (1992). Conceptual graphs: fundamental notions. *Revue d'Intelligence Artificielle* **6**: 365–406.

Choi, N., Song, Il-Y., and Han, H. (2006). A survey on ontology mapping. *ACM Sigmod Record* **35**(3): 34–41.

Christensen, E., Curbera, F., Meredith, G., and Weerawarana, S. (2001). *Web Services Description Language (WSDL) 1.1 – W3C Note 15 March 2001*. W3C (http://www.w3.org/TR/wsdl).

Clark, K.L., and Tärnlund, S.-A., eds. (1982). *Logic Programming*. London: Academic Press.

Clocksin, W.F., and Mellish, C.S. (1981). *Programming in PROLOG*. Berlin: Springer.

Cohen, P.LR., and Levesque, H.J. (1990). Intention is choice with commitment. *Artificial Intelligence* **42**: 213–261.

Common Logic (2007). *Information Technology – Common Logic (CL): A Framework for a Family of Logic Based Languages* (final draft – reference number: ISO/IEC FDIS 24707:2007(E)). Geneva: ISO Copyright Office.

Compton, P., Peters, L., Edwards, G., and Lavers, T.G. (2006). Experience with ripple-down rules. *Knowledge-Based Systems* **19**: 356–362.

Connolly, D., and Miller, L. (2005). *RDF Calendar, an Application of the Resource Description Framework to iCalendar Data – W3C Interest Group Note 29 September 2005*. W3C (http://www.w3.org/TR/rdfcal/).

Cook, W.A. (1979). *Case Grammar: Development of the Matrix Model (1979–1978)*. Washington (DC): Georgetown University Press.

Corbett, D. (2003). *Reasoning and Unification over Conceptual Graphs*. New York: Kluwer Academic/Plenum Publishers.

Corby, O., Dieng-Kuntz, R., and Faron-Zucker, C. (2004). Querying the Semantic Web with the CORESE search engine. In: *Proceedings of the 16th European Conference on Artificial Intelligence (ECAI'2004)*. Amsterdam (2004): IOS Press.

Cranefield, S. (2002). UML and the Semantic Web. In: *The Emerging Semantic Web – Selected Papers from the First Semantic Web Working Symposium*, Cruz, I., Decker, S., Euzenat, J., and McGuinness, D., eds. Amsterdam: IOS Press.

Crofts, N., Doerr, M., Gill, T., Stead, S., and Stuff, M., eds. (2007). *Definition of the CIDOC Conceptual Reference Model – Version 4.2.2*. Heraklion: ICOM/CIDOC Documentation Standards Group (http://cidoc.ics.forth.gr/docs/cidoc_crm_version_4.2.2.pdf).

Cuenca Grau, B., Horrocks, I., Parsia, B., Patel-Schneider, P., and Sattler, U. (2006). Next steps for OWL. In: *Proceedings of the OWLED*06 Workshop on OWL: Experiences and Directions* (CEUR-WS.org/Vol-216), Cuenca Grau, B., Hitzler, P., Shankey, C., and Wallace, E., eds. Aachen: Sun SITE Central Europe (CEUR, http://SunSITE.Informatik.RWTH-Aachen.DE/Publications/CEUR-WS/Vol-216/submission_11.pdf).

Cullingford, R. (1981). SAM and Micro SAM. In: *Inside Computer Understanding: Five Programs Plus Miniatures*, Schank, R.C., and Riesbeck, C.K., eds. Hillsdale (NJ): Lawrence Erlbaum Associates.

Davidson, D. (1967a). Causal relations. *The Journal of Philosophy* **64**: 691–703.

Davidson, D. (1967b). The logical form of action sentences. In: *The Logic of Decision and Action*, Rescher, N., ed. Pittsburgh: University of Pittsburgh Press.

De Bruijn, J., Fensel, D., Keller, U., and Lara, R. (2005). Using the Web Service Modeling Ontology to enable semantic e-business. *Communications of the ACM* **48**(12): 43–47.

De Bruijn, J., Martín-Recuerda, F., Manov, D., and Ehrig, M. (2004). *D4.2.1 State-of-the-Art Survey on Ontology Merging and Aligning V1* (deliverable D4.2.1-WP4, IST-2003-506826 SEKT). Innsbruck: DERI (http://www.inf.unibz.it/~jdebruijn/publications/sekt-d4.2.1-mediation-survey-final.pdf).

Delugach, H. (2005). *CharGer – A Conceptual Graph Editor*. Huntsville (AL): Computer Science Department of the University of Alabama (http://charger.sourceforge.net/).

Dobrev, P., Strupchaska, A., and Toutanova, K. (2001). CGWorld-2001 – new features and new directions. In: *Proceedings of the ICCS 2001 Workshop for Conceptual Graphs Tools* (July 30, 2001, Stanford University, USA, http://www.cs.nmsu.edu/~hdp/CGTools/proceedings/papers/CGWorld.pdf).

Doerr, M. (2003). The CIDOC conceptual reference module – an ontological approach to semantic interoperability of metadata. *AI Magazine* **24**(3): 75–91.

Drummond, N., Rector, A., Stevens, R., Moulton, G., Horridge, M., Wang, H.H., and Seidenberg, J. (2006). Putting OWL in order: patterns for sequences in OWL. In: *Proceedings of the OWLED*06 Workshop on OWL: Experiences and Directions* (CEUR-WS.org/Vol-216), Cuenca Grau, B., Hitzler, P., Shankey, C., and Wallace, E., eds. Aachen: Sun SITE Central Europe (CEUR, http://SunSITE.Informatik.RWTH-Aachen.DE/Publications/CEUR-WS/Vol-216/submission_12.pdf).

Dublin Core (2004). *Dublin Core Metadata Element Set, Version 1.1: Reference Description*. Dublin (OH): Dublin Core Metadata Initiative (http://dublincore.org/documents/dces/).

Dyer, M.G. (1983). *In-Depth Understanding*. Cambridge (MA): The MIT Press.

Ellis, G. (1995). Compiling conceptual graphs. *IEEE Transactions on Knowledge and Data Engineering* 7: 68–81.

Falkovych, K., Sabou, and Stuckenschmidt, H. (2003). UML for the Semantic Web: transformation-based approaches. In: *Knowledge Transformation for the Semantic Web*, Omelayenko, B. and Klein, M. eds. Amsterdam: IOS Press.

Farrel, J., and Lausen, H., eds. (2007). *Semantic Annotations for WSDL and XML Schema – W3C Candidate Recommendation 26 January 2007*. W3C (http://www.w3.org/TR/2007/CR-sawsdl-20070126).

Fast, J. (2005). Structurally underspecified semantics for distributive plural predication. In: *Proceedings of Console XIII 2004*, Blaho, S., Vicente, L., and Schoorlemmer, E., eds. (http://www.sole.leidenuniv.nl/index.php3?m=1&c=24).

Fernández, A., Vasirani, M., Cáceres, C., and Ossowski, S. (2006). Role-based service description and discovery. In: *Proceedings of the AAMAS 2006 Workshop on Service-Oriented Computing and Agent-Based Engineering – SOCABE'2006* (May 8–12, 2006, Future University, Hakodate, Japan).

Ferro, L., Gerber, L., Mani, I., Sundheim, B., and Wilson, G. (2005). *TIDES – 2005 Standard for the Annotation of Temporal Expressions* (2005 Release, updated September 2005). McLean (VA): The MITRE Corporation.

Fikes, R., and Kehler, T. (1985). The role of frame-based representations in reasoning. *Communications of the ACM* 28: 904–920.

Fikes, R., Hayes, P., and Horrocks, I. (2004). OWL-QL – a language for deductive query answering on the Semantic Web. *Journal of Web Semantics: Science, Services and Agents on the World Wide Web* 2: 19–29.

Fillmore, C.J. (1968). The case for case. In: *Universals in Linguistic Theory*, Bach, E., and Harms, R.T., eds. New York: Holt, Rinehart and Winston.

Fillmore, C.J. (1977). The case for case reopened. In: *Syntax and Semantics: Grammatical Relations*, Cole, P., and Sadock, J., eds. New York: Academic Press.

Fillmore, C.J., Wooters, C., and Baker, C. (2001). Building a large lexical databank which provides deep semantics. In: *Language, Information and Computation – Proceedings of the 15th Pacific Asia Conference*, T'sou, B.K., Kwong O.O.Y, and Lai, T. B.Y., eds. Hong Kong: Language Information Sciences Research Centre of the City University.

Franconi, E. (1993). A treatment of plurals and plural quantifications based on a theory of collections. *Minds and Machines* 3: 453–474.

Gangemi, A., and Mika, P. (2003). Understanding the Semantic Web through descriptions and situations. In: *Proceedings of the CoopIS, DOA, and ODBASE03 OTM Confederated International Conferences* (LNCS 2888), Meersman, R., Tari, Z., and Schmidt, D.C., eds. Berlin: Springer.

Gangemi, A., Sagri, M.-T., and Tiscornia, D. (2003). Metadata for Content Description in Legal Information. In: *Proceedings of the Workshop on Legal Ontologies & Web Based Legal Information Management, 9th International Conference on Artificial Intelligence and Law (ICAIL-2003)*. New York: ACM Press.

Gangemi, A., Guarino, N., Masolo, C., Oltramari, A., and Schneider, L. (2002). Sweetening ontologies with DOLCE. In: *Knowledge Engineering and Knowledge Management, Ontologies and the Semantic Web – Proceedings of EKAW'2002* (LNCS 2473), Gómez-Pérez, A., and Benjamins, V.R., eds. Berlin: Springer.

Garshol, L.M., and Moore, G., eds. (2006). *Topic Maps – XML Syntax* (Final Draft International Standard, JTC1/SC34). Geneva: ISO/IEC (http://www.isotopicmaps.org/sam/sam-xtm/2006-06-19/).

Garshol, L.M., Gessa, N., Pepper, S., Presutti, V., and Vitali, F., eds. (2005). *RDFTM: Survey and Interoperability Proposals – W3C Working Draft 23 February 2005*. W3C (http://tesi. fabio.web.cs.unibo.it/view/RDFTM/DraftSurvey?skin = print.pattern).

Gašević, D., Giurca, A., Lukichev, S., and Wagner, G. (2006). Rule-based modeling of Semantic Web Services. In: *Proceedings of the 2nd International Workshop on Semantic Web Enabled Software Engineering at 5th International Semantic Web Conference* (November 6, 2006, Athens, GA, USA).

Gawron, J.M., and Kehler, A. (2004). The semantics of respective readings, conjunction, and filler-gap dependencies. *Linguistics and Philosophy* **27**: 169–207.

Genesereth, M.R., and Fikes, R.E., eds. (1992). *Knowledge Interchange Format, Version 3.0 Reference Manual* (Technical Report Logic-92-1). Stanford (CA): Computer Science Department of the Stanford University.

Gennari, J., Musen, M.A., Fergerson, R.W., Grosso, W.E., Crubézy, M., Eriksson, H., Noy, N.F., and Tu, S.W. (2002). *The Evolution of Protégé: An Environment for Knowledge-based Systems Development* (technical report SMI-2002-0943). Stanford (CA): Stanford Medical Informatics.

Genest, D., and Salvat, E. (1998). A platform allowing typed nested graphs: how CoGITo became CoGITaNT. In: *Proceedings of the Sixth International Conference on Conceptual Structures, ICCS'98* (LNCS 1453), Mugnier, M.-L., and Chein, M., eds. Berlin: Springer.

Gentner, D., Holyoak, K., and Kokinov, B., eds. (2000). *Analogy: Perspectives from Cognitive Science*. Cambridge (MA): MIT Press.

Gerevini, A., and Schubert, L. (1995). Efficient algorithms for qualitative reasoning about time. *Artificial Intelligence* **74**: 207–248.

Goasdoue, F., Lattes, V., and Rousset, M.-C. (2000). The use of CARIN language and algorithms for information integration: the Picsel system. *International Journal on Cooperative Information Systems* **9**: 383–401.

Goddard, C, and Wierzbicka, A. (2002). *Meaning and Universal Grammar: Theory and Empirical Findings* (vol. 1). Amsterdam/Philadelphia: Benjamins.

Goldstein, I., and Papert, S. (1977). Artificial intelligence, language, and the study of knowledge. *Cognitive Science* **1**: 84–123.

Gómez-Pérez, A., González-Cabrero, R., and Lama, M. (2004). ODE SWS: a framework for designing and composing Semantic Web Services. *IEEE Intelligent Systems* **19**(4): 24–31.

Gruber, T.R. (1993). A translation approach to portable ontology specifications. *Knowledge Acquisition* **5**: 199–220.

Guarino, N. (1998). Some ontological principles for designing upper level lexical resources. In: *Proceedings of the First International Conference on Language Resources and Evaluation – LREC 1998*, Rubio, A., Gallardo, N., Castro, R., and Tejada, A., eds. Paris: ELRA.

Guarino, N. (2001). Review of Sowa's knowledge representation. *AI Magazine* **22**(3): 123–124.

Guarino, N., and Giaretta, P. (1995). Ontologies and knowledge bases: towards a terminological clarification. In: *Towards Very Large Knowledge Bases: Knowledge Building & Knowledge Sharing*, Mars, N.J.I., ed. Amsterdam: IOS Press.

Guarino, N., and Welty, C. (2002). Evaluating ontological decisions with OntoClean. *Communications of the ACM* **45**(2): 61–65.

Guarino, N., Carrara, M., and Giaretta, P. (1994). An ontology of meta-level categories. In: *Principles of Knowledge Representation and Reasoning – Proceedings of the Fourth International Conference (KR94)*, Doyle, J., Sandewall, E. and Torasso, P., eds. San Francisco: Morgan Kaufmann.

Guha, R.V., and Lenat, D.B. (1990). Cyc : a midterm report. *AI Magazine* **11**(3): 32–59.

Guha, R.V., and Lenat, D.B. (1993). Re: CycLing paper reviews. In: *The Commonsense Reviews*, Stefik, M.J., and Smoliar, S.W., eds., special section of *Artificial Intelligence* **61**: 149–174.

Guha, R.V., and Lenat, D.B. (1994). Enabling agents to work together. *Communications of the ACM*, **37**(7): 127–142.

Guo, Y., Qasem, A., Pan, Z. and J. Heflin, J. (2007). A requirements driven framework for benchmarking Semantic Web knowledge base systems. *IEEE Transactions on Knowledge and Data Engineering – Special Issue: Knowledge and Data Engineering in the Semantic Web Era* **19**: 297–309.

Güven, S., Podlaseck, M., and Pingali, G. (2005). PICASSO: Pervasive Information Chronicling, Access, Search, and Sharing for Organizations. In: *Proceedings of the IEEE 2005 Pervasive Computing Conference (PerCom 2005)*. Los Alamitos (CA): IEEE Computer Society Press.

Haarslev, V., and Möller, R. (2003). Racer: a core inference engine for the Semantic Web. In: *Proceedings of the 2nd International Workshop on Evaluation of Ontology Tools (EON2003)*, Sanibel Island (October 20, 2003, Florida, USA).

Handler Miller, C. (2004). *Digital Storytelling. A Creator's Guide to Interactive Entertainment.* Burlington (MA): Focal Press.

Higginbotham, J. (1985). On semantics. *Linguistic Inquiry* **16**: 547–593.

Higginbotham, J. (2000). On events in linguistic semantics. In: *Speaking of Events*, Higginbotham, J., Pianesi, F., and Varzi, A.C., eds. Oxford: Oxford University Press.

Hobbs, J.R., and Pan, F. (2004). An ontology of time for the Semantic Web. *ACM Transactions on Asian Language Processing (TALIP): Special Issue on Temporal Information Processing* **3**: 66–85.

Hobbs, J.R., and Pan, F., eds. (2006). *Time Ontology in OWL - W3C Working Draft 27 September 2006*. W3C (http://www.w3.org/TR/2006/WD-owl-time-20060927/).

Hoekstra, R., Liem, J., Bredeweg, B., and Breuker, J. (2006). Requirements for representing situations. In: *Proceedings of the OWLED*06 Workshop on OWL: Experiences and Directions* (CEUR-WS.org/Vol-216), Cuenca Grau, B., Hitzler, P., Shankey, C., and Wallace, E., eds. Aachen: Sun SITE Central Europe (CEUR, http://SunSITE.Informatik.RWTH-Aachen.DE/Publications/CEUR-WS/Vol-216/submission_4.pdf).

Horridge, M. (2004). *A Practical Guide to Building OWL Ontologies with the Protégé-OWL Plugin* (Edition 1.0). Manchester: The University of Manchester.

Horridge, M., Tsarkov, D., and Redmond, T. (2006). Supporting early adoption of OWL 1.1 with Protégé-OWL and FaCT++. In: *Proceedings of the OWLED*06 Workshop on OWL: Experiences and Directions* (CEUR-WS.org/Vol-216), Cuenca Grau, B., Hitzler, P., Shankey, C., and Wallace, E., eds. Aachen: Sun SITE Central Europe (CEUR, http://SunSITE. Informatik.RWTH-Aachen.DE/Publications/CEUR-WS/vol-216/submission_15.pdf).

Horrocks, I., Patel-Schneider, P.F., Boley, H., Tabet, S., Grosof, B., and Dean, M. (2004). *SWRL: A Semantic Web Rule Language Combining OWL and RuleML – W3C Member Submission 21 May 2004*. W3C (http://www.w3.org/Submission/SWRL).

Horrocks, I., Patel-Schneider, P.F., Bechhofer, S., and Tsarkov, D. (2005). OWL rules: a proposal and prototype implementation. *Journal of Web Semantics: Science, Services and Agents on the World Wide Web* **3**: 23–40.

Hunston, S., and Francis, G. (2000). *Pattern Grammar: A Corpus-Driven Approach to the Lexical Grammar of English*. Amsterdam: John Benjamins.

Iannella, R. (2001). *Representing vCard Objects in RDF/XML – W3C Note 22 February 2001*. W3C (http://www.w3.org/TR/2001/NOTE-vcard-rdf-20010222/).

ISO (2004). *8601:2004 Data Elements and Interchange Formats – Information Interchange – Representation of Dates and Times*. Geneva: International Organization for Standardization.

Jackendoff, R. (1990). *Semantic Structures*. Cambridge (MA): MIT Press.

Jahn, M. (2005). *Narratology: A Guide to the Theory of Narrative* (version 1.8). Cologne: English Department of the University (http://www.uni-koeln.de/~ame02/pppn.htm).

Java, A., Finin, T., and Nirenburg, S. (2005). Integrating language understanding agents into the Semantic Web. In: *Proceedings of the AAAI 2005 Fall Symposium on Agents and the Semantic Web*. Los Alamitos (CA): IEEE Computer Society Press.

Java, A., Finin, T., and Nirenburg, S. (2006). Text understanding agents and the Semantic Web. In: *Proceedings of the 39th Hawaii International Conference on System Sciences, HICSS'06*. Los Alamitos (CA): IEEE Computer Society Press. (http://csdl2.computer. org/comp/proceedings/hicss/2006/2507/03/250730062b.pdf).

Johnson, F.L., and Shapiro, S.C. (2001). Redefining belief change terminology for implemented systems. In: *Working Notes for the IJCAI 2001 Workshop on Inconsistency in Data and Knowledge*, Bertossi, L., and Chomicki, J., eds. Menlo Park (CA): AAAI Press.

Kabbaj, A., Moulin, B., Gancet, J., Nadeau, D., and Rouleau, O. (2001). Uses, improvements and extensions of Prolog+CG: case studies. In: *Conceptual Structures: Broadening the Base – Proceedings of the 9th International Conference on Conceptual Structures, ICCS '01* (LNAI 2120), Delugach, H.S., and Stumme, G. eds. Berlin: Springer.

Kabbaj A., Bouzoubaa, K., El Hachimi, K., and Ourdani, N. (2006). Ontology in Amine platform: structures and processes. In: *Conceptual Structures: Inspiration and Application – Proceedings of the 14th International Conference on Conceptual Structures, ICCS '06* (LNCS 4068), Schärfe, H., Hitzler, P., and Ohrstrom, P., eds. Berlin: Springer.

Kahn, K.M., and Gorry, A.G. (1977). Mechanizing temporal knowledge. *Artificial Intelligence* **7**: 87–108.

Kalfoglou, Y., and Schorlemmer, M. (2003). Ontology mapping: the state of the art. *Knowledge Engineering Review* **18**: 1–31.

Kamp, H. (1981). A theory of truth and semantic representation. In: *Formal Methods in the Study of Language*, Groenendijk, J., Janssen, T., and Stokhof, M., eds. Amsterdam: Mathematisch Centrum.

Kamp, H., and Reyle, U. (1993). *From Discourse to Logic. Introduction to Modeltheoretic Semantics of Natural Language, Formal Logic and Discourse Representation Theory*. Dordrecht: Kluwer.

Kautz, H., and Ladkin, P. (1991). Integrating metric and qualitative temporal reasoning. In: *Proceedings of the Ninth National Conference on Artificial Intelligence - AAAI/91*. Cambridge (MA): MIT Press/AAAI Press.

Kim, J. (1993). *Supervenience and Mind: Selected Philosophical Essays*. Cambridge: Cambridge University Press.

Kim, J. (1996). Events as property exemplifications. In: *Events* (International Research Library of Philosophy, 15), Casati, R., and Varzi, A.C., eds. Aldershot: Dartmouth Publishing.

King, M., Ornato, M., Zarri, G.P., Zarri-Baldi, L., and Zwiebel, A. (1977). Ghosts in the machine: an AI treatment of medieval history. In: *Proceedings of the 5th International Joint Conference on Artificial Intelligence – IJCAI/77*. San Francisco: Morgan Kaufmann.

Koster, C.H.A. (2004). Head/modifier frames for Information Retrieval. In: *Proceedings of the 5th International Conference on Computational Linguistics and Intelligent Text Processing – CLing-2004* (LNCS 2945), Gelbukh, A., ed. Berlin: Springer.

Kowalski, R., and Sergot, M. (1986). A logic-based calculus of events. *New Generation Computing* **4**: 67–95.

Kolodner, J.L. (1984). *Retrieval and Organizational Strategies in Conceptual Memory: A Computer Model*. Hillsdale (NJ): Lawrence Erlbaum.

Ladkin, P.B. (1986). Time representation: a taxonomy of interval relations. In: *Proceedings of the Fifth National Conference on Artificial Intelligence – AAAI/86*. Cambridge (MA): MIT Press/AAAI Press.

Ladkin, P.B., and Maddux, R.D. (1987). *The Algebra of Convex Time Intervals: Short Version* (Report KES.U.87.2). Palo Alto (CA): Kestrel Institute.

Landman, F. (2000). *Events and Plurality – The Jerusalem Lectures*. Dordrecht: Kluwer.

Lehmann, F., ed. (1992). *Semantic Networks in Artificial Intelligence*. Oxford: Pergamon Press.

Lenat, D.B., and Feigenbaum, E.A. (1991). On the threshold of knowledge. *Artificial Intelligence* **47**: 185–230.

Lenat, D.B., and Guha, R.V. (1990). *Building Large Knowledge Based Systems*. Reading (MA): Addison-Wesley.

Lenat, D.B., Guha, R.V., Pittman, K., Pratt, D., and Shepherd, M. (1990). CYC: toward programs with common sense. *Communications of the ACM* **33**(8): 30–49.

Levin, B. (1993). *English Verb Classes and Alternations: A Preliminary Investigation*. Chicago (IL): The University of Chicago Press.

Levy, A.Y., and Rousset, M.-C. (1998). Combining Horn rules and description logics in CARIN. *Artificial Intelligence* **104**: 165–209.

Link, G. (1983). The logical analysis of plurals and mass terms: a lattice-theoretical approach. In: *Meaning, Use and Interpretation of Language: Proceedings of 1981 Conference on Meaning, Use, and Interpretation of Language*, Bäuerle, R., Schwarze, C., and von Stechow, A., eds. Berlin: Walter de Gruyter.

Lomuscio, A., and Nute, D., eds. (2005). *Journal of Applied Logic – Special Issue on Deontic Logic in Computer Science* **3**: 369–516.

Lukose, D., Mineau, G., Mugnier, M.-L., Möller, J.-U., Martin, P., Kremer, R., and Zarri, G. P. (1995). Conceptual structures for knowledge engineering and knowledge modelling. In: *Supplementary Proceedings of the 3rd International Conference on Conceptual Structures – Applications, Implementation and Theory*, Ellis, G., Levinson, R., Rich, W., and Sowa, J., eds. Santa Cruz (CA): Department of Computer and Information Sciences of the University of California.

Lumpkin, G., Jakobsson, H., and Colgan, M. (2005). *Query Optimization in Oracle Database 10g Release 2*. Redwood Shores (CA): Oracle Corporation.

Lytinen, S.L. (1992). Conceptual dependency and its descendants. In: *Semantic Networks in Artificial Intelligence*, Lehmann, F., ed.. Oxford: Pergamon Press.

Maamar, Z., Benslimane, D., and Narendra, N.C. (2006). What can context do for Web Services? *Communications of the ACM* **49**(12): 98–103.

Maida, A.S., and Shapiro, S.C. (1982). Intensional concepts in propositional semantic networks. *Cognitive Science* **6**: 291–330.

Manola, F., and Miller, E. (2004). *RDF Primer – W3C Recommendation 10 February 2004*. W3C (http://www.w3.org/TR/rdf-primer/).

Mani, I., and Pustejovsky, J. (2004). Temporal discourse models for narrative structure. In: *Proceedings of the ACL Workshop on Discourse Annotation*. East Stroudsburg (PA): Association for Computational Linguistics.

Mani, I., and Wilson, G. (2000). Robust temporal processing of news. In: *Proceedings of the 38th Annual Meeting of the Association for Computational Linguistics*. Stroudsburg (PA): ACL.

Margolis, E., and Laurence, S., eds. (1999). *Concepts – Core Readings*. Cambridge (MA): MIT Press.

Masolo, C., Borgo, S., Gangemi, A., Guarino, N., Oltramari, A., and Schneider, L. (2002). *WonderWeb Deliverable D17: The WonderWeb Library of Foundational Ontologies* (Preliminary Report, Version 2.0). Padova: IST-CNR.

Masterman, M. (2005). *Language, Cohesion and Form*, Wilks, Y., ed. Cambridge: Cambridge University Press.

Mateas, M., and Sengers, P., eds. (2003). *Narrative Intelligence*. Amsterdam: John Benjamins.

Matuszek, C., Cabral, J., Witbrock, M., and DeOliveira, J. (2006). An introduction to the syntax and content of Cyc. In: *Proceedings of the 2006 AAAI Spring Symposium on Formalizing and Compiling Background Knowledge and Its Applications to Knowledge Representation and Question Answering*. Menlo Park (CA): AAAI.

McDermott, D.V. (1982). A temporal logic for reasoning about processes and plans. *Cognitive Science* **6**: 101–155.

McGuinness, D.L., van Harmelen, F. (2004). *OWL WEB ontology language overview – W3C Recommendation 10 February 2004*. W3C (http://www.w3.org/TR/owl-features/).

McGuinness, D.L., Fikes, R., Hendler, J., and Stein, L.A. (2002). DAML+OIL: an ontology language for the Semantic Web. *IEEE Intelligent Systems* **17**(5): 72–80.

Mehan, J. (1977). TALE-SPIN – an interactive program that writes stories. In: *Proceedings of the 1977 International Joint Conference on Artificial Intelligence – IJCAI/97*. San Mateo (CA): Morgan Kaufmann.

Mel'čuk, I. (1996). Lexical functions: a tool for the description of lexical relations in the lexicon. In: *Lexical Functions in Lexicography and Natural Language Processing*, Wanner, L., ed. Amsterdam/Philadelphia: Benjamins.

Miller, G.A. (1995). WordNet: a lexical database for English. *Communications of the ACM* **38**(11): 39–41.

Miller, S., and Schubert, L.K. (1990). Time revisited. *Computational Intelligence* **6**: 108–118.

Minsky, M. (1975). A framework for representing knowledge. In: *The Psychology of Computer Vision*, Winston, P.H., ed. New York: McGraw Hill.

Mitra, N., ed. (2003). *SOAP Version 1.2 Part 0: Primer – W3C Recommendation 24 June 2003*. W3C (http://www.w3.org/TR/soap12-part0/).

Motik, B., and Horrocks, I. (2006). Problems with OWL syntax. In: *Proceedings of the OWLED*06 Workshop on OWL: Experiences and Directions* (CEUR-WS.org/Vol-216), Cuenca Grau, B., Hitzler, P., Shankey, C., and Wallace, E., eds. Aachen: Sun SITE Central Europe (CEUR, http://SunSITE.Informatik.RWTH-Aachen.DE/Publications/CEUR/WS/Vol-216/Submission_13.pdf).

Motik, B., Sattler, U., and Studer, R. (2005). Query answering for OWL-DL with rules. *Journal of Web Semantics: Science, Services and Agents on the World Wide Web* **3**: 41–60.

Mugnier, M.-L., and Leclère, M. (2007). On querying simple conceptual graphs with negation. *Data and Knowledge Engineering* **60**: 468–493.

Mylopoulos, J., Borgida, A., Jarke, M., and Koubarakis, M. (1990). TELOS: representing knowledge about information systems. *ACM Transactions on Information Systems* **8**: 325–362.

Nazarenko, A. (1993). Representing natural language causality in conceptual graphs: the higher order conceptual relation problem. In: *Conceptual Graphs for Knowledge Representation – Proceedings of the First International Conference on Conceptual Structures* (LNAI 699), Mineau, G.W., Moulin, B., and Sowa, J., eds. Berlin: Springer.

Nazarenko-Perrin, A. (1992). Causal ambiguity in natural language: conceptual representation of "*parce que/because*" and "*puisque/since*." In: *Proceedings of the Fifteenth International Conference on Computational Linguistics – COLING 92* (Nantes, France, August 1992, http://www.cs.mu.oz.au/acl/C/C92/C92-3131.pdf).

Necib, C.B., and Freytag, J.-C. (2005a). Semantic query transformation using ontologies. In: *Proceedings of the 9th International Database Applications and Engineering Symposium, IDEAS'05*, Desai, B.C., and Vossen, G., eds. Los Alamitos (CA): IEEE Computer Society Press.

Necib, C.B., and Freytag, J.-C. (2005b). Query processing using ontologies. In: *Advanced Information Systems Engineering, Proceedings of the 17th International Conference, CaiSE 2005* (LNCS 3520), Pastor, O., and Falcão e Cunha, J., eds. Berlin: Springer.

Němec, P. (2006). Review of "ontological semantics," by Sergei Nirenburg and Victor Raskin. *The Prague Bulletin of Mathematical Linguistics* (86): 55–56.

Niles, I., and Pease, A. (2001a). Towards a standard upper ontology. In: *Proceedings of the International Conference on Formal Ontology in Information Systems (FOIS '01)*. New York: ACM Press.

Niles, I., and Pease, A. (2001b). Origins of the IEEE standard upper ontology. In: *Working Notes of the IJCAI-2001 Workshop on the IEEE Standard Upper Ontology*. Menlo Park (CA): AAAI Press.

Nirenburg, S, and Raskin, V. (2004). *Ontological Semantics*. Cambridge (MA): MIT Press.

Nirenburg, S., Beale, S., and McShane, M. (2004). Evaluating the performance of the Onto-Sem semantic analyzer. In: *Proceedings of the Second Workshop on Text Meaning and Interpretation, ACL-2004*, Niremburg, S., and Hirst, G., eds. East Stroudsburg (PA): ACL.

Noy, F.N., and Rector, A., eds., [Hayes, P. and Welty, C., contributors] (2006). *Defining N-ary Relations on the Semantic Web – W3C Working Group Note 12 April 2006*. W3C (http://www.w3.org/TR/2006/NOTE-swbp-n-aryRelations-20060412/).

Noy, F.N., Fergerson, R.W., and Musen, M.A. (2000). The knowledge model of Protégé-2000: combining interoperability and flexibility. In: *Knowledge Acquisition, Modeling, and Management – Proceedings of EKAW'2000* (LNCS 1937), Dieng, R., and Corby, O., eds. Berlin: Springer.

Oberle, D., Staab, S., and Volz, R. (2005). Three dimensions of knowledge representation in WonderWeb. *Künstliche Intelligenz – Special Issue on Knowledge Representation* 5(1): 31–35.

O'Connor, M., Knublauch, H., Tu, S., Grosof, B., Dean, M., Grosso, W., and Musen, M. (2005). Supporting rule system interoperability on the Semantic Web with SWRL. In: *Proceedings of the Fourth International Semantic Web Conference – ISWC 2005* (LNCS 3729), Gil, Y., Motta, E., Benjamins, V.R., and Musen, M.A., eds. Berlin: Springer.

OKAR Working Group (2005). *Ontology for Knowledge Activity Resources (OKAR) Guide – Draft 2005-03-31*. Fujitsu Laboratories & Ricoh Company. (http://www.ricoh.com/src/rd/img2/ds_okar_draft_20050331_en.pdf).

Ornato. M. (2001). *Répertoire prosopographique des personnages apparentés à la couronne de France aux XIVe et XVe siècles* (préface de Jean-Philippe Genet). Paris: Publications de la Sorbonne.

Ornato, M., and Zarri, G.P. (1976). An application of artificial intelligence in information retrieval: RESEDA project for medieval biographies. In: *Proceedings of 1976 AISB Summer Conference*, Brady, M., ed. Brighton: AISB.

Parson, T. (1990). *Events in the Semantics of English*. Cambridge (MA): MIT Press.

Partee, B.H., ter Meulen, A., and Wall, R. (1990). *Mathematical Methods in Linguistics*. Dordrecht: Kluwer.

Peters, S., and Westerståhl, D. (2006). *Quantifiers in Language and Logic*. Oxford: Clarendon Press.

Peterson, P. (1979). On the logic of *few, many*, and *most. Notre Dame Journal of Formal Logic* 20: 155–179.

Propp, V. (1968) *Morphology of the Folktale*, translated from the Russian by L. Scott, 2 nd ed. Austin (TX): University of Texas Press.

Prud'hommeaux, E., and Seaborne, A., eds. (2007). *SPARQL Query Language for RDF – W3C Proposed Recommendation 12 November 2007*. W3C (http://www.w3.org/TR/2007/PR-rdf-sparql-query-20071112/).

Pustejovsky, J., Ingria, R., Saurí, R., Castaño, J., Littman, J., Gaizauskas, R., Setzer, A., Katz, G., and Mani, I. (2005). The specification language TimeML. In: *The Language of Time: A Reader*, Mani, I., Pustejovsky, J., and Gaizauskas, R., eds. Oxford: Oxford University Press.

Quillian, M.R. (1966). *Semantic Memory* (Ph.D. thesis). Pittsburgh (PA): Carnegie Institute of Technology.

Ramachandran, D., Reagan, P., and Goolsbey, K. (2005). First-orderized research Cyc: expressivity and efficiency in a common-sense ontology. In: *Papers from the AAAI Workshop on Contexts and Ontologies: Theory, Practice and Applications* (Technical Report WS-05-01), Shvaiko, P., Euzenat, J., Leger, A., McGuinness, D.L., and Wache, H., eds. Menlo Park (CA): AAAI.

Randell, D., Cui, Z, and Cohn, A. (1992). A spatial logic based on regions and connection. In: *Proceedings of the 3rd International Conference on Principles of Knowledge Representation and Reasoning – KR'92*, Nebel, B., Rich, C., and Swartout, W.R., eds. San Francisco: Morgan Kaufmann.

Rath, H.H. (2003). *The Topic Maps Handbook* (White Paper, version 1.1). Gütersloh: empolis GmbH (http://www.empolis.com/downloads/empolis_TopicMaps_Whitepaper20030206.pdf).

Rector, A., and Welty, C., eds. (2005). *Simple Part–Whole Relations in OWL – W3C Editor's Draft 11 Aug 2005*. W3C (http://www.w3.org/2001/sw/BestPractices/OEP/SimplePartWhole/).

Riesbeck, C. (1975). Conceptual analysis. In: *Conceptual Information Processing*, Schank, R. C., ed. Amsterdam: North Holland.

Rinaldi, F., Dowdall, J., Hess, M., Ellman, J., Zarri, G.P., Persidis, A., Bernard, L., and Karanikas, H. (2003). Multilayer annotations in PARMENIDES. In: *Proceedings of the K-CAP (International Conference on Knowledge Capture) 2003 Workshop on Knowledge Markup and Semantic Annotation* (October 25–26, 2003, Sanibel Island, Florida, USA).

Rosati, R. (2005). On the decidability and complexity of integrating ontologies and rules. *Journal of Web Semantics: Science, Services and Agents on the World Wide Web* 3: 61–73.

Rosner, M., and Somers, H. (1980). *Case in Linguistics and Cognitive Science* (ISSCO Working Paper 40). Geneva: ISSCO.

Ruppenhofer, J., Ellsworth, M., Petruck, M.R.L., Johnson, C.R., and Scheffczyk, J. (2006). *FrameNet II: Extended Theory and Practice*. Berkeley (CA): International Computer Science Institute (http://framenet.icsi.berkeley.edu/index.php?option=com_wrapper&Itemid=126).

Russel, S., and Norvig, P. (1995). *Artificial Intelligence: A Modern Approach*. Upper Saddle River (NJ): Prentice Hall.

Sarraf, Q., and Ellis, G. (2006). Business rules in retail: the Tesco.com story. *Business Rules Journal* 7(6): http://www.BRCommunity.com/a2006/n014.html.

Scha, R., and Stallard, D. (1988). Multi-level plurals and distributivity. In: *Proceedings of the 26th Annual Meeting of the Association for Computational Linguistics*. Stroudsburg (PA): ACL.

Schank, R.C. (1973). Identification of conceptualizations underlying natural language. In: *Computer Models of Thought and Language*, Schank, R.C., and Colby, K.M., eds. San Francisco: W.H. Freeman and Co.

Schank, R.C. (1980). Language and memory. *Cognitive Science* 4: 243–284.

Schank, R.C. (1982). *Dynamic Memory*. Cambridge: Cambridge University Press.

Schank, R.C., and Abelson, R. (1977). *Scripts Plans Goals and Understanding – An Inquiry into Human Knowledge Structures*. Hillsdale (NJ): Lawrence Erlbaum Associates.

Schank, R.C., and Carbonell, J.G. (1979). Re: the Gettysburg Address – representing social and political acts. In: *Associative Networks*, Findler, N.V., ed. New York: Academic Press.

Schiel, U. (1989). Abstractions in semantic networks: axiom schemata for generalization, aggregation and grouping. *ACM Sigart Newsletter* (107): 25–26.

Schoening, J., ed. (2007). *Data Interoperability Across the Enterprise – Why Current Technology Can't Achieve It*. Ft. Monmouth (NJ): CDSI (http://colab.cim3.net/file/work/SICoP/2007-08-09/JSchoening03272007.doc).

Schubert, L.K. (1976). Extending the expressive power of semantic networks. *Artificial Intelligence* 7: 163–198.

Semy, S.K., Pulvermacher, M.K., and Obrst, L.J. (2004). *Toward the Use of an Upper Ontology for U.S. Government and U.S. Military Domains: An Evaluation* (MITRE Technical Report MTR 04B0000063). Bedford (MA): The MITRE Corporation.

Setzer, A. (2001). *Temporal Information in Newswire Articles: An Annotation Scheme and Corpus Study* (Ph.D. thesis). Sheffield: University of Sheffield (http://www.andrea-setzer.org.uk/PAPERS/thesis.pdf).

Setzer, A., and Gaizauskas, R. (2000). Annotating events and temporal information in newswire texts. In: *Proceedings of the Second International Conference On Language Resources and Evaluation – LREC-2000* (May 31–June 2, 2000, Athens, Greece).

Shadbolt, N., Hall, W., and Berners-Lee, T. (2006). The Semantic Web revisited. *IEEE Intelligent Systems* 21(3): 96–101.

Shaer, B. (2003). "Manner" adverbs and the "association" theory: some problems and solutions. In: *Modifying Adjuncts*, Lang, E., Maienbom, C., and Fabricius-Hansen, C., eds. Berlin: Mouton de Gruyter.

Shapiro, S.C. (1979). The SNePS Semantic Network Processing System. In: *Associative Networks: Representation and Use of Knowledge by Computers*, Findler, N.V. , ed. New York: Academic Press.

Sintek, M., and Decker, S. (2002) TRIPLE – a query, inference, and transformation language for the Semantic Web. In: *Proceedings of the First International Semantic Web Conference – ISWC 2002* (LNCS 2342), Horrocks, I., and Hendler, J.A., eds. Berlin: Springer.

Sirin, E., Parsia, B., Cuenca Grau, B., Kalyanpur, A., and Katz, Y. (2007). Pellet: A Practical OWL-DL Reasoner. *Journal of Web Semantics: Science, Services and Agents on the World Wide Web* **5**: 51–53.

Smith, B. (1996). Mereotopology: a theory of parts and boundaries. *Data and Knowledge Engineering* **20**: 287–303.

Smith, M.K., Welty, C., and McGuinness, D.L., eds. (2004). *OWL Web Ontology Language Guide – W3C Recommendation 10 February 2004*. W3C (http://www.w3.org/TR/owl-guide/).

Soulier, E., ed. (2006). *Le Storytelling, Concepts, Outils et Applications*. Paris: Lavoisier.

Southey, F., and Linders, J. G. (1999). Notio – a Java API for conceptual graphs. In: *Conceptual Structures: Standards and Practices – Proceedings of the 7th International Conference on Conceptual Structures, ICCS '99* (LNAI 1640), Tepfnhart, W., and Cyre, W., eds. Berlin: Springer.

Sowa, J.F. (1984). *Conceptual Structures: Information Processing in Mind and Machine*. Reading (MA): Addison-Wesley.

Sowa J. F. (1988). Using a lexicon of canonical graphs in a semantic interpreter. In: *Relational Models of the Lexicon: Representing Knowledge in Semantic Networks*, Evens M.W. (ed.), Cambridge: Cambridge University Press.

Sowa, J.F. (1991). Toward the expressive power of natural language. In: *Principles of Semantic Networks – Explorations in the Representation of Knowledge*, Sowa, J.F., ed. San Francisco: Morgan Kaufmann.

Sowa, J.F. (1995). Distinctions, combinations, and constraints. In: *Proceedings of the IJCAI'95 Workshop on Basic Ontological Issues in Knowledge Sharing*, Skuce, D., ed. Ottawa: Department of Computer Science of the University of Ottawa.

Sowa, J.F. (1999). *Knowledge Representation: Logical, Philosophical, and Computational Foundations*. Pacific Grove (CA): Brooks Cole Publishing Co.

Sowa, J.F. (2005). Review of "computational semantics," by Sergei Niremburg and Victor Raskin. *Computational Linguistics* **31**: 147–152.

Spärck Jones, K. (2007). Semantic primitives: the tip of the iceberg. In: *Words and Intelligence II: Essays in Honor of Yorick Wilks* (Text, Speech and Language Technology Series 36), Ahmad, K., Brewster, C. and Stevenson, M., eds. Berlin/Dordrecht: Springer.

Spärck Jones, K., and Boguraev, B. (1987). A note on a study of cases. *Computational Linguistics* **13**: 65–68.

Stefik, M.J., and Smoliar, S.W., eds. (1993). The commonsense reviews – eight reviews of B. Lenat and R.V. Guha, "*Building Large Knowledge-based Systems*," and E. Davis, "*Representation of Commonsense Knowledge*," special section of *Artificial Intelligence* **61**: 37–179.

Studer, R., Grimm, S., and Abecker, A., eds (2007). *Semantic Web Services – Concepts Technologies and Applications*. Berlin: Springer.

Sure, Y., Angele, J, and Staab, S. (2002). OntoEdit: guiding ontology development by methodology and inferencing. In: *Proceedings of the Confederated International Conferences CoopIS, DOA, and ODBASE 2002* (LNCS 2519), Meersman, R., and Tari, Z., eds. Berlin: Springer.

Swartjes, I., and Theune, M. (2006). A fabula model for emergent narrative. In: *Technologies for Interactive Digital Storytelling and Entertainment: Proceedings of the Third*

International Conference, Tidse 2006 (LNCS 4326), Göbel, S., Malkewitz, R., and Iurgel, I., eds. Berlin: Springer.

Swartz, A. (2002). *RDF Primer Primer – Editor's Draft, 20 November 2002*. W3C (http://notabug.com/2002/rdfprimer/).

Talmy, L. (1988). Force dynamics in language and cognition. *Cognitive Science* **12**: 49–100.

Talmy, L. (2000). *Toward a Cognitive Semantics Vol. 1: Concept Structuring Systems*. Cambridge (MA): MIT Press.

Tenny, C.L., and Pustejovsky, J. (2000). A history of events in linguistic theory. In: *Events as Grammatical Objects: The Converging Perspectives of Lexical Semantics, Logical Semantics and Syntax*, Tenny, C.L., and Pustejovsky, J., eds. Stanford (CA): CSLI Publications.

Todorov, T. (1969). *Grammaire du Décameron*. The Hague: Mouton.

Troncy, R., van Ossenbruggen, J., Pan, J.Z., and Stamou, G., eds., Halaschek-Wiener, C., Simou, N., and Tzouvaras, V., contributors (2007). *Image Annotation on the Semantic Web – W3C Incubator Group Report 14 August 2007*. W3C (http://www.w3.org/2005/Incubator/mmsem/XGR-image-annotation/).

Tsang, E.P.K. (1987). Time structures for AI. In: *Proceedings of the 9th International Joint Conference on Artificial Intelligence – IJCAI/87*. San Francisco: Morgan Kaufmann.

Tsarkov, D., and Horrocks, I. (2006). FaCT++ description logic reasoner: system description. In: *Proceedings of the International Joint Conference on Automated Reasoning, IJCAR 2006* (LNAI 4130), Furbach, U., and Shankar, N., eds. Berlin: Springer.

Tudorache, T., and Noy, N. (2007). Collaborative Protégé. In: *Proceedings of the Workshop on Social and Collaborative Construction of Structured Knowledge (CKC 2007) – 16th International World Wide Web Conference* (CEUR-WS.org/Vol-273), Noy, N., Alani, H., Stumme, G., Mika, P., Sure, Y, and Vrandecic, D., eds. Aachen: Sun SITE Central Europe (http://ftp.informatik.rwth-aachen.de/Publications/CEUR-WS/Vol-273/paper_93.pdf).

Tuffield, M. M., Millard, D. E. and Shadbolt, N. R. (2006). Ontological approaches to modelling narrative. In: *Proceedings of 2nd AKT Doctoral Symposium*. Aberdeen: Advanced Knowledge Technologies (AKT) Interdisciplinary Research Collaboration.

Uhlir, J., Kremen, P., and Kral, L. (2004). *DNAT – User's Manual* (Cipher IST Deliverable D26/2). Prague: Czech Technical University.

Van Valin, R.D. Jr. (1993). A synopsis of role and reference grammar. In: *Advances in Role and Reference Grammar*, Van Valin, R.D. Jr., ed. Amsterdam: John Benjamins.

Van Valin, R.D. Jr. (1999). Generalized semantic roles and the syntax–semantics interface. In: *Empirical Issues in Formal Syntax and Semantics 2*, Corblin, F., Dobrovie-Sorin, C., and Marandin, J.-M., eds. The Hague: Thesus.

Vendler, Z. (1967). Facts and events. In *Linguistics in Philosophy*, Vendler, Z., ed. Ithaca (NY): Cornell University Press.

Vilain, M., and Kautz, H. (1986). Constraint propagation algorithms for temporal reasoning. In: *Proceedings of the Fifth National Conference on Artificial Intelligence – AAAI/86*. Cambridge (MA): MIT Press/AAAI Press.

Webber, B.L. (1983). So what can we talk about now. In: *Computational Models of Discourse*, Brady, M., and Berwick, R.C., eds. Cambridge (MA): MIT Press.

Westermann, U., and Jain, R. (2006). A generic event model for event-centric multimedia data management in eChronicle applications. In: *Proceedings of the 22nd International Conference on Data Engineering Workshops – ICDE Workshop on eChronicles (ICDEW'06)*. Los Alamitos (CA): IEEE Computer Society Press.

Wierzbicka, A. (1972). *Semantic Primitives*. Frankfurt: Athenäum.

Wierzbicka, A. (1981). *Lingua Mentalis: The Semantics of Natural Language*. Sidney: Academic Press.

Wilensky, R. (1978). *Understanding Goal-based Stories* (Ph.D. dissertation, Research Report #140). New Haven (CT): Computer Science Department of the Yale University.

Wilensky, R. (1987). *Some Problems and Proposals for Knowledge Representation* (UCB/ CSD Report no. 87/351). Berkeley (CA): University of California Computer Science Division.

Wilks, Y. (1975a). An intelligent analyzer and understander of English. *Communications of the ACM* **18**: 264–274.

Wilks, Y. (1975b). Preference semantics. In: *Formal Semantics of Natural Language*, Keenan, E. ed. Cambridge: Cambridge University Press.

Winston, M.E., Chaffin, R., and Herrmann, D. (1987). A taxonomy of part–whole relations. *Cognitive Science* **11**: 417–444.

Witbrock, M., Panton, K., Reed, S.L., Schneider, D., Aldag, B., Reimers, M., and Bertolo, S. (2004). Automated OWL annotation assisted by a large knowledge base. In: *Proceedings of the 4th International Workshop on Knowledge Markup and Semantic Annotation (SEMANNOT 2004) – 3rd International Semantic Web Conference*. Hiroshima (Japan): W3C.

Woods, W.A. (1975). What's in a link: foundations for semantic networks. In: *Representation and Understanding – Studies in Cognitive Sciences*, Bobrow, D.G., and Collins, A. New York: Academic Press.

Zarri, G.P. (1979). From history to computer science: a formalization of the inferential processes of an historian. In: *Proceedings of the 6th International Joint Conference on Artificial Intelligence – IJCAI/79*. San Francisco: Morgan Kaufmann.

Zarri, G.P. (1981). Building the inference component of an historical information retrieval system. In: *Proceedings of the 7th International Joint Conference on Artificial Intelligence – IJCAI/81*. San Francisco: Morgan Kaufmann.

Zarri, G.P. (1986). The use of inference mechanisms to improve the retrieval facilities from large relational databases. In: *Proceedings of the Ninth International ACM Conference on Research and Development in Information Retrieval*, Rabitti, F., ed. New York: ACM.

Zarri, G.P. (1992a). The "descriptive" component of a hybrid knowledge representation language. In: *Semantic Networks in Artificial Intelligence*, Lehmann, F., ed. Oxford: Pergamon Press.

Zarri, G.P. (1992b). Semantic modeling of the content of (normative) natural language documents. In: *Actes des Douzièmes Journées Internationales d'Avignon "Les Systèmes Experts et Leurs Applications" – Conférence Spécialisée sur le Traitement du Langage Naturel*. Nanterre: EC2.

Zarri, G.P. (1995) Intelligent information retrieval: an application in the field of historical biographical data. In: *From Information to Knowledge – Conceptual and Knowledge Analysis by Computer*, Nissan, E., and Schmidt, K.M., eds. Oxford: Intellect Books.

Zarri, G.P. (1997). NKRL, a knowledge representation tool for encoding the "meaning" of complex narrative texts. *Natural Language Engineering – Special Issue on Knowledge Representation for Natural Language Processing in Implemented Systems* **3**: 231–253.

Zarri, G.P. (1998). Representation of temporal knowledge in events: the formalism, and its potential for legal narratives. *Information & Communications Technology Law – Special Issue on Models of Time, Action, and Situations* **7**: 213–241.

Zarri, G.P. (2000). A conceptual model for capturing and reusing knowledge in business-oriented domains. In: *Industrial Knowledge Management: A Micro-Level Approach*, Roy, R., ed. London: Springer-Verlag.

Zarri, G.P. (2003a) *NKRL Manual, Part II – The HClass and HTemp Hierarchies* (Parmenides IST Report). Paris: University of Paris IV/Sorbonne.

Zarri, G.P. (2003b). A conceptual model for representing narratives. In: *Innovations in Knowledge Engineering*, Jain, R., Abraham, A., Faucher, C., and van der Zwaag, eds. Adelaide: Advanced Knowledge International.

Zarri, G.P. (2005). Integrating the two main inference modes of NKRL, transformations and hypotheses. *Journal on Data Semantics (JoDS)* **4**: 304–340.

Zarri, G.P. (2005/2006). *Final Report on the NKRL Component of the IST PARMENIDES Project, IST-2001-39023* (July 6, 2005, revised February 1, 2006). Paris: University Paris4/ Sorbonne.

Zarri, G.P. (2006). Modeling and advanced exploitation of eChronicle "narrative" information. In: *Proceedings of the 22nd International Conference on Data Engineering Workshops – ICDE Workshop on eChronicles (ICDEW'06)*. Los Alamitos (CA): IEEE Computer Society Press.

Zarri, G.P. (2007). Ontologies and reasoning techniques for (legal) intelligent information retrieval systems. *Artificial Intelligence and Law* **15**: 251–279.

Zarri, G.P., and Azzam, S. (1997). Building up and making use of corporate knowledge repositories. In: *Knowledge Acquisition, Modeling and Management – Proceedings of the European Knowledge Acquisition Workshop, EKAW'97* (LNAI 1319), Plaza, E., and Benjamins, R., eds. Berlin: Springer.

Zarri, G.P., and Bernard, L. (2004a). *Using NKRL Inference Techniques to Deal with MoD "Terrorism" Information* (Parmenides IST Report). Paris: University of Paris IV/Sorbonne.

Zarri, G.P., and Bernard, L. (2004b). *NKRL Manual, Part III – The NKRL Software* (Parmenides IST Report). Paris: University of Paris IV/Sorbonne.

Zarri, G.P., and Gilardoni, L. (1996). Structuring and retrieval of the complex predicate arguments proper to the NKRL conceptual language. In: *Foundations of Intelligent Systems – Proceedings of 9th International Symposium on Methodologies for Intelligent Systems, ISMIS'96* (LNAI 1079), Ras, Z., and Michalewicz, M., eds. Berlin: Springer.

Zarri, G.P., Wu, P., Abreu, P., Pires, F., Bertino, E., Ferrari, E., Marcante, A., and Perego, A. (2002). *Software Implementing the Integrated EUFORBIA Prototype* (Rep. Euforbia, Deliverable D11). Paris: CNRS.

Zarri, G.P., Wu, P., Stockinger, P., Bertino, E., Ferrari, E., Perego, A., Abreu, P., Pires, F., Allen, D., and Constable Maxwell, A. (2003). *EUFORBIA, Advanced Indexing and Filtering of Questionable Web Sites – Results and Final Remarks* (Euforbia Publication Report). Milano: Dipartimento di Scienza dell'Informazione dell'Università di Stato di Milano.

Žolkovskij, A., and Mel'čuk, I. (1967). O semantičeskom sinteze [On the semantic synthesis]. *Problemy Kibernetiki* **19**: 177–238. [French translation (1970): Sur la synthèse sémantique. *T.A. Informations* (2): 1–85].

Zúñiga, G.L. (2001). Ontology: its transformation from philosophy to information systems. In: *Proceedings of the International Conference on Formal Ontology in Information Systems (FOIS '01)*. New York: ACM Press.

Index